# Critical Perspectives on
# Safeguarding Children

# Critical Perspectives on Safeguarding Children

*Edited by*

**Karen Broadhurst, Chris Grover and Janet Jamieson**

**WILEY-BLACKWELL**

A John Wiley & Sons, Ltd, Publication

This edition first published 2009
© 2009 John Wiley & Sons Ltd

Wiley-Blackwell is an imprint of John Wiley & Sons, formed by the merger of Wiley's global
Scientific, Technical, and Medical business with Blackwell Publishing.

*Registered Office*
John Wiley & Sons Ltd, The Atrium, Southern Gate, Chichester, West Sussex, PO19 8SQ, UK

*Editorial Offices*
The Atrium, Southern Gate, Chichester, West Sussex, PO19 8SQ, UK
9600 Garsington Road, Oxford, OX4 2DQ, UK
350 Main Street, Malden, MA 02148-5020, USA

For details of our global editorial offices, for customer services, and for information about
how to apply for permission to reuse the copyright material in this book please see our
website at www.wiley.com/wiley-blackwell.

*Library of Congress Cataloging-in-Publication Data*

Critical perspectives on safeguarding children / edited by Karen Broadhurst, Chris Grover,
and Janet Jamieson.
    p. cm.
    Includes index.
    ISBN 978-0-470-68232-6 (cloth) – ISBN 978-0-470-69756-6 (pbk.)  1. Child welfare.
2. Social work with children.  3. Children.  4. Child welfare–Great Britain.  5. Social work
with children–Great Britain.  6. Children.  7. Children–Great Britain.  I. Broadhurst,
Karen.  II. Grover, Chris, 1967–  III. Jamieson, Janet.
    HV713.C743 2009
    362.7–dc22
                                                                              2009021001

A catalogue record for this book is available from the British Library.

Typeset in 9.5/11.5 pt Sabon by Aptara Inc., New Delhi, India.
Printed and bound in Singapore by Fabulous Printers Pte Ltd

1  2009

This book is for:

Jessica, Jay and Julie

# Contents

# List of Contributors

**Professor David Archard** is Professor of Philosophy and Public Policy at Lancaster University. He has previously taught at the Universities of Ulster and of St Andrews. He has written widely in applied ethics and political philosophy, especially on the topic of children, family and the state. He is currently Honorary Chair of the Society for Applied Philosophy, and a member of the Human Fertilisation and Embryology Authority.

**Dr Karen Broadhurst** is a Lecturer in Social Work in the Department of Applied Social Science at Lancaster University. As a former childcare social worker, she has a long-standing interest in the organization of family support and child protection. Karen has undertaken extensive empirical research projects broadly relating to child welfare, that have examined reasons why children are 'missing' from schooling, help-seeking decisions, the nature of family support and more recently the impact of New Public Management on front-line practices, with respect to increasing safety.

**Chris Grover** is Senior Lecturer in Social Policy in the Department of Applied Social Science, Lancaster University. His research interests are concerned with the political economy of relationships between paid work and social security benefits, in particular work-focused coercion and the subsidisation of low-paid work. His recent publications have examined the ideas of living wages and 'making work pay', recent changes to income replacement benefits for sick and impaired people, and relationships between crime and economic and social inequalities.

**Dr Claire Fitzpatrick** (née Taylor) is a Lecturer in Criminology in the Department of Applied Social Science at Lancaster University. She has a long-standing research interest in the welfare of looked after children and more generally in the relationship between youth justice and child welfare. Claire has previously worked at the University of Nottingham, in the Centre for Social Work and School of Law, and for the Home Office Research, Development and Statistics Directorate.

**Professor Malcolm Hill** is Research Professor in the Glasgow School of Social Work, a joint School of the Universities of Strathclyde and Glasgow, UK. His main research interests include: adoption and foster care, children's services, youth justice and young people's participation and he has been a social worker and senior social worker for 9 years. Recent co-edited publications include *Child Protection and Youth Justice* with Lockyer and Stone (Jessica Kingsley Publishers) and *Children, Young People and Social Inclusion* with Tisdall, Davis and Prout (Policy Press).

**Dr Peter Hopkins** is a Lecturer in Social Geography in the School of Geography, Politics and Sociology, Newcastle University, UK. His main research interests include: critical perspectives on young people's geographies, urban geographies of race and ethnicity, geographies of religion and qualitative methods. He is the author of *The Issue of Masculine Identities for British Muslims* (Edwin Mellen Press) and co-editor of *Geographies of Muslim Identities* with Cara Aitchison and Mei-Po Kwan (Ashgate) and *Muslims in Britain: Race, Place and Identities* with Richard Gale (Edinburgh University Press).

**Dr Janet Jamieson** is Senior Lecturer in Criminology in the School of Social Science, Liverpool John Moores University, UK. Her main research interests focus upon children, young people and crime and youth justice policy, with more general regard to related issues including gender, community, exclusion and disadvantage. Her recent publications have addressed the implementation and impacts of anti-social behaviour measures and legislation; youth crime, youth justice and the state (with Joe Yates) and gender and crime (with Karen Evans).

**Dr Ian Paylor** is Senior Lecturer in Applied Social Science in the Department of Applied Social Science at Lancaster University, UK. Prior to taking up his current role as Head of Department, he was the (founder) and Co-Director of the Applied Social Science Research and Evaluation Unit (ASSURE) – a cross-disciplinary unit that works in partnership with the third and statutory sectors offering them support to carry out their own projects, through capacity building and training. His primary research interests are in youth justice and treatment of problematic drug and alcohol use. He is the co-author of the forthcoming book *Social Work and Drug Use* (Open University Press).

**Dr Sue Peckover** is a Senior Research Fellow at the Centre for Applied Childhood Studies at the University of Huddersfield, UK. Sue has professional experience in health visiting. Her teaching and research interests include public health, safeguarding children, domestic violence and professional practice. She has recently worked on two ESRC-funded research studies examining aspects of information sharing, assessment and decision making in child welfare.

**Professor Andy Pithouse** is Director of the Childcare Research Group in the School of Social Sciences at the University of Cardiff. He has been principal investigator of several child safeguarding and family support projects that have helped promote conceptual development, practice innovation and system-building across voluntary and statutory sectors in social work and social care. His particular interests are in theories of childhood and effective interventions.

**Dr Carolyn Taylor** is currently Senior Lecturer in the Department of Applied Social Science at the University of Lancaster, UK and Director of the MA/PgDip in Social Work. A qualified social worker, she has research interests that include childcare practice and policy developments in child welfare past and present and has conducted research about the paths of looked after children and truancy in secondary schools.

**Dr Jo Warin** is a Senior Lecturer in the Department of Educational Research at Lancaster University, UK where she teaches postgraduates on the MA in Education and supervises PhD students as well as teaching on the Psychology in Education undergraduate degree. She has researched widely on family roles and processes of education especially those involving the construction of identity.

**Professor Sue White** is Professor of Social Work in the Department of Applied Social Science at Lancaster University, UK. She is a qualified social worker with extensive practice experience. Her primary research interest is in professional sense-making, and how science, formal knowledge, rhetoric, moral judgement and subjectivity interact in professional practice. She is currently principal investigator for a high profile ESRC funded study of 'error' and 'blame' in child welfare practice, with a particular interest in the impact of New Performance Management.

# Acknowledgements

A number of people have contributed to the writing of this book, in different ways. Thanks are due to Professor Sue White of the Department of Applied Social Science, Lancaster University, who gave us much encouragement at the start of the project. We would also like to thank all the contributors to the volume who helped shape this volume and extend our thinking beyond traditional disciplinary boundaries. Particular thanks are due to Claire Mason, who was involved in the initial design of the book and had she not taken maternity leave to have baby Ava, would have contributed a chapter. At the publishers, we would particularly like to thank Holly Myers, Al Bertrand and Karen Shield who ensured that the book came to fruition. We would also like to thank our referees, Paul Michael Garrett, Barry Goldson and those who remain anonymous to us, for their constructive comments.

# Acknowledgements

# Abbreviations

| | |
|---|---|
| BME | black and minority ethnic |
| CAF | Common Assessment Framework |
| CAMHS | Child and Adolescent Mental Health Services |
| CEAS | Common European Asylum System |
| CONS | Consultant Paediatrician |
| CSA | Child Support Agency |
| DCSF | Department for Children, Schools and Families |
| DfEE | Department for Education and Employment |
| DfES | Department for Education and Skills |
| DHSS | Department of Health and Social Security |
| DoH | Department of Health |
| DSS | Department of Social Security |
| eCAf | electronic Common Assessment Framework |
| ECM | Every Child Matters |
| EU | European Union |
| FRW | Family Resource Worker |
| GCSE | General Certificate of Secondary Education |
| HM | Her Majesty's |
| HO | Home Office |
| HSKE | Home-School Knowledge Exchange |
| HV | Health Visitor |
| ICS | Integrated Children's System |
| ICT | Information and Communication Technology |
| IFS | Institute for Fiscal Studies |
| JAR | Joint Area Review |
| JSA | Jobseekers Allowance |
| LP | Lead Professional |
| LSCB | Local Safeguarding Children Board |
| MP | Member of Parliament |
| NACRO | National Association for the Care and Resettlement of Offenders |
| NAI | non-accidental injuries |
| NAPP | National Academy of Parenting Practitioners |
| NASS | National Asylum Support Service |
| NCRS | National Crime Recording Standard |
| NESS | National Evaluation of Sure Start |
| NFPI | National Family and Parenting Institute |

| | |
|---|---|
| NHS | National Health Service |
| NSPCC | National Society for the Prevention of Cruelty to Children |
| OECD | Organization for Economic Co-operation and Development |
| Ofsted | Office for Standards in Education |
| RAICS | Raising Achievement in Inner City Schools |
| SAT | Standard Assessment Test |
| SEAL | Social and Emotional Aspects of Learning |
| SIS | Social Investment State |
| TM | Team Manager |
| UNCRC | United Nations Convention on the Rights of the Child |
| UNHCR | United Nations High Commissioner for Refugees |
| UNICEF | United Nations Children's Fund |
| UK | United Kingdom |
| USA | United States of America |
| YIP | Youth Inclusion Panel |
| YISP | Youth Inclusion and Support Panel |
| YJB | Youth Justice Board |
| YOI | Young Offender Institute |
| YOP | Youth Offending Panel |
| YOT | Youth Offending Team |

# 1

# Introduction: Safeguarding Children?

Karen Broadhurst, Chris Grover and Janet Jamieson

> The true measure of a nation's standing is how well it attends to its children – their health and safety, their material security, their education and socialization, and their sense of being loved, valued, and included in the families and societies into which they are born. (United Nations Children's Fund [UNICEF], 2007, p. 1)

There can be little doubt that statements from recent New Labour governments accord with the above extract from UNICEF's 2007 *Report Card* – that the lives and well-being of children and young people provide an important measure of a nation's standing. Children and young people, at least at a policy level, are central to what Giddens (1998) has described as New Labour's Social Investment State. Yet when we examine the findings of the UNICEF report, the condition of children in the United Kingdom (UK) is found to be wanting in many respects. Of the 21 countries detailed in the report, the UK performed poorly across a range of indicators of child well-being. Of the six dimensions examined in the report, the UK was in the bottom third in five of them (behaviour and risks, educational well-being, family and peer relationships, material well-being and subjective well-being) and achieved an overall bottom position against the 21-comparator countries.

The government's response to the claims of UNICEF was to deny that much was wrong with the lot of children in the late modern UK. According to a letter from the Minister for Children, Young People and Families, Beverley Hughes MP (The *Guardian*, 16 February 2007), UNICEF's data was out of date and that the government's successes in terms of reducing child poverty and bettering educational achievement were more recent than the data allowed for. Even if such arguments were accepted, and as several chapters in this book suggest they should not be, further concerns about the position of children in the UK were highlighted the following year in a report from the United Nations Convention on the Rights of the Child (UNCRC, 2008).

*Critical Perspectives on Safeguarding Children*   Edited by Karen Broadhurst, Chris Grover and Janet Jamieson
© 2009 John Wiley & Sons, Ltd

The 2008 UNCRC report criticized the UK for not adhering to the UNCRC in several areas of policy, most notably criminal justice and education. In particular, concerns with Anti-social Behaviour Orders were raised, and questions were asked about whether such orders could be reconciled with those aspects of the Convention that relate to the best interests of the child and the development of their personality (UNCRC, 2008). In addition, the dispersal of young people, especially using police powers and ultrasound devices (such as the Mosquito 'Anti-social' Device), were thought to undermine the right to free association and there was concern with the lack of input children had in decisions that led to the restriction of their liberty (UNCRC, 2008). In brief, children were held to be poorly served in the UK because of a lack of commitment to the UNCRC, with it being noted that 'certain regulations were in direct conflict with the Convention' (UNCRC, 2008, para. 7).

These damning reports from extra-national organizations are to some extent surprising, because, as noted, it would appear that recent UK governments have been genuinely concerned with the well-being of children. Yet, these findings, and indeed, many organizations representing children and young people in the UK (Howard League for Penal Reform, 2008; UK Children's Commissioners, 2008) clearly raise questions about a seeming incongruence between discursive commitments to children and young people and the realities of their lives, particularly those who are most vulnerable. It is with this seeming incongruence that this volume is concerned.

*Critical Perspectives on Safeguarding Children* brings together contributors from different disciplinary backgrounds who share in common a concern regarding the direction of social policy with respect to safeguarding children in the UK and who seek to investigate both the coherence and effectiveness of New Labour's policies for *all* children. Drawing contributing authors from criminology, education, geography, health, philosophy, social policy and social work, this volume offers a multi-disciplinary analysis of the New Labour safeguarding project and identifies a number of key limitations which, contributors argue, undermine aspirations to improve the well-being of all children. While much of the critique centres on England and Wales, the book will appeal to a wide readership, given New Labour's reach across the devolved contexts of the UK and the commonalities that the Anglophone countries of Canada, Australia, New Zealand and the United States of America (USA) share in cognate systems of child welfare and protection.

## Safeguarding children: a multi-disciplinary analysis

This book has arisen from conversations that took place between members of staff in the Department of Applied Social Science at Lancaster University who came together to discuss discontents about New Labour's social policies for children and families and the prospects for the ambitious *Every Child Matters:*

*Change for Children Programme* (Department for Education and Skills [DfES], 2004). Catalysed by the 2007 UNICEF report, our intention was to produce a critical text that would draw on our diverse disciplinary backgrounds and bring together some of our growing apprehensions about the safeguarding agenda. As the book took shape, the constituency of the Lancaster group evolved; Janet Jamieson left to take up a post at Liverpool John Moores University and Peter Hopkins migrated to the University of Newcastle. We also called on the assistance of Malcolm Hill based at the University of Glasgow, Andy Pithouse based at the University of Cardiff and Sue Peckover from the University of Huddersfield, to consolidate our project.

In order to appraise New Labour's safeguarding agenda, which is in itself increasingly multi-disciplinary, *Critical Perspectives on Safeguarding Children* considers how child welfare and protection are conceptualized and enacted across diverse fields of policy and provision. In the spirit of 'joined-up government', successive Labour governments have, through a series of incremental steps, culminating in the Green Paper, *Every Child Matters* (Chief Secretary to the Treasury, 2003), enlisted the Home Office (HO), the Department for Work and Pensions (DWP), the Department of Health (DoH) and the now Department for Children, Schools and Families (DCSF) in the project of safeguarding children. This volume aims to elucidate some of the tensions and inconsistencies both *between* and *within* the various policy areas that these ministries have responsibility for and which 'safeguarding' encompasses.

## Safeguarding children: key themes

Early in office, New Labour made a number of confident pledges to children and families, most notably a desire to end child poverty by 2020. A broader safeguarding agenda emerged as concerns about social exclusion coalesced with the more traditional concerns of child protection. The language of safeguarding appeared with the advent of the Children Act 1989, but it was through the New Labour project that, arguably, the family support aspects of this act and a broader notion of 'safeguarding' became central to policy discourses through the introduction of *Working Together to Safeguard Children: A Guide to Interagency Working to Safeguard and Promote the Welfare of Children* (DoH, 1999) and the *Framework for the Assessment of Children in Need and their Families* (DoH *et al.*, 2000).

These developments were taken further with the publication of the Green Paper, *Every Child Matters* (Chief Secretary to the Treasury, 2003) and the passage of the Children Act 2004. While ostensibly responding to the tragic death of Victoria Climbié, the Every Child Matters (ECM) agenda provided the thinking and legislative framework that would further broaden the scope for prevention and early intervention, with the central aim of ensuring the well-being of all children. Nowhere is this more evident than in the priority outcome statements for children, outlined in the *Every Child Matters: Change for Children* programme (DfES, 2004). These statements are that children should achieve economic well-being, be healthy, enjoy and achieve, make a positive contribution and stay safe. They are clearly a far cry from the narrow categories of child protection that dominated practice during the 1980s and 1990s. Thus, we see bold attempts by New Labour to very significantly transform preventative and protective services for children and families.

Given what appears a very positive agenda for children, which seeks to prevent, support and ameliorate childhood harms and disadvantage, how can it be the case this agenda has faltered, such that influential extra-national organizations can give the UK a very poor ranking in their comparative analyses? Of course, the government points to 'local implementation failures' – as the recent case of Baby P demonstrates – rather than failures of policy *per se*. However, chapters in our volume offer alternative explanations. In critiquing New Labour's approach to safeguarding children, this volume aims to shift thinking beyond the persuasive mantras of New Labour, towards detailed examination of the conceptual, ideological and political commitments that underpin New Labour's approach to safeguarding children, commitments that, at best, appear to hinder progress and, at worst, are fatally flawed. In addition, and bound up with these concerns, contributors to this volume also critically examine New Labour's particular approach to policy-making and organizational change. While each contributor brings their own particular interests and understandings to this volume, the following concerns have motivated our contributors:

- There is a serious mismatch between the inclusive rubric of New Labour's safeguarding agenda and the reality of the lives of many of the most vulnerable children and young people.
- New Labour's hegemonic interest in children as future citizen-workers has led to an increasingly narrow and regulated approach to both childhood and parenting.
- New Labour's favoured concept of active citizenship, which places primacy on economic rather than social rights underpinned by a strong moral ethic of self-governance and civic duty, has legitimated a more punitive approach to welfare delivery for those unable to 'play by the rules'.
- Early intervention may be neither positive nor benign, and this is most notable in the field of criminal justice.
- A preoccupation with identifying, assessing and intervening on the basis of 'risk' serves to individualize social problems and to mask the structural, political and individual inequalities which often characterize the lives of vulnerable children and their families.
- The pace of policy-making and rolling out of initiatives has created a confusing and fragmented landscape of welfare provision which, while aiming to produce 'joined-up' solutions for children and families, may have had the contrary effect.

- The size of investment in changes to the infrastructure of safeguarding has been at the expense of investment in areas of policy, notably housing, the tackling of wage inequality and further investment in childcare provision, that might have had a more direct bearing on the lives of children and families.

We briefly introduce these themes here, but they are developed in the analyses of the following chapters.

## Safeguarding: a 'Third Way'?

Safeguarding children is a practical, ethical, but also profoundly political activity. In order to understand social policies with respect to children and families, we need to understand something of the broader welfare commitments of particular governments. A great deal has been written about the 'Third Way' (see, for example, Blair, 1998; Giddens, 1998, 2000), but here we briefly consider some of the basic tenets of this approach and how they relate to safeguarding. The 'Third Way', for many analysts, represents a compromise between the 'old' Left and the New Right, the social justice of the former delivered through the 'free' markets of the latter (see Blair, 1998; Giddens, 1998, 2000). In this sense, state interventions are argued to have a dual role; to strengthen the operation of 'free' markets while affording individuals protection, albeit at a low level, from market failures and inefficiencies. As contributors to this volume identify, the main problem of the union of social justice with 'free' markets in the 'Third Way' is that in the UK, this union has been rather one-sided; the emphasis has been upon buttressing 'free' markets at the expense of social justice concerns. It is this 'bias' in welfare policy that has led to key analysts claiming that New Labour's so-called Social Investment State continues many of the neo-liberal commitments of the former Conservative administration, leading to inevitable inequalities (Perkins *et al.*, 2004).

As discussed in a number of chapters in this volume, New Labour's primary commitment to the free market impacts significantly on those who are most vulnerable (or who fall into vulnerability) because, as Jessop (1994, p. 24) has argued, the re-ordering of social policy in a neo-liberal economic context involves subordinating 'social policy to the needs of labour market flexibility and/or to the constraints of international competition'. This subordination has resulted in UK governments tolerating high levels of economic inequality, out-of-work benefit levels that are below the government's own measure of poverty and conditionality attached to benefits that has, over the past decade, become increasingly punitive and wider in coverage (Grover, 2008).

When we draw on political-economic analyses we can begin to understand some of the mismatch between the rhetoric and the reality of the 'Third Way' in delivering inclusive policies that will secure the well-being of all children.

While New Labour's social policies clearly acknowledge the links between socio-economic circumstances and outcomes for children, 'Third Way' policies are seemingly ineffective in challenging structural inequalities and the poverty that ensues. To understand why this is so, it is important to consider Labour's changing policy position with respect to explanations of poverty and inequality.

The 'Third Way' is not concerned with inequality of outcome. In contrast, it is concerned with inequality of opportunity, a meritocratic notion that is premised upon the idea that, beyond the very minimum, the distribution of material resources is not important, providing that individuals have an *equal* chance of securing them through legitimate means. In a number of chapters in this volume, the contributors make reference to the concept of 'active citizenship' that underpins New Labour's approach to tackling inequality. Contributors argue that notions of active citizenship assume a level playing field and give little credence to the limits for social mobility in the UK. In addition, issues of disability, mental ill health, neighbourhood disadvantage, gender and ethnicity all structure life chances. Narrowly focused on civic duty and an ethic of self-governance, New Labour is rather stunted in viewing life chances as simply a matter of individuals choosing the 'right' path out of disadvantage, primarily through education and paid work.

## Responsibilization, remoralization and adulteration

The idea of the 'Third Way', however, is not just structured by economic concerns. It also has a very strong moral dimension (cf. Rose, 2000) that, although not necessarily discreet from economic concerns, we have separated for analytical purposes. The moral aspects of the 'Third Way' have involved what is described as 'responsibilization' and 'remoralization'. While it would be wrong to suggest that concerns with responsibilities and morals only emerged with the election of New Labour in 1997, it is the case that since 1997 responsibilities and morality have become increasingly important to policy-related discourses and policy interventions. In this sense, New Labour have gone further than previous Conservative administrations in structuring social welfare interventions through concerns with moral standards and the responsibilities of individuals and families.

Of relevance to New Labour's safeguarding agenda is the resultant, and increasing, transfer of responsibilities from the state to children, young people and families. As we have noted, the Social Investment State places great store on the capacity of individuals to avail themselves of the opportunities available to them to secure their own well-being. It is argued (Jamieson, 2008) that the focus upon responsibilities in the 'Third Way' has been informed by the American moral philosopher, Amitai Etzioni (1993, 1995) who calls for a rebalancing of rights and responsibilities. For Etzioni, any rights that are conferred upon individuals and/or their dependent children, bring a set of responsibilities that must be fulfilled in order to access those rights. This is where the New Labour mantra, 'no rights without responsibilities' comes from. As contributors to this volume demonstrate, this mantra has created a set of problems for the safeguarding agenda because (a) it legitimates a more coercive approach to welfare – welfare-related services are seen to have a key role in shaping the values and moral character of its recipients – and (b) it detracts from the social-structural antecedents of disadvantage/need that have a direct bearing on children's welfare (Deacon, 2002). The more corrosive aspects of the rights and responsibilities agenda are discussed in a number of chapters in this volume that draw attention to the iatrogenic effect of New Labour's risk management influenced 'early intervention agenda' that, for example, has resulted in the increasing criminalization of children and young people.

The concept of remoralization is linked to that of responsibilization and refers to the belief that the economic and social dilemmas of late modern society are the consequence of a decline in moral standards, a decline in the moral fibre of individuals and neighbourhoods. In the UK such ideas have been most clearly expressed in concerns about illegitimacy, single parenthood, teenage pregnancy and welfare 'dependency', which, it is argued, have demoralized large numbers of the UK's population (Muncie, 2008a). In order to address these issues and the social and economic dilemmas that are held to be a consequent of them, it is remoralization that is needed. Such arguments, for instance, can be used to explain the increasing number of policies and Acts of Parliament that are aimed at bettering parenting. Indeed, the idea of a 'parenting deficit' (Etzioni, 1993) has, in many ways, come to define the remoralization agenda (Muncie, 2008a).

Responsibilization and remoralization come together in relation to issues that acutely affect the children of economically poor parents, for increasingly they frame access to a range of universal (for instance, education) and more selective (for example, social housing and various social security benefits) welfare benefits and services. The most important implication of the 'rights and responsibilities' agenda for 'safeguarding' children is that it introduces tensions into the 'safeguarding' agenda, because its concern with the well-being of children becomes contingent upon the behaviour and actions of children themselves or that of their parents.

Linked to both responsibilization and remoralization is the concept of 'adulteration'. This concept is mainly used in the youth justice literature to refer to the ways in which over recent years children have been treated in a manner that is increasingly similar to the ways in which adults are treated in the criminal justice system (Muncie, 2008b). In England and Wales, for example, the abolition of *doli incapax*, the possibility of imprisoning children from the age of 12 years and the application of the 'grave crime' provisions point to adulteration (Muncie, 2008b). Adulteration is linked to the concepts of remoralization and responsibilization because it is premised upon the idea that, like adult offenders, child and young offenders, are fully responsible for their actions; that 'child offending is a product of free will and volition and that all offenders should be made fully accountable for their actions' (Muncie, 2008b, p. 10). This view of the moral culpability of children who offend is problematic because it divorces such actions from their material and emotional circumstances that, as we shall see, are often acutely deprived.


## The risk paradigm

New Labour is preoccupied not only with the morals and responsibilities of individuals and families but also with 'risks'. The acceptance of 'risk' within New Labour's approach to policy-making is clearly signalled in Blair's acknowledgement that 'risk management ... is now central to the business of good government' (Blair, 2002, p. 2). Thus, social problems are being increasingly conceptualized in terms of individuals, families, communities and populations deemed to be 'at risk', with interventions targeted to prevent and or ameliorate these risks. Ultimately the management of risk aims to limit the potential for children and young people to develop persistent and intractable patterns of problem behaviour.

While ostensibly concerned with managing uncertainty, given changing social and economic conditions that are perceived to increase risks, the growth and acceptance of the actuarial influenced risk management paradigm within approaches to safeguarding children when examined in detail, finds close links to the responsibilization elements of the 'Third Way' agenda as outlined above. A focus on risk serves to individualize and personalize the problems and vulnerabilities faced by young people and to cut these off from the social, material and cultural context in which they should be situated. This individualization of social problems also serves to mask the responsibilities that the government owes to those children, and their families, whose lived reality is such that they often lack the means and willingness to become the active, economically contributing and law-abiding citizens envisaged in the Every Child Matters policy documents.

As various chapters within this volume highlight, the risk management agenda also has important repercussions for the interactions and interventions that professionals are able to pursue with children and their families. Risk management is premised on structured assessment tools which identify and assess 'risk' as a means to determine the level and specificities of the intervention deemed necessary. A focus on risk is seen to increase the consistency and rigour of assessment and to enable practitioners to adopt a more focused approach to intervention; however, this focus can also conflate and indeed, obscure 'needs'. The risk imperative may also serve to constrain and undermine professional practice and discretion. For example, with specific regard to youth justice, Muncie (1999, p. 150) argues that the prioritization of risk removes such 'transformative' concerns as individual need, diagnosis, rehabilitation and reformation which in effect 'shifts the entire terrain of law and order from one of understanding criminal motivation to one of simply making crime tolerable through systemic co-ordination'.

## The contested nature of childhood in late modern society: New Labour's policy response

The observations we have made about New Labour's 'Third Way' are important in understanding the social meaning(s) that it attaches to childhood. The meaning of childhood is increasingly contested in late modern Britain. On the one hand, children are deemed to be in need of protection from economic and social practices and structures, and from other people who threaten various aspects of their well-being, yet, at the same time, children's agency and their right to self-determination is emphasized (Prout, 2006). In addition, discourses of globalization and a belief that global economic competition requires a highly skilled and flexible workforce has given further priority to childhood as a period of 'investment' – with increasing attention paid to the risks to skill and social capital accumulation arising from 'anti-social' or offending behaviour. Arguably, and faced with these irrefutable tensions, any government will struggle to produce a coherent policy and legislative framework for 'safeguarding' children. However, for New Labour the most pressing concern is that 'support for today's disadvantaged children' will 'help to ensure a more flexible economy tomorrow' (HM Treasury, 2003, para. 5.4).

Social meanings are always contingent, with different societies at various periods in history prioritizing different risks or needs. New Labour's Social Investment State draws children into concerns with the longer-term reproduction of the neo-liberal economic order. As Piper (2008, p. 19) notes:

> The notion of investment is rooted in a particular set of ideas about childhood which construct it as a period of preparation for an economically active and useful working life and for a life-time of law-abiding and making positive contributions to the society.

A close reading of the ECM agenda finds that this theme runs throughout policy documents. It can be argued that ECM is concerned with the child as 'citizen-worker-of-the future' (Williams, 2004, p. 408). Drawing upon Fawcett *et al.* (2004), Lister (2006) argues that this means *Every Child Matters* is more concerned with children as 'becomings', rather than 'beings' and this is problematic because it ignores the views of children that were expressed in the ECM consultation process that clearly emphasized the importance of recreational activities and spaces for children (DfES, 2005). Unfortunately, this is common in the social policy-making process and relates to the ways in which children are constructed in policy-making. Rather than being seen as people with particular needs and voices, children are often seen as a threat to social and economic order or as a 'form of human capital, to be protected and developed' (Ridge, 2002, p. 6).

As many of the contributions to this volume attest, an analysis of New Labour's social policies finds initiatives weighted towards early intervention. They are pre-emptive. This focus is legitimated through an associated rhetoric of economic concerns that foreground costs to the state of children's failure to secure the necessary skills, qualifications and moral dispositions for their future as citizen-workers. Of course, for New Labour concern with children's failure to accumulate social capital in childhood not only reflects anxieties about problems of employability or contribution in adulthood, but also criminality. What we see under New Labour are increasing incursions into the lives of children and their families. Childhood is increasingly regulated. For example, the introduction of the *Birth to Three Matters* framework (DfES, 2002) now means that no part of childhood is exempt from developmental prescription. In addition, further incursions into the lives of families during the early years are legitimated on account of the need to identify not only children, but also infants 'at-risk' of future failings.

It is with respect to the primacy placed on children's contribution to the future economic good that we can understand differential commitment to diverse groups of children, *despite* the language of ECM. New Labour's safeguarding policies are inconsistent with respect to the less 'popular' social groups of children and young people. In particular, children whose residence may be seen as transitory hold a weak place, as they are not easily conceptualized as citizen-workers of the future. Likewise children in conflict with the law are deemed to be threatening and as such forfeit any right they may have had to be 'safeguarded'. Yet, it is often just such children who require most protection.

## Children's services: unremitting change in pursuit of the 'joined-up' solution?

An analysis of New Labour's safeguarding project would be incomplete without consideration of New Labour's very significant investment in the re-engineering of organizational and bureaucratic structures that are seen as central to the delivery of its vision. Early in office, New Labour announced an intention to 'modernize' public services (Cabinet Office, 1999). This essentially amounted to a reform of public services in keeping with the 'Third Way's' commitment to a mixed market of welfare services, but with a new approach to dispersed government founded on a belief in the effectiveness of local networks and partnerships. As a number of our contributors highlight, New Labour's commitment to dispersed government signified a significant shift away from hierarchical bureaucracy, with what was seen as a shift in the balance of power and decision-making to stakeholders, most notably local authorities. 'Modernized' services would deliver centrally driven government ambitions, but through locally negotiated plans, systems and protocols. Of course, this vision required effective collaboration at a local level and, thus, emerged New Labour's mantras of 'joined-up services' and 'seamless solutions'. However, the promise of the seamless delivery of services based on careful local analysis of need and collaborative planning has resulted in an unremitting stream of inter- and intra-organizational changes that, while seeking to remove perceived financial, regulatory and structural obstacles to effective collaboration, may have created further obstacles to good practice.

Since New Labour's arrival in government in 1997 problems in collaboration between agencies, identified in numerous reports of failures to safeguard children, have become a central plank for the safeguarding project. In particular, this line of attribution, which is central in the analyses of the Victoria Climbié inquiry, has served to legitimate the ECM reforms that have required far more radical and far-reaching bureaucratic and organizational change (Laming, 2003). An ever-expanding set of initiatives aims to compel agencies to work more closely together in the name of providing more effective services for children. Children's Trusts, the Common Assessment Framework, ContactPoint, the co-location of workers, joint education and social services appointments, protocols for joint care planning and complaints procedures, as well as pooled budgets and joint commissioning, are all attempts to build a truly integrated service as outlined under ECM (Chief Secretary to the Treasury, 2003).

As the Integrated Children's System (ICS) falters and Children's Trusts receive a pessimistic report from the Audit Commission (Audit Commission, 2008), the observations of critics such as Dowling *et al.* (2004), that New Labour's reforms are complex, costly and possibly dysfunctional, are prescient. During the three New Labour governments, jaundiced organizations and practitioners have been subject to ever more complex and ambitious reforms that in terms of the vision of organizational reform to promote joined up working, may actually have had the contrary effect. As a number of contributions to this volume attest, relentless change in organizational roles and responsibilities can damage, rather than improve, the inter-organizational communication channels, decision processes and shared understandings required for effective collaborative working. Moreover, critics argue that it is only through the day-to-day micro activities and relationship building processes that the shared project of collaborative working can be achieved (McMurray, 2007; Reder and Duncan, 2003). Technical fixes and formal governmental structures are deterministic in their vision, placing great store in compliance through New Performance Management, but they ignore the social context of collaboration that has more to do with 'unwritten and largely non-verbalized sets of congruent expectations held by the transacting parties about each other's prerogatives and obligations' (Ring and Van de Ven, 1994, p. 100).

The problem with New Labour's vision for integrated services is that there is little analysis of their effectiveness or practicability. This is a very important point, because limited public funds mean that money invested in the infrastructure of safeguarding is at the expense of alternative forms of social investment.

## Outline of the book

In chapter 2, Carolyn Taylor traces a recent history of child welfare in the UK by looking back over four decades of state intervention that have seen significant changes in government approaches to safeguarding children. This chapter serves to remind readers of the important antecedents of New Labour's safeguarding agenda. Carolyn's chapter expands on the themes that we have begun to chart in this introduction and provides both a detailed description and analysis of safeguarding within New Labour's 'Social Investment State'.

Further context setting material is provided in chapter 3 and 4 from David Archard and Chris Grover. In chapter 3, and focusing on the central issue of children's rights, David Archard debates the extent to which the commitments of the UNCRC are reflected in the ECM agenda. This chapter is followed by a detailed analysis of the issue of child poverty in chapter 4, with Chris Grover providing a damning critique of New Labour's failure to tackle growing social inequalities, of which the most unacceptable is poverty. The chapter argues that judging by the fact that the government has been unable to meet its own interim targets for tackling child poverty, this policy is likely to fail mainly because of the narrowness of an approach that focuses almost exclusively upon paid work. The chapter argues that governments' lack of success in tackling child poverty is problematic for the safeguarding agenda because it means that the 'economic well-being' outcome of *Every Child Matters* is likely to remain unfulfilled. In this case, children who live in financially poor families appear to be on the margins of the safeguarding agenda.

Chapters 5 and 6 then consider issues of communication and collaboration that are central concerns for New Labour. Chapter 5 provides an analysis of the evidence of the Common Assessment Framework's (CAF's) implementation, clearly illustrating that it is naïve to think that government can simply legislate for 'partnership'. As Andy Pithouse and Karen Broadhurst describe, practitioners bring their own 'qualitative test' to bear on so-called policy goods, and where discretion has not been entirely squeezed out through workflow systems such as ICS, they will choose to take or leave new policy initiatives depending on their fitness for purpose. In chapter 6, Sue White argues that the Laming reforms that have sought to address the communication failures evident in the case of Victoria Climbié inquiry, are based on a number of erroneous assumptions. Drawing on extensive ethnographic observations of practitioners' sense-making activities she argues that 'case formulations frequently emerge from interactions' and 'the facts are rarely simply out there as "information"'. Sue White sees effective communication as deriving from 'professional agility rather than from prescription and standardization'.

The remaining chapters focus on the principal policy areas. Chapters 7 and 8 provide complementary analyses of parenting policy. In chapter 7, and from a social work perspective, Karen Broadhurst argues that support for parenting is increasingly narrow and prescriptive, with initiatives having little impact on the socio-economic factors that undermine parenting capacity. The chapter draws attention to the plight of parents at the sharp edge of New Labour's support and draws links between a less tolerant approach to parents and the sharp rise in care proceedings witnessed over the last decade. In chapter 8, Jo Warin's focus is on parents within education. She is concerned with the ways in which through educational settings, parents are engaged in a manner that privileges 'expert' knowledge about children over parents' own knowledge of their children. In this process, the chapter demonstrates how those parents unable to engage in 'expert' discourse often become pathologized as 'hard to reach' and are seen as perpetuating what are deemed to be patterns of 'poor parenting'.

In chapter 9, Sue Peckover discusses in detail the expansion of safeguarding into the health sector. She makes reference to the size and complexity of the health service and raises questions about the re-engineering of this area of public service in line with new safeguarding demands. At a more practical level, she also draws attention to possible tensions for health professionals, for example health visitors, who on the one hand might consider themselves 'mother's friend', but, on the other hand, are increasingly tasked with monitoring parenting skills. In chapter 10, and continuing the theme of health, Ian Paylor debates problem drug and alcohol use in young people. He draws attention to tensions and contradictions in policy, given that problematic drug and alcohol use are both safeguarding and criminal justice concerns.

Chapters 11 and 12 focus on criminal justice issues for children and young people and the place of safeguarding within youth justice. The title of Janet Jamieson's chapter (chapter 11) hints at the social justice concerns that are central to her analysis, in which, among other issues, she highlights the plight of children in custody who appear left out of any safeguarding agenda. Similarly, in chapter 12, Claire Fitzpatrick addresses the limitations inherent to the safeguarding children agenda with regard to 'looked after' children. She documents the increased risks of criminalization that children in the looked after system, particularly those in residential care, can face and how criminal justice involvement can often negatively impact upon their future well-being.

Finally, and continuing the theme of marginalized children, in chapter 13 Malcolm Hill and Peter Hopkins examine the tensions that exist in the safeguarding agenda with reference to the children of asylum seekers. The authors draw attention to the tensions that arise between humanitarian impulses towards immigrant populations that are more consistent with safeguarding and the desire to control or restrict the number and types of individuals entering the UK or becoming citizens in the case of the asylum and immigration policy. The chapter argues that these tensions are further complicated by the ways in which legislation and policy at various scales – the international, European, British and devolved levels – influences the ways in which practitioners work to maximize the well-being of the children they encounter.

The concluding chapter draws material from across the chapters, and provides a cross-disciplinary analysis of the shortcomings of the New Labour safeguarding project. Drawing attention to the ideological shortcomings of the New Labour project that arise from a creeping welfare conditionality, a preoccupation with risks and responsibilities and over-interference in structures and organizations, the chapter urges caution for those who are optimistic about the inclusive rhetoric of the ECM project. A number of speculative observations are made with respect to a possible change of government and an alternative neo-liberal future for safeguarding.

# References

Audit Commission (2008) *Are We There Yet? Improving Governance and Resource Management in Children's Trusts*, London: Audit Commission.
Blair, T. (1998) *The Third Way: New Politics for the New Century*, Fabian Pamphlet 588, London: Fabian Society.
Blair, T. (2002) 'Foreword by the Prime Minister' in Cabinet Office Strategic Unit, *Risk: Improving Government's Capability to Handle Risk and Uncertainty*, London: Cabinet Office Strategic Unit.
Cabinet Office, The (1999) *Modernising Government*, London: The Stationery Office.
Chief Secretary to the Treasury (2003) *Every Child Matters*, Cm 5860, London: The Stationery Office.
Deacon, A. (2002) *Perspectives on Welfare*, Buckingham: Open University Press.
DfES (2002) *Birth to Three Matters*, London: The Stationery Office.
DfES (2004) *Every Child Matters: Change for Children Programme*, London: The Stationery Office.
DfES (2005) *Every Child Matters Children and Young People Responses*. Analysis of responses to the consultation document, http://www.everychildmatters.gov.uk/_files/2EBFE4007A52D4DCF57FCE9082C6A256.pdf (accessed 10 January 2009).
DoH (1999) *Working Together to Safeguard Children: A Guide to Inter-agency Working to Safeguard and Promote the Welfare of Children*, London: Department of Health, Home Office, Department for Education and Employment.
DoH, Department for Education and Employment and HO (2000), *Framework for the Assessment of Children in Need and their Families*, London: The Stationery Office.
Dowling, B., Powell, M. and Glendinning, C. (2004) 'Conceptualising successful partnerships', *Health and Social Care in the Community*, 12 (4): 309–317.
Etzioni, A. (1993) *The Parenting Deficit*, London: Demos.
Etzioni, A. (1995) *The Spirit of Community: Rights, Responsibilities and the Communitarian Agenda*, London: Fontana Press.
Fawcett, B., Featherstone, B. and Goddard, J. (2004) *Contemporary Child Care Policy and Practice*, Basingstoke: Palgrave Macmillan.
Giddens, A. (1998), *The Third Way: The Renewal of Social Democracy*, Cambridge: Polity Press.
Giddens, A. (2000) *The Third Way and its Critics*, Cambridge: Polity Press.
Grover, C. (2008) *Crime and Inequality*, Cullompton: Willan.
HM Treasury (2003) *Pre Budget Report 2003: The Strength to Take the Long-term Decisions for Britain: Seizing the Opportunities of the Global Recovery*, Cm 6042, London: The Stationery Office.
Howard League for Penal Reform (2008) *Growing Up Shut Up*: New Release, 1 July 2008; http://www.howardleague.org/fileadmin/howardleague/user/pdf/press 2008/Growing Up Shut Up 2 July 2008.pdf (accessed 11 November 2008).
Jamieson, J. (2008) 'Respect (Government Action Plan)', in B. Goldson (ed.), *Dictionary of Youth Justice*, Cullompton: Willan.
Jessop, B. (1994) 'The transition to post-Fordism and the Schumpeterian workfare state', in R. Burrows and B. Loader (eds.), *Towards a Post-fordist Welfare State*, London: Routledge.
Laming, Lord (2003) *The Victoria Climbié Inquiry: Report of an Inquiry by Lord Laming*, Command 5730, London: The Stationery Office.

Lister, R. (2006) 'Children (but not women) first: New Labour, child welfare and gender', *Critical Social Policy*, 26 (2): 315–335.

Maynard, A. and Sheldon, T. (1992) *Agenda for Change*, York: University of York.

McMurray, R. (2007) 'Our reforms, our partnerships, same problems: The chronic case of the English NHS', *Public Money and Management*, 27 (1): 77–82.

Muncie, J. (1999) 'Institutionalised intolerance: Youth justice and the 1998 Crime and Disorder Act', *Critical Social Policy*, 19 (2): 147–175.

Muncie, J. (2008a) 'Responsibilization', in E. McLaughlin and J. Muncie (eds.), *The Sage Dictionary of Criminology*, 2nd edn, London: Sage.

Muncie, J. (2008b) 'Adulteration', in B. Goldson (ed.), *Dictionary of Youth Justice*, Cullompton: Willan.

Perkins, D., Nelms, L. and Smyth, P. (2004) *Beyond Neo-liberalism in the Social Investment State?*, Social Policy Working Paper No. 3, Fitzroy, Brotherhood of St Laurence.

Piper, C. (2008) *Investing in Children: Policy Law and Practice in Context*, Cullompton: Willan.

Prout, A. (2006), *The Future of Childhood: Towards the Interdisciplinary Study of Children*, London: Routledge Falmer.

Reder, P. and Duncan, S. (2003) 'Understanding communication in child protection networks', *Child Abuse Review*, 12 (2): 82–100.

Ridge, T. (2002) *Childhood Poverty and Social Exclusion*, Bristol: Policy Press.

Ring, P. and Van de Ven, A. H. (1994) 'Developmental processes of cooperative interorganisational relationships', *Academy of Management Review*, 19 (1): 90–118.

Rose, N. (2000) 'Community, citizenship, and the Third Way', *The American Behavioral Scientist*; 43 (9): 1395–1441.

The *Guardian* (2007) Letter, 16 February. Available at: http://www.guardian.co.uk/society/2007/feb/16/ childrensservices.guardianletters (accessed 16 February 2009).

UK Children's Commissioners (2008) *UK Children's Commissioners' Report to the UN Committee on the Rights of the Child*, London/Belfast/Edinburgh/Colwyn Bay: 11 Million/NICCY/SCCYP/Children's Commissioner for Wales.

UNCRC (2008) *Consideration of Reports of State Parties. Third and Fourth Periodic Reports of the United Kingdom of Great Britain and Northern Ireland Committee on the Right of the Child*, 49th Session, Summary Record of the 1355th meeting, CRC/C/SR.1355, Geneva: UNCRC.

UNICEF (2007) *Child Poverty in Perspective: An Overview of Child Well-being in Rich Countries – A Comprehensive Assessment of the Lives and Well-being of Children and Adolescents in the Economically Advanced Nations*, Report Card 7, Florence, UNICEF Innocenti Research Centre.

Williams, F. (2004) 'What matters is who works: Why every child matters to New Labour. Commentary on the DfES Green Paper *Every Child Matters*', *Critical Social Policy*, 24 (3): 406–427.

# 2

# Safeguarding Children: Historical Context and Current Landscape

Carolyn Taylor

> The primary focus of official concern has broadened considerably. While in the 1960s it was 'battered babies', in the 1970s 'non-accidental injury to children', in the 1980s 'child abuse', and for much of the 1990s 'significant harm and the likelihood of significant harm', the focus in the new millennium is 'safeguarding and promoting the welfare of the child'. (Parton, 2007, p. 9)

The vocabulary of child protection has undoubtedly undergone considerable change in the last forty years or so. But what exactly do these changes mean? Do they signify important changes in policy and practice relating to the welfare and safety of children and young people or do they merely indicate a more cosmetic, superficial updating of terminology over time while the core framework of services remains intact? Arguably changes in vocabulary up to the 1990s are indicative of refinements in recognizing, managing and intervening in cases of child abuse and neglect since its 'rediscovery' in the 1960s; the safeguarding agenda, on the other hand, may be said to herald more significant change. It has been described as denoting a more systematic and inclusive approach to child welfare issues which has been further extended within the Every Child Matters (ECM) initiative (Chief Secretary to the Treasury, 2003; Department for Education and Skills [DfES], 2004). Introduced in the wake of the inquiry report into the death of Victoria Climbié (Laming, 2003), ECM involves concerted efforts to ensure no child slips through the net of preventative services, through efforts to improve information sharing and working together by professionals, which include the introduction of the Common Assessment Framework, renewed measures to tackle social exclusion and, with the aim of giving children a voice in government and public life, the appointment of the first Children's Commissioner for England (http://www.everychildmatters.gov.uk/aims/).

To explore these developments in child welfare, the chapter is divided into three sections: the first provides an overview of developments within the 'second

*Critical Perspectives on Safeguarding Children*  Edited by Karen Broadhurst, Chris Grover and Janet Jamieson
© 2009 John Wiley & Sons, Ltd

wave' of child rescue from the 1960s; the second explores the safeguarding agenda introduced by the New Labour in the late 1990s while the third section subjects safeguarding to critical scrutiny. Finally, the conclusion returns to consider the changes in vocabulary – from 'protecting' to 'safeguarding' – and asks whether such changes and accompanying policy and legislative developments herald a more positive future for children and young people.

## The 'second wave' of child rescue

It has been suggested that a paper published by the American paediatrician, Henry Kempe, and his colleagues in the early 1960s (Kempe *et al.*, 1962) marks the advent of the second wave of the 'child rescue' movement, eventually placing child abuse centre stage within child welfare not only within the United States of America (USA), but also in the United Kingdom (UK) and Australia (Scott and Swain, 2002, p. 120).[1] Prior to this within the UK, under the Children Act 1948, the attention of Children's Departments had primarily focused upon preventative work with families and the provision of substitute care for children deemed unable to live at home (Holman, 1988; Packman, 1975). The identification of 'battered baby syndrome' was to have far-reaching implications by bringing child abuse to the forefront of concern within child welfare and, at this early stage, making medical staff, and particularly paediatricians, dominant players in this area of work. Professional attention now needed to acknowledge and address the issue of serious physical abuse and injuries to young children which caused permanent injury or death.

   In effect the 'rediscovery' of child abuse led to a shift from a moral model 'based on the exercise of moral authority reinforced by the law' (Scott and Swain, 2002, p. 121) to a medical model based on a 'syndrome' and a disease model in which detection and diagnosis became key (Scott and Swain, 2002). The efficacy of traditional forms of intervention – monitoring, friendly support and advice-giving (in other words, casework of a rather indeterminate kind and length) – was called into question and methods to deal with abusive parents became more specialist and therapeutically oriented (although simultaneously more directive and authoritarian) as the National Society for the Prevention of Cruelty to Children (NSPCC) positioned itself as a primary holder of knowledge and skills in relation to child abuse. Child abuse was not only medicalized, but also psychologized to a much greater extent, as attention was focused upon

---

[1]   The 'first wave' occurred in the latter part of the nineteenth and early twentieth century when voluntary activists established organizations to provide care and refuge for homeless and neglected children. Barnardo's is, of course, the most celebrated of these, although many other organizations existed in the towns and cities of the UK and elsewhere (Ferguson, 2004; Lawrence and Starkey, 2001; Murdoch, 2006; Wagner, 1979; Woodroofe, 1962). With regard to the 'second wave' it should also be added that it is overly simplistic to attribute to Kempe what was undoubtedly a more complex emergence of the 'rediscovery' of child abuse but he and his colleagues seem to have coined the term 'battered baby syndrome' which gained currency in the Anglophone world. Mythic status in the 'battle against child abuse' seems to have followed.

identifying the psychological factors that predisposed certain adults to abuse the children in their care and devising systematic intensive methods of treatment. In this regard knowledge, policy and practice in the UK were heavily influenced by developments in research and practice in the USA (Parton, 2007). However, the mandatory reporting systems widely introduced by state legislatures in the USA in the late 1960s and early 1970s as part of the professional response to child abuse were not adopted in the UK (Munro and Parton, 2007).

Subsumed within the overarching field of child welfare were four discrete strands of endeavour: preventative work with families; work with young offenders; provision for children in public care; and, by the 1970s, systems for dealing with 'non-accidental injury' (NAI), a more generic, less emotive term that displaced 'battered baby syndrome' in professional discourse. This signified the retention of a focus on physical injury while extending the scope of activity beyond young children to any child experiencing alleged injury of a non-accidental kind, including those of a more minor nature such as unexplained bruising. Until the 1970s child abuse work engaged less time and attention within statutory services than preventative work and dealing with children in public care.

The early 1970s saw a major reorganization of the personal social services in England and Wales in the wake of the Seebohm Report (Seebohm Report, 1968) and the Local Authorities Personal Social Services Act 1970 (implemented in April 1971). This Act brought together services for adults, children and older people into newly formed Social Services Departments under the leadership of a Director of Social Services. It established generic working within social work teams with the aim of integrating personal social services across the spectrum of age and need. In this period also, legislation such as the Children and Young Persons Act 1969 gave new powers and duties to social workers. In many ways this can be seen as the high-watermark of the welfarist project with its aim of providing non-stigmatizing, universal services to support individuals and families in need. It assumed a benign role for the state and a neutral, expert role for bureau-professionals charged with assessing and meeting need by supporting families to overcome problems. However, optimism about the capacity of child welfare to provide care and protection within an integrated structure proved short-lived.

The inquiry into the death of Maria Colwell in 1973 caused a sea-change in child welfare priorities as the effects of 'scandal politics' (Butler and Drakeford, 2003) were felt in the arena of child welfare, if not for the first time, to significant effect (Secretary of State for Social Services, 1974). The parameters of the contemporary system of child abuse management were effectively established in response to the Colwell inquiry, initially via a series of circulars and letters from the Department of Health and Social Security (for example, DHSS, 1974, 1976). Inter-agency working under the aegis of Area Review Committees was established, assigning lead responsibility to Social Services Departments to work with local health (community and hospital) services, education and subsequently the police.[2] Case conferencing to assess and review cases was introduced along with NAI registers of children considered to have experienced non-accidental injury (Parton, 1985).

If systems changed fundamentally from the mid 1970s onwards, so too did the focus of practice: within local authorities the Colwell inquiry and subsequent inquiry reports in the 1980s 'had the effect of leading to defensive and bureaucratically constrained procedures and practices' (Corby, 2003, p. 231; see also Harris, 1990; Howe, 1992). Inquiries shone a spotlight upon a central dilemma for social work practice: with hindsight intervention could be deemed both unnecessary and intrusive where agencies were seen to over-react to expressions of concern. At the same time, failures to act in cases of child death or serious injury laid social workers and other professionals open to accusations of ineptitude and gullibility when subsequent inquiries exposed deficits in the sharing and questioning of information and an apparent undue readiness to believe parents. These, it was argued, resulted in the child's vulnerability and needs being lost from view (Corby, 2003; Reder *et al.*, 1993; Reder and Duncan, 1997).

This concern with the limits of intervention also chimed with other public concerns about 'over intrusive and heavy-handed' practice in the general field of child welfare (Corby, 2007, p. 42). There were concerns about the overuse of compulsory powers (Packman, 1986), the use of local authority care as a solution for control and justice issues among young people (for instance, children made the subject of care orders because of their delinquent/offending behaviour – see Morris *et al.*, 1980) and the instabilities and deficiencies of the public care system in relation to 'drift' in care, lack of planning, placement instability, and children's loss of contact with their birth families (DHSS, 1985). Where once social work with children and families had been seen to operate within a framework of welfarism – 'meeting needs, compensating [for] socially caused "diswelfares" and promoting social justice' (Parton, 1996, p. 8) – it came under attack from the 1970s for being woolly-minded and ineffectual in some instances and overly controlling and intrusive in others.

Broader economic constraints in the 1970s also diverted Social Services Departments from the more optimistic vision of welfare services assumed within the Seebohm reforms. Constrained budgetary resources from the mid 1970s and increased demand for services resulted in local authority social work being more narrowly directed at those in the most acute and immediate need, with significant priority given to NAI investigations and statutory work. At the same time social workers were drawn into negotiating with other elements of the welfare system (principally social security, housing and utility companies) on behalf of clients as well as gatekeeping scarce public resources (Langan, 1993). Growing debate about the care and control functions of social work,

---

[2]  Area Review Committees were designed to formulate local policy, procedures and training initiatives; in the early days the majority were chaired by a Director of Social Services but a significant number were chaired by medical personnel (Parton, 1985, p. 105).

the effectiveness of casework and the discretion afforded to social workers contributed to widespread unease about the ability of social work to provide a competent and effective service which has persisted to this day.

By 1978 the term 'child abuse' had supplanted 'non-accidental injury' (which in turn had replaced 'baby/child battering') in government documents (Parton, 1985).[3] This designation more clearly indicated the parameters of professional concern, implying culpability on the part of an abuser and possibly a 'non-protecting' caregiver. The trend towards the proceduralization of child abuse continued with new guidance which extended the categories of abuse or risk of abuse under which a child might be placed on a Child Abuse Register: physical injury, physical neglect, failure to thrive and living in the same household as someone convicted under schedule 1 of the 1933 Children and Young Persons Act (DHSS, 1980). Further inquiries and reports, notably concerning the deaths of Jasmine Beckford (London Borough of Brent, 1985), Kimberley Carlile (London Borough of Greenwich and Greenwich Health Authority, 1987) and Tyra Henry (London Borough of Lambeth, 1987) prompted further soul-searching about the preventability of child deaths and the (in)effectiveness of existing systems and procedures. The response was, again, primarily technical and procedural: in the revised guidance published in 1988 inter-professional coordination and cooperation were given greater prominence under Area Child Protection Committees, which replaced Area Review Committees; child abuse work was reframed as 'child protection', thus shifting emphasis away from the recognition of abuse and neglect to the statutory obligation placed upon local authorities to respond promptly and effectively in concert with other agencies (Corby, 2007, p. 43; DHSS, 1988). The lead responsibility of social workers to act as key worker and to coordinate the 'child protection plan' with core groups and planning meetings was reinforced; Child Abuse Registers were henceforth to be known as Child Protection Registers. The new guidance also contained new definitions of abuse and neglect which gave greater prominence to sexual and emotional abuse (DHSS, 1988).

However, while findings from inquiries into child deaths impelled a more directive and proceduralized approach, events in Cleveland in the late 1980s prompted a rather different reaction. When a large number of children were removed from their parents for suspected child sexual abuse following the use by paediatricians of a controversial diagnostic medical test, social workers and other professionals were pilloried in the media not for their sins of omission as in the cases of child deaths from abuse and neglect, but for their sins of commission. Cleveland, it was argued, exemplified the flagrant breaching of families' rights to privacy and over-zealous interpretation of the statutory duty to protect children from harm (Butler-Sloss, 1988; for discussion of Cleveland see Campbell, 1988;

---

[3] The term NAI is still used to describe a very specific form of injury, but the concept of child abuse encompasses broader notions of harm to children including emotional and sexual abuse. Neglect has also been added to child abuse to indicate another significant form of potential harm to children.

Levy, 1989; Richardson and Bacon, 1991). Attempts to respond to the Cleveland situation, as well as child deaths from physical abuse, led to revisions to the child protection system: parental participation in case conferences was to be encouraged while joint police and social work investigations were recommended in cases of suspected child sexual abuse that for a period of time in the 1980s and 1990s dominated child protection work.

## Child welfare in the 1990s: the 'refocusing' debate

Child welfare in general, and child protection in particular, has for many decades been a contested arena, but this was especially so by the late 1980s. As Parton (2007, p. 17) notes, 'a fine balance had to be struck between protecting the weak and the vulnerable and protection from unwarrantable interference – particularly from the state'. In this context we can see a shift taking place from the socio-medical conceptualization of child abuse and neglect of the 1960s and 1970s to a socio-legal emphasis on child protection established in the wake of Cleveland, although medical diagnosis remained important in child protection inquiries as did expert medical opinion in care proceedings.[4] The enactment of the Children Act 1989 is an important moment in this development and reflects the tensions contained within policy and practice at the time. The Act sought to establish threshold criteria for child protection inquiries and court proceedings ('significant harm' and risk of harm), amended the orders that could be made by the court, set out the powers and duties of the police and local authority to protect children where harm or risk of future harm was indicated or suspected, and required that, where children were made the subject of a court order, a plan for their welfare and protection was available for consideration at the hearing. At the same time the Act, or its accompanying guidance and regulations, clearly established the principles for child care practice, including: acknowledging parental responsibility and the importance of the birth family; the paramountcy principle in relation to the child's welfare; working in partnership with parents and professionals; and the importance of supporting families, as well as protecting children from harm (Allen, 2005; Department of Health [DoH], 1989).

Strains between the child protection and family support elements of the Children Act 1989 were played out in the 1990s. In the years immediately following its implementation the numbers of 'looked after children' (children in public care) declined significantly which provides some evidence that practitioners were endeavouring to work in partnership with parents without recourse to the care

---

[4] Commentators have argued that the rise to prominence of socio-legalism signals a diminution of the influence of psychological and developmentalist approaches as the focus of child welfare narrowed (Otway, 1996; Parton, 1991). Sue White (1998) mounts a convincing argument for the enduring influence of psycho-legalism.

system.[5] However, major problems continued to be exposed. So, for instance, child abuse inquiries continued to cause public alarm as familiar criticisms of practice were repeated and social workers were further damned in the media for either under- or over-protecting children (Parton, 2007). Increased pressures were placed upon child welfare by the exposure of abuse in children's homes which called into question the capacity of the care system to provide a satisfactory substitute for family life (Corby *et al.*, 2001). The existing direction of policy and practice thus came under considerable scrutiny not least because this was a time of broader challenges to the welfare settlement of the post World War II period with the rise of an amalgam of neoliberal economic and neoconservative social policies under Conservative governments from 1979 to 1997. The costs of welfare and its alleged promotion of a 'dependency culture' among welfare recipients were key elements of this challenge.

Thus, before the optimistic agenda of extended and supportive welfare services contained within Seebohm could really take root, it was being undermined not only by economic circumstances but also by a sustained onslaught from New Right thinkers arguing in favour of a radical overhaul of welfare. As part of this process the existing organization and delivery of welfare came under strong attack: rather than being a major (or 'monopoly' according to critics) provider of services, it was argued that the state should adopt a more restricted role as manager and coordinator of services, while the private and voluntary sectors should assume a prominent role in service delivery in a reconfigured 'mixed economy of welfare'.

Managerialism was a further element of this assault upon the classic welfare state and its assumed benign neutrality. Welfare bureaucrats were portrayed as 'building empires at the expense of providing services' (Clarke and Newman, 1997, p. 15), effectively divorced from the 'real' wants and needs of people while welfare professionals were seen as motivated by self-interest and imposing their 'expert' view on passive recipients of services. The 'new managerialism' was advanced as a counter to the deficiencies of bureau-professionalism, placing the manager at the centre of reform in both the public and private sectors. Fundamental to successful reform of an ailing welfare system was the 'right to manage', that is to plan, implement and measure improvements in productivity and outputs in order to deliver the 'three E's' of economy, efficiency and effectiveness (Newman and Clarke, 1994). Welfare needed to be more businesslike,

---

[5] This evidence needs to be treated with some caution. The numbers of children looked after in England and Wales declined from 60,532 in 1990 to 49,100 in 1994 before rising again steadily to exceed the 1990 level by 2003 (there were 60,800 children looked after in that year). However, the proportion of children looked after under care orders increased in the same period (from 55 per cent in 1990 to 63 per cent by 2000 – see Department of Health statistics for the period and Beckett, 2001). The Children Act principle of working in partnership with parents to prevent entry to care seems to have influenced practice and, in consequence, the thresholds for entry to care were raised. When admission to care was deemed necessary, the limits of voluntary arrangements had perhaps been reached and a care order was preferred since it offered greater control to the local authority. It should also be noted that significant numbers of children subject to care orders live with birth parents or family and friends, and are not accommodated by the local authority.

with more clearly stated aims and objectives and standardized criteria by which performance could be measured. The work of frontline staff was thus to be more tightly defined and controlled through new systems of accountability to senior managers.

Given the nature of the attacks on welfare it was perhaps inevitable that social security benefits and community care attracted most attention. However, child and family social work was affected by the discrediting of welfare professionalism that formed part of this challenge to welfarism: 'welfare professionalism was coming under attack for its detachment from the "real world". Trendy theories and liberal or permissive values were seen as eroding both effectiveness and social authority' (Clarke and Newman, 1997, p. 12). Social workers' 'political correctness' in matters of transracial fostering and adoption and their failures in preventing child abuse deaths were all grist to the mill. Notable for its absence though, was any recognition of the effects of poverty and social disadvantage on the lives of those children and families who tended to be the primary users of child welfare services.

Operating within this hostile environment, considerable energies were committed to refashioning child welfare in the 1990s to put in place a new professionalism founded on a clearly articulated knowledge base derived from government-funded academic research. Central to these endeavours was the 're-focusing' initiative which aimed to address the tension between child protection and family support in social work practice. Two publications set the initiative in train: *Seen but not Heard: Coordinating Child Health and Welfare Services for Children in Need* (Audit Commission, 1994) and *Child Protection: Messages from Research* (DoH, 1995). Both documents criticized child welfare work for being overly concerned with child protection to the detriment of family support and a broader understanding of child welfare. In brief, the main criticisms of child protection were that it had become 'too bureaucratised, too proceduralised and over-focused on overt incidents of child abuse, such as bruising and child sexual abuse allegations' (Corby, 2007, p. 66). It was argued that a forensic approach to investigation had come to dominate which, in turn, had led to vast numbers of referrals entering the system, ranging from the apparently minor to the extremely serious, only for the majority of them to be filtered out either before, or at, the case conference stage. Despite being filtered out in this way, a significant proportion of families showed high levels of disadvantage and need which were effectively ignored while resources were concentrated on those families with children placed on the child protection register. Arguably, it became the case that family problems needed to be framed as 'child protection' in order to receive attention and command resources from the local authority.

The investigative system was also found to be profoundly alienating to parents and there was little evidence of professionals working in partnership with them or aiding them through the process (Cleaver and Freeman, 1995; Thoburn *et al.*, 1995). In effect it was argued that child welfare had assumed too narrow a focus and had become a residual set of reactive services primarily organized around child protection and entry to care rather than prevention. In the process a broader construction of the social problems of families with children was effaced. However, the refocusing initiative was careful to avoid any overt political challenge to the government of the day. It presented a depoliticized analysis of child welfare, offering a programme for change that was largely congruent with the managerial agenda promoted within New Right thinking with its focus on increased control and accountability of frontline services.

For these reasons the refocusing initiative has proved contentious. While recognizing the need for family support, critics pointed to the failure of the reformers to acknowledge the difficulties of practising in a highly emotive area of work where social workers were excoriated both for acting and for failing to act to protect children. Moreover, the damning description of child protection was not supplemented by any account of why services might have developed in such a way within a specific political and policy context (Parton, 1997). In this regard the lack of recognition of the 'nature, significance and impact of public inquiries' (Parton, 1997, p. 12) upon policy and practice was a glaring omission since it obscured the reasons why practice might have adopted such defensiveness. The end result was that blame was attributed to professionals and organizational arrangements while solutions were deemed to lie in promoting attitudinal change among managers and frontline staff and modifications to operational perspectives and practice (Parton, 1997). Logistical issues remained about how precisely the child welfare system was to be turned around without an influx of resources. Refocusing was intended to be financed by the resources released from investigation and assessment work in child protection (Parton, 1997), but to critics this clearly represented something of a 'chicken and egg' situation; how precisely would child protection work decrease in volume before family support services had been built up? Regardless of the intentions of advocates of rebalancing, without additional funding to kick-start change, the prospects of achieving a significant shift in focus towards family support appeared seriously hampered.

## Safeguarding: New Labour and the Social Investment State

If the ambitions of refocusing seemed hard to achieve in the political, social and economic climate of the 1990s, nonetheless a wider agenda for child welfare was brought into play in 1997 when New Labour was elected to government. This involved a further change to the vocabulary of child welfare when 'child protection' was subsumed within the broader goal of 'safeguarding and promoting the welfare of the child' (or simply 'safeguarding'):

> Safeguarding and promoting the welfare of the child: the process of protecting children from abuse or neglect, preventing impairment of their health and development, and ensuring they are growing up in circumstances consistent with the

provision of safe and effective care that enables children to have optimum life chances and enter adulthood successfully. (DfES, 2006, p. 27)

For some this represents a radical and not altogether welcome shift of focus. Munro and Calder (2005) warn that eliminating the terms 'child protection', 'abuse' and 'risk' from the vocabulary (and practice) of child welfare is likely to result in a loss of focus on the victims of abuse and a failure to acknowledge both the specificity of child abuse work and the difficulties of working with parents suspected of abuse. New Labour, however, clearly wished to set an agenda for child welfare which embraced a much wider concern 'with parenting, early intervention, supporting the family and regenerating the community more generally' (Parton, 2007, p. 20). The issue of child poverty was 'returned' to social policy having previously been erased from New Right thinking about welfare problems and solutions (see chapter 4 in this volume). This new agenda was firmly located within the New Labour project to construct a 'social investment state' (SIS) (see chapter 1 in this volume). Drawing on a model propounded by the British sociologist, Tony Giddens (1994, 1998), the SIS retained features of the neoliberal approach favoured by previous Conservative administrations, accepting the sovereignty of the market and the need for Britain plc to compete effectively in an increasingly globalized economy, and leaving intact those industries and utility companies privatized under the Conservatives.

There were, however, clear attempts to articulate a New Labour discourse that established distance from its immediate Conservative predecessor and the 'old Labour' approach of the 'classic' post-war welfare state. Both were presented as outdated narratives, unsuited to the conditions facing the UK in the late twentieth century, following changes to work (for example, the decline in manufacturing, the advent of new technologies and women's participation in the workforce), family structures (such as increases in divorce and lone parenthood) and the increased expectations of certain sectors of the population (for instance, among disabled people). Unbridled neoliberalism was castigated because its obeisance to the market, to the detriment of the social, had exacerbated social disadvantage. Despite the expressed desire to 'roll back the state', this had led perversely to increased public spending on social protection. The consequences of the policies pursued by the previous Conservative administrations were multiple: increased poverty, particularly for children; greater inequality between rich and poor; greater dependence on state benefits (the effect of economic restructuring and increased unemployment); and a greater amount of homelessness/rough sleeping (Blair, 1999).

At the same time, the discourse of the SIS was a clear attempt to set New Labour apart from the statism and collectivism of 'old Labour' whose alleged 'tax and spend' philosophy had been so vilified by Conservative administrations between 1979 and 1997. New Labour came to power with a clear agenda to address social issues while transforming the basis for welfare away from a 'something-for-nothing' to a 'something for something' welfare state (Blair,

1999). Welfare was to have an accepted role in the New Labour vision, but neither as a residual safety net, nor as an automatic right to protection. Instead a new, active role for welfare was adumbrated: 'a welfare state that is just about "social security" is inadequate. It is passive where we now need to be active. It encourages dependency where we need to encourage independence, initiative, enterprise for all' (Blair, 1999, p. 13).

Having undermined the claims of its predecessors New Labour used the concept of the SIS as the vehicle to promote an agenda of modernization. Old-style welfare had been reactively oriented towards social protection. New style welfare would be future oriented: 'for state spending to be effective, it must not simply be consumed in the present, to meet current needs, but must be an investment that will pay off and reap rewards for the future' (Jenson and Saint-Martin, 2003, p. 83). Three grounds were articulated as warrants for public spending: addressing the chronic underinvestment in public services which had accumulated during the previous regime; expanding educational and employment opportunities within a knowledge-based global economy; and strengthening communities and citizenship (Brown, 2002, cited in Lister, 2003, p. 429).

Investment in human capital displaced the idea of welfare as income maintenance (Giddens, 1998). Children emerged as key figures in the SIS model since they represented the citizen-workers of the future (Lister, 2003). They were thus prioritized as 'human becomings' in the future rather than 'human beings' in the present (Lee, 2001, p. 5). All children were to be supported and given opportunities to achieve their full potential, although the needs of children growing up in poverty were singled out for particular attention since such disadvantage would not only adversely affect their experiences as adults but also the life chances of their children (HM Treasury, 2003). New parameters were thus established for intervening in families with an emphasis upon a productivist and enabling role for the state (Jenson and Saint-Martin, 2003). In this context, the safeguarding agenda assumes a greater significance since it can be seen as part of an attempt to widen the remit of public services beyond a more narrowly conceived focus on children in need of protection or services to prevent family breakdown:

> Social services for children cannot be seen in isolation from the wider range of children's services delivered by local authorities and other agencies. The Government is committed to taking action through a broad range of initiatives to strengthen family life, to reduce social exclusion and anti-social behaviour among children, and to give every child the opportunity of a healthy, happy, successful life. (DoH, 1998a, para. 3.4)

These themes were echoed across New Labour policy documents. For example, *Supporting Families* acknowledged the familiar concern that 'governments have to be wary about intervening in areas of private life and intimate emotion' (Home Office, 1998, p. 4) but, nevertheless, also argued that advice giving and practical support did not constitute interference (Home Office, 1998, p. 52).

Early intervention was identified as key to these endeavours because of the crucial influence of the child's early years upon future success and happiness (Home Office, 1998, p. 13).

Within *Supporting Families* no reference was made to child abuse, neglect or protection *per se*. Instead, considerable emphasis was placed upon external social issues – poor housing, social exclusion and lack of opportunity – as lying at the root of many serious family problems (Home Office, 1998, p. 40). This set the scene for initiatives that lay outside the scope of existing local authority services for children and families, proposing an integrated approach to family policy ranging from financial support to welfare services. Proposed initiatives included strengthening advice and support via an independent National Family and Parenting Institute and a national helpline for parents; introducing a system of tax credits and increased benefits for working families; and the Sure Start programme which was intended to target help on those 'facing linked problems such as poor educational achievement, health or housing, or unemployment' (Home Office, 1998, p. 13).[6]

Despite lack of acknowledgement within *Supporting Families*, local authority children's services were by no means immune from change. The urgent need for reform and modernization of public services was a key element of the New Labour project from the outset. Serious deficiencies in relation to both adult's and children's services had been identified: failure to protect vulnerable children and adults both in their homes and in institutional care; inflexibility, inconsistencies and lack of coordination of services; lack of clarity regarding service availability and eligibility; and overall inefficiency and lack of cost effectiveness (DoH, 1998a). In relation to children's services the poor outcomes for children in public care were a particular cause of concern, notably in relation to educational achievement, employment, housing, offending and future health and well-being (DoH, 1999b).

The Quality Protects programme, launched in September 1998 as the vehicle to deliver the government's agenda in relation to modernizing children's services was intended to achieve more effective protection for children, better quality care for looked after children and improved life chances for children (DoH, 1998b). This programme set out national objectives, targets and performance indicators for various aspects of children's services,[7] establishing the principle

---

[6]    The first Sure Start programmes were established in 1999 to bring together work in early education, childcare, health and family support for the benefit of young children living in disadvantaged areas and their parents. Their aim was to improve the health and well-being of children aged from birth to four, and that of their families, to provide a platform for successful entry to school and educational achievement. More recently, Sure Start is being extended across England (other countries in the UK make their own provision) with a developing network of Children's Centres. Now greater emphasis is placed on childcare and supporting parents with their aspirations for employment, as well as in parenting. (see http://www.surestart.gov.uk/aboutsurestart/ [accessed 26 August 2008]; see also Clarke, 2006).

[7]    Examples include reducing the number of placement moves experienced by a looked after child within a given year; increasing the number of looked after children adopted during a year as a percentage of all looked after children; making sure that local authorities stay in touch with young people who leave care at 16 until the age of 19 (see DoH, 1999b).

of the local authority as corporate parent with a special duty of care for looked after children, and the development of children's services Management Action Plans which were to be subject to annual review by central government. The initiative was underpinned by a grant of £885 million over a five-year period (DoH, 1998b).

The safeguarding agenda continued apace from the late 1990s. Alongside Sure Start other new agencies were created, notably Connexions and Youth Offending Teams and new programmes set up, such as the Children's Fund, as an early intervention strategy for 5- to 13-year-olds. Significant legislation was enacted, including the Crime and Disorder Act 1998, the Children (Leaving Care) Act 2000 and the Adoption and Children Act 2002, while policy developments included the introduction of a *Framework for the Assessment of Children in Need and their Families* which established new timescales for initial and core assessments along with an abundance of guidance about the conduct of assessments (DoH *et al.*, 2000). The safeguarding agenda received further impetus with the introduction of the Every Child Matters (ECM) framework in the wake of the public inquiry into the death of Victoria Climbié (Chief Secretary to the Treasury, 2003; Laming, 2003). While ostensibly a response to concerns arising from Victoria's horrific death at the hands of her great aunt and the latter's partner, *Every Child Matters* reaffirms a commitment to safeguarding and promoting the welfare of children within a wider framework of supportive services aimed at early intervention.

Within this wider framework, ECM also addresses the organizational and procedural issues raised by the Laming inquiry with regard to information sharing, decision-making and inter-agency working. Integrated working is placed centre stage, which has led to significant reorganization and realignment of children's services to promote joined-up working between agencies and professionals. In particular, it has brought together education and child and family social work in a single local authority department and established broader integration of services including health, police and voluntary organizations in Children's Trusts (see Audit Commission, 2008). Information collecting and sharing were identified as central to early identification and intervention across agencies and emphasized in policy developments. This has led to an upsurge of information and communication technology (ICT) initiatives which form part of social work's 'electronic turn' (Garrett, 2005) and which parallel technology initiatives across the public sector (Selwyn, 2002). Developments in children's services include ContactPoint,[8] the electronic version of the Common Assessment Framework (eCAF) and the Integrated Children's System (ICS). ContactPoint, (formerly the Information Sharing Index), is a proposed online directory that will hold data about all children with the aim of enabling quick access by authorized staff to ascertain who is working with a child and which children are

---

[8] At the time of writing the introduction of ContactPoint has been delayed (Murray, 2008).

causing concern (DCSF, 2007). eCAF is an electronic version of the Common Assessment Framework designed to provide a simple, standardized initial assessment tool for all agencies working with children and families (DCSF, 2008). The Integrated Children's System (ICS) is the electronic successor to the *Looking after Children* materials (Ward, 1995), to be used for assessment, planning, intervention and review in detailed assessments, creating an e-record for children in need, especially looked after children (DCSF, 2007).

Within the ECM framework child protection procedures have been subject to further revision and reinforcement. Multi-agency working is re-emphasized in a new version of *Working Together to Safeguard Children* (DfES, 2006). The former Area Child Protection Committees (ACPCs) have been replaced by Local Safeguarding Children Boards which are now placed under statutory arrangements. Section 11 of the Children Act 2004 places a duty upon key people and bodies to make arrangements to safeguard and promote the welfare of children. Statutory guidance has been issued with the intention of strengthening lines of accountability between frontline staff and their managers, and emphasizing staff training needs (DfES, 2007). Joint planning and commissioning of services are also emphasized while inspection is newly configured to reflect a multi-agency approach with the introduction of the Joint Area Review (JAR) framework with primary responsibility for inspection transferred to Ofsted.

## Safeguarding: a critique

Making sense of the safeguarding agenda and its implications is no easy matter given the range of initiatives encompassed by it and the pace of change since 1997. However, any critical assessment of New Labour's project of 'safeguarding children' must consider both the context of its delivery and obstacles to the realization of the vision of a more effective and inclusive agenda for children. New Labour's commitment to further disperse children's services, the process by which '"agency" is being distributed from and by a strategic centre' (Clarke and Newman, 1997, p. 25), together with increased regulation and inspection while aiming to increase efficiency and safety, may have had the reverse effect. This, coupled with the pace at which new policies have been rolled out, has been described as creating an extremely testing environment for practitioners, leading to recurring crises in staff recruitment and retention (Audit Commission, 2002; Gupta and Blewett, 2007).

The National Childcare Strategy, Quality Protects, Sure Start, the Children's Fund, Choice Protects, Youth Inclusion and Support Panels, Every Child Matters, Multi-Agency Panels, Championing Children, the Children's Workforce Development Council, National Service Frameworks and National Standards, the Children's Plan – these are just some of the child welfare/safeguarding initiatives introduced by New Labour since 1997 (see https://www.everychildmatters. gov.uk/socialcare for an overview of current policies and projects). They provide incontrovertible evidence of New Labour's 'initiativitis'or 'hyperactivism' which has proved both 'exhausting and confusing' (Fawcett *et al.*, 2004, pp. 159–60). It is not simply the pace of change which is so troubling. Despite its overt commitment to evidence-based practice, New Labour has not always waited for evidence nor abided by its findings before introducing new policies. Sure Start provides a classic example. The programme has been evaluated since its inception but there have been strong criticisms of the leeway given to local programmes in England which seriously inhibited evaluation (Axford, 2007; Rutter, 2006). The lack of conclusive evidence of effectiveness has not, however, held back the rolling out of Sure Start Children's Centres across the country, prompting Professor Sir Michael Rutter to question: 'in what sense can it be claimed that the Sure Start policy is evidence-based?' (Rutter, 2006, p. 140).

Dispersal and initiativitis have been accompanied by a renewed emphasis upon managerialism by New Labour. This continues to cause problems by further constraining front-line practice and curtailing the scope for professional discretion which, arguably, ought to be central to effective safeguarding work (Broadhurst *et al.*, 2008). At the core of public service reform have been attempts to bring a rational, business-like view of service delivery to public sector organizations. Within this discourse, managers are differentiated from other social actors within organizations, notably welfare professionals. The latter are pejoratively connoted as inclined to make choices on the basis of sectional interests and to rely on 'particularistic knowledge' whereas managers are held to 'bring to bear an open and transparent rationality' in their decision-making (Clarke, 2004, p. 36). Given their propensity to stray from the business goals of the organization, possibly even to be '"captured or coopted" by [service users] ... and their demands for greater equity or redress' (Clarke and Newman, 1997, p. 11), professionals have to be made accountable to a managerial hierarchy. This is clearly evident within child welfare services with the introduction of audit and performance management tools and techniques from the late 1990s (DoH, 1999b). Tightly specified performance indicators have been embedded within local authority practice alongside the publication of league tables and the 'naming and shaming' of failing authorities/services. However, there is little evidence that child welfare has been improved by this audit culture (British Association of Social Workers, 2008; Broadhurst *et al.*, 2008).

ICT is central to this managerial agenda since its proponents claim that it offers more sophisticated means of standardizing recording, monitoring work and gathering data for strategic planning. Criticisms have been expressed about the practical application of ICT and its implications for civil liberties (Garrett, 2005; Munro, 2004). With regard to the former, security is a major issue after recent high profile losses of electronically stored data by government departments or those contracted to work on their behalf. This has led to a delay in the nationwide introduction of ContactPoint despite its centrality to New Labour's information-sharing vision. Staffing and training are also a concern if accurate, up-to-date databases are to be properly established and maintained for an ever-changing population of children. The government has also been accused of misplaced confidence about the capacity of ICT to generate useful and unambiguous information, particularly when systems play so large a role in shaping what is recorded (Munro, 2004). Overall, it is argued, there is little evidence that ICT is a panacea for deficiencies in communication and information-sharing between professionals.

Tensions also abound in New Labour's adherence to a 'dispersed state' (Clarke, 2004) which has deepened political commitment to a 'mixed economy of care' in which a greater role in service delivery is assigned to the private and voluntary sectors (for example, assessment, therapeutic work and foster/residential care). To a significant extent local authorities have shifted from being providers to enablers, coordinators and commissioners of services.[9] A further element has been the creation of additional state agencies separate from local authority children's services either in terms of funding, for example Sure Start and Connexions, or in terms of accountability, for example the Youth Justice Board bears responsibility for Youth Offending Teams. Multiplying the number of agents and agencies involved in service delivery, of course, generates new problems of fragmentation which the government has attempted to counteract by its invocation of partnership working, 'joined-up' services and information sharing but, as the case of Baby P so vividly indicates, exhortation and even system reform do not necessarily achieve the desired effect.[10]

Child welfare services are also being adversely affected by the marketization of services. For example, local authority foster carers have migrated to the independent sector, lured by the offer of better pay and conditions which has created problems with contracting and partnerships (Sellick, 2006). This has led to shortages of local authority placements and, perversely, placement instability as children are moved from out-of-authority to in-house provision as a cost-saving measure. Despite the claims to the contrary by the government, it is hard to avoid the conclusion that recent reforms have created a highly complex, confusing and competing array of services which conform more to an ideological model of welfare reform than the espousal of a 'what works', evidence-based approach.

In sum, the safeguarding project is far from seamless. It has involved a significant degree of dispersal of agents and agencies, creating tensions in terms of regulation and control that managerialist initiatives struggle to resolve. The energies and focus of organizations can easily be diverted towards audit and inspection to the detriment of services to children in need and their families, and

---

[9]   There is a need to be cautious about over-emphasizing the innovatory aspects of the mixed economy of care. Voluntary and private sector organizations did not disappear in the classic period of the welfare state. They were, however, marginalized while state activity was accorded privileged status in commentaries.

[10]   Baby P was a 17-month-old child who died in the London Borough of Haringey in August 2007. The subsequent conviction of his mother, mother's partner and their lodger for 'causing or allowing the death of a child' in November 2008 has resulted in an enormous media furore, not least because Baby P lived in the same London borough as Victoria Climbié but, unlike Victoria, was subject to a child protection plan and seen many times by health and welfare professionals right up to his death (see Haringey Local Safeguarding Children Board, 2008).

to staff morale. Managerialism combined with the 'electronic turn' is radically changing front-line social work practice in assessment and court work which is now dominated by the demands of computerized recording. At the same time, technological fixes such as electronic recording seem unlikely to successfully address the deficiencies in information collecting and sharing that so trouble policy-makers and auditors. Coherent, 'joined-up' services are much more difficult to deliver than New Labour governments have seemed prepared to accept, while policy initiatives invariably have unintended, as well as intended, consequences, creating new problems while simultaneously attempting to resolve ones previously identified. Inevitably there is a great deal lost from this model of social inclusion. Rather than a 'social distributionist' discourse of poverty and inequality there is a tendency to revert to a 'social integrationist' model predicated upon the individual reform and responsibilization of parents (Clarke, 2006; see also chapters 7 and 11 in this volume).

## Conclusion

To what extent do the changes in vocabulary since the 1960s constitute fundamental change to child welfare and how should we evaluate these developments? While changes in vocabulary can sometimes mask the maintenance of the *status quo*, it is undeniable that a focus on safeguarding is very different from that of 'battered baby syndrome'. The latter focused narrowly on a very specific form of harm to young children while the former operates within a broad agenda to promote children's welfare and to address social disadvantage. A focus on battered babies encouraged a narrow concern with extreme physical injury which foregrounded the role of the paediatrician in physical examination and diagnosis. While this role remains important in child protection it has itself come under increasing scrutiny with criticisms of diagnostic failures in child deaths and challenges to the competence of expert witnesses in high-profile court cases. In contrast, safeguarding presumes far wider involvement by a range of agencies and workers within a mixed economy of care and a dispersed state. Not only do legal specialists and the courts assume a more influential role where a care order is deemed necessary as part of the protection process, the scope of child welfare is considerably widened, giving rise to new roles and functions within a broader framework of early intervention measures to prevent social exclusion.

Safeguarding clearly signals change, yet there remain notable continuities with the past. In terms of organization and procedures there has been a series of incremental changes since the 1970s to refine child protection systems with the aim of improving recognition of abuse, assessment and information sharing, interprofessional working and working (in partnership) with parents. While the contemporary system is significantly different from that established thirty or so years ago it nonetheless bears its imprint in several important ways, notably: the increasingly precise definitions and categories of abuse and the setting of threshold criteria for 'significant harm'; the focus on abuse and neglect as an intra-familial problem which demands psychological rather than societal explanations, thus largely perpetuating a pathological model of abuse and neglect, and the continued onus on professionals to get it right in detecting and responding to harm in conformity with high expectations from the public and media.

In the light of this complex picture, to what extent can safeguarding be perceived as a move towards a more positive way of working in and for child welfare? By locating children within a context of social exclusion and addressing their wider needs, the SIS appears to offer a significant contribution to advancing the cause of children and families. However, this should not obscure the more problematic aspects of its implementation in terms of its bureaucratizing tendencies and adherence to the 'rituals of verification' so beloved of the 'audit society' (Power, 1997); its continuing distrust of professionals; its authoritarian desire to responsibilize parents as 'choice-making, self-directing subjects' (Clarke, 2005, p. 451) regardless of their economic and social circumstances, and the creation of a landscape of child welfare of mind-boggling complexity.

While aims to lift children out of poverty and to offer them greater opportunities and better life chances are commendable, it is nonetheless difficult to avoid considerable misgivings about the nature and coherence of current initiatives. But this should not induce nostalgic aspirations for some past golden age; intrinsic to child welfare policy and practice over the decades is debate about how best to define and provide for children's needs in the present while setting them on the road to active, purposeful citizenship in the future. Such debate inevitably involves value positions and normative assumptions about the nature of childhood and the needs of children, the responsibilities of parenthood, and relations between the family and the state.

Some elements of safeguarding indicate New Labour's preparedness to adopt a more interventionist stance in child welfare, notably in relation to supporting families and addressing 'anti-social' and offending behaviour. Child protection, however, continues to tread the fine line between unwarranted interference in family life and acceptable, indeed necessary, intervention. The case of Baby P has assumed great importance in this regard. Statements from central government suggest that 'the usual suspects' for blame – poor communication, failures in interprofessional working, inadequate assessment – might prevail. In the past defining problems in this way has typically led to managerial, technical-procedural responses of the kind outlined in earlier sections. At the same time, there are some encouraging signs of debate and resistance not previously seen in response to child deaths with frontline social work staff, academics and the professional social work body speaking out in various media about the difficulties in protecting and safeguarding children within the current configuration of children's services. It is perhaps too much to hope that managerialism and initiativitis will easily be set aside, nonetheless wider exposure of safeguarding's problematic enactment in practice is a welcome development. It remains to be seen whether positive change results.

# References

Allen, N. (2005) *Making Sense of the Children Act 1989: A Guide for Welfare and Social Services*, 3rd edn, Chichester: John Wiley & Sons.

Audit Commission (1994) *Seen but not Heard: Coordinating Child Health and Welfare Services for Children in Need*, London: HMSO.

Audit Commission (2002) *Recruitment and Retention: A Public Service Workforce for the Twenty-first Century*, London: Audit Commission.

Audit Commission (2008) *Are We There Yet? Improving Governance and Resource Management in Children's Trusts*. London: Audit Commission.

Axford, N. (2007) 'Learning the moral of the Sure Start story', *Prevention Action*, 8 November, Available at: http://www.preventionaction.org/comment/learning-moral-sure-start-story (accessed 19 December 2008).

Beckett, C. (2001) 'The great care proceedings explosion', *British Journal of Social Work*, 31 (3): 493–501.

Blair, T. (1999) Beveridge Lecture, Toynbee Hall, 18 March, London. Reprinted as 'Beveridge revisited: A welfare state for the 21st century' in R. Walker (ed.) *Ending Child Poverty: Popular Welfare for the 21st Century?* Bristol: Policy Press, pp. 7–21.

British Association of Social Workers (2008) *Lord Laming Review: Progress Report on Safeguarding*, Birmingham: British Association of Social Workers.

Broadhurst, K., Wastell, D., White, S., Hall, C., Peckover, S., Thompson, K., Pithouse, A. and Davey, D. (2009) 'Performing initial assessment: Identifying the latent conditions for error in local authority children's services', *British Journal of Social Work*, Advance Access, 19.1.2009, DOI:10.1093/bjsw/bcn162.

Butler, I. and Drakeford, M. (2003) *Scandal, Social Policy and Social Welfare*, 2nd edn, Bristol: Policy Press.

Butler-Sloss, Lord Justice E. (1988) *Report of the Inquiry into Child Abuse in Cleveland 1987*, Cmnd 412, London: HMSO.

Campbell, B. (1988) *Unofficial Secrets*, London: Virago Press.

Chief Secretary to the Treasury (2003) *Every Child Matters*, Cm 5860, London: The Stationery Office.

Clarke, J. (2004) 'Dissolving the public realm? The logics and limits of neo-liberalism', *Journal of Social Policy*, 33 (1): 27–48.

Clarke, J. (2005) 'New Labour's citizens: Activated, empowered, responsibilized, abandoned?', *Critical Social Policy*, 25 (4): 447–463.

Clarke, J. and Newman, J. (1997) *The Managerial State*, London: Sage.

Clarke, K. (2006) 'Childhood, parenting and early intervention: A critical examination of the Sure Start national programme', *Critical Social Policy*, 26 (4): 699–721.

Cleaver, H. and Freeman, P. (1995) *Parental Perspectives in Cases of Suspected Child Abuse*, London: HMSO.

Corby, B. (2003) 'Towards a new means of inquiry into child abuse cases', *Journal of Social Welfare and Family Law*, 25 (3): 229–241.

Corby, B. (2007) *Child Abuse: Towards a Knowledge Base*, 3rd edn, Buckingham: Open University Press.

Corby, B., Doig, A. and Roberts, V. (2001) *Public Inquiries into the Abuse of Children in Residential Care*, London: Jessica Kingsley.

DCSF (2007) *ICS, CAF and ContactPoint: An Overview*, London: DCSF.

DCSF (2008) *National e-CAF Fact Sheet*, London: DCSF.

DfES (2004) *Every Child Matters: Next Steps*, London: The Stationery Office.

DfES (2006) *Working Together to Safeguard Children: A Guide to Inter-Agency Working to Safeguard and Promote the Welfare of Children*, London: The Stationery Office.

DfES (2007) *Statutory Guidance on Making Arrangements to Safeguard and Promote the Welfare of Children under Section 11 of the Children Act 2004*, London: DfES.

DoH (1989) *An Introduction to the Children Act*, London: HMSO.

DoH (1995) *Child Protection: Messages from Research*, London: HMSO.

DoH (1998a) *Modernising Social Services: Promoting Independence, Improving Protection, Raising Standards*, London: The Stationery Office.

DoH (1998b) *The Quality Protects Programme: Transforming Children's Services*, LAC98 (28), London: DoH.

DoH (1999a) *Me Survive? Out There? New Arrangements for Young People in and Leaving Care*, London: DoH.

DoH (1999b) *The Government's Objectives for Children's Services*, London: DoH.

DoH, Department for Education and Employment and Home Office (2000) *Framework for the Assessment of Children in Need and their Families*, London: The Stationery Office.

DHSS (1974) *Memorandum on Non-accidental Injury to Children*, London: DHSS.

DHSS (1976) *Non-accidental Injury to Children: The Police and Case Conferences*, LASSL (76) 2, London: HMSO.

DHSS (1980) *Child Abuse: Central Register Systems*. LASSL (80)4, London: HMSO.

DHSS (1985) *Social Work Decisions in Child Care: Research Findings and Their Implications*, London: HMSO.

DHSS (1988) *Working Together: A Guide to Inter-Agency Cooperation for the Protection of Children from Abuse*, London: HMSO.

Fawcett, B., Featherstone, B. and Goddard, J. (2004) *Contemporary Child Care Policy and Practice*, Basingstoke: Palgrave Macmillan.

Ferguson, H. (2004) *Protecting Children in Time: Child Abuse, Child Protection and the Consequences of Modernity*, Basingstoke: Palgrave Macmillan.

Garrett, P.M. (2005) 'Social work's "electronic turn": Notes on the deployment of information and communication technologies in social work with children and families', *Critical Social Policy*, 25 (4): 529–553.

Giddens, A. (1994) *Beyond Left and Right*, Cambridge: Polity Press.

Giddens, A. (1998) *The Third Way: The Renewal of Social Democracy*, Cambridge: Polity Press.

Gupta, A. and Blewett, J. (2007) 'Change for children? The challenges and opportunities for the children's social work workforce', *Child and Family Social Work*, 12 (2): 172–181.

Haringey Local Safeguarding Children Board (2008) *Serious Case Review Child 'A'* [Baby P]: *Executive Summary*, London: Haringey Local Safeguarding Children Board.

Harris, N. (1990) 'Defensive social work', *British Journal of Social Work*, 17 (1): 61–69.

HM Treasury (2003) *Budget Report: Building a Britain of Economic Strength and Social Justice*, http://www.hm-treasury.gov.uk./budget/bud_bud03/budget_report/bud_bud03_repindex.cfm (accessed 21 July 2008).

Holman, B. (1988) *Putting Families First: Prevention and Child Care*, Basingstoke: Macmillan.

Home Office (1998) *Supporting Families: A Consultation Document*, London: The Stationery Office.

Howe, D. (1992) 'Child abuse and the bureaucratisation of social work', *Sociological Review* 40 (3): 491–508.

Jenson, J. and Saint-Martin, D. (2003) 'New routes to social cohesion? Citizenship and the social investment state', *Canadian Journal of Sociology*, 28 (1): 77–99.

Kempe, C.H., Silverman, F.N., Steel, B.F., Droegemuller, W. and Silver, H.K. (1962) 'The battered child syndrome', *Journal of the American Medical Association*, 181: 17–24.

Laming, Lord Herbert (2003) *The Victoria Climbié Report: Report of an Inquiry by Lord Laming*, Cm 5730, London: HMSO.

Langan, M. (1993) 'The rise and fall of social work', in J. Clarke (ed.), *A Crisis in Care? Challenges to Social Work*, London: Sage, pp. 47–67.

Lawrence, J. and Starkey, P. (eds.) (2001) *Child Welfare and Social Action in the Nineteenth and Twentieth Centuries: International Perspectives*, Liverpool: Liverpool University Press.

Lee, N. (2001) *Growing Up in an Age of Uncertainty*, Buckingham: Open University Press.

Levy, A. (ed.) (1989) *Focus on Child Abuse: Medical, Legal and Social Work Perspectives*. London: Hawksmere.

Lister, R. (2003) 'Investing in the citizen-workers of the future: Transformations in citizenship and the state under New Labour', *Social Policy and Administration*, 37 (5): 427–443.

London Borough of Brent (1985) *A Child in Trust: The Report of the Panel of Inquiry into the Circumstances surrounding the Death of Jasmine Beckford*, London: London Borough of Brent.

London Borough of Greenwich and Greenwich Health Authority (1987) *A Child in Mind: Protection of Children in a Responsible Society, The Report of a Commission of Inquiry into the Circumstances surrounding the Death of Kimberley Carlile*, London: London Borough of Greenwich.

London Borough of Lambeth (1987) *Whose Child? The Report of the Inquiry into the Death of Tyra Henry*, London: London Borough of Lambeth.

Morris, A., Giller, H., Szwed, E. and Geach, H. (1980) *Justice for Children*, London: Macmillan.

Munro, E. (2004) 'State regulation of parenting', *Political Quarterly*, 75 (2): 180–184.

Munro, E. and Calder, M. (2005) 'Where has child protection gone?', *Political Quarterly*, 76 (3): 439–445.

Munro, E. and Parton, N. (2007) 'How far is England in the process of introducing a mandatory reporting system?', *Child Abuse Review*, 16 (5): 5–16.

Murdoch, L. (2006) *Imagined Orphans: Poor Families, Child Welfare, and Contested Citizenship in London*, New Brunswick, NJ: Rutgers University Press.

Murray, J. (2008) 'Why the delay in launching database?', *Education Guardian*, 2 September.

Newman, J. and Clarke, J. (1994) 'Going about our business? The managerialization of public services', in J. Clarke, A. Cochrane and E. McLaughlin (eds.), *Managing Social Policy*, London: Sage, pp. 13–31.

Otway, O. (1996) 'Social work with children and families: From child welfare to child protection', in N. Parton (ed.), *Social Theory, Social Change and Social Welfare*, London: Routledge, pp. 152–171.

Packman, J. (1975) *The Child's Generation: Child Care Policy from Curtis to Houghton*, Oxford: Basil Blackwell.

Packman, J. (1986) *Who Cares? Social Work Decisions about Children*, Oxford: Basil Blackwell.

Parton, N. (1985) *The Politics of Child Abuse*, Basingstoke: Macmillan.

Parton, N. (1991) *Governing the Family: Child Care, Child Protection and the State*, Basingstoke: Macmillan.

Parton, N. (1996) 'Social theory, social change and social work', in N. Parton (ed.), *Social Theory, Social Change and Social Work*, London: Routledge, pp. 4–18.

Parton, N. (1997) 'Child protection and family support: Current debates and future prospects', in N. Parton (ed.), *Child Protection and Family Support: Tensions, Contradictions and Possibilities*, London: Routledge, pp. 1–24.

Parton, N. (2007) 'Safeguarding children: A socio-historical analysis', in K. Wilson and A. James (eds.), *The Child Protection Handbook: The Practitioner's Guide to Safeguarding Children*, 3rd edn, Edinburgh: Baillière Tindall, pp. 9–30.

Power, M. (1997) *The Audit Society: Rituals of Verification*, Oxford: Oxford University Press.

Reder, P. and Duncan, S. (1997) *Lost Innocents: A Follow-Up Study of Fatal Child Abuse*. London: Routledge.

Reder, P., Duncan, S. and Gray, M. (1993) *Beyond Blame: Child Abuse Tragedies Revisited*, Basingstoke: Macmillan.

Richardson, S. and Bacon, H. (1991) *Child Sexual Abuse Whose Problem? Reflections from Cleveland*, Birmingham: Venture Press.

Rutter, M. (2006) 'Is Sure Start an effective prevention intervention?, *Child and Adolescent Health*, 11 (3): 135–141.

Scott, D. and Swain, S. (2002) *Confronting Cruelty: Historical Perspectives: Historical Perspectives on Child Protection in Australia*. Carlton South, Victoria: Melbourne University Press.

Secretary of State for Social Services (1974) *Report of the Committee of Inquiry into the Care and Supervision Provided in Relation to Maria Colwell*, London: HMSO.

Seebohm Report (1968) *Report of the Committee on Local Authority and Allied Personal Social Services*, Cm 3703. London: HMSO.

Sellick, C. (2006) 'Opportunities and risks: Models of good practice in commissioning independent foster care', *British Journal of Social Work*, 36 (8): 1345–1359.

Selwyn, N. (2002) '"E-stablishing" an inclusive society? Technology, social exclusion and UK government policy making', *Journal of Social Policy*, 31 (1): 1–20.

Thoburn, J., Lewis, A. and Shemmings, D. (1995) *Paternalism or Partnership? Family Involvement in the Child Protection Process*, London: HMSO.

Wagner, G. (1979) *Barnardo*, London: Eyre & Spottiswoode.

Ward, H. (ed.) (1995) *Looking after Children: Research into Practice*. London: The Stationery Office.

White, S. (1998) 'Interdiscursivity and child welfare: The ascent and durability of psycho-legalism', *Sociological Review*, 46 (2): 264–292.

Woodroofe, K. (1962) *From Charity to Social Work in England and the United States*, London: Routledge, Kegan & Paul.

# 3

# Every Child's Rights Matter

## David Archard

*Every Child Matters* (ECM) purports to be a child protection policy document and yet it is clearly much more (Chief Secretary to the Treasury, 2003). Its drafting was prompted by, and its publication accompanies, a full response to the findings of the Victoria Climbié inquiry (Laming, 2003). This latter, sadly, is yet another investigation into the failings of those agencies charged with preventing child abuse; and it is not likely, even more sadly, to be the last such investigation. ECM is thus clearly motivated by an official concern, always re-animated by each successive failure, to learn the lessons from the death of a child at the hands of abusive or neglectful guardians. In this regard, it is one more document striving to provide some kind of answer to the question: How can we best protect those of our children who are at risk of serious harm?

Yet the document outlines an approach which is much broader than that of child protection. Indeed, it essays a comprehensive strategy for the promotion of the welfare of all children. There are, of course, important questions about whether or not the document's publication has been followed by the introduction and execution of policies which have redeemed its promise. It is also possible – as with so many official documents – that ECM simply serves as a rationalization for policies whose real justification is pragmatic or narrowly political in the worst sense. However, I am interested with the ideas that underpin the strategy outlined in ECM and my intention is the modest one as a moral and political philosopher of identifying and evaluating normative issues: How should a society devise laws and policies in respect of children? What are the moral justifications for any approach that is taken? In particular, I want to address the question of how the strategy outlined in ECM is to be evaluated from a children's rights perspective.

## The holism of *Every Child Matters*

ECM's strategy has itself, or is associated with broader policy and legal initiatives that have, a number of features which might fairly be characterized as

*Critical Perspectives on Safeguarding Children*   Edited by Karen Broadhurst, Chris Grover and Janet Jamieson
© 2009 John Wiley & Sons, Ltd

'holistic' or 'comprehensive'. Let me spell these out. First, there is a commitment to what we could call 'integrated governance' and what is more fashionably termed 'joined up government' by the present administration (Bogdanor, 2005). The general idea is that the provision of all services to children – welfare, educational, health, child protection, family, juvenile justice – should be provided in a systematically coordinated fashion. This should ensure that there is both an elimination of overlap and an avoidance of a shortfall in any area. The justification of such coordination is both positive and negative. The negative justification is a pressing concern that no child should fall 'through the cracks between different services' (Chief Secretary to the Treasury, 2003, para. 3). Thus it is important that children at risk can be reliably and efficiently identified wherever their condition or behaviour gives cause for concern; further, that speedy and effective solutions can be provided through a range of appropriate actions.

The positive justification of the coordination is to be found in the second and perhaps the most important 'holistic' feature of the strategy. This is a commitment to the view that child protection must be seen in the context of efforts to promote the general well-being of all children. We might call this the 'whole child' approach. A roughly contemporaneous report from the Australian State of Victoria's Department of Human Services declares itself indebted to the UK legislative framework whose 'defining characteristic' is 'the acknowledgement that child protection cannot be separated from policies to improve children's lives as a whole' (Victorian Department of Human Services, 2003, pp. ix; x, 51 and 73).

It is worth commenting that this commitment has a number of possible justifications. The first derives from a broadening of our understanding of abuse and neglect beyond what is occasioned by the actions of individuals to encompass a more general shortfall in welfare. This shortfall may, in turn, be attributed to the culpable failures of society and not just individuals. Thus children can be described as institutionally or socially abused if they are brought up in conditions of extreme poverty. Influential work in the 1970s by David Gil sought to define child abuse as 'inflicted gaps or deficits between circumstances of living which would facilitate the optimal development of children to which they should be entitled, and their actual circumstances, irrespective of the sources or agents of the deficit' (Gil, 1975, pp. 346–7).

The second justification for the 'whole child' approach relies on a view about the causal aetiology of abuse and neglect. Instead of seeing abuse as episodic and attributable to individual psychological failures it is viewed as symptomatic of a dysfunctional relationship between a child and her guardian which in turn is attributable to, or in large part caused by, broader situational factors. Hence, abuse is argued to be more prevalent within lower income families, or those experiencing a wide range of social and economic difficulties.

The third justification for the 'whole child' approach is a view that child protection alone is simply not good enough. Merely ensuring that children do not suffer abuse and neglect is insufficient. Note also that although much child protection practice is preventative much also is reactive and after the event. We want children not to fall below a minimum threshold of decent nurture because we believe that children deserve protecting. But if, as a society, we care about our children then we need to do more than only to take some steps to prevent their being harmed. We are surely also obliged to attend to all of their needs and to make every reasonable effort to promote their general welfare. If children do indeed matter then they must be adequately schooled and housed, they must have proper leisure and sporting facilities, their health must be safeguarded and enhanced, and so on.

For my part, I think that the first justification of the whole child approach relies on a tendentious definition of abuse. Allowing that a society can abuse its children by failing to raise them to a certain level of welfare may serve useful political and rhetorical purposes. But it deprives the condemnatory term 'abuse' of its considerable power in picking out comparatively rare, exceptional and grave maltreatments of a child. The second justification rests on a contentious and unhelpfully narrow theory of the aetiology of abuse. Social and economic factors may serve as a context to some forms of abuse. But there is no simple and fixed correlation between every instance of abuse and the abuser's social or economic circumstances. It is, thus, more helpful – and more credible as the normative basis of any comprehensive strategy – to see the 'whole child' approach as motivated by a positive concern to go beyond the prevention of harm and to be, rightly, concerned with the general welfare of children.

The third feature of a 'holistic' approach to child welfare is what the Victoria report calls 'a unifying framework for most aspects of the law relating to the care and upbringing of children' (Victorian Department of Human Services, 2003, p. 46). The Children Act 1989 of England and Wales is praised in this regard. Certainly this legislative instrument was important not simply for reforming child care law but for bringing under the umbrella of a single statute all of the key principles and guarantees of provision that might otherwise have been scattered across different laws and policies. Such a single unified legal instrument sets forth the basic underpinning principles and defines the essential responsibilities of all those within society who may be entrusted with the care of children. As will be suggested later a more radical and preferable alternative is the incorporation of the United Nations Convention of the Rights of the Child (UNCRC) into domestic legislation, just as the European Convention of Human Rights was incorporated into UK law as the Human Rights Act 1998.

The fourth feature of a 'holistic' approach is the creation of official positions whose remit is a specific and exclusive concern with children. So there is now a Minister for Children and Young People, and a Children's Commissioner in England.[1] The latter is defined as an 'independent champion' articulating the views and opinions of children that might otherwise be drowned out. This is subtly different from, but need not exclude, the possibility of also having an

---

[1] England was the last of the four UK jurisdictions to appoint a Children's Commissioner.

Ombudsman who could investigate claims directly reported to him or her of abuse and mistreatment, a role mooted in recent years in England and Wales. The first Children's Ombudsman appointed by Norway 25 years ago, and whose example has been followed by others such as Sweden and Ireland, fulfils the role accorded to the new Children's Commissioner in England.

Obviously, the ultimate value to children of such institutional innovation depends upon the financial allocations made to, and the executive powers of, any Minister or Commissioner. In the UK, for instance, it makes a difference if a Minister is a full member of Cabinet. Nevertheless, the creation of these positions represents a formal acknowledgement of the state's obligations to children, a recognition of its duty to ensure that the welfare of children within its jurisdiction is promoted.

The fifth and final feature of a holistic strategy is that it encompasses all children. *Every* child – irrespective of his or her background or circumstances – matters. The commitment to inclusivity is very important, but it is egalitarian only in an extremely restricted and weak sense. First, the strategy contains no commitment to ensuring that all children's welfare will be raised to the same level. 'Opportunities' is a term used frequently throughout ECM. But, of course, opportunities can be maximized for all while it remains the case that children derive unequal benefits from their various opportunities and, thus, society continues to exhibit substantive and entrenched social inequality. It is a familiar criticism of any principle of equal opportunity that while it is formally or procedurally egalitarian it need not be substantively egalitarian in outcomes. Second, it is every child within England and Wales who matters. The scope of 'every' is thus national and not global. This is a matter to which I will return.

## *Every Child Matters* and the United Nations Convention on the Rights of the Child

The strategy of ECM has much to commend it: its comprehensiveness, its broad 'whole child' vision and its official acknowledgement of a statutory responsibility for the welfare of children. Yet there is one extraordinary shortcoming. There are no more than a couple of references to the rights of the child and these taken in their context clearly see children as having human rights inasmuch, and only inasmuch, as they are young humans. There is thus no appreciation of the possibility that children might have rights as children. Most striking is the fact that ECM contains not a single reference to the UNCRC,[2] not even an acknowledgement that the UK has ratified this Convention.

Ratification entails certain obligations on ratifying states beyond a commitment to do everything reasonable to implement the rights listed in the UNCRC.

---

[2]   The UNCRC can be found at: http://www2.ohchr.org/english/law/crc.htm (accessed 10 December 2008).

In particular, all ratifying states are duty bound to provide reports every five years 'on the measures they have adopted which give effect to the rights recognised [in the CRC] and on the progress made on the enjoyment of those rights' (UNCRC, Article 44). It is in consequence notable that the 2008 Report – the first submitted conjointly by all four Children Commissioners from the constituent countries of the UK – commented in its conclusion on the increasing 'gap between rich and poor ... along with associated disparities in the well-being of children and respect for their rights' (UK Children's Commissioners, 2008, p. 4).

The Government has subsequently produced an ECM website[3] and there it offers an account of how the ECM agenda 'maps' onto the UNCRC framework, a claim to which I will return. For now, it is sufficient to make the following two brief points. First, some European countries – such as Belgium, Cyprus, Finland, Norway, Portugal and Spain – have incorporated the UNCRC into their domestic law. UNICEF has called upon the UK to follow suit (UNICEF, 2008). The failure of the UK government to do so may reasonably be taken as clear evidence of a less than whole-hearted commitment to the rights of the child.

Second, the UK took the decision to opt out of some of the provisions of the UNCRC when this was ratified in 1991. This – as discussed in Chapter 13 – has been true, with worrying implications, in the domain of asylum and immigration policy. In effect, the UK has determined that the provisions of the UNCRC, and thus a respect for the rights of the children in question, do not constrain those measures of immigration control which its government considers expedient. This opting out further reinforces the impression of a half-hearted commitment to the UNCRC, and to its internationalist implications.

Despite the official claim that the ECM agenda simply 'maps' onto the UN-CRC agenda for children there are significant differences. Let me indicate the most salient. First, ECM lists a set of desirable outcomes for children: being healthy; staying safe; enjoying and achieving; making a positive contribution; and, economic well-being. By contrast, the UNCRC accords to children a set of basic rights possessed insofar as they are children. These, according to a now familiar typology, comprise rights to the provision of certain goods, rights to protection against certain harms, and participation rights. There is a great difference between the specification of desirable outcomes for persons and the ascription to those persons of fundamental entitlements.

For example, it is perhaps ideal that I should receive certain goods and services. But agreement on the desirability of this outcome – even if enforced and thus guaranteed – is considerably weaker in force and in character from the acknowledgement that I have a *right* to those goods and services. The difference lies, as has been recognized by philosophers writing on rights, in the idea that

3  The ECM website can be found at: http://www.everychildmatters.gov.uk/ (accessed 4 January 2008).

someone can *claim* of right what is due to them and not simply have to rely on their beneficent treatment by others. This difference matters even if the beneficent treatment can be regarded as assured. This is why rights have extraordinary value to their possessors (Feinberg, 1970). Joel Feinberg's elucidation of this critical claim has led to his article being justifiably described as 'one of the three most important essays written on rights in the twentieth century' (Wellman, 2005, p. 213). For Feinberg, the fact that someone can claim their due and is recognized as being a rights-holders makes all the difference to their status – as moral agents and as citizens. The UNCRC acknowledges that children have rights; the ECM agenda merely prescribes better ways to treat children.

A second difference between the ECM and UNCRC agendas lies in the voice that is given to children. Article 12 of the UNCRC reads:

> 1 States Parties shall assure to the child who is capable of forming his or her own views the right to express those views freely in all matters affecting the child, the views of the child being given due weight in accordance with the age and maturity of the child.
> 2 For this purpose, the child shall in particular be provided the opportunity to be heard in any judicial and administrative proceedings affecting the child, either directly, or through a representative or an appropriate body, in a manner consistent with the procedural rules of national law.

Thus, this is a right not only to have a voice but to have the institutional opportunities to exercise that voice. This second clause is important for it imposes a duty upon the authorities to give practical effect to the basic right and to ensure that the child really is heard. A right to speak is of little value even to adults unless there are real and effective opportunities to speak.

By contrast, the ECM report accords a consultative role to children but it does so only in two places. Moreover, the context and character of such consultation suggests, as Fiona Williams (2004, p. 412) points out, that 'children's views are not very important'. It is not simply that children's views do not matter much, that they are given only a limited or insignificant weight in the practical deliberations of law and policy-makers. It is also that they matter only instrumentally. The value of hearing the child for those concerned with designing services and provisions for children lies in ensuring that these services are well designed. The value of hearing the child is consultative and it is as a means to others' ends. It is not intrinsic and it does not reflect a view, enshrined in Article 12, that the child has a basic right to express an opinion on all matters which touch on his or her interests. In this regard, the ECM report expresses a more widespread devaluation of the nature and significance of a child's right to be heard (Archard and Skivenes, 2009a).

A third difference between the ECM agenda and the UNCRC agenda lies in their respective views of the child. We can speak of the interests a child has as a child and those which the child has as a future adult. Equally, we can speak of the interest society has that its children should enjoy certain goods both in so far as they are and remain children, and in so far as they will grow into future adult members of that society. For instance, a child has an interest in a safe, healthy and flourishing childhood, and does so for so long as he or she is a child. At the same time, the future adult has an interest in growing into a physically healthy and psychologically well-balanced person. And society has a clear interest that its future members should be well-formed, functioning characters able to contribute to its prosperity and good order.

The UNCRC is concerned with the interests of children as, and insofar as, they remain children. It does not see children as future members of society, and its Preamble makes explicit reference to 'childhood [as] entitled to special care and assistance'. However, it is clear that, by contrast, the ECM agenda views the child in the light of the future adult he or she will become, and as both a present and future contributing member of society. Thus, the 'achieving' half of the desirable outcome 'enjoying and achieving' is summarized as 'developing the skills for adulthood'; the outcome 'making a positive contribution' is defined as 'being involved with the community and society and not engaging in anti-social or offending behaviour'; and the outcome 'economic well-being' is future- and society-oriented being defined as 'not being prevented by economic disadvantage from achieving their full potential in life' (Chief Secretary to the Treasury, 2003, pp. 11–12). It is clear though, that there is no neat and clear separation of interests in this context. A healthy child is more likely to grow into a healthy adult whose contribution to his or her society is a productive one. However, the critical question is where the principal justification of policies lies: is the focus upon the child as a child or as an adult-to-be and as a contributing productive member of society?

A fourth difference between the UNCRC and the ECM agenda is to be found in the scope of 'every' when applied to children as a group. The UNCRC is an international covenant signed and ratified by all but two states; the rights it accords to children it accords to children wherever they live in the world. Now, of course, the UNCRC does not enjoin each ratifying state to protect the rights of children outside its own national boundaries. Article 2 requires that 'States Parties shall respect and ensure the rights set forth in the present Convention to each child *within their jurisdiction*' (emphasis added) but continues, importantly, 'without discrimination of any kind'. This means, *inter alia*, 'irrespective of the child's or his or her parent's or legal guardian's national, ethnic or social origin'. By contrast, ECM is a document addressed only to the needs of the children of England.[4] Moreover, as chapter 13 shows, the ECM agenda does not provide the protection the UNCRC affords to refugee children. In addition to Article 2 already quoted, Article 22 imposes upon any governments a duty to afford to refugee children within its jurisdiction all of those rights listed in the Convention and, hence, the very same rights accorded to any child normally resident within the state.

---

[4] Although where ECM relates to non-devolved responsibilities, such as Home Office services, it also applied to Wales (Chief Secretary to the Treasury, 2003, p. 11).

## Rights and wrongs

The four respects in which the UNCRC differs from the ECM agenda – the according to children of basic rights; the recognition of a child's entitlement to a voice; the acknowledgement of the child as a child; and the international scope – are respects in which the ECM agenda is poorer. These differences also serve to reinforce the sense that the UK government's commitment to the ideal of the child and to her fundamental rights to which UNCRC gives expression is lukewarm. This is not, however, to deny that a rights-based approach to children has its problems. Let me indicate the principal ones.

In the first place, the language of rights is notoriously vague and imprecise. Understandably, perhaps the conditions under which agreement to an international covenant is secured from a number of very differently placed states ensure that the wording of any final clause is open to different interpretation. Any particular right will be couched in terms from which no one party can dissent. The price paid for such unanimity may be fuzziness and equivocation. In lots of respects this does not make an international charter of rights so very different from national laws and general statements of policy intent. The desirable outcomes of ECM are perhaps not much better and may, indeed, be worse. However global rights have a binding force upon ratifying states that are, in consequence, all the keener to make sure that their ratification does not tie them to impossibly demanding measures. Thus, it is not obvious that a rights-based approach of the kind represented by the UNCRC, even if incorporated into domestic law, would give a clearer statement of what ought to be done for children than the ECM agenda.

Second, the UNCRC accords every child a range of rights. These, as indicated earlier, comprise three kinds of right: to the provision of certain goods, to protection against certain harms, and to participation. It has been often noted that there is a fundamental tension between the latter two kinds of right (Archard, 2004, p. 60). This is most dramatically represented in the gap that exists between the two central rights of the UNCRC: the right of a child to have its voice heard and given weight (Article 12) and the obligation imposed on parties by Article 3 that 'in all actions concerning children, whether undertaken by public or private social welfare institutions, courts of law, administrative authorities or legislative bodies, the best interests of the child shall be a primary consideration'. Article 12 is essentially empowering of children and views them as, at least in part, autonomous self-determining agents; Article 3, by contrast, is essentially paternalist and views children as in need of protection by those more able and better placed to make decisions for them.

Article 2 of the UNCRC requires states to 'respect and ensure the rights set forth in the present Convention to each child within their jurisdiction'. It does not thereby indicate that these rights have an order of importance or priority; indeed it suggests that all of the listed rights have the same status. Articles 3 and 12, in other words, should reasonably be taken as giving expression to two imperatives of equal weight and significance. It may be that, in the final analysis, the requirement to hear the child can be taken as subordinate to the promotion of the child's best interests (Marshall, 2001, p. 26). Some jurisdictions may indeed make this explicit. However, this lexical ordering of the two rights is nowhere explicitly stated in the UNCRC. Moreover, as an interpretation of the UNCRC, it sits uneasily with the ascription to the child of a range of free-standing participation rights, such as those of freedom of expression (Article 13), of conscience and of religion (Article 14), and of association (Article 15). The key point to be noted here is that the UNCRC agenda is beset by a tension between its animating principles. This presents difficulties for any attempt straightforwardly to translate the agenda into laws and policies.

Third, laws and general statements of legislative intent only have as much value as the means of implementing and enforcing them; they are also only as robust as the measures for holding governments accountable for their success and failure in realizing them. In this respect the UNCRC is likely to lose out when set against the ECM agenda. The latter at least represented a statement of clear intent, and it has moreover been followed by further developments in distinct areas of child policy, such as early years and child care, youth justice, young people's health, and young people's training and employment. These have sought to give practical effect to the stated desiderata of the original ECM agenda.

By contrast the UNCRC although ratified by the UK government has not yet been incorporated into domestic law. The government is, as a ratifying state, accountable for its failures to implement the Convention. Yet this in effect reduces to an obligation to submit a regular report to the UN Committee on the Rights of the Child. Since ratification in 1991 the UK government has submitted only four reports. Moreover, those charged with overseeing the government's implementation of the Convention have regularly commented on the government's failings in this regard. The report to the UN Committee from the four Children's Commissioners in 2008 states 'that, not only do some of the Committee's concluding observations of 2002 still lack any effective implementation, but some things have actually got worse' (UK Children's Commissioners, 2008, p. 4).

## Rights and youth justice

'Developments in juvenile justice' are one salient respect in which matters have got worse, and the Commissioners cite the following as evidence:

> There is a very punitive approach to misbehaviour by children and young people and the criminal justice system is used too readily. Compared to other European countries, England has a very low age of criminal responsibility and high numbers of children are locked up. (UK Children's Commissioners, 2008, p. 5)

Fiona Williams notes that a central concern of the Joint Committee on Human Rights in respect of the Government's failure 'to publish an overarching strategy for children with the UNCRC as its framework' (House of Lords and House of Commons Joint Committee on Human Rights, 2003, para. 9) 'was the failure of *Every Child Matters* to increase the age of criminal responsibility from 10 to 12 years, and to condemn the use of custodial sentences for 12–14 year olds even when they have not been persistent offenders' (Williams, 2004, p. 421). Chapter 11 in this volume similarly argues that the promise of the ECM agenda is gainsaid by the authoritarian and punitive policies on youth justice pursued by the present government.

However, it is here in particular that it is well worth spelling out the implications of a rights approach to children and young people. More particularly still, it is worth making at least one key distinction. The incarceration of young people in increasing numbers is an expensive, inefficient, and counterproductive way of dealing with persistent young offenders. It puts huge pressures on an already overcrowded prison system and probably serves only to increase the number of adult career criminals.

This has, in recent years, been the repeated mantra of Professor Rod Morgan, distinguished criminologist, erstwhile Chair of the Youth Justice Board, and longstanding critic of the government's youth justice policies (Morgan, 2007). Consistent with that line of criticism Article 37 (b) of the UNCRC clearly states that:

> No child shall be deprived of his or her liberty unlawfully or arbitrarily. The arrest, detention or imprisonment of a child shall be in conformity with the law and shall be used only as a measure of last resort and for the shortest appropriate period of time.

Thus, there is a strong presumption against the imprisonment of young people. But such a presumption is perfectly consistent with recognition that young people may properly be held accountable under certain conditions for their criminal behaviour. Hence, the impermissibility of incarcerating the young should carefully be distinguished from the permissibility or otherwise of holding the young to account for their culpable wrongdoing. Article 40.1 of the UNCRC enshrines:

> the right every child alleged as, accused of, or recognized as having infringed the penal law to be treated in a manner consistent with the promotion of the child's sense of dignity and worth, which reinforces the child's respect for the human rights and fundamental freedoms of others and which takes into account the child's age and the desirability of promoting the child's reintegration and the child's assuming a constructive role in society.

Article 40.3 spells out this requirement by insisting that each ratifying state should establish 'laws, procedures, authorities and institutions' that are 'applicable to children' who may have infringed the penal law. That, in turn, requires the establishment of a minimum age of legal responsibility, and the adoption, 'whenever appropriate and desirable' of 'non-judicial proceedings' for dealing with children below that age. Finally, Article 40.4 indicates a variety of dispositions that may be adopted to deal with child offenders that are 'appropriate to their well-being and proportionate both to their circumstances and the offence'. The Article instances 'care, guidance and supervision orders, counselling; probation; foster care; education and vocational training programmes and other alternatives to institutional care'.

In short, it is wrong to imprison children but not necessarily to hold at least some of them responsible for their crimes, and to develop appropriate measures in the light of such a holding. Both processes and outcomes in respect of young offenders must be appropriate to their age. If incarceration is wrong, so also may be the use of adult judicial proceedings. It helps then to see that we can understand the age of criminal responsibility in two ways (Scottish Law Commission, 2002). Such an age will, in a first sense, indicate the point at which children may be presumed to have the capacity to understand the difference between right and wrong and to act accordingly. In a second sense, the age of criminal responsibility fixes that time at which it is thought appropriate for children to be subject to certain kinds of juridical processes, in particular, appearing before a court determining guilt or innocence and apportioning the appropriate penalties.

It is, thus, worth remembering that the 1999 judgment of the European Court of Human Rights in respect of the defendants in the Jamie Bulger trial of 1993 did not exonerate them. There is no question that they were guilty of a heinous murder. It also seems reasonably evident that the two defendants did have some sense of right and wrong, and did, in retrospect, understand their behaviour to be seriously immoral. However, the Court found that the proceedings violated the Bulger defendants' right to a fair hearing. More particularly, the Court determined that these proceedings – held within with an adult Crown Court with its attendant formality, a specially built dock to accommodate their childish stature, exposed to a hostile public gallery – 'must be regarded in the case of an eleven-year-old child as a severely intimidating procedure' which 'deprived him of the opportunity to participate effectively in the determination of the criminal charges against him' (European Court of Human Rights, 1999a, 1999b). The Lord Chief Justice, in response to the judgment of the European Court, introduced new rules – governing the use of robes and wigs, as well as a police presence in the courtroom – to ensure that any judicial process should not expose any young defendant to 'avoidable intimidation, humiliation or distress' (Lord Chief Justice of England and Wales, 2000).

Children, in short, may be held responsible for their criminal acts but it follows neither that they should, in consequence, be held accountable before an adult court, nor that they should be punished by incarceration or other penal measures that an adult might suffer for the same criminal act. The UNCRC's insistence upon a child's right to 'appropriate' treatment for his or her wrongdoing is exemplary. It is also yet more evidence of that Convention's concern, by contrast with the ECM strategy, to attend to the child as a child.

It is a further question whether the treatment 'appropriate' to the child offender should attend only to the child's welfare. The Scottish Hearings System is unique in this regard (Lockyer and Stone, 1998). It enshrines the principles of the 1964 Kilbrandon Report (Lord Kilbrandon, 1995) which sees the child offender as being as much in need of care and protection as the child who is the victim of abuse and neglect. In recent years in response to persistent offending from young persons in Scotland, widespread public perceptions of the Hearings System as 'soft' on such offenders and a political concern with addressing crime have led to pressures on the original system. This has resulted in experiments in the 'fast tracking' of persistent offenders and a Youth Court (Whyte, 2003).

The original system and its underlying principles are consonant with the holistic approach to child protection recommended by the ECM strategy. The broader context – social, familial, educational and economic – is that within which the abuse of a child and a child's offending might be understood and addressed.

However, the system is seen as exemplifying a *welfare* model which views the appropriate approach to child offending as one of taking measures, social and individual, to meet the needs of the child. By contrast, a *justice* model views the child offender as properly accountable to society for her actions, and hence subject to a proportionate punishment. It is moot whether a welfare model of this kind violates canons of judicial fairness (Archard, 2007). What is worth remarking is the extent to which seeing the child as a rights-holder, and especially as one entitled to be a participant in the determination of outcomes affecting her interests, predisposes one to see the child as responsible for her actions. In other words, a rights agenda constructs children as agents whereas a protectionist approach of the kind represented by ECM, by contrast, envisages the child as in need of protection and provision for her needs. The child as agent is much more likely to be seen as someone who ought to be held accountable to society for her wrongdoing. Hence, the rights approach is much more congenial to those who think children ought not to escape penalties for their offences.

Consider, then, the case of 15-year-old Jerry Gault. He was tried and convicted in 1964 of an offence (making 'a lewd or indecent' telephone call) before an Arizonan juvenile court, and sentenced to six years in juvenile detention. He and his parents appealed on the grounds that the juvenile court process violated due process. The US Supreme Court decision in 1967 (*In re Gault* 1967) is generally acknowledged as a landmark judgment in the recognition of children's rights. It established that under the Fourteenth Amendment to the Constitution, juveniles accused of offences in a delinquency proceeding must be accorded many of the same procedural rights as adults, including the right to confront witnesses and the right to counsel. However, what is notable is precisely that the judgment did not argue for the right of young offenders to be tried in their own courts, but rather to be accorded the same due process rights as adults.

# Conclusion

A rights-based agenda for policy and legislation in respect of children, and one deriving most obviously from the UN Convention, has many virtues that the ECM agenda does not. Most fundamentally, it envisages children as *entitled* to outcomes which a policy statement couched in the manner of the ECM document sees merely as desiderata. This is to the advantage of a rights-based agenda even if the policy statement is of the highest order and backed by clear statements of executive intent. In very practical terms what is due to one as of right can serve as the basis of challenges to juridical and policy practice in the courts. It is, thus, instructive to compare how the Human Rights Act has accorded adult citizens rights that they can now use to effect legal or policy changes, whether it is in forcing the reform, the initiation, or the repeal of laws.

Furthermore, it obviously remains unacceptable that a state which has ratified the UNCRC should fail so obviously to couch its policies in respect of children in the terms of that Convention. The repeated criticisms of the UK Children's Commissioners points to the failures of the Government to see its ratification of the Convention as not much more than token. However, there is very real tension at the heart of that rights agenda. This is between seeing children as agents or participants, as claimants to a say in their own lives and, by contrast, as vulnerable dependants in need of protection and provision. This will always beset any policies and practices which give effect to it. Indeed, the fundamental tension between seeing children as entitled to be heard on matters affecting their interests and as having interests that adults should promote on their behalf remains unresolved in child protection and child welfare policies (Archard and Skivenes, 2009a, 2009b). Although the ECM agenda does not address this tension, it is there also in the provisions of the Children Act. The crucial point is that the adoption of a children's rights discourse does not resolve this tension; it merely couches it in different, if clearer, terms.

In the area of juvenile justice there is a real problem in reconciling a welfare view of children, even those who offend, as having interests that must be promoted and a justice view of the child offender as a responsible agent. Of course, there is still a distinction to be made between an ascription of responsibility and a punitive disposal of any offence. Children can be responsible, as adults also may be, for their wrongdoing but not punished, as adults are, for such wrongdoing. This will not satisfy those who see extensions of responsibility to young offenders as somehow justifying their criminalization. Nevertheless, any move in the direction of attributing agency to children is an achievement whose price is a retreat of some significance from a welfarist or protectionist stance towards them.

The ambiguity and ambivalence inherent in our attitudes to children are also there in the ECM agenda. They are not resolved by the adoption of a rights-based agenda which will, if anything, render them more obvious and more pronounced.

# References

Archard, D. (2004) *Children, Rights and Childhood*, 2nd edn, London: Routledge.
Archard, D. (2007) 'Children's rights and juvenile justice', in M. Hill, A. Lockyer, and F. Stone (eds.), *Youth Justice and Child Protection*, London and Philadelphia: Jessica Kingsley Publishers, pp. 250–265.
Archard, D. and Skivenes, M. (2009a) 'Balancing a child's best interests and a child's views', *International Journal of Children's Rights*, forthcoming.
Archard, D. and Skivenes, M. (2009b) 'Hearing the child', *Child and Family Social Work Journal*, forthcoming.
Bogdanor, V. (ed.) (2005) *Joined-up Government*, British Academy Occasional Paper 5, Oxford: Oxford University Press.
Chief Secretary to the Treasury (2003) *Every Child Matters*, Cm. 5860, London: The Stationery Office.
European Court of Human Rights (1999a) *Case of T. v. The United Kingdom* (Application no. 24724/94), 16 December.
European Court of Human Rights (1999b) *Case of V. v. The United Kingdom* (Application no. 24888/94), 16 December.
Feinberg, J. (1970) 'The nature and value of rights', *Journal of Value Inquiry*, 4 (4): 243–260.
Gil, D. (1975) 'Unravelling child abuse', *American Journal of Orthopsychiatry*, 45 (2): 346–356.
House of Lords and House of Commons Joint Committee on Human Rights (2003) *The Government's Response to the Committee's Tenth Report of Session 2002–03 on the UN Convention on the Rights of the Child, Eighteenth report of Session 2002–2003*, HL Paper 187, HC 1279, London: The Stationery Office.
*In re Gault*, 387 U.S. 1 (1967) http://supreme.justia.com/us/387/1/case.html (accessed 10 December 2008).
Kilbrandon, Lord (1995) *The Kilbrandon Report: Children and Young Persons, Scotland*, 3rd edn, London: Stationery Office Books.
Laming, Lord (2003) *The Victoria Climbié Inquiry: Report of an Inquiry by Lord Laming*, Command 5730, London: The Stationery Office.
Lockyer, A. and Stone, F. (eds.) (1998) *Juvenile Justice in Scotland: Twenty-Five Years of the Welfare Approach*, London: Butterworths.
Lord Chief Justice of England and Wales (2000) *Practice Direction: Trial of Children and Young Persons in the Crown Court*, http://www.dca.gov.uk/ypeoplefr.htm (accessed 10 December 2008).
Marshall, K. (2001) 'The history and philosophy of children's rights in Scotland', in A. Cleland and E. Sutherland (eds.), *Children's Rights in Scotland*, 2nd edn, Edinburgh: W. Green, pp. 11–28.
Morgan, R. (2007) 'A temporary respite', The *Guardian*, 19 February.
Scottish Law Commission (2002) *Report on the Age of Criminal Responsibility*, Edinburgh: The Stationery Office.
UK Children's Commissioners (2008) *UK Children's Commissioners' Report to the UN Committee on the Rights of the Child (2008), United Nations Convention on the Rights of the Child*, http://sccyp.org.uk/UK_Childrens_Commissioners_UN_Report.pdf (accessed 10 December 2008).
UNICEF (2008) *UNICEF calls for UNCRC to be incorporated into law*, http://www.unicef.org.uk/press/news_detail_full_story.asp?news_id=1203 (accessed 10 December 2008).
Victorian Department of Human Services (2003) *Protecting Children: The Child Protection Outcomes Project*, Melbourne: The Allen Consulting Group.

Wellman, C. (2005) 'Feinberg's two concepts of rights', *Legal Theory*, 11 (3): 213–226.

Whyte, B. (2003) 'Young and persistent: Recent developments in youth justice policy and practice in Scotland', *Youth Justice*, 3 (2): 74–85.

Williams, F. (2004) 'What matters is who works: Why every child matters to New Labour. Commentary on the DfES Green Paper *Every Child Matters*', *Critical Social Policy*, 24 (3): 406–427.

# 4

# Child Poverty

Chris Grover

## Introduction

In Britain the life chances of children are set by the financial well-being of the families into which they are born. The children of the least well off are more likely to die as children, and if they reach adulthood die younger than their better off peers (Roberts and Power, 1996). In the meantime, they will have to live with the stigma of being poor in a deeply unequal society where the status of individuals is often measured by their ability to consume (Bauman, 2005). They are also less likely to gain a set of 'good' educational qualifications, are more likely to be excluded from school and to be involved with criminal justice agencies, and to be working in low paid, casualized sectors of the economy (Grover, 2008; Whitty, 2001). Moreover, children born into poor families today are likely to die poor and have children who will remain poor because intergenerational social mobility in the UK is low and falling (Blanden *et al.*, 2005).

It is within this broader context that this chapter examines the safeguarding children agenda. The chapter starts by focusing upon the location of poverty within the Green Paper, *Every Child Matters* (Chief Secretary to the Treasury, 2003). It then goes on to discuss the extent and nature of child poverty in the UK and to critically examine central government attempts to tackle it. Finally, it examines the tension between, on the one hand, getting parents (especially lone parents) into paid work as *the* means of tackling child poverty and, on the other hand, a concern with parenting that is linked to issues related to offending and 'anti-social' behaviour.

## *Every Child Matters* and child poverty

We have seen in chapter 2 that *Every Child Matters* extended traditional notions of child protection to broader notions of safeguarding and promoting the welfare of children (see also Parton, 2006a, 2006b; Penna, 2005). In this wider sense,

*Critical Perspectives on Safeguarding Children*   Edited by Karen Broadhurst, Chris Grover and Janet Jamieson
© 2009 John Wiley & Sons, Ltd

children are deemed to be in need of protecting from a range of socio-economic phenomena, poverty in particular.

In *Every Child Matters* poverty appears in two main, and related, contexts. First, it is identified as a 'risk factor' related to poor life chances and high public expenditure, although it is not made clear how much of a risk it is. In the case of education, for instance, *Every Child Matters* notes in a manner, reflecting a parent-blaming discourse that structures it (Munro, 2004), that: 'Parental involvement in education seems to be a more important influence than poverty, school environment and the influence of peers' (Chief Secretary to the Treasury, 2003, para. 1.12). However, having noted this, the Green Paper goes on to discuss relationships between social status and educational performance across a range of ages. This clearly shows a positive relationship between poor material circumstances and poor educational performance. More generally, addressing poverty is described as one factor in tackling the 'key drivers of poor outcomes' for children (Chief Secretary to the Treasury, 2003, para. 1.18). In contrast, in this general sense parenting is not described as a driver of poor outcomes, although the Green Paper does note a need for a '*stronger focus upon parenting and families*' (Chief Secretary to the Treasury, 2003, para. 1.18) because of the 'strong impact on a child's educational development, behaviour, and mental health' that parenting is held to have (Chief Secretary to the Treasury, 2003, para. 3.1).

This apparent confusion is a consequence of the Green Paper's aim to address poor life chances; parenting is held to be important for the life chances of all children, although in reality parenting interventions are focused upon the poorest parents (Goldson and Jamieson, 2002), while, in addition, poverty is important only to the life chances of those children living in households with the lowest incomes. It also reflects the general thrust of the safeguarding children agenda that is structured through 'rights and responsibilities' (Balls, 2007); that if parents want, for instance, to access state benefits then they and their children must act in a manner deemed responsible. In this sense, parenting and poverty become inextricably linked through the potential of the state to impoverish the already poor (Grover, 2008).

The second way in which child poverty appears in *Every Child Matters* relates to the policies that New Labour have introduced as a means of meeting its aim (discussed below) of abolishing child poverty by 2020. The policies aimed at doing this are described as one of the 'strong foundations to improve services for children and young people' that the government has already put in place (Chief Secretary to the Treasury, 2003, p. 25). In this context, *Every Child Matters* argues that the 'best way to tackle child poverty is to widen opportunities for parents to work, and raise the incomes of working families' (Chief Secretary to the Treasury, 2003, para. 2.1), and outlines the government's approach to doing this through what is described elsewhere as the 'employment model' (Adler, 2004; for critique see Grover, 2006); helping parents to secure paid work through the New Deals[1]; removing barriers, such as a lack of affordable childcare, to paid work, and 'ensuring work pays through the national minimum wage and the introduction of tax credits for working families' (Chief Secretary to the Treasury, 2003, para. 2.1).

As an inhibitor of life chances child poverty was most closely linked in *Every Child Matters* to one – economic well-being – of the 'five key outcomes' around which there was apparently 'broad agreement' among the children and adults consulted in its development (Chief Secretary to the Treasury, 2003, para. 1.3). These outcomes were later enshrined in the Children Act 2004 (section 10(2)) and they are the measure by which: 'Public services are now judged' (Balls, 2007, p. 2). Ensuring the economic well-being of children was defined in *Every Child Matters* as being important for children in 'overcoming socio-economic disadvantages to achieve their full potential in life' (Chief Secretary to the Treasury, 2003, para. 1.3). The Green Paper was pointing towards the need to ensure that children did not face constrained life chances as a consequence of the socio-economic circumstances into which they were born. This was because constrained life chances were argued in *Every Child Matters* to have a detrimental impact upon economic and social well-being at a societal level (Chief Secretary to the Treasury, 2003, para. 1.5). In brief, *Every Child Matters* implies that with early identification and intervention the economic burden of social problems could be reduced. While the Green Paper does not explicitly say so, the implication is that it is poor children who are particularly burdensome because the targeted and specialist services it says are required within a universal context are, generally speaking, those aimed at, and imposed upon, poorer children and their parents. In this context, and as was argued in chapter 1 in this volume, it is possible to understand *Every Child Matters* as reflecting, and helping to constitute, the so-called social investment state, a project that is as much concerned with economic and social governance as it is with the well-being of children.

## Child poverty

When New Labour was elected in 1997 it 'inherited levels of poverty and inequality unprecedented in post-war [World War II] history' (Stewart and Hills, 2005, p. 1). However, it was unclear in the first two years of its reign if New Labour was to be able to do much about it. While the then Chancellor of the Exchequer and now Prime Minister, Gordon Brown was (and is) concerned about child poverty, driven partly by his understanding of the anti-poverty agenda

---

[1] The New Deals are employment programmes for particular groups in the population; for disabled people, lone parents, partners of unemployed people, people over the age of 25, people over the age of 50 and young people. The programmes vary in terms of their mandatory requirements and are being replaced by a new 'flexible New Deal' (Secretary of State for Work and Pensions, 2007).

of the 'Red Clydeside' MPs of the 1920s (see Brown, 1988), his concern also with making Labour electable on a platform of economic competence meant that it was committed in its first two years to the tough spending plans of the outgoing Conservative government. This was reflected in the fact that child poverty increased by a percentage point in 1998/99 before falling back to 33 per cent in 1999/2000 (Department for Work and Pensions [DWP], 2007, p. 52). By 2005/06 the proportion of children living in poverty in the UK had fallen 3 percentage points to 30 per cent (DWP, 2007, p. 52). Such figures though, disguise important differences in the extent of child poverty between the devolved constituencies of the UK and between social groups.

## Child poverty in the devolved constituencies

According to the government's headline measure of child poverty – income below 60 per cent of the median – the devolved constituencies of the UK all have lower rates of child poverty compared to the UK rate of 30 per cent. For instance, in the 3-year period 2004/5 to 2006/7 the rate of child poverty averaged 25 per cent in Scotland. This was the lowest of the devolved constituencies and 5 percentage points lower than England (DWP, 2008, Table 4.14ts), although, of course, it still means that a quarter of Scotland's children are living in poverty. At 26 per cent, a quarter of the North of Ireland's children also lived in poverty, while at 29 per cent the proportion of children living in poverty in Wales is closest to that of England. Moreover, between 1998/9–2000/1 and 2004/5–2006/7 the proportion of children living in poverty in Scotland fell by 7 percentage points, 6 percentage points in Wales and 4 percentage points in the North of Ireland (DWP, 2008, Table 4.14ts). In England child poverty fell by 3 percentage points.

Quite why there are such differences between, on the one hand, England and Wales and, on the other hand, the North of Ireland and Scotland is difficult to say, for the main ways of addressing child poverty are the same over the four constituencies. Social security and labour market policies are not devolved responsibilities. Palmer *et al.* (2006) suggest that the differences between England and Scotland are more to do with the poor performance of two areas of England – London and the West Midlands – in terms of child poverty than anything unique to the Scottish experience of reducing child poverty. This, of course, raises the question of why those two areas of England appear to have performed so poorly in terms of child poverty, for Palmer *et al.* (2006, p. 4) argue that the fall in child poverty in Scotland is due to 'increases in tax credits and in out-of-work benefits for families with children', policies that are equally applicable to London and the West Midlands in England as they are to Scotland. In the case of the North of Ireland the lower rate of child poverty compared to England is somewhat surprising given that it 'has a higher proportion of people than any GB region not in paid work, receiving an out-of-work benefit' (Kenway *et al.*, 2006, p. 17). It might, therefore, be expected to have a higher rate of poverty compared to the other regions. This apparent contradiction points to the complexities of the social security system, in particular relationships between means-tested and social insurance benefits, the consequence of which is that 'it is wrong to assume that receipt of out-of-work benefits automatically signals income poverty' (Kenway *et al.*, 2006, p. 17).

## Social divisions and child poverty

A quarter (25 per cent) of white children are living in poverty (Platt, 2007, Table 4.3, p. 40). Children from black and minority ethnic (BME) groups, however, are far more likely to be living in poverty. At 32 per cent, Indian children are from the BME group that are least likely to be living in poverty, although they are a third more likely to be living in poverty compared to white children. Black Caribbean (50 per cent living in poverty) and black African (56 per cent living in poverty) children are around twice as likely to be living in poverty compared to white children. The situation is even worse for Pakistani and Bangladeshi children, of whom 60 per cent and 74 per cent respectively are living in poverty (Platt, 2007, Table 4.3, p. 40). Children with impairments are also particularly vulnerable to poverty, especially if their parents do not receive disability-related social security benefits for them (Burchardt and Zaidi, 2008; Northway, 2005). These observations regarding the social divisions of child poverty have important implications for the government's main method – getting the parents of poor children into work – for tackling poverty. This is because BME people face employment disadvantages due to racism and the parents of disabled children face great problems in accessing childcare services to free them for paid work (Daycare Trust, 2008; Grover, 2008).

However, there is a group of children – those whose parents are seeking asylum – who are excluded from the government's plans, discussed below, to eradicate child poverty by 2020 (Reacroft, 2008). This is because there is little hope of tackling their poverty, for while the rate of financial support for the children of asylum seekers is the same as the tax credit rate for indigenous children, their parents receive 30 per cent less than the adult rate of Income Support. The government argues that this is because asylum seekers do not have to pay utility bills, although this is not necessarily the case (Reacroft, 2008). In contrast, the lower rate of financial support for asylum seeking families can be explained as a mechanism to deter people from seeking asylum in Britain. As Cunningham and Tomlinson (2005, p. 254) note: 'Justified by the claim that welfare acts as a "magnet", encouraging "bogus" asylum applications, governments have set about dismantling asylum seekers' social rights'. Similar sentiments lay behind the withdrawal of the 'work concession' in 2002 that now prevents asylum seekers from partaking in paid employment (Refugee Council, 2005), which recent governments have argued, as we shall see below, is *the* means of tackling child poverty. Moreover, under section 9 of the Asylum and Immigration (Treatment of Claimants, etc.) Act 2004, the Home Office is able to stop all forms of welfare support available to asylum seeking families 'whose applications have been turned down and who fail to take "reasonable steps" to leave the UK' (Cunningham and Cunningham, 2007, p. 278). The effect of this is to push some of the most vulnerable children and their families in the UK into destitution, something that is exacerbated by the prohibition of local authorities to use section 17 of the 1989 Children Act to support those children and families (Cunningham and Cunningham, 2007). It would appear that to recent governments every child does not matter (Cunningham and Tomlinson, 2005) because policies aimed at discouraging asylum seeking and encouraging repatriation condemn the children of asylum seekers to live in households that are especially impoverished by the actions of the state.

Article 27 of the Convention of the Rights of the Child notes that: 'state Parties recognize the right of every child to a standard of living adequate for the child's physical, mental, spiritual, moral and social development'. In the UK the state is failing to do this for a large proportion of all children, but for the children of asylum seekers in particular. This is, perhaps, not surprising given that the Convention of the Rights of the Child is not part of UK law (see chapter 3 in this volume) and that under its ratification the UK secured opt-outs in relation to asylum and immigration (see chapter 13).

## Abolishing child poverty

In 1999 the then Prime Minister, Tony Blair, in a lecture in memory of the architect of the post-World War II welfare state, William Beveridge (see Beveridge, 1942), committed New Labour to 'end child poverty forever' within a generation[2] (by 2020) (Blair, 1999, p. 7; see also HM Treasury, 1999; for discussion Brewer *et al.*, 2006; Dornan, 2004; Fimister, 2001). Given that its main measure of success was relative to the median income this was a bold commitment because as the median increases so too does the amount below which the government argues people are living in poverty. Initially, there were advances made towards the interim target of reducing child poverty by a quarter between 1998/99 and 2004/05. However, the target was missed by 200,000 children and between 2004/5 and 2005/6 the number of children living in poverty actually increased by 200,000 (Brewer *et al.*, 2007), the first time the figure had increased in seven years (Brewer *et al.*, 2007; DWP, 2007). Officials for the DWP argued that the reason why child poverty was increasing again was because of the under-reporting of income by self-employed people (*The Times*, 28 March 2007). However, the increase in child poverty and the missing of the first target

---

[2]    Child poverty will be deemed abolished when it reaches a level that is 'amongst the best in Europe' (DWP, 2003, para. 70). This will mean that up to 10 per cent of children will, at any one time, be living in poverty (Child Poverty Unit, 2009).

reflected the fact that relative measures of poverty are, by their definition, a moving target. This was confirmed by the DWP (2008, para. 60) which noted the 2010 target to halve child poverty would not be met

> because of economic and demographic changes. For example, higher average incomes for all households and trends towards more lone parents living on their own with their children work against the target to reduce the number of children in relatively low income and workless households.

The DWP's arguments for missing the 2004/5 target, however, is not strong, for the economic and demographic factors that they point to as explanations were not difficult to forecast. Average earnings and the number of lone parents, hereafter described as lone mothers as the vast majority (about 90 per cent – National Statistics, 2006) are women, have been increasing for many years. These trends do not preclude tackling child poverty, but they undoubtedly make it more expensive, for the higher the median income is, the more people there are who are likely to be living below the point used as the measure of poverty.

The Institute for Fiscal Studies (IFS) (Brewer *et al.*, 2007), for example, calculated that in order to have a 50:50 chance of meeting the 2010 target of reducing child poverty by a half, substantially more money – £4 billion per year by 2010/11 – is required to increase the social security benefits (child tax credit in particular) for children whose parents and guardians are not in work or who are in low paid work. However, while the 2008 budget did find an additional £0.85 billion for tackling child poverty by increasing consumption taxes on motor vehicles and alcoholic drinks, this is well short of the figures calculated by the IFS and there is little indication that future budgets will be able to raise even this inadequate amount for addressing child poverty. In this context, perhaps the biggest challenge for the government relates to the politics of child poverty. If it is the case, as the then Secretary of State for Social Security, James Purnell MP, was reported as saying: that the 'political demand to halve child poverty was small' (The *Guardian*, 3 March 2008), then there seems little chance of abolishing child poverty by 2020. This is so for all the constituencies of the UK. In Scotland, where, unlike the other constituencies, the target of a decrease in child poverty of a quarter between 1998/9 and 2004/5 was met (Palmer *et al.*, 2006), the fear is that the reduction in such poverty has now stalled (cf. House of Commons Scottish Affairs Committee, 2008), as it has also done in Wales (Kenway and Palmer, 2007).

These observations are particularly pertinent because, at the time of writing, the UK had just entered what many believe will be a deep and prolonged recession. With unemployment increasing,[3] the target of abolishing child poverty

---

[3] Over the year to October 2008 the claimant count measure of unemployment increased by 154,800 to 980,900. Over the year to September 2008, according to the Independent Labour Office measure, unemployment increased by 182,000 to 1.82 million, an unemployment rate of 5.2 per cent (http://www.statistics.gov.uk/cci/nugget.asp?ID=12, accessed 9 November 2008).

by 2020 seems even more remote, unless, and this is the irony of measures of poverty related to incomes, the median income reduces during the recession while the income of the poorest remains stable. That said, in the 2009 Queens Speech it was announced that the government intended to introduce a Bill that will enshrine in legislation the commitment to abolishing child poverty by 2010. While such a move may keep child poverty on the political and policy agenda over the next decade or so, it is doubtful whether it will result in its successful abolition. It is unclear, for example, what redress there will be if the target is not met and we already have statutory targets[4] for tackling fuel poverty, targets that are unlikely to be met. Legal pressures seem as equally ineffective as moral pressure when it comes to the issue of poverty.

The implication of this discussion regarding child poverty for the safeguarding agenda is clear. The government is unable to fulfil one of the five outcomes – the social and economic well-being of children – that was enshrined in the 2004 Children Act, for while poverty is, in the main, measured in monetary terms, it is often felt in terms of exclusion; exclusion from events and activities that many young people take for granted.

So, for example, in developing a child-centred approach to understanding child poverty, Ridge (2002) demonstrates how poverty structures the ability of children to make and sustain friendships, inclusion within, and exclusion from, peer groups, and the ability of children to 'fit in'. She (Ridge, 2002, p. 133), for instance, found that clothing had a particular salience for children, for wearing the '"right" clothes allayed fears of bullying and were also seen as valuable for developing self-esteem and confidence'. In social policy-making, however, concerns that children have are often either ignored or relegated to concerns about them as adults-to-be (see chapter 1 in this volume). Even in the narrow concerns of the government, however, it is the case that the effects of child poverty are deeply problematic, for not only are the development of self-esteem and confidence important for securing employment as an adult, the opportunities for education and learning are also constrained by poverty. This was highlighted in Ridge's (2002) research with children and young people who, along with their parents and guardians, highlighted difficulties with paying for events such as school trips and the materials required for projects linked to GCSE courses, while West (2007, p. 284) notes that poorer children leave education 'because of the need to earn money or because their parents could not afford for them to continue'.

On its own terms these observations are problematic for the government, for it is clear that poverty is having an adverse impact upon the development of the human capital of poor children. This is problematic because, as we have seen,

---

[4]  The Warm Homes and Energy Conservation Act, passed in 2000, introduced the legally binding targets of eradicating fuel poverty in England among vulnerable people (such as pensioners, impaired and long-term sick people) by 2010 and eradicating fuel poverty across the UK by 2016–18. However, it is 'likely that in 2007 there were about 2.9 m households and 2.3 m vulnerable households in fuel poverty in England – the highest levels for nearly a decade' (Fuel Poverty Advisory Group, 2008, p. 2).

the concern in *Every Child Matters* with children as 'becomings' is manifested in a concern with their human capital, the development of which is crucial to the longer-term aim of tackling child poverty. So, the argument goes, developing the human capital of today's children will increase their earning potential so that when they have children those children will not be consigned to a life of poverty. A focus upon the long term, however, tells us little about what the government is doing to tackle poverty in the current cohort, and those up to 2020, of children. It is this shorter-term approach that the remainder of this chapter focuses upon.

## Paid work: the solution to child poverty?

> Work, for those who can, remains the most sustainable route out of poverty. The Government are supporting families to escape poverty by increasing employment and raising incomes for those who can work. (Stephen Timms, Employment and Welfare Minister, House of Commons Debates 2008, col. 2805W)

The words of Timms summarizes the government's view that paid work is *the* way of tackling poverty, particularly for those children in workless households. For a variety of economic reasons linked to macroeconomic stability and social reasons linked to the so-called 'dependency culture' the focus has been upon getting at least one adult from such households into paid work (Grover, 2005; Grover and Stewart, 2002). These trends are particularly visible in relation to lone mothers who are particularly problematized in terms of worklessness because of the alleged affect that not seeing the adult in paid work they live with has upon male children (Grover and Stewart, 2002). So concerned have New Labour governments been with the worklessness of lone mothers that they have set a target of getting 70 per cent of them – a similar percentage to married women – into paid work by 2010, although it is another target that will be missed (see evidence of Paul Gregg in Work and Pensions Committee, 2007, p. 63).

In order to get parents into paid work the government, as was noted in *Every Child Matters*, has taken an approach characterized by three elements. First, it has involved increasing the pressure upon parents and guardians to take paid work through changes to social security and labour market policies. Second, it has increased financial incentives to encourage people to take work through a 'making work pay' strategy that combines the national minimum wage with in-work benefits (tax credits) (Grover, 2005; Rake, 2001). Third, it has focused upon barriers to paid work, the most important of which for lone mothers is held to be a lack of affordable childcare (Brewer and Browne, 2006).

However, it is not clear that the government will be able to address child poverty through paid work. There are several reasons why this might be the case. Most notable is the issue of those families with dependent children who are not in paid work. We have seen that Timms argues that child poverty can be addressed by increasing employment levels and increasing (through the National Minimum Wage and tax credits) the income of those in paid work. This argument reflects the first half of the government's mantra 'work for those that can and security for those that cannot' (see Hyde *et al.*, 1999). The second part of this mantra – 'security for those that cannot' work – has been more problematic. In fact, it is argued (for instance, Becker, 2002, 2003) that it has been neglected by the government. This is arguably because the government believes that worklessness is explained by what economists called the 'supply side'; that it is the consequence of workless people not having the 'right' attitude to paid work and/or the skills that employers demand (Peck and Theodore, 2000). In this sense, the government's argument suggests there is not a group of working-aged claimants that can legitimately claim to be unable to work, even if they have physical or intellectual impairments, or, in the case of lone mothers, they have responsibility for caring for dependent children.

Such ideas conjoin with a long-standing discourse framing social security policy that suggests if benefits are too high, or are too easily available, they will deter people from taking paid work at prevailing wage levels and encourage them to secure their income through out-of-work benefits. This powerful combination of supply-side economics and 'dependency culture' discourse has a particular impact upon the income of poorer families. For instance, a lone mother with two children at 2005/06 benefit rates would have received £160.08 per week (excluding Housing Benefit and Council Tax Benefit) if she were not in work and claiming social security benefits. If she took a job at 16 hours per week at the minimum wage her gross income would be £246.19 per week, of which £165.39 per week (more than if she did not have a job) would be paid as tax credits and child benefit. Out of work her family's income is below the government's measure of poverty of 60 per cent of the median. In work, it is above it. The figures demonstrate, however, that contrary to popular belief, receiving social security benefits, either in or out of work, does not bring riches. £160.08 per week, for instance equates to £22.97 per day to cover all the expenses (except rent and council tax) of three people.

These observations link to a further problem with government attempts to address child poverty; paid work is not the panacea that it is held up to be. Over a half (54 per cent) of children living in poverty live in households where at least one adult is in paid work (Child Poverty Action Group, 2006). Moreover, it is also the case that the government's approach to getting people into paid work may actually exacerbate poverty. So, for example, the government's policy is to 'make work pay' (to ensure there is a financial incentive for people not in employment to take paid work) in order to encourage individuals into low paid work. This is a very different matter to tackling child poverty that for many children (46 per cent of those living in poverty) is caused by their parents not being in paid work. It also means that the redistribution of resources through the social security system have not been to the very poorest families, but have been to the not-quite-so-poor (cf. Brewer *et al.*, 2004, 2008). The consequence is that 1.3 million (10.2 per cent) children live in what Magadi and Middleton (2007) describe as 'severe poverty'.[5]

Recent changes in social security policy also have the potential to push people further into poverty. The case of such changes for lone mothers makes the point. From the 1970s to the mid 1990s the policy relationships between lone mothers and paid work were framed by the Finer Report (Department of Health and Social Security, 1974). While the Finer report was premised upon rather dated ideas regarding the needs of children to be cared for by their mothers (Millar, 2000), it did at least suggest that lone mothers should have a *choice* of whether or not they should take paid work. However, since the mid 1990s there has been increasing pressure upon lone mothers, as well as other claimants, to take paid work through what is now called the 'work first' approach (Peck and Theodore, 2000). What this means is that lone mothers have to engage with work-focused interviews with Jobcentre Plus staff in order to initiate and to continue their claims for benefits. Unless the lone mother has 'good reason' for not engaging with these interviews she is sanctioned (her benefit is reduced for a specified period). While only a small proportion of the lone mothers are sanctioned (between April 2001 and December 2005, for example, 77,400 sanctions were applied – House of Commons Debates, 2006, col. 943W), those that are, lose, on average, more than £10 per week.

The sanctioning of lone mothers in this way is of concern for at least two reasons. First, such sanctions reduce incomes that we have seen are less than the 'poverty line' of 60 per cent of the median income. In brief, already low incomes are reduced further, impacting upon the financial position of lone mothers and their children:

> Sanctioned lone parents highlighted the difficulties they faced managing on reduced income, especially paying utility bills and rent. Customers only had money for essentials and missed out on extras, such as socialising. Lone parents also reported being unable to buy treats for their children, provide pocket money or pay for school trips. (Joyce and Whiting, 2006, p. 3)

In the context of *Every Child Matters* this approach is problematic, for it contradicts concerns with the financial well-being of children contained in it. We have already seen that, even on the government's own view of children as 'becomings', attempts to tackle child poverty are failing. Attempts to get lone mothers into paid work by sanctioning them will exacerbate this.

Second, the nature and extent of sanctioning lone mothers is to be greatly extended. This is because from November 2008 new lone mothers have had

---

[5]  Magadi and Middleton (2007, p. 24) define children as living in 'severe poverty' if they live in households with a very low income (below 50 per cent of the median) *and* where there is also material deprivation. In their work material deprivation is represented by deprivation of both adult and child necessities (that include, for instance, living in households unable to afford a week's holiday once a year, to make regular savings of £10 per week, and/or unable to afford to replace worn-out furniture). Households unable to afford two or more of the adult or child (or both) necessities are held to be living in deprivation.

to claim Jobseeker's Allowance (JSA), rather than Income Support, when their youngest reaches the age of 12 (before that it was 16 years or 18 if the child was still in full-time education). From 2012 it will be when their youngest child reaches the age of 7, and possibly in the future when the youngest child reaches the age of one year (Gregg, 2008). This means that the out-of-work benefit income for lone mothers is likely to become more unstable as sanctions under the JSA sanction regime are far more common. For instance, in the quarter ending November 2006 there were nearly as many (65,000) sanctions applied to JSA claimants as had been applied in nearly 6 years under the 'work first' regime for lone mothers (77,400) (National Statistics, 2007; House of Commons Debates, 2006, col. 943W). In brief, the sanctioning of claimants is far more frequent under the JSA regime and, therefore, lone mothers face an even more precarious financial situation in the future.

Moreover, the use of wage subsidies (tax credits) to 'make work pay' for lone mothers is also problematic. Underpinning New Labour's approach to paid work is the idea that its policies contribute to labour markets that are essentially meritocratic; that once on the first rung of the metaphorical employment ladder lone mothers – as well as other disadvantaged groups – will be able to climb it. While the experience of BME people, women and impaired people in labour markets demonstrate that the idea of meritocracy in labour markets is deeply problematic, there is a danger that New Labour's policies have something approaching an opposite effect; entrenching the poor labour market position of many lone mothers and women more generally (Grover, 2008). There is some evidence to suggest, for example, that the Family Credit (the less generous predecessor of tax credits) was encouraging lone parents 'to take up jobs below their full potential, finding later that they have the wrong work experience to move upward' (Gray, 2001, p. 195). Moreover, the macroeconomic idea behind tax credits is to put downward pressure on wages. In brief, they were designed in the hope of maintaining low wages (Grover and Stewart, 2002).

## Poverty, parenting and work: tensions in *Every Child Matters*

We have seen that in *Every Child Matters* children appear as beings that need protecting from society, but also from whom society needs protecting. There is an obvious tension here in the need to both care for children and to control them. Penna (2005) argues that these tensions operate through electronic technologies that surveil children and their families. However, these tensions are also reflected in, and constituted by, the policies we have been concerned with in this chapter. This is most notable in our context by the drive to get at least one adult from workless households into paid work as, so the government argues, a means of tackling child poverty. We have seen that for many children this is a rather spurious argument for getting their parents or guardians into paid work because of the high proportion of children living in poverty in households where at least one adult is in paid work. However, there are other reasons for getting people into paid work that relate to the role models that it is thought are important that parents should demonstrate to their children. So, for example, in order to tackle the inter-generational transmission of the so-called 'dependency culture' there has been a concern that the parents of children should be able to demonstrate to their children, particularly their male children, that when they are adults they must earn their income, rather than receiving it through social security benefits. This is particularly the case for lone mothers (Grover and Stewart, 2002).

Such concerns are consistent with the broadening of child protection beyond emotional, physical or sexual abuse to 'encompass the prevention of factors that impact adversely on children considered to be "socially excluded"' within the safeguarding children agenda (Penna, 2005, p. 146). In brief, such concerns are consistent with the idea that children need protecting from broad socio-economic factors. However, they are arguably inconsistent with the idea that society also requires protecting from children. This is particularly so in the case of lone mother headed households, which continue in the public and political imagination to be associated with social disorder and criminality, because it raises the question of care for children while their parents are at work. While demonstrating the value of paid work may, for New Labour governments, be a signifier of a good parent, having children at home with no parent present certainly is not. It is at this juncture that the tensions in policies around what is deemed to be good for children are most visible, for there appears to be an inconsistency in thinking about relationships between paid work and 'good' parenting that is also of great concern to New Labour governments in the tackling of offending and 'anti-social' behaviour (see, for example, Goldson and Jamieson, 2002; Scourfield and Drakeford, 2002). If lone mothers are at work how can they be expected to be fully involved in the parenting of their children?

There have been attempts to deal with these tensions through social policy interventions to address what is described as the problem of 'latch-key kids'. First, the tax-benefit system is designed, providing – and they are not always – employers are cooperative (cf. Lakey *et al.*, 2002), to enable lone mothers to balance work with paid employment. This is reflected in the fact they only have to work 16 hours per week in order to claim tax credits. The setting of such a low number of hours to qualify for wage subsidies was done to help lone mothers to 'combine work with their responsibilities for their children' (Tony Newton MP, then Secretary of State for Social Security, House of Commons Debates, 1990, col. 731). In other words, it was hoped that setting a relatively low (16 hours) threshold for claiming in-work support would help enable lone mothers balance the two issues – paid employment and the care of their children – thought to be important in preventing offending and 'anti-social' behaviour among their children. This policy move had at least two advantages. First, it was hoped that through having a role model in paid employment the children of lone mothers would recognize the importance of paid employment when they were adults. Second, the children of lone mothers would not be at risk of engaging in offending and 'anti-social' behaviour because the one parent they lived with was at work before or after (or both) they went to, and came home from, school (Grover, 2008; Grover and Stewart, 2002).

Second, there has been a focus upon increasing the availability of childcare, most recently wrap-around childcare supplied in, but not necessarily by, schools. Such policy developments involve the commodification of parenting through making paid workers responsible for the caring and socialization of the children attending childcare services. For New Labour such services offer the advantage of socializing children in an environment away from parents who, the recent focus upon parenting suggests – including that in *Every Child Matters* – cannot be trusted to raise their children 'adequately' (Munro, 2004). Blair (2004, pp. 3–4) hinted at such issues when in a speech about childcare he argued that he wanted 'an end to latch key kids' and that the provision of childcare 'was not about children being abandoned in schools for ten hours a day, all year round. It's about providing a service that engages children, helping them to flourish through sports, play, music while meeting the needs of working parents'. In this sense, childcare is held to have multiple roles. It frees parents to work while helping to manage potential problems with the behaviour of the children whose parents are working through providing them with an environment in which they can develop. This is in contrast, as the impression is often given, to children floundering at home because they are being raised by adults with poor parenting skills.

## Conclusion

Despite child poverty being an issue that is concerning to many in New Labour, policies to tackle it are failing. The latest figures suggest that it is increasing once again after several years of decline. These observations are particularly pertinent to the safeguarding children agenda. This is because in its widening of concerns about children, poverty is defined as one of the issues that they need protecting from if they are not to be disadvantaged by the financial situation into which they are born and they are not to be an economic and social 'burden' upon the state and tax payers.

The problem for the government, and poor families, is the former's fixation upon paid work as being the solution to child poverty. As we have seen, in its current configuration paid work is unable to deliver above-poverty incomes for many families. The problem here is not paid work *per se*, but the way in which it is organized, for it is structured in a way that allegedly rewards personal effort and skill (although such notions are, of course, themselves structured through social divisions such as gender and 'race') without taking into account the familial responsibilities of workers. This has been a familiar criticism of wages in capitalism since its early days. In contemporary society it has particular pertinence because of the pledge to abolish child poverty. It is unclear how this can be done when essentially tax payers are left to pick up the bill of meeting the costs for social reproduction. It is unlikely, given contemporary politics, that any of the mainstream political parties will commit themselves to the amount of spending required to eradicate child poverty, despite the fact that the aim of abolishing it by 2020 is to be enshrined in law. Moreover, because it is argued that child poverty can only be tackled through paid work, the government is resorting to increasingly authoritarian means of getting people into it, a strategy that, ironically, is predicated upon impoverishing the very poorest people in society; their children will find it particularly difficult to get out of poverty and in this regard the safeguarding agenda is likely to fail the most vulnerable children in the UK.

# References

Adler, M. (2004) 'Combining welfare-to-work measures with tax credits: A new hybrid approach to social security in the United Kingdom', *International Social Security Review*, 57 (2): 87–106.

Balls, E. (2007) *Speech by the Economic Secretary to the Treasury, Ed Balls MP, at the Rachel Squire Memorial Lecture*, 20 February.

Bauman, Z. (2005) *Work, Consumerism and the New Poor*, 2nd edn, Maidenhead: Open University Press.

Becker, S. (2002) '"Security for those who cannot": Labour's neglected welfare principle', *Poverty*, 112, www.childpoverty.org.uk/info/Povertyarticles/Poverty112/welfare.htm (accessed 23 April 2008).

Becker, S. (2003) '"Security for those who cannot": Labour's neglected welfare principle' in J. Millar (ed.), *Understanding Social Security: Issues for Policy and Practice*, Bristol: Policy Press.

Beveridge, W. (1942) *Social Insurance and Allied Services*, Cmd. 6404, London: HMSO.

Blair, T. (1999) Beveridge Speech, Toynbee Hall, 18 March. Published as 'Beveridge revisited: A welfare state for the 21st century', in R. Walker (ed.), *Ending Child Poverty: Popular Welfare in the 21st Century*, Bristol: Policy Press.

Blair, T. (2004) PM's speech to the Daycare Trust, http://www.pm.gov.uk/output/Page6564.asp (accessed 20 March 2007).

Blanden, J., Gregg, P. and Machin, S. (2005) *Intergenerational Mobility in Europe and North America, A report supported by the Sutton Trust*, London: Centre for Economic Performance, London School of Economics.

Brewer, M. and Browne, J. (2006) *The Effect of the Working Families Tax Credit on Labour Market Participation*, IFS Briefing Note No. 69, London: Institute for Fiscal Studies.

Brewer, M., Goodman, A., Myck, M., Shaw, J. and Shephard, A. (2004) *Poverty and Inequality in Britain: 2004*, Commentary No. 96, London: IFS.

Brewer, M., Goodman, A., Sha, J. and Sibieta, L. (2006) *Poverty and Inequality in Britain*, Commentary No. 101, London: IFS.

Brewer, M., Goodman, A., Muriel, A. and Sibieta, L. (2007) *Poverty and Inequality in the UK: 2007*, Briefing Note No. 73, London: IFS.

Brewer, M., Sibieta, L. and Wren-Lewis, L. (2008) *Racing Away? Income Inequality and the Evolution of High Incomes*, Briefing Note No. 76, London: IFS.

Brown, G. (1988) Maxton, Edinburgh: Mainstream Publishing.

Burchardt, T. and Zaidi, A. (2008) 'Disabled children, poverty and extra costs' in J. Strelitz and R. Lister (eds.), *Why Money Matters: Family Income, Poverty and Children's Lives*, London: Save the Children.

Chief Secretary to the Treasury (2003) *Every Child Matters*, Cm 5860, London: The Stationery Office.

Child Poverty Action Group (2006) *Poverty: The Facts*, http://www.cpag.org.uk/publications/extracts/PtheFsummary06.pdf (accessed 7 March 2007).

Child Poverty Unit (2009) *Ending Child Poverty: Making it Happen*, London: Child Poverty Unit.

Cunningham, J. and Cunningham, S. (2007) '"No choice at all": Destitution or deportation? A commentary on the implementation of Section 9 of the Asylum and Immigration (Treatment of Claimants, etc.) Act 2004', *Critical Social Policy*, 27 (2): 277–298.

Cunningham, S. and Tomlinson, J. (2005) '"Starve them out": Does every child really matter? A commentary on Section 9 of the Asylum and Immigration (Treatment of Claimants, etc.) Act, 2004', *Critical Social Policy*, 25 (2): 253–275.

Daycare Trust (2008) 'Childcare – parents of disabled children speak out', *Press Release*, 23 April.

Department of Health and Social Security (1974) *Report of the Committee on One-Parent Families*, Cmnd. 5629, London: HMSO.

DWP (2003) *Measuring Child Poverty*, London: DWP.

DWP (2007) *Households below Average Income (HBAI) 1994/95–2005/06*, http://www.dwp.gov.uk/asd/hbai/hbai2006/contents.asp (accessed 7 April 2008).

DWP (2008) *An analysis of the productivity of the Department for Work and Pensions 2002/03 to 2007/80*, Leeds: DWP.

Dornan, P. (ed.) (2004) *Ending Child Poverty by 2020: The First Five Years*, London: Child Poverty Action Group.

Fimister, G. (2001) *Tackling Child Poverty in the UK: An End in Sight?*, London: Child Poverty Action Group.

Fuel Poverty Advisory Group (2008) *Sixth Annual Report 2007*, London: Department for Business, Enterprise and Regulatory Reform.

Goldson, B. and Jamieson, J. (2002) 'Youth crime, the "parenting deficit" and state intervention: A contextual critique', *Youth Justice*, 2 (2): 82–99.

Gray, A. (1998) 'New Labour – new labour discipline', *Capital and Class*, 65: 1–8.

Gray, A. (2001), '"Making work pay": Devising the best strategy for lone parents in Britain', *Journal of Social Policy*, 30 (2): 189–208.

Gregg, P. (2008) *Realising Potential: A Vision for Personalised Conditionality and Support. An Independent Report for the Department for Work and Pensions*, Norwich: The Stationery Office.

Grover, C. (2005) 'Living wages and the "making work pay" strategy', *Critical Social Policy*, 25 (1): 5–27.

Grover, C. (2006) 'Welfare reform, accumulation and social exclusion in the United Kingdom', *Social Work and Society*, 4 (1), http://www.socwork.net/2006/1/articles/grover (accessed 2 April 2008).

Grover, C. (2008) *Crime and Inequality*, Cullompton: Willan.

Grover, C. and Stewart, J. (2002) *The Work Connection: The Role of Social Security in Regulating British Economic Life*, Basingstoke: Palgrave.

HM Treasury (1999) *Tackling Poverty and Extending Opportunity*, The Modernisation of Britain's Tax Benefit System Number Four, London: HM Treasury.

House of Commons Debates (1990) *Child Maintenance*, 29 October, vol. 178, cols. 729–749.

House of Commons Debates (2006) *New Deal*, 28 March, vol. 444, part 2, cols. 940W–943W.

House of Commons Debates (2008) *Child Poverty*, 6 March 2008, issue no. 2126, col. 2805W.

House of Commons Scottish Affairs Committee (2008) *Child Poverty in Scotland*, HC 277, London: The Stationery Office.

Hyde, M., Dixon, J. and Joyner, M. (1999) '"Work for those that can, security for those that cannot": The United Kingdom's new social security reform agenda', *International Social Security Review*, 52 (4): 69–86.

Joyce, L. and Whiting, K. (2006) *Sanctions: Qualitative Summary Report on Lone Parent Customers*, DWP Working Paper No 27, Leeds: Corporate Document Services.

Kenway, P., MacInnes, T., Kelly, A. and Palmer, G. (2006) *Monitoring Poverty and Social Exclusion in Northern Ireland 2006*, York: Joseph Rowntree Foundation.

Kenway, P. and Palmer, G. (2007) *Monitoring Poverty and Social Exclusion in Wales 2007*, York: Joseph Rowntree Foundation.

Lakey, J., Parry, J., Barnes, H. and Taylor, R. (2002) *New Deal for Lone Parents: A Qualitative Evaluation of the In-Work Training Grant Pilot (IWTG)*, London: Policy Studies Institute.

Magadi, M. and Middleton, S. (2007) *Severe Child Poverty in the UK*, London: Save the Children.

Millar, J. (2000) 'Lone parents and the New Deal', *Policy Studies*, 21 (4): 333–345.

Munro, E. (2004) 'State regulation of parenting', *The Political Quarterly*, 75 (2): 180–184.

National Statistics (2006) *Social Trends 36*, Basingstoke: Palgrave Macmillan.

National Statistics (2007) *DWP Quarterly Statistical Summary*, London: DWP.

Northway, R. (2005) 'Disabled children', in G. Preston (ed.), *At Greatest Risk: The Children Most Likely to Be Poor*, London: Child Poverty Action Group.

Palmer, G., MacInnes, T. and Kenway, P. (2006) *Monitoring Poverty and Social Exclusion in Scotland 2006*, York: Joseph Rowntree Foundation.

Parton, N. (2006a) '"Every Child Matters": The shift to prevention whilst strengthening protection in children's services in England', *Children and Youth Services Review*, 28 (8): 976–992.

Parton, N. (2006b) *Safeguarding Childhood: Early Intervention and Surveillance in a Late Modern Society*, Basingstoke: Palgrave Macmillan.

Peck, J. and Theodore, N. (2000) 'Beyond "Employability"', *Cambridge Journal of Economics*, 24: 729–749.

Penna, S. (2005) 'The Children Act 2004: Child Protection and Social Surveillance', *Journal of Social Welfare and Family Law*, 27 (2): 143–157.

Platt, L. (2007) *Poverty and Ethnicity in the UK*, York: Joseph Rowntree Foundation.

Rake, K. (2001) 'Gender and New Labour's social policies', *Journal of Social Policy*, 30 (2): 209–231.

Reacroft, J. (2008) *Like Any Other Child? Children and Families in the Asylum Process*, London: Barnardos.

Refugee Council (2005) *The Forbidden Workforce: Asylum Seekers, the Employment Concession and Access to the UK Labour Market*, London: Refugee Council.

Ridge, T. (2002) *Childhood Poverty and Social Exclusion*, Bristol: Policy Press.

Roberts, I. and Power, C. (1996) 'Does the decline in child injury mortality vary by social class? A comparison of class specific mortality in 1981 and 1991', *British Medical Journal*, 313: 784–786.

Scourfield, J. and Drakeford, M. (2002) 'New Labour and the "problem of men"', *Critical Social Policy*, 22 (4): 619–640.

Secretary of State for Work and Pensions (2007) *In Work, Better Off: Next Steps to Full Employment*, Cm 7130, London: The Stationery Office.

Stewart, K. and Hills, J. (2005) 'Introduction', in J. Hills and K. Stewart (eds.), *A More Equal Society? New Labour, Poverty, Inequality and Exclusion*, Bristol: Policy Press.

West, A. (2007) 'Poverty and educational achievement: Why do children from low-income families tend to do less well at school?', *Benefits: The Journal of Poverty and Social Justice*, 15 (3): 283–297.

Whitty, G. (2001) 'Education, social class and social exclusion', *Journal of Education Policy*, 16 (4): 287–295.

Work and Pensions Committee (2007) *The Government's Employment Strategy, Third Report of Session 2006–07*, HC63-I, London: The Stationery Office.

# 5

# The Common Assessment Framework: Effective Innovation for Children and Young People with 'Additional Needs' or Simply More Technical Hype?

Andy Pithouse and Karen Broadhurst

## Introduction

In this chapter we focus on a recent initiative – the Common Assessment Framework (CAF). This assessment tool is promoted by governments in England and Wales as a means of safeguarding children through the early identification of children's needs and the bringing together of agencies to determine how best those needs can be addressed. As a key component of the vision of integrated children's services as outlined in the *Every Child Matters: Change for Children Programme* (Department for Education and Skills [DfES], 2004a), CAF, in its basic electronic assessment format will help share key information between children, families and service providers. CAF aims to help children and families attain the priority outcomes set by government in England for the well-being of all children (see DfES, 2004b) and likewise in Wales, but in regard to a more extended set of key outcomes contained in Welsh Assembly policy (see Welsh Assembly Government, 2004).

At the time of writing in late 2008, CAF had only just been rolled out (to varying extents) in England and was still being piloted in Wales. Hence, it is premature to claim some definitive picture. However, there are some evident issues and illuminating insights from recent research that we think merit attention and will be of interest to policy, practitioner and management constituencies (Brandon *et al.*, 2006a, 2006b; Gilligan and Manby, 2007; Mason *et al.*, 2005; Peckover *et al.*, 2008a, 2008b; Pithouse, 2006; Ward *et al.*, 2002). With that

*Critical Perspectives on Safeguarding Children*   Edited by Karen Broadhurst, Chris Grover and Janet Jamieson
© 2009 John Wiley & Sons, Ltd

proviso, we start by outlining the thinking behind the CAF's design and its associated applications and processes, before moving on to provide a broad-ranging discussion of CAF's effectiveness. We focus on CAF's impact on service outcomes and CAF's potential to elicit standardized and holistic assessments of children's needs, before considering in some detail the impact of CAF on outcomes for children, young people and families. Finally, given its proposed integration with the information database ContactPoint, we engage with discussion that raises critical questions about the panoptical and net-widening potential of CAF. The chapter concludes by drawing together evidence to date and flagging priority areas for future research.

## What is the Common Assessment Framework?

As we have noted, the essence of CAF is that it provides a single assessment tool that practitioners from a range of professions can use to identify children and young people with 'additional needs' at an early point. Such needs tend to be relatively moderate and thus, the category 'additional needs' would not include 'children at risk of significant harm' or 'children in need' because of significant health, developmental and/or other domestic difficulties which might necessitate intensive intervention by more specialist childcare services. CAF is also a central vehicle for ensuring that key agencies, across the sectors of health, welfare, education and criminal justice, share in the responsibility for children's welfare and collaborate to prevent children slipping through the net of relevant agencies (Department for Children Schools and families [DFCS], 2007; DfES *et al.*, 2005; Youth Justice Board, 2008). In this sense, CAF connects strongly with New Labour's commitment to early intervention in that it 'shifts the focus from dealing with the consequences of difficulties in children's lives to preventing things from going wrong in the first place' (DfES, 2004b, para 1.5). Therefore, it can be read as adding to New Labour's portfolio of strategies for tackling what are perceived as 'cycles of disadvantage' (see chapter 7 in this volume) and promoting social inclusion. In essence, CAF is meant to target issues at an early point so that these can be dealt with quickly by relevant, often universal services, and *before* needs become entrenched and more serious.

Legally, the CAF is located within various statutes and guidance that refer to multi-agency collaboration to support children and parents. The Children Act 1989 section 27 (1) and (2) may be used to facilitate sharing of information between authorities about children in need. In respect of the well-being of children more generally, the Children Act 2004 sections 10 and 11 place a duty on the local authority and relevant partners to cooperate to promote the well-being of children. CAF was originally paper-based, but is now e-configured and a future is envisaged in which CAF is linked to the proposed database, ContactPoint, to facilitate information sharing. Its computer-based functionality not only stores evidence that a CAF exists, but it can also provide strategic management information in regard to the multiple and spatial characteristics of additional needs.

Completion of CAF requires key demographic and family details about the child. The assessment process requires that the practitioner comments briefly upon needs and strengths in relation to developmental, parenting and environmental domains. Much here depends upon the CAF design, training and quality oversight in regard to the depth and standard of assessment, as we discuss in the following section. CAF aims to reduce the number of assessments to which families are exposed and to enable professionals to gather together information about a child in one place, facilitating a common understanding of a child's needs. It is envisaged that information then follows the child, enabling a range of agencies to more easily garner the details necessary to provide an early and joined up response (see DfES, 2004a). While a relatively simple assessment tool, CAF nonetheless bears the weight of much government aspiration in relation to improving collaborative practice to safeguard children. Through the breaking down of boundaries between agencies that have previously been thought to hinder effective early intervention, CAF is deemed to play a key role in preventing poor outcomes for children. The policy vision of integrated assessment that underpins CAF is undoubtedly positive, depicted through the descriptors; 'holistic', 'strengths focused' and 'seamless' (DfES, 2004b) but, as we discuss below, is argued to be particularly problematic with regard to communication across professional boundaries.

In introducing the specific category of children with 'additional needs', CAF reflects New Labour's commitment at a policy level to carve out a service space where agencies can respond to children and young people with what are held to be lower levels of need. In this regard, a CAF would be less likely to be completed by more specialist workers, such as child care social workers, whose cases typically comprise children with more significant concerns. Nor would a CAF normally be used where children have already come to the attention of Local Authority Children's Social Care and are receiving a service after their needs have been assessed. The CAF is more likely to be used for children who come to the notice of relevant professionals for the first time or where some previous involvement by professionals has resulted for some time in a 'closed case'. A CAF is usually intended to invoke a coordinated response and usually results in the calling of a multi-agency meeting (sometimes called a Child with Additional Needs Meeting) to agree a plan for the child. At such a meeting, a Lead Professional (LP) may be appointed and tasked to coordinate services identified at the meeting and to provide a single point of contact for families and professionals alike. The LP thus oversees and coordinates the provision of what might otherwise be overlapping and/or fragmented services. In addition, and of considerable importance, the LP is ideally someone that families know and trust. A CAF LP may be from a local voluntary organization, school or health service, and has the potential to provide more immediate, relationship-based support for families in their help-seeking.

However, the many voluntary and statutory agencies that provide local services for children while under a general duty to cooperate to promote the well-being of children, are not *compelled* by law to complete CAF forms in order to assess or refer cases to one another. Much depends upon the way CAF is taken up at the local authority level by consortia or steering groups that represent key agencies that provide services for children. As we shall see, this is by no means without difficulties in providing a coherent standardizing approach to assessment. Nor is the idea of some overarching electronic assessment system linked to a database without its critics. We turn now to some of the findings and critical questions about CAF's implementation and future potential.

## CAF and service outcomes – mixed findings from England and Wales

A number of studies suggest some positive findings in respect of CAF impact on service outcomes. For example, from recent evaluations in England (Brandon *et al.*, 2006a, 2006b; Peckover *et al.*, 2008a) and Wales (Pithouse, 2006), we know that diverse professionals view CAF as helping to improve multi-agency working and information sharing and that CAF appears to have had some positive effect on reducing referral rates to the local authority in some pilot areas.

Evaluation by Pithouse *et al.* (2004) of the first Welsh CAF comprised a semi-experimental comparative design involving detailed examination before and after implementation of the common assessment in one pilot authority. Analysis of some 88 completed CAFs revealed a notable decrease in missing information in regard to basic background demographic detail compared to pre-implementation referrals and notifications used by a range of local providers. It was also noted that implementing CAF as a pre-condition of referring children in need had the effect of reducing the number of referrals to social services. This suggests that CAF may have made professionals more discriminating in their decision to refer. In addition, the reduction in referrals did not appear to have perverse consequences. There was little evidence, for instance, that more child protection referrals were being made because of cases moving into crisis as a consequence of professionals being averse to using the CAF to refer. There was also little evidence that professionals were using child protection procedures instead of the CAF system to inappropriately fast-track referrals.

Pithouse *et al.* (2004) also revealed a modest increase in the recording of health-related information; much more information on education needs and, notably, more emphasis in assessments upon parent and family strengths. It was also evident that there were changes before and after in relation to the impact of CAF on social services. There were indicators of a more focused response from social services whereby the CAFs they received led to more initial assessments, fewer referrals leading to no further action or advice only, or referred on to other agencies, and more referrals accepted for direct action by social services teams. Interviews with a cross-section of CAF writers (27 in total) in occupational settings other than social work (for instance, education, health, the courts and voluntary organizations) revealed that most thought the CAF design (domains, thresholds of concern, prompts and examples of need) helped them think more holistically about the child. Moreover, although most respondents thought the CAF form burdensome because of the completion time (60–90 minutes), they nearly all considered it, if it could be streamlined, a valuable tool that ought to survive beyond the pilot.

The findings from England report mixed successes to date. In a DfES commissioned evaluation of CAF and the LP role in 12 local authority areas, Brandon *et al.* (2006a) describe their findings as tentative, given that a quarter of the participating sites described themselves as slow to implement CAF at the time of the evaluation. However, they did find enthusiasm for CAF was widespread, with practitioners from diverse professional backgrounds believing that CAF was a very important initiative for children, young people and families. The study reported evidence that some good assessment work was being undertaken outside of local authorities and that services were being offered. For example, the researchers found that in some areas, because the CAF process drew together a multi-agency team that met and agreed the CAF, even where the assessment did not highlight that further services were required outside the immediate reference group, the process served to formalize the needs of the child in question and reminded participating agencies of their responsibilities to the particular child. Thus, the process in itself, can be seen as a vehicle for strengthening the existing safety net for children and young people. Participants indicated that the CAF was stimulating the sharing of information in ways that would not previously have happened, both between professionals and with service users. For example, the researchers describe that when CAFs were completed in collaboration with parents, this formed a good basis for partnership working and facilitated shared understandings of needs. When further meetings were held, parents were not surprised by concerns expressed or described needs. Brandon *et al.*'s study provides some preliminary evidence that CAF is enabling practitioners to think beyond their own circumscribed area of practice, towards the consideration of a broader network of relevant agencies.

However, the researchers made clear that further evaluation was needed to substantiate these positive findings, for they also found a number of obstacles to participation in CAF work. These included school staff not attending training and an unwillingness to follow the CAF process. The police were also described as difficult to engage in a number of areas due to a 'perceived conflict of interests between "keeping the community safe" and "child first priorities"' (Brandon *et al.*, 2006b, p. 405). A more recent study by Gilligan and Manby (2007) in two CAF pilot projects in a northern England town, also reported commitment and enthusiasm from practitioners, but detailed analysis of the site found the reality of practice differed from the rhetoric, with few practitioners offering to take up the LP role. The findings from these studies resonate with concerns expressed by respondents to the initial DfES (2004b) consultancy that reported concerns on the part of diverse professional groups about the additional work that CAF could bring to already over-stretched agencies. Indeed, from studies in both England and Wales, it is evident that CAF is not budget neutral in terms of training investment, IT system operating costs, time-costs in CAF completion and, given that it aims to identify a population of low-level additional need that might otherwise not have had some early attention, it would seem inevitably to generate more work for local agencies. Whether a prompt intervention via CAF ultimately offsets these additional costs by tackling problems before they deepen, and therefore become more expensive, is not yet known.

In contrast to the Wales evaluations, the studies of CAF in England also reveal less consistent findings about the impact of CAF on *referral* processes and indeed the 'traffic' at the front-door of local authorities. Reduction in referrals to social services consequent to CAF implementation were noted in early evaluation studies in England (Peel and Ward, 2000) and more recently in a study in one pilot area by Mason *et al.* (2005). However, subsequent studies are less conclusive, largely due to the variability in how CAF is being used. In some English authorities, CAFs are used by service providers for intra-agency assessment and planning purposes only. Indeed, CAF is seen as more appropriate for this purpose and *inappropriate* as an information sharing tool beyond the agency. By contrast, other authorities use them as a means of identifying needs or raising concerns in order to activate some response, both intra- and inter-agency (see Peckover *et al.*, 2008a, 2008b). In other authorities CAF seems to be used less as a means of multi-agency assessment and collaboration around some child's need, and more as a means of referral to a single agency (see Ofsted *et al.*, 2008, para. 24). Thus, we see the emergence of CAF in some areas as the predominant means of basic assessment and/or referral by all local agencies working with children, and in other areas we can detect a more selective and prescribed use of CAF by a more narrow membership of agencies.

The Wales pilot (Pithouse *et al.*, 2004) was instructive in revealing the varied and uneven knowledge base of local professionals who frequently come into contact with children. The results were also a valuable reminder that terms such as the local childcare 'system' or 'network' imply much more coherence and competence than is likely to exist. A key lesson from this study was that the mantra of joined-up services to promote a more standardized approach to information construction and sharing seemed based on the rule of optimism – that somehow a common assessment framework was simply an uncomplicated opportunity waiting to be exploited. As with Brandon *et al.* (2006b), it became evident that the CAF system and the assessment capacities of participating workers needed careful nurturing over time via ongoing training, clearly agreed protocols for information sharing and mechanisms for coordination and problem-solving across complex occupational boundaries. Even then, as Brandon *et al.* (2006b, p. 405) note, where agencies fail to engage with CAF, there are 'no sanctions or inducements to rectify this, as there are no national performance indicators'. In addition, the legislative framework that supports CAF, in common with Part III of the Children Act 1989, allows for considerable discretion in terms of services that agencies are required to provide under the law (see Masson, 2006 for a fuller discussion). CAF is designed to assist agencies to fulfil their obligations as set out under sections 10 and 11 of the Children Act 2004. However, in practice, while social workers and other professionals have a duty to cooperate to promote the well-being of children, it will be difficult to enforce engagement with the CAF process in 'relevant agencies'. In particular, statute does not compel any particular agency to undertake the role of the LP and the associated duties of overseeing the coordination of services agreed under a CAF plan, while acting as a single point of contact for the child and/or the family. This is a particular issue because the LP role is critical to the effectiveness of CAF. While we would not advocate further regulation of relevant agencies, motivations and resources to complete CAF as well as CAF's utility for diverse agencies, needs further analysis. As Munro (2005, p. 376) suggests, tools may be being designed 'with an unrealistic picture of the practice world in which they will be used'.

At root also lies something of a paradox in that CAF policy seems to have been drafted in the absence of what a 'good' (or 'bad') CAF and its operating system might actually be like. Thus, while CAF training and exemplars outline the sorts of issues and information needed there is no sense of some agreed mode or content scenario. This raises the issue, to which we now turn, of whether CAF's standardizing potential can be realized, given the range of professionals expected to contribute to it, and the diverse and often multi-faceted nature of the needs of service users.

## Achieving a common language of need? Assessing CAF's standardizing potential

As Reder and Duncan (2003, p. 82) note, 'problems of communication seem to haunt professional practice'. CAF is seen as a vehicle for not only stimulating 'network' thinking among practitioners, but also for resolving communication issues related to a lack of common knowledge base about children's needs that has been highlighted in reviews of child protection services (Sinclair and Bullock, 2002). In providing a single assessment tool, with many stimulus subheadings that aim to orient the practitioner to a common set of issues, CAF is seen as the vehicle for improving the clarity, consistency and relevance of both assessment and information sharing.

Notwithstanding some differences between England and Wales and revisions to the CAF form since its inception, CAFs have in common a conceptual base within the domains contained in the *Framework for the Assessment of Children in Need and their Families* (Department of Health [DoH], 2000). Take for example, the first (paper-based) Welsh CAF pilot (Pithouse, 2006; Pithouse *et al.*, 2004). It focused on children in need as defined by section 17 of the Children Act 1989 (note that this denotes a higher threshold than 'additional needs' and is thereby unlike versions in England). It contained three thresholds of concern (mild, moderate and serious, each containing prompts and examples) which were linked to four different age-bands of children and geared to the key assessment domains of developmental milestones, parenting capacities and environmental themes. Its design drew upon earlier pioneering work in England (Peel and Ward, 2000; Ward *et al.*, 2002) and was intentionally detailed, highly schematic and very much intended as a heuristic device for multiple and diverse workers at a local level. By contrast, the models adopted in England (and in the current 2007/8 Welsh pilots of CAF that shares much with the English models) are much more functional and minimalist in assessment input. The same domains exist but usually as assessment topic-headings with relatively less guidance and prompts around their content and completion. While this no doubt reduces the time involved in completing these forms, it is unknown whether this also reduces the depth and consistency of the information entered compared with the CAF deployed in the first Welsh pilot, and in earlier models in England. This is because, as far as we are aware, no comparisons have been undertaken. However, what research (Gilligan and Mamby, 2006; Peckover *et al.*, 2008a, 2008b) does reveal to date is that the standardizing aspirations of CAF regarding *common* assessment are yet to be fully realized.

Predictably, and appropriately, the sorts of ICT-based policy 'goods' claimed by government for CAF regarding its capacity to harmonize the language and practice of assessment and to provide swift and safe access to e-system information, have not been taken at face value by academic, professional and media observers. The idea that the CAF template, training and procedures might somehow be sufficient to standardize professional activity across multiple agencies may well be over-optimistic, particularly (as discussed above) because many relevant agencies are not constrained by statute.

Technology is rarely a wholly determining force. Professionals and their agencies often bring their own overriding interpretation or moderating expertise to find ways to work around new systems that they find difficult or incongruent with their existing practices (Hudson, 2005). They will bring their own qualitative 'test' to bear upon CAF based upon day-to-day practice experience, and the practical demands of the setting. Research suggests that CAF writers shape and deploy the CAF for various purposes, while some also *avoid* using the CAF altogether and use alternative or pre-existing (and often preferred) methods of communication (Peckover *et al.*, 2008a, 2008b). Whether these are the residual effects of an e-system yet to fully assert its authority is not yet known (the Assessment Framework for Children and Families on which the CAF is based also took some years to become fully embedded in England and in Wales – see Cleaver and Walker, 2004). However, what can be noted is that where discretion exists there will be those who simply will not operate the CAF system. For example, in the most recent trialling of the CAF in five local authorities across Wales in 2007–8 (see Cleaver *et al.*, 2008), anecdotal evidence suggests scant completion of the e-CAF and more use of the paper-based version in the first months of implementation. Cleaver *et al.* (2008) attribute such problems of implementing CAF to worker anxiety over switching to an unfamiliar IT system and the reluctance on the part of service users to participate in an assessment that would leave a non-erasable electronic trace.

Similarly, in a study of four local authorities in England implementing CAF (Peckover *et al.*, 2008a) it was noted that one authority had some 2,500 workers trained in the CAF, but less than 2000 had logged on to register as CAF users. In another authority, 800 staff had trained but only some 300 had used the system to complete a CAF. There was a significant proportion of staff (a third to a half) in two of the four authorities that did not complete a CAF online but used a paper-based source. Peckover *et al.* (2008a) describe some disengagement by staff in the early stages of implementation. This is perhaps predictable because, as we noted earlier, CAF places a general duty on professionals, but the undertaking of the LP role lacks legal mandate. Of course, compulsion and monitoring bring their own dangers regarding the quality of information recorded. A more fruitful line of enquiry might be to examine the CAF design with respect to its fitness for purpose, in the context of universal and non-statutory providers.

It is likely that some agencies, particularly education and health, will play a more pronounced part in CAF activity compared to others, and that smaller organizations, for instance, many in the voluntary sector, may more slowly be adopted into a local system somewhat dominated by large statutory providers. In the Welsh study by Pithouse *et al.* (2004) the CAFs were constructed mainly by health and education professionals who would typically complete CAF domains that elided with their occupational knowledge base and task orientation. Thus, teacher commentaries in CAFs predictably referred to educational or school-based matters and rarely commented upon parenting or aspects of the child's domestic circumstances. Health professionals tended to emphasize child development and/or parenting support, and were less likely to stray into issues of local/home environment or family income. Most CAF writers, including the voluntary sector, rarely entered comments in those domains that called upon some literacy around more complex areas such as child identity and the emotional world of family members. Perhaps such topics were seen as too intrusive, obscure, or beyond the skill base of the writer. More generally, the needs of parents are not well featured within the formal categories and purpose of the common assessment (see also Corby *et al.*, 2002; Featherstone and Manby, 2006). Official CAF guidance imagines CAF as a generic, rather than specialist assessment, but, inevitably, organizational relevance frames the completion of professional responses (May-Chahal and Broadhurst, 2006).

Conventional wisdom in social theory argues that we have witnessed in late modernity a transformation of 'knowledge', whereby the informational (knowledge stripped of its context, compressed and unitized for manipulation in new information and communication technologies) has taken prominence over the social (knowledge with more discursive properties of narrative that denote context and voice). In brief, the 'information-age', itself a term now somewhat over-worked, is believed to have shifted our lives more towards the world of networks (virtual and actual) in which knowledge is defined by its utility and by its partializing, standardizing and universalizing functionality (see Lash, 2002; Parton, 2008). Such a view finds some resonance in the term 'descriptive tyranny' (see Gubrium *et al.*, 1989) to capture the ways in which ICT systems (such as CAF forms) pre-determine the categories and formats in which knowledge is encoded. Yet, the CAF is not some impermeable externality but is a set of practices and technologies that the worker will likely engage with and make 'their own'. What was clear from the early Welsh pilot was the tendency for all workers to complete the concluding summary section and some would complete this only and leave the assessment domains empty. This may be because the summary section allows a more traditional narrative to build around a 'story' rather than the account being broken into discrete elements linked to assessment categories.

At a 'common-sense' level we might expect a CAF to possess accuracy, clarity, economy, and an 'evidence base' of commentary free of bias or discriminatory phrasing. Yet research (Peckover *et al.*, 2008a; Pithouse *et al.*, 2006) suggests all manner of linguistic modes can be noted in which alleged fact, professional opinion, hunches, suspicions and other *ad hominem* assertions would mingle or dominate commentary driven from particular occupational positions. Thus, while the CAF may disrupt traditional temporal and narrative displays, it does not displace these entirely – narrative as colour and complexity is never wholly squeezed out. CAF narratives noted by Peckover *et al.* (2008a) were often lively evocations of people and events, particularly where reported speech of characters was used, which seemed to lend accounts more authenticity. Similarly, dialogic comments from CAF writers (for example, use of the first person) were sometimes deployed to report action or make direct requests for services. Nevertheless, these 'workarounds' or local adaptations do suggest that the design format does not readily fit practitioners' preferred or established ways of recording.

Peckover *et al.* (2008a) detected 'tautological shimmer' in the way some writers seemed to re-produce the very text within the CAF form itself and accompanying guidance as an easy way to construct some basic vocabulary about need or concern. In this sense, the CAF format and guidance sometimes became little more than a 'sentence bank' for writers who use these 'resources' to construct their accounts. Again, this suggests that practitioners were struggling with the format of CAF. In addition, the orientation of many CAFs towards traditional 'problem-reporting' reflected established methods of reporting concerns to the local authority. Practitioners appeared to struggle to focus more broadly on needs, strengths and actions that should be taken as demanded by the CAF. Reporting concerns was for many CAF writers their usual way of doing business but this became something of a speculative moment when attempting to enter data into CAF domains that were not typically areas in which, conceptually and practically, they operated with any degree of comfort.

CAFs typically feature *selective* completion in relation to what a worker may or may not know about the needs of service users. However, a common assessment where there is no text in relation to some domains raises the question of interpretation for other CAF readers. Are we to see this as evidence that there are no issues or needs, or that these exist, but remain unknown? The multiple subheadings that comprise CAF are not only confusing for the reader, but can be just too much of a challenge for the CAF writer. Likewise, the search systems and criteria that will identify the existence of a CAF on a database require the inputting and matching of reliable information. This is by no means a given as Peckover *et al.* (2008a, 2008b) describe in relation to staff accounts that reveal the interpretative challenges presented by missing or unknown data on the CAF e-system. CAF aims to produce holistic assessments of the needs of children and their families, but this neglects evidence that formal records are inherently selective and elliptical, and that the 'whole story' pertaining to cases is neither feasible, nor required in most instances.

Reder and Duncan (2003, p. 84) argue that practical measures, such as shared protocols or procedures, 'only address a small part of the complexity' of communication difficulties. In particular, they argue that communication is an interpersonal process and, as the evidence above illustrates, without attending to the psychological and interactional dimensions of human communication, practical measures are likely to have limited success. They offer (Reder and Duncan, 2003, pp. 95–6) the following prescient observation that resonates with the analysis in chapter 6 in this volume:

> reorganisation fundamentally misses the point about the psychology of communication: that individuals and groups create their own boundaries based on beliefs, attitudes, work pressures, and so on. Furthermore each episode of communication has an interpersonal dynamic of its own and clarity of understanding will not necessarily be enhanced by different organisational structures. In our view, efforts to enhance professionals' capacity to think and therefore to communicate, would be more rewarding.

## Does CAF enable closer working between key agencies, parents, children and young people?

The aim of CAF is to facilitate a more participative, shared approach to assessment. In this case we might expect to see more reference to the views of parents and children, and to their consent to a CAF and its subsequent uses. While CAF appears to have generated more explicit documenting of consent than hitherto, much of this is consent from adults (see Peckover *et al.*, 2008a; Pithouse, 2006). In Wales, the early pilot revealed no discernible change in getting either consent or the explicit views of children within the assessment process. Also, it was evident from the Welsh pilot that around 16 per cent of CAFs had missing information about whether consent had been obtained from adults. This leaves room to doubt whether it had ever been sought. The notion that some users are more likely to be informed about the CAF as a prelude to its use, rather than being asked for permission to commence an assessment, is a possibility according to research by Peckover *et al.* (2008a, 2008b). Some of the problems in evidencing consent may have more to do with the electronic configuration of e-CAF and the unintended consequences that its electronic format has created. Practitioners cannot easily share e-CAF with service users. Therefore, they tend to draft a first version of the e-CAF and then take this as a paper-based form to the adult and child for them to read. The worker then needs to enter the users' views into the e-version. Such a process of sharing and iteration inevitably prolongs a process that has as its core aim a swift approach to information exchange. These transaction costs, together with the additional time involved in completing a CAF (it is likely that whatever was in place before CAF would have been less elaborate and perhaps more informal), may mediate against the documenting of consent, even when it has been sought. Again, what appears obvious from the above studies is significant variation within and across occupational groupings in relation to procedures and mandates for gathering users' views. In some instances, the utilization of broader information-sharing agreements, signed by service users at initial contact with a particular agency or professional, were seen to suffice.

CAF aims to open up help-seeking pathways for children, young people and families, in that they can now approach a variety of individuals for help in the first instance and can choose to access services via a trusted individual. The DfES (2004b) consultation indicated that this was an important consideration for children and young people. However, to date, we know little of whether this aspiration is being realized. Brandon *et al.* (2006b, p. 402) describe how the development of CAF practices in schools enabled parents to approach school inclusion staff, such as learning mentors for 'a CAF' and, thus, they were able to access support for parenting. However, such evidence is scant and far more systematic analysis of CAF practices is required in order to make more definitive claims about CAF and help-seeking pathways. In addition, the available evidence suggests that irrespective of the outcome of a CAF assessment, professionals may be reluctant to refer on to the local authority, due to perceived stigma and that service users will not consent to this avenue for help (Horwath and Buckley, 2004). The issue of CAF's relationship with child protection and the ongoing negative image of the local authority as dealing primarily with child abuse (Broadhurst *et al.*, 2007), may continue to inhibit help-seeking. In addition, there is some evidence to suggest that where CAF does facilitate help-seeking, it does not necessarily follow that services will be provided to meet need due to resource constraints. In this context, CAF may be interpreted as raising the expectations and hopes of families that are then dashed in the face of what are well-documented problems of resources shortages, particularly with respect to adequate housing, income poverty, access to additional support in school and children's mental health needs. A CAF evaluation by Gilligan and Manby (2007) in two locations in the north of England suggested that rationed resources and agency priorities meant that only a small number of children with additional needs received a service despite genuine enthusiasm from practitioners about using the common assessment.

In addition, there is some research evidence that in relation to CAF's aspiration to stimulate a more inclusive service response, it is failing to address well-documented gender differences in service use (Daniel *et al.*, 2005; Featherstone, 2006). As Gilligan and Manby (2007) observed in their recent study, fathers had no involvement in the majority of assessments. Moreover, we know little about CAF's ability to ensure representation of Black and minority ethnic (BME) groups (Chand, 2008). A number of commentators (Chand, 2008; Lane, 2007) have argued that it is all too easy to *'partition off'* a child's 'race' and/or ethnicity from the core business of an assessment (Chand, 2008, p. 8), and have argued that the issue of the needs of diverse groups is not well addressed in the policy documents of *Every Child Matters*.

The extent to which CAF is realizing its aims in opening up help-seeking options and promoting a more inclusive and collaborative approach to assessment is not yet fully evidenced. Where there are tentative positive findings (Brandon *et al.*, 2006a) these seem swiftly followed by more negative observations (Gilligan and Manby, 2007). It may be that tensions and dilemmas that were played out at the front-door of the local authority, such as the relationship between family support, child protection and associated stigma, as well as issues of inclusion, participation and consent, are simply displaced to CAF.

## The e-CAF: security, surveillance and integrity issues

CAF databases in authorities in England are intended to link and integrate with a planned national data base of children known as ContactPoint that at the time of writing was not operational. The government in Wales is yet to decide if it wishes to set up a similar system. ContactPoint will allow approved users to search for previous service involvement with children and families, and facilitate contact and information sharing between professionals. The idea of a national children's database has attracted notable criticism and concerns have been expressed that it will create the potential for unwarranted interference from what has been cast by some as an emergent 'surveillance state' (see Parton, 2006) whose new technologies, by design or default, erode further the traditional divide between the private realm of the citizen (families in particular) and the limited, but necessary, intrusions of the state into individual domestic affairs (see Garrett, 2004, 2005a, 2005b; House of Commons Education and Skills Select Committee, 2005; Hudson, 2002; Munro, 2005; Penna, 2005). A national database that contains sensitive details about children is thought to create direct and collateral risks to privacy, safety and rights. It is not necessary to be an easily convinced 'conspiracy theorist' to suspect that citizen-sensitive databases can be susceptible to misuse, mismanagement and, as worryingly, to being casually mislaid by a state with a growing appetite for exploiting its new technology-driven panoptical capacities. Likewise, the proposition that government can create secure databases that are impermeable to external criminal threat seems a risky claim given the techno-ingenuity of determined individuals and groups. If our well-defended money and identities can be electronically (and frequently) stolen, what barrier is there to people accessing what is likely be a less well-defended common assessment database?

As important, is the concern that what may lie within the official accounts (such as a common assessment) about citizens that can be shared via local and national databases is inevitably selective, partial, potentially inaccurate, sometimes based on impressions or intuitions and typically biased towards occupational or professional interest about the subject matter. This familiar point about the variable quality and contingent nature of organizational records in human service professions finds new salience precisely because of the capacity for CAF systems to universalize and preserve indefinitely workers' judgements about the lives of children and those who care for them.

The above concerns about the uses and abuses of new welfare technologies have been marshalled by various critics (Hudson, 2002; Parton, 2006; Penna, 2005) whose views, for the most part, are vigorous rather than sensational, albeit the latter can be seen in the more febrile imaginings of some academy and media doomsayers. In summary, most concerns about state-sponsored ICT systems in children's services sensibly raise issues about inappropriate surveillance and net-widening, threats to citizen privacy, data security, assessment quality, and the unreflective assumptions within policy about new technology innovations, such as CAF, to engage effectively with the complexity of child and family needs. These concerns about CAF and its databases reside more at the level of potential threats to its integrity and such cautions merit serious attention.

## Can CAF deliver for children with additional needs?

At this juncture it would be decidedly unwise to attempt some definitive verdict upon whether CAF is delivering for children with additional needs. There is certainly some evidence that in places, CAF is stimulating 'network' thinking and prompting practitioners to think beyond their immediate field of concern to coordinate early intervention for children and young people. However, this evidence is tentative as CAF is emerging as an assessment and referral *option* that is variably applied. It is evident that for some CAF is used mainly as a referral. For others, it is used as an internal memorandum to progress some planning. For perhaps most, it seems to be a means to register with other agencies the particular concerns of the writer around a child's problems which are constructed in light of their own professional standpoint. Moreover, as we have seen, in some local authority areas staff avoid using CAF altogether or do not comply fully with its requirements. This evidence suggests, as Hudson (2004, p. 77) has argued, that attempts to stimulate collaborative networks via top-down centrally driven mandates tend to be naïve about the 'widespread discretion' that impacts on implementation. This is particularly so for CAF, given, as we have argued, that the underpinning legislation of the Children Act 1989 and 2004 does not actually compel practitioners to complete the CAF or take on the LP role. Nevertheless, CAF, in keeping with many other of New Labour's 'innovations', such as the Integrated Children's System (ICS), is being rolled out in England and Wales.

There are those who argue that CAF can be described as a low-cost technical fix to deliver early intervention without additional funding to agencies that are expected to deal with an increased demand that may arise from CAF's widespread uptake (Gilligan and Manby, 2007). The frequent integrative organizational changes in children's services at local government level that assume added value by being ever more 'joined up' may well overlook the possibility that children's additional needs – the focus of CAF – have as much to do with resource distribution for which central and not local government has prime responsibility (see Masson, 2006; O'Brien *et al.*, 2006). There has been a consistent critique of the moves towards integration, not least that more organizational and bureaucratic change will not challenge broader structural inequalities that plague poor families. Masson (2006, p. 223) writes that 'Laming's perspective on what had to be joined up was partial. Particularly, his focus was almost entirely confined to the local level, ignoring the contributions and responsibilities of central government'. It is important that future research differentiates between local implementation problems and problems that have more to do with tensions and contradictions in New Labour's policies for inclusion. Again, as Masson (2006) notes, it is not clear that the closer integration of children's services would have helped Victoria Climbié, particularly given her marginal status as an illegal immigrant, and that, in common with many other vulnerable children and infants, she did not attend school.

To date, the evidence suggests that there are problems with CAF that transcend local context. CAF cannot always guarantee a service. It does not appear to engage effectively adult males as the carers/parents of children. There appear to be limits to children and young people's participation. These are all tentative findings that suggest CAF may have displaced, but not necessarily remedied, problems previously manifest at the front door of the local authority that relate to patterns of inclusion and the representation of BME groups and gender. Local skirmishes about how, or by whom CAFs should be completed, should not mask the 'bigger' questions that relate to the direction of national policy with respect to inclusion and hinge on income, housing and, for example, the status of particular minority groups.

CAF introduces the category 'additional needs'. Whenever a new category is created so too is a boundary that, in the context of rationed resources, can serve to exclude families from services. From what we know from our related research (Broadhurst *et al.*, 2009) local authorities have well-established methods of preserving manageable workloads through the situated 'adjustment' of the boundary between lower level and priority work. There is an inherent risk that there will be an increase in the filtering out of children 'in need' at the door of the local authority, through their strategic re-categorization as 'children with additional needs'. Thus, clarity and agreement is required about what is meant by 'additional needs' and the boundaries of this category with regard to the other official criteria of 'children in need' or 'children at risk of significant harm' as defined in sections 17 and 47 of the Children Act 1989. The official guidance describes the definition of 'additional needs' as a broad term that is used to describe all those children at risk of poor outcomes as defined by *Every Child Matters* (DfES, 2008). We can envisage the obvious difficulties posed by this definition of additional needs. So, for example, it allows agencies (as does Part III of the Children Act 1989 that relates to the category: 'children in need') to exercise considerable discretion and, thus, 'establish their own priorities' with respect to service provision (Masson, 2006, p. 235). It is likely that priorities around child protection and child developmental needs will predominate as they do now. In part, this is due to the fact that agencies struggle to respond to other needs that are systemic in nature. These are environmental factors, such as housing and neighbourhood. Whether, as an early intervention, CAF will invite a shared and resolute response by agencies to lower level additional needs has as much to do with the available resources of agencies, as it does the presenting need.

At the other end of the spectrum, critics of CAF see it as having far-reaching 'colonizing' potential, the potential to suck in families and agencies that may bear negatively on both. The former may come to official notice and be listed on a database as in need of a child welfare service when a more informal, anonymous and low-key response may be all that was required. Indeed, some parents will rightly question why an *assessment* is required and view this as intrusive and stigmatizing. They may even ask why someone cannot simply put in a request for help for these additional needs, particularly when the solution is, in their view at least, fairly obvious. And will parents who refuse to participate in a CAF get the same service as those that do? There may also be a downside for those children's agencies for whom assessing and being a part of a local child welfare system is not their expressed purpose. Such agencies may assert a more 'external' role in which, for example, they advocate on behalf of children's interests and rights rather than seek to assess and exchange information about their needs. Such roles may be weakened through the incorporation of these sorts of voluntary sector organizations into the CAF system.

CAF's potential to be a timely and effective innovation that will improve children's outcomes thanks to the possibilities brought by information technology-assisted assessment is yet to be proven. Given the centrality of CAF to the *Every Child Matters* agenda and priority outcomes for children, it is important to note that there is little evidence of its effect on children's outcomes and its cost-effectiveness. This is perhaps surprising when considering the many aspirations held by government for CAF, as a transformative mechanism, to standardize practice and speed up intervention and communication.

## Conclusion

How should we conceive of the CAF project? Is it more an information technology 'fix' that, without the resources to tackle additional needs, will ultimately fail to make an impact on children's lives? Is it more a colonizing administrative system, part of a new imperial ordering of early assessment and referral in children's welfare services at the local level? Or, is it a timely and effective innovation to tackle needs swiftly and help children towards appropriate outcomes? All three perspectives may, of course, be well wide of the mark in charting the gradual emergence of CAF across England and Wales. However, insofar as CAF is developing variably across different authorities it is likely that these tendencies may apply to varying extents in different areas. The challenge for future research is to examine the polarities of applications and debates, and provide a substantive evidence base about CAF's effectiveness. Children with lower level needs have a long history of being neglected by child welfare agencies. However, it is imperative that services work towards optimizing outcomes for all children, including those most at risk of marginalization. In sum, the current CAF, as a classification system, has been designed without much anticipation of its situated use. Yet, it is here that the tensions, limitations and potential of CAF will be played out, reflecting both local implementation issues and challenges for central government.

## References

Brandon, M., Howe, A., Dagley, V., Salter, C., Warren, C. and Black, J. (2006a) *Evaluating the Common Assessment Framework and Lead Professional Guidance and Implementation in 2005–6*. Nottingham: DfES Publications.

Brandon, M., Howe, A., Dagley, V., Salter, C. and Warren, C. (2006b) 'What appears to be helping or hindering practitioners in implementing the common assessment framework and lead professional working', *Child Abuse Review*, 15 (2): 396–414.

Broadhurst, K., Mason, C. and Grover, C. (2007) 'Sure Start evaluation and the "re-authorisation" of Section 47 child protection practices', *Critical Social Policy*, 27 (4): 443–461.

Broadhurst, K., Wastell, D., White, S., Hall, C., Peckover, S., Thompson, K., Pithouse, A. and Dolores, D. (2009) 'Performing initial assessment: Identifying the latent conditions for error in local authority children's services', *British Journal of Social Work*. Advance Access at DOI: bcn162v1-19.

Chand, A. (2008) 'Every Child Matters? A critical review of child welfare reforms in the context of minority ethnic children and families', *Child Abuse Review*, 17 (1): 6–22.

Cleaver, H. and Walker, S. (2004) 'From policy to practice: The implementation of a new framework for social work assessments of children and families', *Child and Family Social Work*, 9 (1): 81–90.

Cleaver, H., Walker, S., Scott, S., Cleaver, D., Rose, W., Ward, H. and Pithouse, A. (2008) *The Integrated Children's System: Enhancing Social Work and Inter-agency Practice*, London: Jessica Kingsley.

Corby, B., Millar, M. and Pope, A. (2002) 'Assessing children in need assessments: A parental perspective', *Practice*, 14 (4): 5–15.

Daniel, B., Featherstone, B., Hooper, C. and Scourfield, J. (2005) 'Why gender matters for every child matters', *British Journal of Social Work*, 35 (8): 1343–1355.

DCSF (2007) *Every Parent Matters*, London: The Stationery Office.

DfES (2004a) *Every Child Matters: Change for Children Programme*, London: The Stationery Office.

DfES (2004b) *Every Child Matters, Next Steps*, London: The Stationery Office.

DfES (2006) *The Common Assessment Framework for Children and Young People: Managers Guide*. Available at http://www.everychildmattters.gov.uk/caf (accessed 12 December 2008).

DfES, Home Office and DoH (2005) *Every Child Matters: Change for Children. Young People and Drugs*, Nottingham: DfES.

DoH (2000) *Framework for the Assessment of Children in Need and their Families*, London: The Stationery Office.

Featherstone, B. (2006) 'Why gender matters in child welfare and protection', *Critical Social Policy*, 26 (2): 294–315.

Featherstone, B. and Manby, M. (2006) 'Working with families: Messages for policy and practice from an evaluation of a school based project', *Children and Society*, 20 (1): 30–39.

Garrett, P. (2004) 'The electronic eye: Emerging surveillance practices in social work with children and families', *European Journal of Social Work*, 7 (1): 57–71.

Garrett, P. (2005a) 'New Labour's new electronic "telephone directory": The Children Act 2004 and plans for databases on all children in England and Wales', *Social Work and Social Sciences Review*, 12 (1): 5–21.

Garrett, P. (2005b) 'Social work's "electronic turn": Notes on the deployment of information and communication technologies in social work with children and families', *Critical Social Policy*, 25 (4): 529–553.

Gilligan, P. and Manby, M. (2007) 'The Common Assessment Framework: Does the reality match the rhetoric?' *Child and Family Social Work*, 13 (2): 177–187.

Gubrium, J., Buckholdt, D. and Lynott, R. (1989) 'The descriptive tyranny of forms', *Perspectives on Social Problems*, 1: 195–214.

Horwath, J. and Buckley, H. (2004) 'Looking for common ground', *Community Care*, 22 July.

House of Commons Education and Skills Committee (2005) *Every Child Matters. Ninth Report of Session 2004–05*, vol. I, London: The Stationery Office.

Hudson, B. (2004) 'Analysing Network Partnerships: Benson re-visited', *Public Management Review*, 6 (1): 75–94.

Hudson, B. (2005) 'Information sharing and children's services reform in England: Can legislation change practice?', *Journal of Interprofessional Care*, 19 (6): 537–546.

Hudson, J. (2002) 'Digitising the structure of government: The UK's information age government agenda', *Policy and Politics*, 30 (4): 515–531.

Lane, J. (2007) 'Culture, ethnicity, language, faith and equal respect in early childhood: Does "getting it" matter?' *Education Review*, 20 (6): 101–107.

Lash, S. (2002) *Critique of Information*, London: Sage.

Mason, C., May-Chahal, C., Regan, S. and Thorpe, D. (2005) *Differentiating Common Assessment Cases from Other Types of Cases: The Research Evidence for CAF*

*Responses*. Available at: http://www.lums.lancs.ac.uk/files/ccips/7115/download/ (accessed 26 January 2007).

Masson, J. (2006) 'The Climbié Inquiry – context and critique', *Journal of Law and Society*, 33 (2): 221–243.

May-Chahal, C. and Broadhurst, K. (2006) 'Integrating objects of intervention and or-ganisational relevance: The case of safeguarding children missing from education systems', *Child Abuse Review*, 15 (6): 440–455.

Munro, E. (2005) 'What tools do *we* need to improve identification of child abuse?', *Child Abuse Review*, 14 (6): 374–388.

O'Brien, M., Bachmann, M., Husbands, C., Shreeve, A., Jones, N. and Watson, J. (2006) 'Integrating children's services to promote children's welfare: Early findings from the implementation of children's trusts in England', *Child Abuse Review*, 15 (6): 377–395.

Ofsted, Health Care Commission and HM Inspectorate of Constabulary (2008) *Joint Area Review: Haringey Children's Services Authority Area*, London: Haringey.

Parton, N. (2006) *Safeguarding Childhood: Early Intervention and Surveillance in a Late Modern Society*, Basingstoke: Palgrave.

Parton, N. (2008) 'Changes in the form of knowledge in social work: From the "social" to the "informational"?' *British Journal of Social Work*, 38 (2): 253–269.

Peckover, S., White, S. and Hall, C. (2008a) 'Making and managing electronic children: E-assessment in child welfare', *Information, Communication and Society*, 11 (3): 375–394.

Peckover, S., Hall, C. and White, S. (2008b), 'From policy to practice: Implementation and negotiation of technologies in everyday child welfare', *Children and Society*, 23 (2): 136–148.

Peel, M. and Ward, H. (2000) *North Lincolnshire Parenting Project: Report to Area Child Protection Committee*, Loughborough: Loughborough University.

Penna, S. (2005) 'The Children Act: Child protection and social surveillance', *Journal of Social Welfare and Family Law*, 27 (2): 143–157.

Pithouse, A. (2006) 'A common assessment for children in need? Mixed messages from a pilot study in Wales', *Child Care in Practice*, 12 (3): 199–217.

Pithouse, A., Batchelor, C., Crowley, A., Ward, H. and Webb, M. (2004) *Developing a Multi-agency Pre-referral Common Assessment Approach to the Identification of Children in Need in the Community*. A report submitted to and held by Welsh Assembly Government, Child and Family Policy Section, Cardiff.

Reder, P. and Duncan, S. (2003) 'Understanding communication in child protection networks', *Child Abuse Review*, 12 (2): 82–100.

Sinclair, R. and Bullock, R. (2002) *Learning from Past Experience: A Review of Serious Case Reviews*, London: DoH.

Ward, H., Smith, N., Garnett, L., Booth, A. and Everett, G. (2002) *Evaluation of the Introduction of Inter-agency Referral Documentation (Children in Need and in Need of Assessment Consent Form) in North East Lincolnshire, Loughbor-ough University*. Available at: http://www.lboro.ac.uk/research/ccfr/Publications/Interagencyreferral.pdf (accessed 20 August 2007).

Welsh Assembly Government (2004) *Children and Young People: Rights to Action*, Cardiff: Welsh Assembly Government.

Youth Justice Board (2008) *Youth Crime Action Plan Consultation Document*, London: Youth Justice Board.

# 6

# Arguing the Case in Safeguarding

Sue White

## Introduction

MR GARNHAM: What is emerging with increasing clarity in this Inquiry is that your diagnosis [of scabies] was regarded as decisive by junior doctors, social workers and police officers.... And that as a consequence of your apparently firm diagnosis, those other people took no further steps to investigate the allegations of physical abuse.

DR SCHWARTZ: It is not entirely my responsibility for the actions of others. I would have liked them to have pursued it further; I was concerned. I know there was a faxed letter sent through to Social Services, it was not our practice at that time to fax referrals of that nature to Social Services. It was so unusual that we did send one through.

MR GARNHAM: I do not want it to be taken that I am suggesting that the fact that what I have just put to you is true excuses junior doctors, police officers or social workers from their responsibility, but as a matter of fact, Doctor, your opinion appears, does it not, to have been treated by these other people as being decisive of the question?

DR SCHWARTZ: *I cannot account for the way other people interpreted what I said. It was not the way I would have liked it to have been interpreted.*

MR GARNHAM: Was it not known to you at the time that that is the way social workers and police officers would treat the opinion of a person as eminent as yourself?

DR SCHWARTZ: In the past, when we have had problems like this, we have had discussions directly, and I would have explained why I reached my conclusion with regard to scabies. I would have

---

*Critical Perspectives on Safeguarding Children*   Edited by Karen Broadhurst, Chris Grover and Janet Jamieson
© 2009 John Wiley & Sons, Ltd

> hoped that they would have heard what I was saying about
> other aspects about which we were concerned.
> (Victoria Climbié Inquiry, 2001, http://www.victoria-climbie inquiry.org.uk/
> Evidence/Archive/Oct01/121001latestp3.htm: emphasis added)

The extract above is taken from the transcribed evidence given to the Victoria Climbié Inquiry, by Dr Ruby Schwartz, Consultant Paediatrician at the Central Middlesex Hospital, one of many senior child welfare professionals who had been in contact with Victoria before her death in 2001. Victoria died in London, England as a result of long-standing cruelty at the hands of her great aunt, Marie-Therese Kouao and Kouao's partner, Carl John Manning (for a full review of the case, see Laming, 2003), sparking a highly influential inquiry into professional and institutional failure, which proved a pivotal catalyst in New Labour's modernization agenda for children's services. Resulting legislative changes first outlined in the *Every Child Matters* Green Paper (Chief Secretary to the Treasury, 2003), include the establishment of Local Children's Safeguarding Boards, with the responsibility for safeguarding children and conducting reviews on all child deaths, and increased regulation and audit of child protection responses. Government put in place a series of measures intended to enhance information sharing and early intervention drawing heavily upon Information and Communication Technologies (ICTs) to support their ambitions (Hudson, 2002). These included the establishment of a children's database (currently known as ContactPoint), which is intended to hold basic information on all children in an area, with an option for practitioners to record their involvement with a child/young person and as an early warning, place a 'flag of concern' on a child's records. Aspirations for a 'Common Assessment' process were also outlined. The Common Assessment Framework (CAF) has been developed as the standard tool for all professionals working with children and families, which can be used for both assessment and referral purposes (Department for Education and Skills [DfES], 2006a, 2006b). It is hoped that, as a result, a 'common language' may develop to improve information sharing and communication between professionals.

It is difficult to fault Laming's broad diagnostics of the professional and systemic failures that contributed to Victoria's death, they are many and obvious, and usually accepted by the main professional actors involved. However, I shall argue here that the policy responses, particularly the much lauded 'information sharing' initiatives outlined above, have been based on a set of somewhat erroneous assumptions:

(1) That errors in safeguarding are a result of professionals failing to share information.
(2) That it is always possible to distinguish between competing explanations for a child's presenting problems and that it is the job of referrers to do so.

(3) That a common language of child welfare can be developed.
(4) That technologies, including ICTs, can assist with this.

We have seen, in the recent tragic case of Baby P[1] in England, that these erroneous assumptions led to a raft of reforms which arguably have done little to make children safer. Of particular note has been the failure to acknowledge the essentially interpretative nature of interprofessional *communication*, to which Dr Schwartz refers in her testimony above in the Victoria Climbié case. There were plenty of instances of information sharing in the Climbié and the Baby P case, but the information was contradictory and often misinterpreted.

This chapter puts forward alternative ways of conceptualizing and assisting inter-professional communication. It posits that professional interaction about particular cases is intrinsically argumentative in nature, in that facts are ordered with intent to persuade the listener of a particular reading of a case and are centrally concerned with sorting cases into institutional categories, which are probably not shared between agencies. Once the categorization has taken place, it is very difficult to shift. Arguably the tight assessment timescales imposed by the *Framework for the Assessment of Children in Need and their Families* (Department of Health [DoH], 2000) have exacerbated this problem (Broadhurst *et al.*, 2009; Fish *et al.*, 2008). Using exemplars from ethnographic work and professional experience, this chapter posits that professionals must be prepared to seek to understand the knowledge used by other occupations and that attempts to develop a common language of child concern often result in the use of *habitualized and stereotyped phrases with little 'diagnostic' meaning* (White *et al.*, 2008). Implications for professional education are also drawn out. But first we must revisit some salient data from the inquiry into the death of Victoria Climbié and re-interrogate what they mean for practice.

## The Laming inquiry revisited: the 'almost right' diagnosis and the poisonous prescription

The extract with which this chapter begins relates to Dr Schwartz's clinical opinion that scratches and lesions to Victoria's arms and hands were self-inflicted due to her experiencing intense itching from an alleged scabies infection. This opinion was in contrast to a previously expressed and documented diagnosis by a locum registrar Dr Ajayi-Obe, who produced detailed body maps of Victoria's

---

[1] Baby P aged 17 months, from the London Borough of Haringey, was killed in August 2007. He died as result of a blow to the head which knocked out one of his teeth, subsequently found in his stomach. He had a broken back and multiple rib fractures, numerous bruises and other lesions. His mother, her partner and their lodger were convicted in November 2008 of causing or allowing his death. The case then received intense media coverage and has sparked a further appraisal of child protection procedures and practices in England.

injuries and was of the view, having listened to Victoria's history, that there was a strong possibility that she had been physically abused. While Dr Schwartz testified to the inquiry that she had made it clear to social services that she could not exclude physical abuse, the production of a medical explanation for some of the injuries proved a highly consequential red herring.[2] The contact with social services to inform them of the 'change' of diagnosis was made by Dr Dempster a junior doctor unfamiliar with social services and the child protection system.

In his evaluation of the professional practices surrounding Victoria's death, Lord Laming asserts:

> Improvements to the way information is exchanged within and between agencies are imperative if children are to be adequately safeguarded. Staff must be held accountable for the quality of the information they provide. Information systems that depend on the random passing of slips of paper have no place in modern services. Each agency must accept responsibility for making sure that information passed to another agency is clear, and the recipients should query any points of uncertainty. In the words of the two hospital consultants who had care of Victoria:
>
> > "I cannot account for the way other people interpreted what I said. It was not the way I would have liked it to have been interpreted."
> >
> > (Dr Ruby Schwartz)
>
> > "I do not think it was until I have read and re-read this letter that I appreciated quite the depth of misunderstanding."
> >
> > (Dr Mary Rossiter)
>
> The fact that an elementary point like this has to be made reflects the dreadful state of communications which exposed Victoria to danger. (Laming 2003, Paragraph, 1.43, http://www.victoria-climbie-inquiry.org.uk/finreport/introduction.htm)

This is a noteworthy statement, in which the words 'information' and 'communication' appear to be conflated. It is easy to see why Laming came to this view. Documentation of observations, procedures, professional reasoning and decision-making in the hospitals charged with Victoria's care was at best haphazard and 'slips of paper' were indeed operating as a make-shift information system.

While this is clear, formal organizational systems are Janus faced and have a more sinister countenance beneath their superficially rational allure. Janus, the Roman God of *gateways* is an apt metaphor here in more ways than one. Victoria became defined through the locally rational, but ultimately dysfunctional *gatekeeping* practices in Brent Social Services. Actions to safeguard Victoria were road-blocked by institutional practices that were *excessively* rigid and formalized. Social services operated with institutional categories completely opaque to

---

[2] The production by Baby P's mother of a 'medical' explanation for his injuries, namely that he had behavioural disturbances and was injuring himself, also proved a very significant distraction for professionals in this more recent case.

the doctors making the referrals. For example, it was imperative for social workers to make an early distinction between a child in need and a child protection referral because different teams would respond to each. They, thus, demanded impossible levels of certainty from doctors who were simply trying to seek advice and enlist support in investigating ambiguous, but potentially extremely consequential circumstances, and attempting to address a migrant family's social needs. What is striking about the professional activity in Victoria's case is the suspension of ordinary aspects of mundane reasoning (Pollner, 1974) in favour of precipitous categorization and swift disposal, particularly by social services and the police.

My observations here are hardly novel. In their excellent paper on the subject Reder and Duncan (2003, p. 87) posit:

> Attributing a shared meaning involves everything from receiving the same message content that was sent, through having similar understandings of the words, phrases, sentences and shorthands, to obtaining feedback on hypotheses about how the overall message content and its meta-communications should be understood.

French philosopher, Michel Serres argues that communications within a system are embedded in a range of interpretative dichotomies – signal/non signal; information/noise and pattern/randomness (Serres, 2007) – each with semi-permeable boundaries. One reader/hearer may find information, where another detects only noise. For the receivers of the referrals, the categories 'non-accidental injury' or 'child protection case' were the pattern, the genuine deliberations of the doctors simply noise. Over again in the medical testimony, it is recounted that while the signs of physical abuse were ambiguous, general anxieties about neglect and emotional abuse were not, yet there was no easy disposal route within social services for such woolly musings. There were, quite simply, plenty of instances of information sharing in the Climbié case, but the information was contradictory and often misinterpreted. Signal and noise were frequently confused. This was no doubt exacerbated by the impact of globalization and migration (Parton, 2006) and cultural assumptions relating to West Africa, for example, the presumed increased likelihood of Victoria being infected with scabies, and by her racial characteristics, which made bruising more difficult to detect for Dr Schwartz and the lesions look less 'angry' against her skin. Laming has been criticized for failing adequately to engage with these matters of 'race and place' and for his failure to emphasize the disadvantage and exclusion caused by UK immigration policies (Garrett, 2006).

So, let us examine in more detail what the Laming Report concludes about the contact between Dr Dempster, the junior doctor and social services:

> Whatever the precise form of words she used, Dr Dempster had some difficulty in securing a satisfactory response from social services. She recalled that she ended up having at least two or three lengthy conversations with social services due to the fact that she was having trouble ascertaining who was going to take

responsibility for seeing Victoria. Her impression was that the change in diagnosis from non-accidental injury to scabies meant that a different person was now to take responsibility for the case. She said, 'Whoever I talked to made it a lot more complicated, actually, because I thought that whoever I talked to would come in and see her and it would be very straightforward. But it was not'. (Laming, 2003, pp. 250–1)

Dr Dempster followed up the conversation with the following letter:

Thank you for dealing with the social issues of Anna Kouao [Kouao was believed to be Victoria's mother and Victoria was known by Kouao as Anna]. She was admitted to the ward last night with concerns re: possible NAI (non-accidental injuries). She has however been assessed by the consultant Dr Schwartz and it has been decided that her scratch marks are all due to scabies. Thus it is no longer a child protection issue. There are however several issues that need to be sorted out urgently: 1) Anna and her mother are homeless. They moved out of their B & B accommodation 3 days ago. 2) Anna does not attend school. Anna and her mother recently arrived from France and do not have a social network in this country. Thank you for your help. (cited in Laming, 2003, p. 251)

The communicative intent in this letter was to prompt a visit to the hospital by a social worker, but was read by social services as a recategorization of the case and it triggered a quite different organizational response. Brent children's social services had two initial assessment teams – the duty team and the child protection team alongside six long-term teams. Initial referrals were considered first by the duty team. If the referral appeared to relate to 'a child in need', the case would remain in the duty team for initial assessment. If it was agreed that it contained child protection concerns, it would be transferred to the child protection team for urgent action. Thus, within the assumptive world of Brent Social Services, the crucial line of this letter becomes 'Thus it is no longer a child protection issue' and not the 'urgent' social matters catalogued by Dr Dempster in the understandable, but mistaken belief that they would trigger a response. Once the case was recategorized thus, it entered a bottle neck of less urgent cases held in an extremely over-stretched duty team, dealing with 200–300 backlog cases a week and an influx of unaccompanied asylum-seeking children with complex needs. This was compounded by the fact that, like most other social services departments and contrary to practices in health (Fish *et al.*, 2008), there was no routine system in Brent for notifying those making a referral of the action taken in relation to that referral. This simple dysfunction has not been rectified in the raft of reforms rolled out post-Climbié.

## Making a case in child welfare

I have discussed elsewhere the ways in which cases in child welfare get 'told' by professionals (for example, White, 2002; White and Featherstone, 2005).

Here, I am particularly concerned with the interface between children's social care and health, where things went so badly wrong for Victoria Climbié. In child health settings, the attribution of causation can be particularly complex. We saw the impact of the 'scabies' diagnosis on the professional reasoning in Victoria's case. It turned her into a 'medical' case. In accomplishing diagnosis and establishing causation in cases where there may be a co-existent medical diagnosis, the boundary between problems with biological and those with psychological or psychosocial causes is particularly important for professionals and is discussed at length in professional literature (for instance, Garralda, 1996; Woodward *et al.*, 1998). The diagnostic categories themselves frequently reflect the same preoccupation (for example, 'failure to thrive' is routinely subdivided into organic [intrinsic] and non-organic [psycho-social] varieties). The decision about whether a problem is seen to be part of the child's biological make-up, or a product of their environment, or both, clearly has a direct bearing on the management of a case. For example, the suspicion that poor weight gain is not the result of genetics, or a metabolic disorder, but is an indication that the child is not being fed, or is emotionally deprived may precipitate referral to social workers, rather than admission to a paediatric bed.

There are some contexts and situations in which professionals talk directly to each other about cases. Such talk takes place in formal meetings where very detailed formulations of cases are delivered often in long narrative turns. It takes place in abridged form in regular 'updates' before clinics, or during ward rounds or nursing 'handovers'. It takes place over the telephone and over coffee. Wherever it takes place, this talk does particular work. It turns symptoms and events into cases which are recognizable to professionals and can be processed using one or more of a range of potential disposals. I have noted that these disposals are saturated with institutional categories as we saw in the example from Brent Social Services above, which required an instant categorization as either child protection or not; and also with the operational contingencies of the time – for example, the 200–300 cases in the allocation bottle-neck and the imperative imposed by government to complete an initial assessment within seven working days (Broadhurst *et al.*, 2009; Fish *et al.*, 2008).

That is, professional talk does not straightforwardly describe different kinds of cases, rather the case is, at least in part, *constituted* through the telling and other possible readings are closed down. In other words, the same case may be told in many different ways and often this happens when a new professional becomes involved and sees it differently. We saw this in the Climbié case in the competing diagnoses of Drs Schwartz and Ajayi-Obe. Moreover, where there are ambiguous symptoms and moral evaluations, particularly of parents/carers, these frequently authorize particular readings and the whole process is in turn affected by differential professional status and organizational hierarchies. Despite the fact that there was no face-to-face discussion, nor arguments offered to refute Dr Ajayi-Obe's alternative reading of Victoria's injuries, as Laming notes, the veracity of Dr Schwartz's expert opinion was taken as read. Nobody asked the simple questions, 'what made you change your mind?', or 'are you sure?'

It is worth illustrating this process with an example of a case discussion where there were competing views of what might be happening in a family.

## Telling the case: an exemplar

The data are taken from an ethnographic study (see White, 2002) and were gathered during 2000/1. The extract is taken from a meeting about a family with three children aged five, four and eight months, the eldest of whom (Paul in the transcript) has severe physical problems and learning disabilities for which no definitive diagnosis has been found. The meeting has been convened by the social work team manager in a hospital-based team in response to a number of concerns raised by the social worker and other professionals about all three children who have poor weight gain and developmental problems. The purpose of the meeting is to decide whether to 'move' the case into a child protection arena, with the standard institutional response – convening a case conference. Present are the social work team manager (TM), the family resource worker (FRW) from social services, who has been providing practical help, the health visitor (HV), who was monitoring development, and the head teachers of the eldest child's school for children with disabilities and from the middle child's school. The dietician and speech therapist have sent their apologies but have provided reports for the meeting. The consultant paediatrician (CONS) is invited but has arrived late. During the meeting the professionals, in the absence of the paediatrician, have together been building an argument that the children are failing to develop appropriately due to less than adequate parenting. I have called cases like this one 'not just medical' cases (White, 2002) as their telling often involves a good deal of rhetorical work, since any problems the child may be experiencing could potentially be attributed to their medical condition. Professionals must work up a version in which the child's problems are 'not just medical' (see White, 2002, for further detail).

All professionals have given accounts of the children being smelly and of parents failing to follow advice. The paediatrician eventually joins the meeting some 45 minutes late. At this point, the team manager summarizes the case so far for the benefit of the paediatrician who has clinical responsibility for the child and also undertakes sessional input to the school for children with physical disabilities. He is known informally as something of a disability specialist in the paediatric service:

TM:     Now we accept that Paul has special needs ehm and his attendance at [special school] has improved slightly, I would say it's not sufficient well it's not as much as we would've liked and we still think that his sort of ehm development may be being impaired by his parents' lack of doing the things that they should for him ... On the 4th of January it was 12.6 kg on 1 February it was 13.2, so there was a slight increase between January and February but he was having Pediasure [a calorific food supplement] to supplement his diet. We don't think the children are being fed adequately and we don't think they're being stimulated adequately either, but the other issue, the thing that occurred at the planning meeting, was they actually made a statement that they didn't, if they were concerned about feeding Paul too much, because it would make him too heavy to carry upstairs, ehm so obviously that was sort of put back to them that you know that wasn't a good, an acceptable reason for not feeding him, but we wondered whether he does attend [school] but he doesn't attend regularly. He also doesn't attend on a Tuesday morning which is when I understand you go. We wondered whether you would perhaps have a look at him.

CONS:   Well I can do yes, yes, you could say that he was failing thrive and there is that way his weight creeps up and it was a bit higher in the first year, it has dropped off a bit through the second year in fact it's crept up from the bottom centile, reasonably satisfactorily I would say.

HV:   – but it's probably due to the Pediasure that he's having not to his –

CONS:   – I don't know how Paul feeds, and whether he he's, they obviously feed him don't they ... I don't know how well or how easy he is to feed.

FRW:   Terrible apparently.

CONS:   Oh I imagine he's very ...

FRW:   I think he has everything pureed

CONS:   Yeah, ... I think given the parents' limitations and ... They find it difficult to set time aside to feed him, I don't know, but I think that might be one part. If he gains weight better on the Pediasure then I must say I think ... I mean I find it very difficult to say whether he's worse because of lack of stimulation than he would otherwise be. Whether he would be slightly better in a different family, who can know ... Trouble is we don't have a diagnosis for Paul, I thought I had but I haven't ehm and he is waiting to see the geneticists to see if they have more ideas about ehm ... I find this very difficult because here we are with a family, who have a fairly handicapped child who appears to be getting by and is their parenting of that child good enough? I don't know.

TM:   Well I think that I think that's why we're here really because that's what we're not sure about. It's not sure whether it is good enough or not whether it's acceptable enough.

CONS:   and how could we make it better for them

TM:   Well we're trying to make it better. I think what we're being faced with is the resistance of the family to accept some of the supports that we're putting, or even if even if they don't totally resist it, they certainly make it very difficult for professionals to provide the sort of help.

Here we can see the powerful definitional privilege that paediatricians have in marking cases as 'not just medical'. The Team Manager's telling of the case so far is often explicitly moral in tone, for example:

> ... and we still think that his sort of ehm development may be being impaired by his parents' lack of doing the things that they *should* for him

> We don't think the children are being *fed adequately* and we don't think they're being *stimulated adequately* either

> because it would make him too heavy to carry upstairs, ehm so obviously that was sort of put back to them that you know that *wasn't a good, an acceptable reason* for not feeding him. (emphases added)

This is typical of social workers' talk in situations where parenting is being judged (for instance, White and Stancombe, 2003).

The consultant responds by stating that there had been some failure to thrive, a term he is using in the clinical sense – meaning the child is failing to grow properly, for some as yet undetermined reason. He mitigates this by arguing that the weight has crept up 'reasonably satisfactorily'. This is met by an immediate interjection by the health visitor who claims this as a success for Pediasure, a food supplement. Considerable character work in relation to the parents had taken place before the consultant arrived at the meeting. For example, there had been a number of florid accounts of the children's smelly condition and the parents' intellectual limitations, the mother's traumatic childhood which was alleged to be affecting her ability to parent. Yet, the consultant shifts the frame away from moral category 'less than adequate parent' into the sceptical language of clinical science:

> I find it very difficult to say whether he's worse because of lack of stimulation than he would otherwise be. Whether he would be slightly better in a different family, who can know ... Trouble is we don't have a diagnosis for Paul, I thought I had but I haven't ehm and he is waiting to see the geneticists to see if they have more ideas about ehm ... I find this very difficult because here we are with a family, who have a fairly handicapped child who appears to be getting by and is their parenting of that child good enough? I don't know.

This is an area of monopoly expertise for the doctor, who would be difficult to challenge except by medical colleagues. Indeed, the paediatrician's first few turns were enough to destabilize what had hitherto been a very robust 'parents as culpable' version. There is a recognizable moral struggle towards the end of the extract with the consultant constructing the family as 'in need of help', which receives a powerful 'tried but failed' rebuttal by the team leader. The consultant's version certainly did not return this case to a 'just medical' reading, but it problematized the positions that the other speakers had taken and rendered further practical work necessary to 'persuade' the consultant that the child's parents and not his body were the problem. In this instance a pragmatic arrangement was made for Paul to be fed at school so that the 'difficult feeder' hypothesis could be tested. Had the consultant not attended the meeting, the outcome may have been quite different.

Afterwards, the paediatrician, whom I knew very well, expressed his exasperation at what he called the 'zealotry' of social services in their reaction to child welfare issues. He said he wanted somewhere to go to talk things through, without 'the balloon going up'. Clearly, this contextual evaluation of the general proportionality of the response from his social work colleagues will also have affected his telling of the case in the meeting. Similarly, the social workers had their own versions of the paediatrician as 'nice but naïve', or more pejoratively as 'soft on parents'. They would also make routine ironic references to 'medical power'. For example, in response to me asking what use was made of a certain office, one of them replied, 'oh that's where God's children hang out', referring to the paediatric secretaries. All of this identity work impacts on sense-making in the case and the notion that it can somehow be neutralized by a common-language, or an assessment pro forma appears preposterous.

This case illustrates that case formulations frequently emerge from interactions. The facts are rarely simply out there as 'information'. They are worked up and assembled in this kind of way. However, as in Victoria's case there is an expectation upon medical staff, including psychologists and psychiatrists to deliver to social services unequivocal case formulations in relation to the safeguarding of children. Is it, or is it not a child protection case? This vastly underestimates the difficulties in making such a definitive diagnosis in many cases, but since the very first step of allocating a case to a social worker relies on this categorization having been accomplished, we can see the problems.

In the case discussed above, at least the locus for discussion was a family whom the members of the meeting knew in their full embodied state, dirt, smells and all, and the outcome of a process of hypothesis testing which would do little harm to the child, or to the family. What is so seriously disturbing in the case of Victoria Climbié, is that, while there was still a great deal of 'arguing the case' taking place, this was often simply in order to place her into a bureaucratic category. The common-sense action of visiting the child in the hospital, to 'see for themselves', which seemed to the referring doctors so self-evident and pragmatic a response from social services, was outside the repertoire for the hard-pressed social work team in cases that were not designated as section 47 (immediate child protection concerns). This point was made by Dr Schwarz in the extract at the start of this chapter:

> In the past, when we have had problems like this, we have had discussions directly, and I would have explained why I reached my conclusion with regard to scabies. I would have hoped that they would have heard what I was saying about other aspects about which we were concerned.

So, how has this been affected by the raft of government driven initiatives we have seen the wake of Victoria's death?

## Arguing the case in contemporary children's departments

The Greek word, Pharmacon, means both a medicine and a poison, serving to remind us that good intentions can be toxic. While Laming's assessment of the various errors and failures that contributed to Victoria Climbié's death is sound enough, the raft of reforms rolled out in its wake are likely to have exacerbated the problems facing those whose work involves safeguarding children. The Laming Report marks a watershed in the history of child welfare services in England (Laming, 2003; Parton, 2006). The conceptual shift away from child protection towards 'safeguarding' required all agencies and professionals working with children to fulfil their responsibilities. In order to achieve this the government put in place a series of measures including service reorganization and integration, workforce reform, enhanced information sharing and early intervention drawing heavily upon an e-government agenda to support some of these ambitions. However, based on detailed empirical work,[3] I would argue here, and have discussed elsewhere (Broadhurst *et al.*, 2009; Peckover *et al.*, 2008; White *et al.*, 2008) these may well exacerbate, rather than ameliorate the difficulties we saw in Victoria's case. For example, timescales introduced with the Assessment Framework (DoH, 2000) are now e-configured providing little room for practitioner manoeuvre: there is an imperative to assign a 'contact' to a category within 24 hours of the contact being made; if a case is identified for 'initial assessment', this must be completed within 7 days, and a Core Assessment must be completed within 35 days. In addition, centrally prescribed and standardized forms circumscribe professional assessment that break down the child and family's situation into a number of needs and capacities across a range of areas.

Moreover, the post-Climbié reforms have somehow concatenated with the government's e-government agenda and the newly established referral and assessment teams are often located centrally with referrals being taken initially by Customer Relations Managers, unqualified administrative agents who enter the details of the referred child onto a database to be 'workflowed' by qualified staff (Broadhurst *et al.*, 2009; Fish *et al.*, 2008). This means there are more, rather than fewer layers between those referring and those who may or may not decide on a response.

---

[3]    Since 2005, I have been involved in two Economic and Social Research Council funded ethnographic studies. The first under the e-Society Programme, examined electronic information sharing and the second, which is ongoing, examines the impact on everyday practice of performance management in children's services.

The imperative at the point of referral has become to assign the case, on the basis of limited information, to a particular disposal pathway. Obviously, this process, like any other, can be done well, or badly, but it clearly has no hope of ameliorating the communication disjunctures which contributed to the death of Victoria Climbié. The imperative at the point of referral has become to assign the case, on the basis of limited information, to a particular disposal pathway. Practitioners must make rapid decisions as to whether cases are first, the business of the agency, and then whether cases will follow a 'child protection' [CP] or 'children in need' [CIN] pathway. Obviously, such work flow processes, like any other, can be done well, or badly, but these e-configured pathways clearly have little hope of ameliorating the communication disjunctures which contributed to the death of Victoria Climbié as discussed.

In addition, as discussed in the introduction to this chapter, with the superficially laudable aim of creating a common-language of child welfare the government has introduced the CAF. Professionals are encouraged to evaluate strengths, needs, actions and solutions for children across three domains derived from the Framework for Assessment of Children and Need and their Families (DoH, 2000): 'Development of unborn baby, infant, child or young person', 'Parents and carers' and 'Family and environmental'. There are subsections, prompts and trigger questions provided under each of these domains. Under 'Development of unborn baby, infant, child or young person', for instance, there are seven subsections and further divisions within these. The subsections include 'Emotional and social development' that itself includes feeling special; early attachments; risking/actual self-harm; phobias; psychological difficulties; coping with stress; motivation, positive attitudes; confidence; relationships with peers; feeling isolated and solitary; fears, and often unhappy. 'Behavioural development' includes lifestyle; self-control; reckless or impulsive activity; behaviour with peers; substance misuse; anti-social behaviour; sexual behaviour; offending; violence and aggression; restless and overactive; easily distracted, and attention span/concentration.

The CAF is designed to be evidence-based, focused on needs and strengths, rather than 'concerns'. Crucially, stories – the usual medium for case formulation – are designed out. This can make the completed CAF very hard to understand, even for seasoned child welfare professionals (see White *et al.*, 2008).

It is noteworthy in the discussion of Paul's development above that many of the professionals had the ability to be *multi-lingual*. They all knew what Pediasure was, they all understood the salience of the fact that the paediatrician was unsure of the diagnosis (that he did not know in sufficient detail what impact the child's intrinsic problems could reasonably be expected to have on his development). That there was argumentation in the case is undeniable, that there were competing accounts is clear, that some players were more influential than others is self-evident, but the outcome was a sensible re-engagement with the family's circumstances. I am certainly not implying that the government's reforms mean this kind of dialogue is no longer possible, but it thrives from professional agility, not from prescription and standardization. If practitioners retain this in the current environment it will be in spite of structures not because of them.

Policy under Gordon Brown's premiership in the UK shows some sign of acknowledging these systemic problems, although it is unfortunately wrapped in hyperbolic fog. *The Children's Plan* (Department for Children, Schools and Families [DCSF], 2007, p. 18), for example, proclaims:

> Delivering the vision set out in the Children's Plan will require a series of system-wide reforms to the way services for children and young people work together. By putting the needs of children and families first, we will provide a service that makes more sense to the parents, children and young people using them, for whom professional boundaries can appear arbitrary and frustrating. By locating services under one roof in the places people visit frequently, they are more likely to find the help they need. And by investing in all of those who work with children, and by building capacity to work across professional boundaries we can ensure that joining up services is not just about providing a safety net for the vulnerable – it is about unlocking the potential of every child.

Let us hope that this is done after a proper diagnostic engagement with the way services work now, with what works and why, and what sorts of people we need in children's services. Moreover, government must pay adequate attention to the interface with hospitals and acute paediatrics where the possibility of matters getting lost in translation and in the blur of admission and discharge is greatest.

I have referred already to the recent case of Baby P. Baby P had been subject to a child protection plan for the 8 months prior to his death. The multi-agency system was mobilized. He had several inpatient episodes during which bruising was noted and two days before he died was taken by his mother to a developmental check with a locum paediatric consultant who did not examine him because he was 'cranky'. This child's death is obviously the responsibility of his killer, but it is clear that the system failures were not in 'sharing information', but in having the time and space and argumentative flexibility to debate and make sense of what was being seen and recorded. Professionals in the case appear to have been distracted from the forensic work they really needed to do, by the mother's explanation for his injuries. Baby P's mother alleged that he had intrinsic behavioural disturbances, for which he had been referred to Great Ormond Street hospital for specialist investigation. Baby P was seen to 'head bang' by professionals and thus it seems evidence which may have disconfirmed this reading of the case was neither properly attended to, nor interrogated. Micromanagement and the onerous, prescriptive recording and audit, embedded in e-enabled standardized processes are indeed noxious remedies for any system charged with managing this kind of variety and complexity.

# The denouement

When professionals engage with the lives of people who come to the attention of their services, they undertake an often grave activity. A transitional object like a standardized assessment form, or an easy institutional category, is no more than an *ignis fatuous* luring professionals, or more importantly the children and families with whom they work, onto slippery and sometimes fatally jagged rocks. Multi-professional work can only be worthwhile if we allow the variety of different vocabularies and a curiosity about them, alongside an understanding that we do not *find* facts, we *make* them. If we do not understand what another is saying, we need to ask them what they mean, but we need to recognize when this is necessary. If we are, for example, an unqualified customer relations officer in a busy service with limited expectation of understanding the detail of the work, why would we ask, and with what vocabulary? The very best, and most experienced practitioners need to be at the nodes of information exchange, all else is utter folly.

For those of us who educate professionals, let us teach our students modesty, and let us attend to the dangers of jealously biting at the backs of other occupational groups – doctors and the medical model are a particular delicacy at such banquets within in my own discipline. Instead, let us educate for uncertainty, compassion, carefulness and wisdom. A cloying concoction? Maybe, but not a poisonous one! After 25 years of practising, managing, educating and researching in child welfare, I am convinced that only those who have these qualities are able to work (relatively) safely and soundly with children and families placed under their charge.

This 'workforce issue' is the hardest and most intractable part of the problem and the least amenable to quick-fix policy-making. As I have argued elsewhere (for instance, Balen and White, 2007; Taylor and White, 2006), nurturing practitioners who have these kinds of qualities requires us to provide a broad educatedness – competency-based, skills training and easy-read assessment guides will not do. For example, we may see child welfare assessment as a form of social research. Along with compassionate engagement with their work, practitioners need to learn rigorous data collection and analysis skills. They need to be aware of their limitations as human information processors and they need at the same time to attend to the impact of taken-for-granted institutional short-cuts. They need to understand and interrogate the fallibilities of their own and other's reasoning processes. This needs intelligence, dialogue, respect and caution and it also needs *time*.

I shall leave the last words to Gerald de Montigny (1995). For social workers, read 'child welfare professionals':

> Social workers know how to inscribe everyday or mundane occasions as proper instances into institutional categories. Such inscriptive work quiets the tumultuous

noise of drunken shouting between husband and wife. It cools out a child's hot tears. It manages the welts from a beating. Simply put, it modulates the noise, multiple dimensions and uncertainties of an immediately experienced reality. It substitutes regulated tonal symmetries provided through professional categories and texts for the noise of daily life. (de Montigny, 1995, p. 28)

If the tumultuous noise of Victoria Climbié's life had not been so efficiently quieted, she would almost certainly not have died.
'BRING ON THE NOISE!'

# References

Balen, R. and White, S. (2007) 'Making critical minds: Nurturing "not-knowing" in students of health and social care', *Social Work Education*, 26 (2): 200–206.
Broadhurst, K., Wastell, D., White, S., Hall, C., Peckover, S., Thompson, K., Pithouse, A., Davey, D. (2009) 'Performing "initial assessment": Identifying the latent conditions for error at the front-door of local authority children's services', *British Journal of Social Work*. Advance Access at DOI: bcn162v1-19.
Chief Secretary to the Treasury (2003) *Every Child Matters*, Cmnd 5860, London: The Stationary Office.
DCSF (2007) *The Children's Plan*; www.dcsf.gov.uk/publications/childrensplan/downloads/The_Childrens_Plan.pdf (last accessed 29 October 2008)
de Montigny, G. (1995) *Social Working: An Ethnography of Front Line Practice*, Toronto: University of Toronto Press.
DfES (2006a) *Common Assessment Framework for Children and Young People: Managers' Guide*, London: DfES.
DfES (2006b) *Common Assessment Framework for Children and Young People: Practitioners' Guide*, London: DfES.
DoH (2000) *Framework for the Assessment of Children in Need and their Families*, London: The Stationery Office.
Fish, S., Munro, E. and Bairstow, S. (2008) *SCIE Report 19: Learning Together to Safeguard Children: Developing a Multi-agency Systems Approach for Case Reviews*, http://www.scie.org.uk/publications/reports/reports19.asp (last accessed 29 October 2008)
Garralda, M. (1996) 'Somatisation in children', *Journal of Child Psychology, Psychiatry and Allied Disciplines*, 37 (1): 13–33.
Garrett, P.M. (2006) 'Protecting children in a globalized world', *Journal of Social Work*, 6 (3): 315–336.
Hudson, J. (2002) 'Digitising the structure of government: The UK's information age government agenda', *Policy and Politics*, 30 (4): 515–531.
Laming, Lord (2003) *The Victoria Climbié Inquiry: Report of an Inquiry by Lord Laming*, Cm 5730, London: The Stationery Office.
Parton, N. (2006) *Safeguarding Childhood: Early Intervention and Surveillance in a Late Modern Society*, Basingstoke: Palgrave Macmillan.
Peckover, S., Hall, C. and White, S. (2008) 'From policy to practice: The implementation and negotiation of technologies in everyday child welfare', *Children & Society*, 23 (2): 136–148.
Pollner, M. (1974) 'Mundane reasoning', *Philosophy of the Social Sciences*, 4 (1): 35–54.
Reder, P. and Duncan, S. (2003) 'Understanding communication in child protection networks', *Child Abuse Review*, 12 (2): 82–100.

Serres, M. (2007) *Parasite*, Minneapolis: University of Minnesota Press.

Taylor, C. and White, S. (2006) 'Knowledge and reasoning in social work: Educating for humane judgement', *British Journal of Social Work*, 36 (6): 1–18.

White, S. (2002) 'Accomplishing the case in paediatrics and child health: Medicine and morality in interprofessional talk', *Sociology of Health and Illness*, 24 (4): 409–435.

White, S. and Featherstone, B. (2005) 'Communicating misunderstandings: Multi-agency work as social practice', *Child and Family Social Work*, 10 (3): 207–216.

White, S., Hall, C. and Peckover, S. (2008) 'The descriptive tyranny of the common assessment framework: Technologies of categorization and professional practice in child welfare', *British Journal of Social Work*. Advance access available at: DOI: 10.1093/bjsw/bcn05.

White, S. and Stancombe, J. (2003) *Clinical Judgement in the Health and Welfare Professions: Extending the Evidence Base*, Maidenhead: Open University Press.

Woodward, L., Taylor, E. and Dowdney, L. (1998) 'The parenting and family functioning of children with hyperactivity', *Journal of Child Psychology and Psychiatry*, 39 (2): 161–169.

# 7

# Safeguarding Children through Parenting Support: How Does *Every Parent Matter*?

Karen Broadhurst

## Introduction

> To judge by the attention given to parenting by UK policy makers in recent years, you could be forgiven for thinking that there were few headlining social problems – from anti-social behaviour on our streets to childhood obesity and falling standards in schools – for which 'better parenting' was not the solution.
>
> (Moran and Ghate, 2005, p. 329)

Support for parenting has found increasing emphasis in England and Wales under successive New Labour governments. Since the publication of the consultation document, *Supporting Families* (Home Office, 1998), New Labour has made it clear that it sees effective parenting as critical to the health and welfare of the nation and has been hyperactive in the rolling out of parenting support initiatives. As we see in this chapter's opening epigraph, better parenting is increasingly viewed as the solution to a range of social problems. The Every Child Matters (ECM) agenda reflects and helps constitute this approach by linking the five priority outcomes for children[1] with good parenting, most notably in the document *Every Parent Matters* (Department for Education and Skills [DfES], 2007).

This chapter initially considers why parenting has been centre-staged under New Labour before providing a critical discussion of the raft of parenting initiatives that have emerged both pre- and post-ECM. ECM promised a radical reform of children's services, but in focusing upon parenting policy, this chapter will point to continuity, rather than fractures, across New Labour's time in government. Parenting skills training, the provision of expert guidance to

---

[1] The five priority outcomes for children that are central to the ECM agenda are: being healthy, staying, safe, enjoy and achieve, make a positive contribution and achieve economic well-being.

---

*Critical Perspectives on Safeguarding Children*   Edited by Karen Broadhurst, Chris Grover and Janet Jamieson
© 2009 John Wiley & Sons, Ltd

improve parenting capacity, as well as strategies that aim to engage parents in their children's learning have been, and are, central and enduring elements of New Labour's approach.

The principal argument of this chapter is that while the ECM agenda stresses the inter-connectedness of issues that impact on parenting capacity, clearly identifying an association between socio-economic disadvantage and life chances, New Labour's programme of parenting support focuses intervention narrowly on individual lifestyle and behavioural change. Breaking the so-called 'cycle of deprivation' has been an enduring theme under New Labour (Department of Social Security [DSS], 1999, p. 5), but in terms of parenting, intervention is weighted towards tackling a perceived 'poverty of ambition' or attainment, rather than tackling the multi-faceted socio-economic causes of disadvantage (Deacon, 2003, p. 133). Intervention is organized around guidance, incentives and sanctions that steer individual parents into paid work, encourage parents to become active consumers of parenting knowledge and remind parents to become partners with schools/early years settings in their children's education, while modest 'flanking measures' (Jessop, 2003), such as in-work benefits, have largely left intact inequalities that structure the parenting experience.

The chapter concludes with a detailed discussion of the position of families considered 'at risk' and who, on account of their social position, often find themselves on the receiving end of New Labour's targeted parenting support (Social Exclusion Taskforce, 2008, para. 1.4). While this group of parents (for example, those subject to statutory social work intervention) might receive short-term help in the form of funded day-care for children or emergency financial assistance, such help is frequently accompanied by a mandate for change that can result in more serious sanctions for those unable to improve their parenting skills.

## The centre-staging of parenting under New Labour: a brief history

> Parents and the home environment they create are the single most important factor in shaping children's well-being, achievements and prospects. (DfES, 2007, p. 1)

The three New Labour governments constitute the longest period in office for the parliamentary Labour Party and has enabled a distinct political and policy climate to evolve (Alcock, 2005). A notable feature of New Labour's welfare policy is the designation of parenting as a discrete area of policy intervention. A confident and persuasive rhetoric places parents centre-stage in securing children's well-being, legitimating a raft of parenting support interventions. The above quote, taken from the foreword to the document, *Every Parent Matters* (part of the ECM Series, DfES, 2007), illustrates the centrality of parents within the ECM project and echoes the bold and factive claims that first emerged in New Labour's signature family policy document, *Supporting Families* (Home Office, 1998).

Early in office, the publication of the consultation document *Supporting Families*, resulting from the work of the Ministerial Group on the Family centre set up in 1997, provided New Labour's first formal governmental family policy statement and placed parenting at the heart of policy (Maclean, 2002). Proposing that contemporary parenthood was increasingly difficult, due to the changing nature of household composition and roles, this document legitimated a more interventionist role for the state to ensure that strong families remained the 'building blocks' of society. In keeping with New Labour's broader project of tackling social exclusion through paid work, a programme of support for parenting began to emerge that included in-work benefits, a national childcare strategy, improvements to maternity and paternity leave, and support through universal and selective services to more directly aid the parenting task. Good parenting was not only linked to children's well-being, but, wrapped up in a new language that emphasized civic responsibility, parents were also implicated in the successes and failures of 'community'. Gillies (2005, p. 77) has argued that *Supporting Families* presented new family support measures as 'neutral attempts to promote families and benefit children', but when examined, they 'are in fact structured around a distinct, value-laden vision of how responsible, competent parents should behave'.

*Supporting Families* clearly underlined the values of personal responsibility and paid work and suggested that the disconnection of parents and children from these 'common' values was linked to problems of crime and social breakdown. Parents were seen to need expert advice, to ensure they acquired the 'skills' and values of good parenthood. A number of commentators have argued that New Labour's programme of support to families amounts to a remoralization of parents – an elevation and extension of parental responsibility, with a very clear message from government, that governments will support but not *replace* parents (Maclean, 2002; Piper, 2008).

In attempting to understand why parents have been centre-staged under New Labour, it is important to briefly consider the legacy of the preceding 18 years of Conservative administration. There is a general consensus that the closing two decades of the twentieth century saw a significant transformation of the relationship between the state and its citizens, precipitated by the rise of neo-liberalism (cf. Garland, 2001; Jessop, 2003; Marquand, 2004; Miller and Rose, 2008). Under successive Thatcher administrations, new forms of neo-liberal governance began to emerge that aimed to govern differently with an aim of reducing the perceived costs and inefficiencies of 'big government'. What has been described as an emergent anti-statist neo-liberal orthodox led to a renegotiation of the welfare state, most notably a shift away from the direct provision of state welfare support to families and an increasing reliance on a mixed economy of social protection. In this context, parents were required to be increasingly agentic, securing the conditions of their own independence and financial security, largely through paid work. In England and Wales, the influence of Thatcher governments during the 1980s has been seen as instrumental in destabilizing a hitherto largely uncontested social imperative for government through a focus upon *individual* responsibility (Rose, 1999). While it was argued that the state would maintain an infrastructure of law and order, it was envisaged that there would be a shift away from what was described as 'the nanny state' that was held to inhibit the virtues of individual responsibility and enterprise, towards an enabling state that would help individuals to help themselves. No longer would the state be answerable for all problems of individual security, needs, health or occupation, rather rational social actors, would secure their own futures, by taking on at least a proportion of the responsibility for their own well-being (cf. Miller and Rose, 2008; Rose, 1999). Such anti-statist sentiments were supported by a shift away from socio-structural accounts of disadvantage, towards explanations that clearly located the causes of disadvantage *within* the family or the behaviour of individuals who failed to embrace the values of paid work and enterprise (Deacon, 2003; Jones and Novak, 1999; Levitas, 1998).

A number of clear differences can be drawn between New Labour and previous Conservative administrations with regard to family and parenting policy. Most notable is New Labour's more *active* approach to supporting families (part of what we have seen described as the Social Intervention State – see Chapter 1) and the clear designation of parenting as a discrete area of social policy. However, there is a general consensus that the elevation of individual responsibility and the curtailment of the social obligations of the state – initiated by the Conservative governments of the 1980s and 1990s – have influenced the direction of New Labour's family policy (cf. Jessop, 2003; Muncie, 2006). To substantiate this point, a brief discussion of New Labour's particular appropriation of the 'cycle of deprivation' hypothesis – an explanatory framework popularized through the work of former Secretary of State Sir Keith Joseph (1972) – is useful. This concept is central to an understanding of, first, New Labour's particular methodology for supporting parenting and, second, why successive Labour governments place parenting as being central to good outcomes for children.

The concept of the 'cycle of deprivation' has a long history and has been subject to debate and revision[2] (Deacon, 2003). However, during the Conservative administrations of the 1980s and 1990s harsher explanations of the inter-generational transmission of disadvantage were reinvigorated.[3] These firmly located the causes of poverty and disadvantage in the alleged faulty mores and errant behaviours of individuals and families. While New Labour has very clearly acknowledged that life-chances are diminished by the experience of poverty in childhood (HM Treasury, 1999) and has undertaken a series of

---

[2]   While all variants of the 'cycle of disadvantage' hypothesis stress the inter-generational continuity of disadvantage, there are clear differences between perspectives that acknowledge the role of structure and those that place more emphasis on individual attitudes and norms. Deacon (2003) provides a detailed analysis of a number of competing perspectives.

[3]   Concerns with the problem family have an enduring history in the UK. Goldson and Jamieson (2002), for instance, trace a history of state interest in 'problem families', identifying, for example, nineteenth-century concerns with the relationship between juvenile crimes and problems of 'faulty' family morality or conduct.

'flanking measures'[4] to attempt to lift families out of poverty, there is a clear continuity between New Labour and the preceding Conservative administrations in terms of the proposition that disadvantage is, at least in part, a product of maladaptive cultural norms, attitudes and behaviours[5] (Clarke, 2006; Deacon, 2003; Gewirtz, 2001; Stepney *et al.*, 1999). In this context, New Labour's appropriation of the cycle of deprivation reflects what Deacon (2003, p. 128) describes as 'the adaptive explanation', that clearly implicates the aspirations and behaviours of families in the inter-generational reproduction of disadvantage.

New Labour has been keen to stress that low aspirations are a reaction to a range of adversities (Home Office, 1998; Social Exclusion Taskforce, 2008), but nevertheless it is strong communities and strong families that are called upon to take up opportunities offered by government to secure the route out of disadvantage (Stepney *et al.*, 1999). In a speech early in the first New Labour government made by then Prime Minister, Tony Blair, on the Aylesbury estate[6] in London, he called for attitudinal change and the need to tackle the 'the dead weight of low expectations' that was seen to characterize such neighbourhoods (Blair, 1997). Indeed, so strong is New Labour's faith in the ability of the individual to secure his/her own fate, that many so-called 'opportunities', such as parenting orders, are offered not just on a voluntary basis, but can carry sanctions for non-compliance. It has been observed that such policy interventions are informed by what is described as Anglicanised Communitariansim[7] (Deacon, 2002; Grover, 2008), a particularly authoritarian version of communitarianism that, on the one hand, espouses an anti-individualist position with appeals to community and social cohesion, but, on the other hand, has increasingly instantiated *individual* responsibility in policy and legislation (see, for example, Etzioni, 1994).

The language of parenting ecology that characterizes many of New Labour's policy documents and practice guidance (for example, *Framework for the Assessment of Children in Need and their Families*, Department of Health [DoH], 2000) suggests that parenting needs to be understood in context; that is housing, neighbourhood, household composition and so forth matter. However, examination of the *loci* of parenting interventions, as this chapter illustrates, finds intervention predominantly directed at *individual* behaviour or lifestyle change. Etzioni's (1993) *Parenting Deficit*, has been particularly influential in this regard.

---

[4]   Jessop (2003) describes the redistributionist elements of New Labour's anti-poverty strategy, such as the various tax credits, as simply flanking measures that achieve modest reductions in income inequalities that inevitably arise in a neo-liberal free market economy.
[5]   An alternative way of understanding intergenerational continuities in social exclusion would be to consider the possibilities for social mobility in England and Wales (cf. Gregg *et al.*, 2007; Hills and Stewart, 2007).
[6]   The area in which the Aylesbury estate is located is in the 'lowest' category on the ACORN classification for inner city adversity (http://www.caci.co.uk/acorn/acornmap.asp). This indicates that the area is characterized by extremely high levels of social disadvantage.
[7]   A full discussion of this concept is beyond the scope of this chapter. However, a number of commentators have argued that the communitarian philosophy emphasizes responsibility and personal agency, but New Labour's 'Anglicanised Communitarianism' is a particularly authoritarian version, manifest in the range of sanctions and orders that are attached to the new welfare 'opportunities' (Deacon, 2002; Grover, 2008).

Etzioni's emphasis on the moral commitments of parenthood, to both children and community, has paved the way for the further elevation of parental responsibility and has legitimated an interventionist stance on the part of government to promote 'good', moral conduct on the part of individual parents (Deacon, 2002; Grover, 2008; Heron and Dwyer, 1999).

Finally, in linking parenting *style* to disadvantage, New Labour has legitimated the targeting of intervention on families 'at risk' because they are seen as most likely to transmit low aspirations and reproduce 'cycles of deprivation' (Social Exclusion Taskforce, 2008, paras. 1.4–1.8). The point of 'progressive universalism'[8] that helps to frame ECM is that the most significant incursions will be into the lives of families living in conditions of acute economic and social deprivation (Department for Children, Schools and Families [DCSF], 2007; DfES, 2007), namely families where the parents are poor, young, single and not in work and, of whom, the majority will be women (Featherstone, 2006; Grover, 2008). Successive New Labour governments have favoured the concept of the family 'at-risk' acknowledging the impact of systemic factors on parenting, but for parents at the sharp edge of targeted support programmes, parenting support can give way to more coercive interventions in the form of parenting contracts, orders, fines and imprisonment, legitimated by a strong moral discourse that emphasizes duty, respect and obligation.

## Information, expert guidance and skills training

> Parents are demonstrating a growing appetite for discussion, information and advice... (DfES, 2007, p. 1)

In 1999 the creation of the National Family and Parenting Institute (NFPI) signalled the changing face of parenting support under the new government, endorsing the central role of the expert in providing advice for parents, practitioners and agencies. As a centre of expertise, the NFPI offers an authoritative version of good practice in parenting and draws on parents' positive accounts of expert help to promote the role of the professional in family life. At the time of writing this chapter, the NFPI was running a campaign to draw attention to 'health visitors – an endangered species'. Its campaign to expand the workforce of health visitors drew on a YouGov poll (2008) and claimed that 'parents love health visitors' (www.familyandparenting.org/healthVisitors, accessed 12 November 2008).

---

[8]    Progressive universalism is the term adopted by the government to describe an approach which aims to provide 'support for all and more help for those who need it most when they need it most' (HM Treasury, 2003, para. 5.1). However, in practice, this approach still focuses intervention narrowly on the poorest families. Indeed, the approach suggested in the recent policy document from the Social Exclusion Taskforce (2008) *Reaching Out: Think Family*, suggests an even tighter focus on families suffering forms of socioeconomic disadvantage.

The NFPI was followed by the development of the helpline, Parentline Plus, a national telephone helpline offering individual advice and guidance to parents, as well as signposting relevant courses and workshops for them. As Edwards and Gillies (2004) have described, New Labour has offered a pedagogy of parenting, based on the notion that expert advice and guidance will assist parents to maximize parenting capacity. Sure Start, Extended Schools, Children's Fund initiatives, helplines and internet based resources, all organized according to nationally agreed indicators, offer the templates of good parenting and avenues for parent education in one guise or another. Given the central role that women play in the lives of children, it is mothers who have found themselves bearing the brunt of the new prescriptions. Even prior to the birth of their children they are offered extensive guidance on matters to do with the consumption of coffee, shellfish and alcohol, as well as exercise and sun-bathing.

Group-based parenting skills programmes have become the favoured vehicle for the delivery of the government's parent information and education agenda, provided by an expanded workforce of health, education and welfare professionals. Programmes typically offer parenting skills advice and training on either a voluntary or referral basis, with estimates that mothers constitute some 80 per cent of those referred (Ghate and Ramella, 2002). Parents are given expert advice on matters ranging from the management of children's behaviour to the improvement of children's learning. Implicit in these programmes is an assumption that parenting can be reduced to the acquisition of a set of skills or a toolkit, ignoring the complex relationships and contexts that also structure parenting. Utting (1995), for instance, concluded that while it is difficult to argue that conditions of socio-economic adversity cause parenting problems, they do certainly make parenting more difficult.

The success of parenting classes is mixed and a consistent finding is that the open access programmes tend to be popular with white middle-class parents, but that there are significant problems with enrolment and attrition for more disadvantaged families and minority groups (Social Exclusion Taskforce, 2008). A number of programmes report problems of low uptake of services following referral and that there are issues of cost-effectiveness given that many programmes operate with very small numbers of participants or low levels of attendance (Barlow *et al.*, 2005; Barnes *et al.*, 2006; Thurston, 2007). The receptiveness of parents to professional advice or instruction has been found to depend on mode of entry to services and the social location of parents (Edwards and Gillies, 2005; P. Graham, 2007; Vincent and Ball, 2007). Middle-class parents who actively seek out parenting advice are more likely to view themselves as consumers of parenting services. In contrast, referred parents, typically targeted by area-based initiatives, may be less receptive to advice offered (or imposed) that explicitly aims to change existing ways of parenting. A key study by Edwards and Gillies (2005) found that working-class parents were dismissive of what they described as the textbook help offered by professionals and took pride in their own successes as parents in difficult circumstances. Pamela Graham

(2007) warns that care needs to be taken in terms of the subtle messages that parenting skills classes transmit to vulnerable parents concerning skills deficits. Parents' confidence can be undermined by professional expertise, particularly when professionals set unrealistic standards for both parents' and children's development.

Parenting skills classes have become increasingly standardized offering a uniform model of what is held to be good parenting, such as Webster Stratton's 'Incredible Years' (http://www.incredibleyears.com, accessed 15 October 2008). However, research suggests that classes are more positively received when class facilitators are responsive rather than instructive in their approach, finding space to offer emotional support and befriending (P. Graham, 2007). Indeed, a number of evaluations have claimed that group-based support derived from the experience of meeting and talking with parents facing similar difficulties has more of an impact on parents than information or expert guidance (Ghate and Ramella, 2002).

There is *some* evidence that parenting skills classes can impact positively on parent-child relationships, particularly if they are combined with home visiting and attention is paid to promoting relationships of trust (Moran and Ghate, 2005). However, studies consistently report that practical help in the form of respite childcare, launderette facilities, toy libraries and financial support overwhelmingly meets the needs of parents experiencing socio-economic disadvantage (Brophy, 2006; Fernandez, 2007; P. Graham, 2007; Penn and Gough, 2002; Pithouse and Tasiran, 2000). As Williams (2004, p. 419) notes, 'what parents need is time and support to follow their responsibilities through rather than reminders to carry them out'. While a number of Sure Start projects and family centres have attempted to continue to provide practical help, in recent years there has been a significant shift away from the informal open-access family centres that were found to be popular with families (Pithouse and Tasiran, 2000). Under New Labour, the emphasis on targeted, standardized and structured programmes of behaviour modification (Furedi, 2006) have seen the demise of informal, negotiated welfare spaces. Local authority family centres may set aside time for drop-in, but frequently operate on a referral only basis, offering supervised contact and structured parent education programmes dictated by family support or child protection plans.

There have been a number of developments in the Third Way politics of parenting. However, the importance of expert guidance and the training of parents in the skills of good parenthood are enduring themes. The post-ECM landscape offers further initiatives, such as the National Academy of Parenting Practitioners (NAPP), launched in 2007 which aims to further develop the knowledge base for an expanded parenting practitioner workforce. The Children's Plan drawn up by the reconfigured DCSF under the government of Gordon Brown (DCSF, 2007) details further investment in specialist parent advisers in schools. This plan has also announced an expanded role for health visitors, who, trained via the 'One-to-One'[9] programme, will listen for and spot problems between couples following the birth of a baby, intervening with expert help. A *Parent Know-How* service will provide parents with access to quality web materials, with targeted information helplines and printed material for parents described as 'at higher risk' or unable to access other channels of support (DCSF, 2007).

The priority placed on the provision of information and expert guidance – a key continuity in New Labour's parenting policy – might, arguably, be described as part of a broader UK wide transition towards a knowledge-based economy. However, this priority serves to occlude other needs that parents may have and that impact on priority outcomes for children. Information and expert guidance have a differential appeal depending upon the audience (Clarke, 2006) and for parents who are struggling, for example, to ensure their children 'achieve economic well-being', the narrow focus on the provision of information and knowledge acquisition, will do little to ameliorate low income, poor housing and the lack of material goods – aspirations instantiated in the five ECM priority outcomes and associated aims. For the most disadvantaged families, the solution may lie, as Penn and Gough (2002) noted, in the price of a loaf of bread.

## Engaging parents in children's learning

One of the main continuities in New Labour's welfare policies has been the argument that there is a clear link between educational attainment and life chances (Chief Secretary to the Treasury 2003, DfES, 2004; DSS, 1998). In this context, it is no surprise that a key aim of New Labour's programme of parenting support, has been to facilitate parents' engagement in their own and their children's learning (see Chapter 8 in this volume). Under New Labour, a vision of the good parent who reads to her children, ensures family life provides regular educational opportunities and sets time aside to engage with children's homework, has been increasingly promoted (Gewirtz, 2001).

Sure Start offered the early prototype of 'family learning' aiming to engage parents in positive learning activities with their young children, as well as offering parents back-to-work learning opportunities (Schneider *et al.*, 2007). While each Sure Start project was required to respond to its local community, enabling some scope for flexibility and innovation, individual centres were also required to report on their progress towards specific targets that included the impact of intervention on a child's ability to learn and the percentage increase in the number of children having 'normal' levels of communication, learning and literacy (Schneider *et al.*, 2007). Thus, to a large extent Sure Start projects were tied into

---

[9] The 'One-to-One' programme describes the support that health visitors can provide on a one-to-one basis to new mothers as part of a routine and universal service. However, and consistent with the idea of progressive universalism the One-to-One programme is also seen as a vehicle for identifying those mothers who need to be assisted to access additional or more specialist support compared to the majority of mothers.

an agenda of early intervention and early education that required the delivery of a number of common core activities and aimed to structure, *a priori*, the nature of parenting support.

Education is, arguably, even more clearly the organizing principle through which the ECM agenda is configured (Williams, 2004). This emphasis is reinforced through the five priority outcome statements with education and achievement as central themes. For instance, if we examine the priority outcome, 'enjoy and achieve', the associated aims are that children should be 'ready for school' and 'achieve stretching national educational standards' (DCFS, 2008). Under ECM, the reconfigured Sure Start Children's Centres will continue the theme of early learning, adopting an even earlier,[10] early learning curriculum – the Foundation Stage – which was outlined in the *Birth to Three Matters Quality Framework* (DfES, 2002). Schools will become more involved in the provision of parent education and under the Children Act 2004 (section 10) they can also play a greater role in both the defining and commissioning of services to meet local needs. Since the launch of ECM a number of subsequent documents, notably *Every Parent Matters* (DfES, 2007) and *Reaching Out: Think Family* (Social Exclusion Taskforce, 2008) suggest a series of further initiatives to promote parental engagement with children's learning and offer additional incentives to agencies who are able to more assertively engage families. For parents, incentives such as Bookstart will provide free books to all families in England with children aged 6–9 months, 18 months and 3 years.

We have seen that New Labour are especially concerned with those families thought to be 'at risk' of transmitting deprivation to their children. This is particularly visible with regard to education. The Sure Start programme commenced in designated areas of social exclusion (Barnes *et al.*, 2003) and was premised on a firm belief in the economic value of intervening early in a child's life to counter 'cycles of deprivation'. This initiative was followed by the setting up of the Children's Fund, to provide funding for targeted family support projects concerned with the education and achievement of disadvantaged families with *older* children. Valerie Wigfall (2006) describes *Families in Focus*, a project set up through the Children's Fund and aimed at children and young people aged 4–16. Initially piloted on an estate in a south London borough considered a 'crime hotspot' and characterized by a high percentage of workless households, the aim of the project was to help people to help themselves primarily through education and attitudinal change (Wigfall, 2006, p. 18). In the spirit of what New Labour have termed 'positive welfare', *Families in Focus* offered activities for children and young people ranging from sports to litter picking, with the aim of raising aspirations and building respect for and engagement with community.

---

[10] Sure Start projects already operated according to a pre-school curriculum. The introduction of *Birth to Three Matters* now means that no part of childhood is curriculum free, unless a child is not in a formal early years or educational setting.

While the provision of services to families who might otherwise be unable to purchase support is welcome, the narrow focus of many of the initiatives such as *Families in Focus* is problematic, particularly with respect to meeting all the priority ECM outcomes for children. Educational attainment targets for disadvantaged children and young people remain disappointing (Hills and Stewart, 2007) and certainly the findings from the national evaluation of Sure Start suggest that the programme has not had the expected broader impact on children's development (Buchanan, 2007; Carpenter *et al.*, 2005; Schneider *et al.*, 2007). Gewirtz (2001, p. 374) questions the ubiquitous orientation to parent/child education of much of New Labour's social inclusion agenda and considers whether we really want our children to become subject to 'the kind of parent who turns every household task into a learning experience?' Research has found that middle-class parents demonstrate what has become something of a preoccupation with enrichment activities for their children (Vincent and Ball, 2007). However, for families who are struggling with the basic necessities of life due to problems of disability or mental health, the benefits of infant massage or baby Mozart fail to meet presenting needs (Fernandez, 2007; Ghate and Hazel, 2002; Williams, 2004). All too often parents' requests for respite childcare, financial assistance and better housing are not met, and instead parents are vilified for failing to engage with the 'opportunities' on offer. However, as the recent report from the Social Exclusion Taskforce (2008) identifies, a key reason families fail to engage with formal services is that they are not offered in a form that meets families' needs.

## Parents at the sharp edge of New Labour's support programme

> Don't be surprised if the penalties are tougher when you have been given the opportunities but don't take them. (Blair, 1997, in Vaughan, 2000, p. 347)

Children living in poverty and/or experiencing other forms of disadvantage, such as living with a parent with a disability or chronic illness, are most at risk of failing to achieve the five priority outcomes of ECM (Dorling, 2006; Hills and Stewart, 2007). However, if we examine the impact of New Labour's programme of support, there is no doubt that those who live in conditions of socio-economic disadvantage have found themselves at the sharp edge of Labour's Social Intervention State (see Chapter 2 in this volume). As the above quote indicates, welfare interventions have become more coercive under New Labour, with penalties for those who fail to take up the 'opportunities' offered, namely work and education. This controlling impulse within Labour's Third Way politics has been well documented (see, for instance, Garrett, 2008; Muncie, 2006; Rose, 2000).

Early in office, the spirit of a zero tolerance government emerged in the form of compulsory parenting orders that can require parents to attend parenting classes for training and guidance in how to better manage their children's behaviour. New Labour has opened up a multitude of new governable, quasi-welfare spaces (Rose, 2000) – schools and pre-schools in particular – for the monitoring and assessment of parents. The pre-school provides an early in-road into families 'at-risk', enabling earlier identification and structured intervention, the cornerstones of Labour's interventionist state. The White paper, *Higher Standards Better Schools* (DfES, 2005), enabled schools to apply for parenting orders and fixed penalties in cases of alleged aggravated truanting, cases where parents are argued to condone the truancy. While these kinds of sanctions have been heavily criticized, particularly in relation to Human Rights (Garrett, 2008), they have remained a key strand of the new welfare contract, along with child safety orders, anti-social behaviour orders and curfews.

Perhaps one of the greatest paradoxes of New Labour's targeted support is that, on the one hand, disadvantage is considered geographic or spatial, acknowledging the negative impact of multiple factors at the level of neighbourhood (for example, housing and schooling), but, on the other hand, the majority of safeguarding activity serves to identify and abstract the individual family from this context. Not least because the entry ticket to many services (particularly the gate-keeping local authority) is the identification of some kind of parenting deficit. In this way, the problems of disadvantage are personalized, with social work, health and educational assessments all tending to identify individual deficiencies. Thus, in practice, and beyond the rhetoric of social exclusion, children's services play a key role in locating causality within individual families. Skilled and compassionate child welfare workers may try to buffer the stigmatizing effects of the child welfare system but the continued coding of children within family support/child protection plans as subject to, or at risk of 'sexual abuse', 'physical abuse', 'emotional abuse' and 'neglect' serves to erase the contextual aspects of the lives of vulnerable families. Work undertaken by Lancaster University's Child Welfare Research Unit (Broadhurst *et al.*, 2005) with children categorized as 'missing' from school systems found that in order to understand children's disengagement from schooling, a number of socio-structural factors needed careful consideration, notably homelessness, and the social and economic obstacles that mothers face when they flee domestic violence. We found disengagement from schooling had as much to do with the reluctance of schools to offer places to children in homeless persons or temporary accommodation, than parents' wilful disengagement with schooling.

The Victoria Climbié Inquiry preceded the launch of the ECM agenda and serves as a powerful reference for all those involved in the work of safeguarding children:

> Some children's lives are different. Dreadfully different. Instead of the joy, warmth and security of normal family life, these children's lives are filled with risk, fear,

and danger: and from what most of us would regard as the worst possible source – from the people closest to them. (Chief Secretary to the Treasury, 2003, p. 1)

However, there are a number of problems with the foregrounding of parental maltreatment within the ECM agenda, resulting from this tragic but extreme case. First, the report serves to skew thinking about the majority of families who may need assistance to bring up children, but where there is no intention to harm them. Issues of risk and the fear of child deaths continue to disproportionately influence child welfare services. Second, a focus on child maltreatment serves to obscure children's broader social needs. As Masson (2006) has observed in her critique of the Climbié Inquiry, the inquiry overlooked the policy tensions clearly implicated in the agencies' failure to respond to Victoria. The request from Victoria's carer for housing was declined – intervention in this area of need could have proved an important point of engagement with this family, yet, as Masson (2006, p. 223) notes, 'making destitute children and families who are not supposed to be in the United Kingdom appears to be government policy'.

A fundamental tension structures the ECM agenda with respect to safeguarding. On the one hand, ECM is couched in an inclusive rhetoric of 'every parent' and 'every child', but at the same time the backcloth of the Climbié Inquiry can only serve to reinforce discourses of risk that have more to do with child maltreatment than broader risks emanating from socio-structural inequalities. In this context, while ECM and the Common Assessment Framework (DfES, 2004) aim to facilitate access to services at an earlier point, families may still find their social need overlooked as priority is given to investigating concerns about child maltreatment. Notwithstanding the seriousness of a small percentage of cases that come to the attention of the local authority, it is important, particularly in the context of recent high profile cases such as Baby P, that proportionate attention is placed on ensuring a supportive welfare-orientated approach to children in need.

Parents who are involved with statutory social work services are subject to family support and child protection procedures that are increasingly standardized. Work recently undertaken by the Child Welfare Research Unit at Lancaster University (Broadhurst, 2008) found that parents (frequently lone mothers living in conditions of socio-economic deprivation) of children subject to either child protection or family support plans are set clearly defined targets for 'behavioural' improvement, according to standardized norms (for instance, to maintain hygiene standards, to engage their child(ren) in quality play and to attend dental appointments) with little consideration paid to the context of parenting capacity (for example, income, transport, working hours, physical/emotional capacity). The focus of practitioners is on the parents' ability to achieve these targets and little help is offered (or indeed possible) by way of the amelioration of poor housing, income poverty or network capacity. Acute crises may result in the provision of a broader short-term package of support, such as funded day-care for children or emergency financial assistance. However, longer-term support has become something of a taboo. While skilled practitioners may try to work around these constraints, practitioners find their practice increasingly regulated through performance management targets that penalize local authorities for too many 're-registrations'[11] of children and for cases that are deemed open too long by a case holding social worker (Broadhurst *et al.*, 2009).

Any analysis of safeguarding work needs to consider worker discretion and the ways that skilled workers will try to carve out space to work effectively with families (Broadhurst *et al.*, 2009). However, as noted, practice is increasingly constrained through performance management targets and, since the introduction of the Integrated Children's System (ICS), excessive administrative demands mean that safeguarding can amount to not much more than the defining of a moral mandate for change and the monitoring of poor parents (frequently mothers). The space for therapeutic engagement is increasingly limited, although research has suggested that this is a very important aspect of child welfare work (Quinton, 2004). In the context of increasing demands on mothers to work, to be more involved in education and so forth, it has been too easy for them to fall foul of the newly structured approach to safeguarding children that can result in the compulsory removal of children.

# New Labour's parenting support: what works?

Establishing the success of Labour's programme of support to parents is difficult, not least because there are significant problems with the evaluative research as exemplified by the much publicized Sure Start evaluation. First, families most in need are less likely to participate in services or their evaluation (Social Exclusion Taskforce, 2008). Second, evaluations tend to be narrowly focused on clearly defined/desired effects of services that often do not give adequate insights into the impact of services on the ecology of parenting (Quinton, 2004). Third, the rapidly changing and constantly evolving world of children's services renders any longitudinal studies very hard to achieve. As Hilary Graham (2007) has noted, the government's fixation with rolling out and the pace at which initiatives are rolled out, leaves little space for detailed qualitative analysis. A systematic review of the international parenting research 'highlighted the patchiness of knowledge about what works' in parenting support (Moran and Ghate, 2005, p. 331).

Nevertheless, there is evidence that a population of parents have taken advantage of the new parenting education and that for those who can get into work, the in-work financial benefits have lifted a proportion of families out of

---

[11] The child protection register no longer exists, but the expression 're-registration' is still current. Children now become subject to a child protection plan and local authorities are required to report to Ofsted on the number of children who have been de-registered, but, following reappraisal of concerns, become subject to a further child protection plan.

poverty (see Chapter 4 in this volume for a fuller discussion). However, many of the families *most* in need have not benefited from the current organization of parenting support (Moran and Ghate, 2005), with children and young people who live in families with complex difficulties still failing to achieve many of the five ECM priority outcomes (Buchanan, 2007; Social Exclusion Taskforce, 2008; Williams, 2004). While a comprehensive analysis of social inequality is beyond the scope of this chapter, it is important to note that a number of studies continue to report that the world of New Labour remains significantly socially stratified (Dorling, 2006; Greener, 2002; Hills and Stewart, 2007; Joseph Rowntree Foundation, 2007).

Statistical data concerning the numbers of young people in the most excluded spaces are illuminative. School exclusions remain high, having initially dropped from an all time high in 1997/8. Exclusions rose significantly in 2003/4 to a figure of 9,880. Exclusions in 2005/2006, were up by about 1,000 compared to 1999/2000 (DfES, 2007). The numbers of children in custody stands at around 3,000 (Howard League for Penal Reform, 2008), a figure that is far in excess of those for our European counterparts (see Chapter 11 in this volume). Statistics that relate to care proceedings are very concerning, with a three-fold increase reported between 1992 and 2002 (McKeigue and Beckett, 2004). The continued rise in care proceedings led to a comprehensive national review in 2006 that has forecast further increases (Department for Constitutional Affairs, 2006). Early evidence suggests the figures for care proceedings will be subject to further increase given the high profile Baby P case (Child and Family Court Advisory Support Service, 2008).

Policy and practice approaches that in large part reduce parenting capacity to ability or 'skills' do not take into account inequality or the social and material contexts of the lives of families that *do* matter. Fairclough (2000) has described the reduction of parenting to a set of skills that can be acquired, *generic of context*, as one of the most pernicious aspects of New Labour's 'support' programmes, rendering those who are unable to pick up the technical skills of parenting as failing. ECM promises a radical reform of children's services to provide integrated services to more closely meet need. However, if what is 'common' in common assessment is a narrow focus on individual behaviour and lifestyles, then ECM is unlikely to deliver the intended outcomes for children that are central to its mission. As Gregg *et al.* (2007, p. iiii) note:

> many aspects of growing up in poverty are harmful to children's development, and that narrowly-targeted interventions are unlikely to have a significant impact on intergenerational mobility.

Moran and Ghate's (2005, p. 332) systematic analysis of the research and evaluation of parenting support interventions concluded that in order to increase the effectiveness of intervention, the wider ecology of parenting needed to be recognized and they concluded that without tackling 'broader social inequalities', parent support intervention would have limited success.

## Conclusion

ECM held out a potential radical reform of children's services, but when parenting support initiatives are examined, there appears to be something of a recycling of New Labour's favoured 'enabling' methods of education and skills training that emerged in the context of *Supporting Families*. The inclusive rubric of ECM suggests a broader and positive agenda for children and priority outcome statements such as 'be healthy' or 'enjoy and achieve' cannot fail to appeal to a broad audience. However, detailed examination of its less popularized outcomes for children, such as the numbers of children in care or incarcerated, raises serious questions about the iatrogenic effect of New Labour's narrow and potentially coercive parenting support programme.

The inclusive rhetoric of New Labour's family support programme provides a smokescreen behind which the continued stripping of welfare protection together with the increase in punitive measures that fall disproportionately on those most in need, renders vulnerable those individuals who maybe 'cannot' play by the rules (see Chapter 4 in this volume). A key limitation in New Labour's programme is the underpinning rational view of behaviour, that individuals secure the conditions of their own experience, largely based on instrumental or economic rationalities. This objectifies learning; anyone can learn what are seen increasingly as the *skills* of good parenting if provided with the right training. This conception of learning runs counter to the wealth of research evidence that finds learning highly socially stratified (Gewirtz, 2001; Hills and Stewart, 2007; Hirsh, 1995). Under successive New Labour governments, principles of inclusion assume a level playing field and, as Gillies (2005, p. 86) notes, 'structural hurdles and barriers to individual action are obscured by a focus on the role of agency and personal responsibility in determining life chances'.

The most likely benefactors of New Labour's parent support programme are the parents who can most easily help themselves. For example, parents who can negotiate education league tables and who enjoy the possibility of social mobility can steer their way to a more prosperous existence for themselves and their families (Vincent and Ball, 2007). Those who can benefit in the new choice economy have been able to sort themselves into communities of choice – enclaves of the good life – but those who cannot participate in active citizenship are left behind (Dorling, 2006). If New Labour is serious about breaking 'cycles of deprivation' and promoting the ECM priority outcomes for *all* children, then, as Fernandez (2007, p. 14) notes, from her comprehensive review of the international family support literature, we need to 'keep social disadvantage and social exclusion in focus and address the structural dimensions of parenting environments'.

# References

Alcock, P. (2005) 'From social security to social inclusion: The changing policy climate', *Benefits: The Journal of Poverty and Social Justice*, 43 (2): 83–88.

Barlow, J., Stewart-Brown, S. and Hilton, D. (2005) 'Hard to reach or out of reach? Reasons why women refuse to take part in early interventions', *Children and Society*, 19 (3): 199–210.

Barnes, J., Broomfield, K., Frost, M., Harper, G., Mcleod, A., Knowles, J. and Leyland, A. (2003) *Characteristics of Sure Start Local Programmes Areas: Rounds 1 to 4 National Evaluation Summary*, London: Department for Education and Schools, Sure Start Unit.

Barnes, J., Macpherson, K. and Senior, R. (2006) 'Factors influencing the acceptance of volunteer home-visiting support to families with new babies', *Child and Family Social Work*, 11 (2): 107–117.

Blair, T. (1997) *The Will to Win*, speech delivered at the Aylesbury Estate, London, 2 June.

Broadhurst, K. (2008) 'Constructing active citizenship in safeguarding work' (departmental seminar paper, available from author).

Broadhurst, K., May-Chahal, C. and Paton, H. (2005) 'Children missing from school systems: Exploring divergent patterns of disengagement in the narrative accounts of parents, carers, children and young people', *British Journal of Sociology of Education*, 26 (1): 105–119.

Broadhurst, K., Wastell, D., White, S., Hall, C., Peckover, S., Thompson, K., Pithouse, A. and Davey, D. (2009) 'Performing "initial assessment": Identifying the latent conditions for error at the front-door of local authority children's services', *British Journal of Social Work*. Advance access available at DOI:10.1093/bjsw/bcn162.

Brophy, J. (2006) *Care Proceedings under the Children Act 1989: A Research Review*, Research Series/06, London: Department for Constitutional Affairs.

Buchanan, A. (2007) 'Including the socially excluded: The impact of government policy on vulnerable families and children in need', *British Journal of Social Work*, 37 (2): 187–207.

Carpenter, J., Griffin, M. and Brown, S. (2005) 'Prevention in integrated children's services: The impact of Sure Start on referrals to social services and child protection registrations', *Child Abuse Review*, 16 (1): 17–31.

Child and Family Court Advisory Support Service (2008) *CAFCASS Notes Sharp Rise in Care Order Applications*, http://www.cafcass.gov.uk/news/2008/increase_in_care_cases.aspx (accessed 12 December 2008).

Chief Secretary to the Treasury (2003) *Every Child Matters*, Cm 5860, London: The Stationery Office.

Clarke, K. (2006) 'Childhood, parenting and early intervention: A critical examination of the Sure Start national programme', *Critical Social Policy*, 26 (4): 699–721.

Deacon, A. (2002) *Perspectives on Welfare*, Buckingham: Open University.

Deacon, A. (2003) 'Levelling the playing field: Activating the players New Labour and the "cycle of disadvantage"', *Policy and Politics*, 31 (2): 123–137.

DCSF (2007) *The Children's Plan: Building Brighter Futures*, London: The Stationery Office.

DCSF (2008) *The Every Child Matters Revised Outcomes Framework*, http://publications.everychildmatters.gov.uk/eOrderingDownload/DCSF-00331-2008.pdf (accessed 1 November 2008).

Department for Constitutional Affairs (2006) *Review of the Child Care Proceedings System in England and Wales*, http://www.dca.gov.uk/publications/reports_reviews/childcare_ps.pdf (accessed, 10 September 2008).

DfES (2002) *Birth to Three Matters: A Framework to Support Children in the Earliest Years*, http://www.standards.dfes.gov.uk/primary/publications/foundation_stage/940463/ss_birth2_3matters_birth.pdf (accessed 10 September 2008).

DfES (2004) *The Common Assessment Framework*, London: The Stationery Office.

DfES (2005) *Higher Standards Better Schools for All*, http://www.dcsf.gov.uk/publications/schoolswhitepaper/pdfs/DfES-Schools%20White%20Paper.pdf (accessed 5 September 2008).

DfES (2007) *Every Parent Matters*, London: The Stationery Office.

DoH (2000) *The Framework for the Assessment of Children in Need and their Families*, London: The Stationery Office.

Dorling, D. (2006) 'Inequalities in Britain 1997–2006: The dream that turned pear-shaped', *Local Economy*, 21 (4): 353–361.

DSS (1998) *New Ambitions for our Country: A New Contract for Welfare*, Cmnd 3805, London: HMSO.

DSS (1999) *Opportunity for All*, Cm 4445, London: The Stationery Office.

Edwards, R. and Gillies, V. (2004) 'Support in parenting: Values and consensus concerning who to turn to', *Journal of Social Policy*, 33 (4): 627–647.

Edwards, R. and Gillies, V. (2005) *Resources in Parenting: Access to Capitals Project Report*, Families and Social Capital ESRC Research Group, London: London South Bank University.

Etzioni, A. (1993) *The Parenting Deficit*, London: Demos.

Etzioni, A. (1994) *The Spirit of Community*, New York: Crown.

Fairclough, N. (2000) *New Labour, New Language*, London: Routledge.

Featherstone, B. (2006) 'Why gender matters in child welfare and protection', *Critical Social Policy*, 26 (2): 294–315.

Fernandez, E. (2007) 'Supporting children and responding to their families: Capturing the evidence on family support', *Children and Youth Services Review*, 29 (10): 1368–1394.

Furedi, F. (2006) *Save Us from the Politics of Behaviour*, www.Spikedon-line.com (accessed 11 September 2008).

Garland, D. (2001) *The Culture of Control: Crime and Social Order in Contemporary Society*, Oxford: Oxford University Press.

Garrett, P. (2008) 'How to be modern: New Labour's neoliberal modernity and the change for children programme', *British Journal of Social Work*, 38 (2): 270–289.

Gewirtz, S. (2001) 'Cloning the Blairs: New Labour's programme for the re-socialisation of working-class parents', *Journal of Education Policy*, 16 (4): 365–378.

Ghate, D. and Hazel, N. (2002) *Parenting in Poor Environments: Stress, Support and Coping*, London: Jessica Kingsley.

Ghate, D. and Rhamella, M. (2002), *Positive Parenting: The National Evaluation of the Youth Justice Board's Parenting Programme*, London: Youth Justice Board.

Gillies, V. (2005) 'Meeting parents' needs? Discourses of "support" and "inclusion" in family policy', *Critical Social Policy*, 25 (1): 70–90.

Goldson, B. and Jamieson, J. (2002) 'Youth crime, the "parenting deficit" and state intervention: A contextual critique', *Youth Justice*, 2 (2): 82–99.

Graham, H. (2007) *Unequal Lives: Health and Socioeconomic Inequalities*, Buckingham: Open University Press.

Graham, P. (2007) 'Partnership between parents and professionals', in J. Schneider, M. Avis and P. Leighton (eds.), *Supporting Children and Families: Lessons from Sure Start for Evidence-Based Practice in Health, Social Care and Education*, London: Jessica Kingsley, pp. 101–110.

Greener, I. (2002) 'Agency, social theory and social policy', *Critical Social Policy*, 22 (4): 688–705.

Gregg, P., Propper, C. and Washbrook, E. (2007) *Understanding the Relationship between Parental Income and Multiple Child Outcomes: A Decomposition Analysis*, available at: http://sticerd.lse.ac.uk/dps/case/cp/CASEpaper129.pdf (accessed 5 July 2008).

Grover, C. (2008) *Crime and Inequality*, Cullompton: Willan.

Heron, E. and Dwyer, P. (1999) 'Doing the right thing: Labour's attempt to forge a new welfare deal between the individual and the state', *Social Policy and Administration*, 33 (1): 91–104.

Hills, J. and Stewart, K. (2007) *A More Equal Society: New Labour, Poverty, Inequality and Exclusion*, Bristol: Polity Press.

Hirsh, F. (1995) *Social Limits to Growth*, London: Routledge.

HM Treasury (1999) *Tackling Poverty and Extending Opportunity: The Modernisation of Britain's Tax and Benefit System*, No. 4. London: HMSO.

HM Treasury (2003) *Pre-budget Report 2003: The Strength to Take the Long-term Decision for Britain: Seizing the Opportunities of the Global Recovery*, Cm 6042, London: The Stationery Office.

Home Office (1998) *Supporting Families: A Consultation Document*, London: The Stationery Office.

Howard League for Penal Reform (2008) *Growing Up Shut Up: Fact Sheet*, http://www.howardleague.org/fileadmin/howard_league/user/pdf/press_2008/Growing_up_Shut_Up_factsheet.pdf (accessed 10 September 2008).

Jessop, B. (2003) 'From Thatcherism to New Labour: Neo-liberalism, workfarism, and labour market regulation', in H. Overbeek (ed.), *The Political Economy of European Unemployment: European Integration and the Transnationalization of the Employment Question*, London: Routledge.

Jones, C. and Novak, T. (1999) *Poverty, Welfare and the Disciplinary State*, London: Routledge.

Joseph, K. (1972) 'The cycle of deprivation', speech to Conference of Pre-School Playgroups Association, Westminster, 29 February.

Joseph Rowntree Foundation (2007) *Poverty across Britain, 1968 to 2005*, London: Joseph Rowntree Foundation.

Levitas, R. (1998) *The Inclusive Society? Social Exclusion and New Labour*, London: Macmillan.

Maclean, M. (2002) 'The Green Paper Supporting Families, 1998', in A. Carling, S. Duncan and R. Edwards (eds.), *Analysing Families: Morality and Rationality in Policy and Practice*, London: Routledge.

Marquand, D. (2004) *The Decline of the Public: The Hollowing Out of Citizenship*, Cambridge: Polity Press.

Masson, J. (2006) 'The Climbié Inquiry – context and critique', *Journal of Law and Society*, 33 (2): 221–243.

McKeigue, B. and Beckett, C. (2004) 'Care proceedings under the 1989 Children Act: Rhetoric and reality', *British Journal of Social Work*, 34 (6): 831–849.

Miller, P. and Rose, N. (2008) *Governing the Present: Administering Economic, Social and Personal Life*, Cambridge: Polity Press.

Moran, P. and Ghate, D. (2005) 'The effectiveness of parenting support', *Children and Society*, 19 (4): 329–336.

Muncie, J. (2006) 'Governing young people: Coherence and contradiction in contemporary youth justice', *Critical Social Policy*, 26 (4): 770–793.

Penn, H. and Gough, D. (2002) 'The price of a loaf of bread: Some conceptions of family support', *Children and Society*, 16 (1): 17–32.

Piper, C. (2008) *Investing in Children: Policy, Law and Practice in Context*, Cullompton: Willan.

Pithouse, A. and Tasiran, A. (2000) 'Family support or family control? A statistical exploration of worker and "representative client" perceptions of local authority family centre services', *Child and Family Social Work*, 5 (2): 129–141.

Quinton, D. (2004) *Supporting Parents, Messages from Research*, London: DfES.

Rose, N. (1999) *Powers of Freedom: Reframing Political Thought*, Cambridge: Cambridge University Press.

Rose, N. (2000) 'Government and control', *British Journal of Criminology*, 40 (2): 321–339.

Schneider, J., Avis, M. and Leighton, P. (2007) *Supporting Children and Families: Lessons from Sure Start for Evidence-Based Practice in Health, Social Care and Education*, London: Jessica Kingsley.

Social Exclusion Taskforce (2008) *Reaching Out: Think Family*, London: The Cabinet Office.

Stepney, P., Lynch, R. and Jordan, B. (1999) 'Poverty and exclusion and New Labour'. *Critical Social Policy*, 19 (1): 109–127.

Thurston, M. (2007) 'Understanding family support', in J. Schneider, M. Avis and P. Leighton (eds.), *Supporting Children and Families: Lessons from Sure Start for Evidence-Based Practice in Health, Social Care and Education*, London: Jessica Kingsley, pp. 185–194.

Utting, D. (1995) *Family and Parenthood: Supporting Families, Preventing Breakdown*, York: Joseph Rowntree Foundation.

Vaughan, B. (2000) 'The government of youth: Disorder and dependence', *Social and Legal Studies*, 9 (3): 347–366.

Vincent, C. and Ball, S. (2007) '"Making up" the middle-class child: Families, activities and class dispositions', *Sociology*, 41 (6): 1061–1077.

Wigfall, V. (2006) 'Bringing back community: Family support from the bottom up', *Children and Society'*, 20 (1): 17–29.

Williams, F. (2004) 'What matters is who works: Why every child matters to New Labour. Commentary on the DfES Green Paper: *Every Child Matters'*, *Critical Social Policy*, 24 (3): 406–427.

# 8

# Safeguarding Children's Well-being within Educational Settings: A Critical Review of Inclusion Strategies

Jo Warin

## Introduction

Education is central to the safeguarding children agenda. In protecting children and maximizing their potential *Every Child Matters* (Chief Secretary to the Treasury, 2003) argued that the plans it outlined would reduce the educational failure of children. There are several ways in which education is held to be important in safeguarding children; it is central to the 'enjoying and achieving' outcome of *Every Child Matters* and to the longer-term concerns with the economic well-being of children. In addition, education has not been immune from the idea that we see in several chapters in this volume that in order to safeguard children then parenting needs to be improved. We shall see in this chapter that these concerns about education in the safeguarding agenda are, in fact, closely related.

In their consideration of the 'dividing line between family autonomy and legitimate state intervention', the Commission on Families and the Wellbeing of Children (2005, p. ix) emphasize that children's educational sites provide ideal venues for parenting interventions. This is reflected in the role of education in the pre-school and compulsory school years in the transmission of parenting advice and information, a trend that has been particularly visible since the introduction of *Every Child Matters*. This might be welcomed as education is one of a diminishing number of universal services in the UK, and hence, theoretically at least, all parents – rather than just the poorest – with dependent children could be open to pressures aimed at 'encouraging' them to conform to New Labour's version of the responsible parent. The theory somewhat diminishes, however, when one takes account of the fact that those parents wealthy enough to opt

*Critical Perspectives on Safeguarding Children*   Edited by Karen Broadhurst, Chris Grover and Janet Jamieson
© 2009 John Wiley & Sons, Ltd

out of everyday parenting by sending their children to fee-paying boarding schools are not subjected to such pressures, and that it is those children from economically deprived and/or black and minority ethnic (BME) families who – and their parents – are labelled as being problematic in education policy and practice (Crozier, 2005; Lupton, 2005). The class and 'race' dimensions of the problematizing of parenting, however, are lost in a discourse about marginalized parents who are alleged to be 'hard to reach' (for instance, Social Exclusion Taskforce, 2007a, 2007b), a discourse that, as we shall see, risks pathologizing poorer parents, rather than taking account of the various pressures and barriers they face to participating in the formal education of their children.

This chapter challenges the idea that parents are 'hard to reach'. It does this by examining national and local policy strategies that have been directed at two specific categories of parents identified as such; BME parents and fathers. I problematize the concept of 'reach' arguing that many parents in these categories do not believe that their own parental knowledge and expertise is recognized, sought out or valued by education professionals. I then go on to discuss the idea of 'mutual reach' between parents and educational institutions as a means of valuing the knowledge of parents before examining the concept of knowledge exchange.

The chapter discusses these issues in policy and practice, not just within compulsory schooling, but also within related educational institutions such as Children's Centres and extended schools. The central argument of this chapter – that education policy needs to take account of parents 'funds of knowledge' (Gonzalez *et al.*, 2005) – has been developed through my involvement in three empirical studies. The first was an evaluation of a five-year development project known as Raising Achievement in Inner City Schools (RAICS). Under the RAICS project 70 schools received funding through the Single Regeneration Budget to raise school achievement by devising strategies for increasing the quality and quantity of the involvement of parents in the education of their children (Edwards and Warin, 1999). The research was based in one local education authority in the mid 1990s. The second was a large-scale qualitative study of family life in Rochdale, Lancashire, focusing on aspects of parental care and control in families with teenagers. It provided insight into the 'funds of knowledge' that parents possess and the many informal ways that children are educated in the home and local community. This research revealed tensions between the valuing in schools of efforts expended on academic achievement and efforts expended in different, but equally valuable and educational activities, such as caring for younger siblings, and sporting activities outside of school (Langford *et al.*, 2001; Solomon *et al.*, 2002; Warin *et al.*, 1999). The third study that this chapter is based upon is an evaluation of Early Excellence Centres in Cumbria in the North of England (Warin, 2000). Early Excellence Centres were the pre-cursors to Sure Start Children's Centres and were seen as spearheading the way for inclusive practices with families and the integration of the different professional services. The Cumbrian centres had a particular brief for reaching isolated rural families and for working with fathers.

## Parental involvement practices

There are many opportunities for parental involvement in the schooling of their dependent children. So, for instance, the RAICS project outlined above included opportunities (such as parents' evenings, open days, homework diaries and Parent Teacher Association meetings) that will be familiar to readers who may have engaged with them as pupils and/or parents. Other strategies (for example, bingo and cheese and wine evenings) were social events developed by the RAICS schools in order to attract parents on to school territory in order to raise the profile of parental involvement in them.

Since the time of the RAICS project (the mid 1990s) some of these practices have become more firmly entrenched within school procedures, especially under the influence of the Office for Standards in Education's (Ofsted) inspection focus on communication between school and parents (Ofsted, 1999). An updated list would now include the use of school websites for accessing information about the school and, demonstrating the authoritarian drift in school-parent/parenting relationships, the introduction of Parenting Contracts (formal agreements between school and parents introduced in 2003 to address pupil behaviour and attendance) and Parenting Orders which the 2006 Education and Inspections Act allows schools to apply for in cases of exclusion and where a pupil has 'seriously misbehaved, but has not been excluded' (Department for Education and Skills [DfES], 2006, p. 291).

We could also update this list through the many formal and informal opportunities for parent communication with education staff that have proliferated through the development of Children's Centres, and the creation of extended schools services. In the Cumbria Early Excellence cluster of Sure Start centres (now Children's Centres) there were specific events for enskilling, informing and educating parents, such as talks on aspects of 'Healthy Living' (for example, nutrition and first aid), drop-in counselling for parents, and courses on behaviour management, as well as certificated evening classes, for example, a NVQ3 in Early Years Care and Education. Looking ahead, there are two relevant recommendations for action in *Every Parent Matters* (DfES, 2007). First, that all schools should have information sessions organized by the school as part of the induction of new pupils when they move into primary schooling and, again, at transfer to secondary schooling (many already do this). Second, parents should have access to school-based 'Parent Support Advisers'. The intention is that this new professional role should ensure 'effective exchanges of information' between home and school, provide basic parenting classes and recommend parents to specialist services where they are deemed necessary (DfES, 2007, p. 25).

Taken together, the activities discussed above represent different opportunities, backed by various levels of compulsion, for professional educators to *transmit* knowledge, and underlying values, into the home via parents with dependent children. The discussion, however, demonstrates that the opportunities for parents to initiate meaningful communication with the school and to present their own values, hopes, and information about their children, are often very thin on the ground. This one-way flow of information has been revealed in a number of studies of home-school contact (Bastiani, 1997; Cairney, 2000; Crozier, 1997; Edwards and Warin, 1999). While the Children's Plan (Secretary of State for Children, Schools and Families, 2007, p. 5) in noting that the 'government does not bring up children – parents do' seems to cede to parents' expertise as people who know what is best for their children, educational policy and practice looks much more like strategies for correcting perceived parental inadequacies than acknowledging that parents might have knowledge and expertise in raising children. So, while educational institutions and services provide a means of engaging in the private world of families and parenting, the expectation that is built into the policies and practices of home-school communication is that parents are to be influenced by the values and purposes of the educational institution rather than the other way round. The implication is that children can only be successfully safeguarded through a one-way flow of information from educationalists to parents; from 'expert' to 'novice'.

## Reach and 'hard to reach'

In spite of the increasing policy focus on influencing parenting, and the proliferation of practices discussed above, the government is concerned it is constrained in accessing many parents, parents that in government discourse are constructed as 'hard to reach'. Such discourse, however, is problematic because it has various potential meanings. The way it is employed by the government is as a proxy for those groups who are perceived not to be engaged with public services. Its usage in this manner, however, says little about why people do not engage with such services and it also often involves judgements about the quality of parental engagement. In their research on relationships between policing and 'hard to reach' groups, for instance, Jones and Newburn (2001, p. 13) note that '"hard to reach" actually means "hard to engage with on a positive level"'. Moreover, it is clear that treating so-called 'hard to reach' groups as a homogeneous mass is deeply problematic and potentially stigmatizing because of the power relationships involved in defining who exactly is 'hard to reach' (Cook, 2002). Cook (2002), for instance, points to dissonance between those doing the defining and those defined as 'hard to reach'.

Reflecting some of these issues, typologies of those people deemed 'hard to reach' have been developed. Doherty *et al.* (2004), for instance, suggest three categories of not mutually exclusive 'hard to reach' families: minority groups ('traditionally under-represented groups, the marginalized, disadvantaged or socially excluded' – Doherty *et al.*, 2004, p. 4); those who 'slip through the net' (those who for various reasons are 'invisible' to service providers), and those who are deemed service resistant (those who are 'unwilling to engage with service providers, the suspicious, the over targeted or disaffected' – Doherty *et al.*, 2004,

p. 4). As we shall see, the latter group is particularly pertinent to discussions about engagement with educational institutions.

Despite these difficulties with the conceptualizing of 'hard to reach' it has become a taken-for-granted concept in government discourse. The recent Social Exclusion Taskforce (2007b, p. 4) paper, *Reaching Out: Think Family*, for example, aims to tackle a minority (2 per cent) of families with 'complex and multiple problems' who are held to be disproportionately responsible for 'anti-social' acts. It suggests that such families are 'hard to reach' because, first, they make up such a small proportion of the population and, second, because of a disjuncture between the views of 'the system' of such families and the view of such families of 'the system'. The 'net effect' of this is 'that families and services fail to engage effectively' (Social Exclusion Taskforce, 2007b, para. 2.7). The implication, as was highlighted by Jones and Newburn (2001) in relation to policing, is not the difficulty of accessing 'hard to reach' families, but perceptions of *their* engagement with the services on offer.

While the *Reaching Out: Think Family* paper recognizes that the perceptions and experiences of the so-called 'hard to reach' help structure their non-engagement (or their lower than the expected/demanded level of engagement) with public services, the paper is also structured by the tensions in the government's desire to 'support' families. The reader of *Reaching Out: Think Family*, for instance, is left in little doubt of the tools of the state (Anti-Social Behaviour Orders, eviction and Parenting Orders) that 'can, as a last resort, be used to enforce engagement with services' (Social Exclusion Taskforce, 2007b, para. 2.2). In this context, it is difficult to conclude anything but that reaching the so-called 'hard to reach' implies a one-way transmission of influence from government via public services to parents and families.

With the caveats about the concept of 'hard to reach' in mind, however, it is also the case that researchers and evaluators of family-based services, nursery education and childcare, at local and national levels, have noted that certain categories of parents, most notably BME and fathers, remain excluded from such services.

## BME parents

Lloyd and Rafferty (2006) undertook a synthesis of local evaluations of Sure Start programmes and found a scarcity of work involving BME families. They suggest that while service providers recognize the under-representation of BME families in service usage, they do not provide specific plans for addressing the issue. They also point out that more effort is expended on reaching South Asian communities compared to African and African Caribbean communities. However, exceptions to these more general trends do exist. The Sure Start Centre at Higham Hill, Waltham Forest, for instance, has a particular focus on, and understanding of, problems of engagement with parents in specific BME groups

(NESS, 2004). These are portrayed as language problems, family responsibilities, insecurities about immigration status and a concern about providing personal information. Some of the families are portrayed as being tied to the domestic sphere by their cultural traditions. Others feel they lack the confidence to approach strangers when they do manage to attend some of the Sure Start services. A further example comes from Wilson and Refson (2007) in their evaluation of the organization, Place2Be, a therapeutic service operating inside some schools. They claim that its work with families from BME groups is a hallmark of its success: 'The proportion of non white children accessing individual or group interventions in the Place2Be was 35% (on average, across all hubs). This compares with 7.5% in the general population as indicated in the National Statistics Census, 2001' (Wilson and Refson, 2007, p. 132). Wilson and Refson (2007, p. 136) attribute this success to the fact that while the Place2Be is an 'external service' it is embedded within the inner workings of a primary school: 'it retains its own authority and standards and yet fits into the fabric of the school, working alongside teachers and others close to the children' (Wilson and Refson, 2007, p. 136). The familiarity and proximity of the Place2Be programme within the school means that access to children's counselling has been improved.

While the above examples are testament to positive efforts to engage some 'hard to reach' families, the strategies described are based on the assumption that reach is both necessary and desirable. However, I will suggest below that what is required is a much more democratic basis for engagement with families based on a concept of mutual reach. A fundamental part of this re-conceptualization of parents as reciprocal partners with services is a need for research on the parenting values, beliefs and practices of BME families. In the consultation phase for preparation of the Children's Plan, the Department for Children, Schools and Families (DCSF, 2007, p. 155) formed focus groups and consultation events including a 15 per cent representation from BME groups. While this is a step in the right direction there is currently too little research on which policy might be based. As Arrighi (2007, p. 109) points out, 'ethnic differences in parenting styles ... are neither well documented nor understood'. If BME families are to be fully included in pre-school and compulsory school age services and their children able to engage with the five outcomes of *Every Child Matters* they need to be.

## Fathers

A focus on engaging with fathers has been a key concern in the development of Sure Start Children's Centres. Of the original group of Early Excellence Centres (set up in 1997) which pioneered the practices that became enshrined within Sure Start and then in Children's Centres, a small number had a particular focus on working with fathers. Including fathers, for instance, was a specific part of the work at the Pen Green Centre, a flagship Early Excellence/Children's Centre in Corby, Northamptonshire, and the Sheffield Children's Centre (Broadhead and Meleady, 2008; Chandler, 1997; Whalley, 1997) and it was also a key focus in one of the Cumbrian centres I worked with as local evaluator. This centre, based in an area of high male unemployment, developed a specific set of practices to increase the involvement of fathers and male carers, discussed more fully in Warin (2007). Various strategies were attempted to involve such men. So, for example, a local musician was engaged to set up a fathers' band, recording nursery rhymes and songs, drawing in men who would not otherwise have been involved, attracted by the 'carrot' of professional music recording. The success of the 'Dads work' at this centre was largely due to the drive of a nursery teacher, himself a father of young children and a longstanding member of the immediate local community. However, such practices were not widespread or lasting within the national picture of Sure Start. In their exploratory study of engaging fathers in Sure Start, Lloyd *et al.* (2003) revealed a strong mother focus in service management and delivery, and found that only 12 per cent of programmes were categorized as 'highly involving fathers'. Lloyd *et al.* (2003) make a number of recommendations, prioritizing the need for male workers and recognizing that services should be tailored to the differing needs of fathers in diverse circumstances. Ferguson and Hogan (2004), in their analysis of father-inclusive practices, recommend that professionals should address the anxieties that can lead to fathers excluding themselves. They identify fears of professionals' assumptions about dangerous and feckless masculinities, fears about being discovered defrauding social security or any other illegal activities, and fears about their personal relationships with children. They suggest that father-inclusive policies must overcome classism and prejudice against men working with children. They recommend that agencies who work with children and families develop explicit father-inclusive policies and practices, a recommendation that *Every Child Matters* also makes.

## Enduring barriers for accessing parents

There is an increasing identification of specific groups of 'hard to reach' families and a growing understanding, arising from the research and evaluations of service usage, about some of the barriers to engaging with services for those families. Anning *et al.* (2007) in the National Evaluation of Sure Start final report, reveal that potential service users who do not engage are articulate about what the barriers to them accessing services are, but that providers find it very difficult to surmount them. In this section I consider why some of the identified barriers seem so immoveable.

One of the reasons lies in the gap between the cultural worlds of professionals and the families they are attempting to engage. This is implied in the argument of Ferguson and Hogan (2004) that the development of father inclusive practices will have to include tackling classism and prejudices. A number of commentators ask challenging questions about the nature of the relationship between families who are deemed 'hard to reach' and the professionals involved in trying to reach them (Anning *et al.*, 2007; Pomerantz *et al.*, 2007; Wilson and Refson, 2007). They suggest that professionals may find it difficult to move beyond their comfort zones and their traditional ways of working: 'They may be so institutionalised in their practice that, from an organisational point of view, they are not set up or prepared to extend beyond their traditional procedures' (Wilson and Refson, 2007, p. 132). With specific reference to the reach of schools, Crozier and Davies (2007, p. 295) point out that schools frequently inhibit accessibility for certain parents and we should perhaps pay attention to the concept of 'hard to reach schools' rather than 'hard to reach parents'.

Researchers into communication between secondary school staff and parents find that parents often feel powerless and infantilized in their contact with school staff. So, for example, Crozier (2002) quotes a parent who noted: 'Sometimes when I go into school and they're talking to you, I feel intimidated because ... you feel as if you're the kid'. Walker and MacLure (2001, p. 12), in their study of parents' evenings, note that even those parents who are themselves teachers, often feel powerless: 'When such parents attend parents' evenings they experience them emphatically as parents – i.e. the relatively powerless actors in the encounter'. A further aspect of cultural communication barriers between professionals and parents lies in the specifics of professional cultural discourses. For example, professional educational language often mystifies and intimidates parents. During the local evaluation of the Cumbrian Early Excellence centres, a parent told me about her lack of confidence to stand up to the centre staff when they had misunderstood the 'bad behaviour' of her 4-year-old son during a school bus trip. Following her involvement in a parenting programme at the centre, she felt, not a 'better' parent as perhaps had been the intention, but better able to communicate with staff on their own terms, for example, to use the term 'cognitive development' to discuss her son's needs. While recognizing the value of her new-found confidence, the story was depressing in that it illustrated that she had to speak an unfamiliar professional language before she felt 'part of the club' and, thus, able to communicate with staff. Parents who slip through the net of services may do so for the simple reason that they do not recognize themselves in the language used to engage them. This point is made by Sheriff (2007) who discusses why young fathers do not access services. He points to the gendered language used in publicizing services and suggests that the simple strategy of harnessing the gender neutral term 'parent' to replace the ubiquitous 'mother' would have a considerable benefit.

Where professionals are themselves embedded in the cultures and communities of potential service users it is possible to build up a greater mutual trust and overcome parental insecurities. We have already seen examples of this in the Cumbrian male nursery worker who created a crucial 'bridge' between fathers and the centre. His 'Dads work' was based on a democratic model in which he and the other fathers shared their parental expertise and knowledge of their children (Warin, 2007). The work of the Sheffield Children's Centre is exemplary in this respect. Broadhead and Meleady (2008, p. 61) describe how the centre appoints and supports staff who are representative of 'hard to reach' groups, staff who knowingly place 'their collective heads above the parapet through their work'. They present a frank account of the challenges faced by their staff. So, for example, some staff were leafleted with race hate flyers, a disabled worker experienced considerable harassment, and male staff had to struggle to overcome the prejudices of some people in the local community.

Recognizing the important bridging function that certain service employees may fulfil, and paying attention to the inclusive and exclusive features of language, are certainly strategies that may go some way towards engaging the categories of families who 'slip through the net'. However, these approaches do not help to engage families who may be characterized as 'service resistant' in Doherty *et al.*'s (2004) typologies of 'hard to reach'. Relevant here are findings from studies with BME families that reveal that a lack of so-called help-seeking behaviour may be explained by a resistance to the perceived values of UK liberalism (Beishon *et al.*, 1998; Hylton, 1997). Beishon *et al.* (1998, p. 77), for instance, report a resistance to 'an excessive individualism and materialism, in which personal gratification and fulfilment undermine more family-orientated values'. In the Moyenda project (Hylton, 1997, p. 3), an African-Caribbean woman makes the following comment on service provision: 'the values they passed down to your children are worse than what you would give'. These studies suggest that parents in these families are likely to feel they have little to learn about parenting from the UK's educational establishments, a finding echoed in Dosanjh and Ghuman (1996, p. 155), who reported that 'Punjabi fathers are more involved than their white counterparts in the education of their children'. Reay and Mirza (2002) and Crozier (2002) discuss how black parents may often feel driven by the wish to *compensate* for schooling rather than to cooperate with schooling. In an account of their small-scale study of four black (African-Caribbean) supplementary schools Reay and Mirza (2002) show how the practices within them demonstrate an effective and collectivized agency that represents a response to a mainstream educational system which is perceived to be failing black pupils. They show that: 'The black women through their involvement, as both educators and parents, in supplementary schooling were producing resources to compensate for perceived deficits in state educational provision' (Reay and Mirza, 2002, p. 9).

These observations are important because they demonstrate that resistance to inclusion in services is not born out of deviancy or pathological failings. The observations suggest that it is the ways in which educational institutions are embedded in a deeply socially and culturally unequal society that is the problem for the 'hard to reach', rather than the 'hard to reach' being the problem. If children are to be safeguarded, if they are to fulfil the Every Child Matters outcomes, then educational services will have to work harder to include those families labelled as 'hard to reach' in their services. This will necessarily involve a questioning of the social, cultural and linguistic relationships between families and service provision. One aspect of this that I want to highlight is the recognition that ought to be given to the contribution that parents can make when their own values and practices are not only recognized, but welcomed, by educational institutions and where there is an expectation that educational professionals have as much, perhaps more, to learn from parents than parents have to learn from educational professionals.

## Mutual reach

We need to think much more radically about 'reach'. I suggest that we need a very different concept, a counter-discourse – that of 'mutual reach' – on which to base education policy and practice. Many parents, including those identified in the examples above, do not recognize the contributions they have to make to a partnership with staff in Children's Centres and schools. While policy documents may use the rhetoric of respect for parents there are, in fact, few arenas for creating a genuine partnership or exchange of information between parents and educationalists about children. There are very few opportunities, places or spaces for a more democratic and genuine knowledge exchange to occur. There are also very low expectations of what parents can contribute. There is policy blindness to the idea that professional educators can learn from parents. It is, perhaps, little wonder that so many parents become identified as 'hard to reach'.

In order to establish models of a more democratic and cooperative exchange between parents and teachers we need to locate and build on pockets of existing practice where a concept of 'mutual reach' is operating. We need to find examples of democratic practice as advocated by the Organization for Economic Cooperation and Development (2006, p. 220) in their description of early childhood services as: 'a life space where educators and families work together to promote the wellbeing, participation and learning of young children ... based on the principle of democratic participation'.

An exceptional study by Gonzalez *et al.* (2005), focusing on parents' 'funds of knowledge' enshrined this principle. It provides both a concept and a model of educational intervention which could inspire policy on home-school communication. The 'funds of knowledge' concept turns on its head the parental deficit model that underlies so much of current parent-school policy. The starting point is that education needs a counter-discourse in a period when it is dominated by a discourse of accountability through testing. Gonzalez *et al.* (2005, p. x) base the concept of 'funds of knowledge' on the premise that 'people are competent, they have knowledge, and their life-experiences have given them that knowledge'. In the Funds of Knowledge Project, carried out in Tucson, USA, the research team, including a teacher, anthropologist and educational researcher, set out to document the competences and knowledge held within the families whose children attended participating schools, and the communities in which the schools were located. They aimed to explore the pedagogical implications that come about through gaining a deep and personal understanding of the children's families, and recognizing the resources contained within them. They conclude that this rich understanding of the lives of their pupils can provide the basis for learning and teaching in the classroom. They engaged teacher/researchers to conduct in-depth interviews with parents in order to access an understanding of the family/community lives of their pupils. An important aspect of the study was that the teacher/researchers were themselves well-recognized members of these communities and, therefore, were in a good position to build the trust necessary for knowledge exchange.

The 'funds of knowledge' concept illuminates ways that teachers and childcare workers can learn from parents, since this approach seems to be attempting to operationalize a concept of 'parent as expert'. It also suggests a need for researchers to undertake a wide trawl of families, going into homes and community settings to engage with parents to understand their funds of knowledge. One such example comes from Maddock (2006, p. 153) who has conducted ethnographic case studies of children's learning outside of school, exploring contexts where learning was 'not an obligation or purpose'. She reveals the learning opportunities in a range of activities including DIY, and sports and leisure activities. The children's home learning is fuelled by social and emotional dimensions and offers opportunities for learning about the human condition. She suggests that if teachers close their eyes to learning which occurs outside school, and are required to impose school models of learning onto children's home learning, 'they miss important parts of the whole picture of learning' (Maddock, 2006, p. 155). In the Rochdale study, referred to at the outset of this chapter, the extensive family interviews we conducted on a one-to one basis with different family members enabled us to glimpse the many informal educational activities that were ongoing in the home, providing a further illustration of funds of knowledge. So, for example, one father was teaching his 14-year-old son to make a Sunday roast dinner; another enjoyed walks with his daughter in the local conservation area in which he shared his knowledge of wild life; one mother was helping her daughter with interior decorating, and another father was teaching basic woodworking skills to his daughter through the construction of a rabbit hutch.

Another significant example is the recent work of Martin Hughes and colleagues in the Home-School Knowledge Exchange project (HSKE, 2007). Mindful of previous critiques of the one-way flow of values and information from school to home this project set out to ensure an exchange of knowledge about the child from home to school and from school to home. Knowledge exchange strategies included video viewings, shoe boxes filed with artefacts from home and photographic displays of both environments (Hughes and Greenhough, 2006). Hughes and Greenhough (2006) suggest that it is necessary to raise the profile of home-school communication both inside and outside school. This is a far cry from the practice revealed in the evaluation of the RAICS project, described above, where the over-riding concern of the teachers was 'getting the parents in' and where improvements in parental involvement were measured by counting the numbers of parents crossing the school threshold (Edwards and Warin, 1999). The all-important issue of the location, or territory, for home–school knowledge exchange that Hughes and Greenhough (2006) draw attention to has also been noted in the development of practice with parents in Children's Centres.

The evaluation of the Cumbrian Early Excellence/Children's Centres revealed the significance of home visits for developing mutual trust between parents and professionals. Here, concerns about mutual reach were compounded by the rural isolation of some of the families concerned. Home visits were seen as a crucial first step in developing rapport between staff and parents in order for staff to gain a rich insight into the child's home life, to understand their interests, activities and preferences, and their family relationships. Home visits may, of course, be fraught with parental concerns about surveillance from their child's professional educators, especially among parents who have a history of mistrust of professionals visiting their homes. However, the staff concerned were well aware of these issues and handled them sensitively. So, for instance, they were aware of managing first impressions through attention to non-intimidating dress and body language, and in order to build a rapport they engaged in play with children and parents together in a relaxed manner. A further example comes from Pen Green Children's Centre, which like the example above, illustrates that the establishment of trust is a necessary pre-cursor to knowledge exchange between parents and professionals. Whalley (2001) describes the innovative practice in parent-staff collaboration that takes place at the centre. Parents are loaned camcorders and encouraged to make videos of their children learning and playing at home while nursery staff also make recordings of the child in the centre. She explains that parents were anxious about showing staff the videoed footage because they were worried about the judgements that nursery staff might make about their interventions with their child without having access to the parents' perspectives. She also points out that members of the nursery staff were equally concerned about parents' judgements. Consequently, parents and staff were brought together to watch the videos simultaneously and to exchange their understandings about the child, building a trust that would pave the way to further cooperation.

How far could these practices filter up the school system from early years to primary schooling and to secondary schooling? These practices are undoubtedly resource intensive and they happen in contexts that are relatively free from the performance constraints of national tests and league tables. The practice described by Whalley (2001) is possible because, despite the introduction of the curriculum for 3–5s (the Foundation Stage), there is clearly much less public pressure on this age group to perform, compared to older children whose achievements are examined and measured through SATs and public exams.

Consequently, educational purposes are focused on social and emotional aspects of education as much as academic achievement. Given this much wider brief for the welfare of the child, parents are more likely to recognize their contribution in cooperating with staff. This is because, in particular, parents can contribute to a knowledge exchange with professionals in educational institutions their experience of their child's social and emotional life. We need models where there is a mutual exchange of knowledge about the interests and emotional concerns of children, as well as their more academic abilities.

There are several recent policy developments in education which, taken together, appear to offer a move away from the very narrow conception of academic ability and achievement which has underlined the policies of New Labour to date. One is the emphasis on social and emotional aspects of learning (SEAL), which has now been introduced into primary schooling and is currently being piloted in secondary education (Social, Emotional and Behavioural Skills [SEBS], 2008). The second development is the policy emphasis on 'personalized' learning, intended to be based on a 'sound knowledge and understanding of every child's needs' (Miliband, cited in James and Pollard, 2004). Sceptics suggest that personalized learning is wide open to interpretation and, therefore, while it could be about the development of learner identities, it could equally produce more frequent assessment and target setting (James and Pollard, 2004). Nevertheless, I believe that personalized learning, along with SEAL, offer a potential move towards a more holistic approach to schooling and perhaps indicate an upward extension of the pedagogic aims and purposes that characterize some of the best practice in Children's Centres. It remains to be seen how such policy turns will be realized in practice in a climate that is still strongly dominated by the performance goals and measurable outcomes reified in league tables, SAT scores and public exams results, a climate in which, according to Shuayb and O'Donnell (2008, p. 3), 'what matters is measured and what cannot be measured does not matter'. Shuayb and O'Donnell (2008) also suggest that UK education policy now seems caught between two goals: a traditional economic pressure to compare educational performance favourably with international competitors, and a return to philosophies of personalized teaching rooted in earlier child-centred values, aimed at improving a broader notion of child well-being. These, however, make uncomfortable bedfellows.

## Conclusion: the way forward

This chapter has been concerned with issues that are important to the safeguarding children agenda. First, education is central to the five outcomes of *Every Child Matters*. It is seen by the government as *the* means of developing the human capital of children as 'becomings'. While the 'education, education, education' mantra of New Labour is now not heard as loudly as it once was, it is clear that education is seen by the government as being the main mechanism for tackling a range of economic and social dilemmas in the longer term. Second, the chapter has focused upon families – those deemed to be 'hard to reach' – that are central to the safeguarding agenda. The government is keen to highlight that it believes a very small minority of families are the cause of a disproportionate amount of 'anti-social' behaviour, but even these are not lost causes; they can be brought into the normative fold. Hence, the focus upon how the so-called 'hard to reach' can be 'captured' in policy terms.

The chapter has exposed the tensions that exist in the education-related aspects of safeguarding children. It suggests, for instance, tensions between the 'enjoy and achieve' outcome of *Every Child Matters* and the longer-term economic well-being outcome that is related to developing the human capital of children. Education seems to be failing children on both of these accounts. The recent UNICEF (2007) report, *Child Poverty in Perspective: An Overview of Child Well-being in Rich Countries*, for instance, found that only 19 per cent of children aged 11, 13 and 15 in the UK said they liked school 'a lot'. Fifteen OECD nations scored higher than the UK on this measure and the UK's score was about half of the top scoring OECD nation, Norway. With so few enjoying their schooling in the UK it is perhaps not surprising that many children are not achieving. While such observations are clearly at odds with the 'enjoy and achieve' outcome of *Every Child Matters*, they also undermine the longer-term aims of increasing the human capital of children so that they can contribute when they are adults.

The point that I want to make is that parental engagement with educational institutions in a way that respects and harnesses the former's 'funds of knowledge' could help safeguard children's likelihood of being able to 'enjoy and achieve' within their schooling and in their broader lives. In order to protect children from misery, boredom and a low engagement in learning we need two-way communication between parents and education professionals with the goal of sharing holistic knowledge about children. In particular, parents can contribute knowledge about their children's interests, preferences, home activities, culture and also about their emotional lives, drives and family relationships. However, constraints to the realization of this goal lay in the current emphasis of educational policy on a narrowly defined academic performance and the educational professional as 'expert'.

Within current government policy the expertise of educational professionals is intended to enrich the life of the child within their family by improving parenting. In this chapter I have presented a critique of the assumptions behind this approach and made the case for a counter-discourse, a turn in policy that suggests that parental expertise is accessed in order to enrich children's educational experiences and outcomes. Instead of trying to correct so-called 'poor parenting', communication between parents and education professionals could be harnessed to the cooperative goal of safeguarding children's enjoyment of school and of their wider lives.

# References

Anning, A., Stuart, J., Nicholls, M. and Goldthorpe, J. and Morley, A. (2007) *Understanding Variations in Effectiveness amongst Sure Start Local Programmes: Final Report*, Research Report NESS/2007/FR/024, London: DfES.

Arrighi, B. (2007) *Understanding Equality: The Intersection of Race/Ethnicity, Class and Gender*, Lanham, MD: Rowman and Littlefield.

Bastiani, J. (1997) *Home-School Work in Multicultural Settings*, London: David Fulton.

Beishon, S., Modood, T., and Virdee, S. (1998) *Ethnic Minority Families*, London: Policy Studies Institute.

Broadhead, P. and Meleady, C. (2008) *Children, Families, and Communities. Creating and Sustaining Integrated Services*, Maidenhead: Open University Press.

Cairney, T. (2000) 'Beyond the classroom walls: The rediscovery of the family and community as partners in education', *Educational Review*, 52 (2): 163–174.

Chandler, T. (1997) 'Daring to care – men and childcare', in M. Whalley (ed.), *Working with Parents*, London: Hodder and Stoughton.

Chief Secretary to the Treasury (2003) *Every Child Matters*, Cm 5860, London: The Stationery Office.

Commission on Families and the Wellbeing of Children (2005) *Families and the State: Two-way Support and Responsibilities: An Inquiry into the Relationship between the State and the Family in the Upbringing of Children*, Bristol: Policy Press.

Cook, D. (2002) 'Consultation, for a change? Engaging users and communities in the policy process', *Social Policy and Administration*, 36 (5): 516–531.

Crozier, G. (1997) 'Empowering the powerful: A discussion of the interrelation of government policies and consumerism with social class factors and the impact of this upon parent interventions in their children's schooling', *British Journal of Sociology of Education*, 18 (2): 187–200.

Crozier, G. (2002) *Beyond the Call of Duty: The Impact of Racism on Black Parents' Involvement in their Children's Education*, paper presented at the ESRC Sponsored Seminar Series, 'Parents and Schools: Diversity, Participation and Democracy', University of East Anglia, 20 June.

Crozier, G. (2005) '"There's a war against our children": Black educational underachievement revisited', *British Journal of Sociology of Education*, 26 (5): 585–598.

Crozier, G. and Davies, A. (2007) 'Hard to reach parents or hard to reach schools? A discussion of home-school relations, with particular reference to Bangladeshi and Pakistani parents', *British Educational Research Journal*, 33 (3): 295–313.

DCSF (2007) *The Children's Plan: Building Brighter Futures*, http://www.dcsf.gov.uk/publications/childrensplan/downloads/The_Childrens_Plan.pdf (accessed 20 May 2008).

DfES (2006) *Final Regulatory Impact Assessment for the Education and Inspections Act 2006*, London: DfES.

DfES (2007) *Every Parent Matters*, London: DfES.

Doherty, P., Stott, A. and Kinder, K. (2004) *Delivering Services to Hard to Reach Families in On Track Areas: Definitions, Consultation and Needs Assessment*, Home Office Development and Practice Report, No. 15, London: Home Office, Research, Development and Statistics Directorate.

Dosanjh, J. and Ghuman, P. (1996) *Child-rearing in Ethnic Minorities*, Clevedon: Multilingual Matters.

Edwards, A. and Warin, J. (1999) 'Parental involvement: for what? An exploration of the rationales for the involvement of parents in schools', *Oxford Review of Education*, 25 (3): 325–341.

Ferguson, H. and Hogan, F. (2004) *Strengthening Families through Fathers*, Waterford: Centre for Social and Family Research.

Gonzalez, N., Moll, L. and Amanti, C. (2005) *Funds of Knowledge: Theorizing Practices in Households, Communities and Classrooms*, London and Hillsdale, NJ: Lawrence Erlbaum.

HSKE (2007) 'Home-School Knowledge Exchange' project, http://www.tlrp.org/proj/phase11/phase2e.html (accessed 23 May 2008).

Hughes, M. and Greenhough, P. (2006) 'Boxes, bags and videotape: Enhancing home-school communication through knowledge exchange activities', *Educational Review – Special Issue*, 58 (4): 471–487.

Hylton, C. (1997) *Family Survival Strategies: A Moyenda Black Families Talking Project*, Social Policy Research 135, London, Exploring Parenthood, http:www.jrf.org.uk/knowledge/findings/socialpolicy/sp135 (accessed 18 April 2008).

James, M. and Pollard, A. (2004) *Personalised Learning: A Commentary by the Teaching and Learning Research Programme*, Swindon: Economic and Social Research Council, www.tlrp.org.pub (accessed 23 May 2008).

Jones, T. and Newburn, T. (2001) *Widening Access: Improving Police Relationships with Hard to Reach Groups*, Police Research Series Paper 138, London: Home Office.

Langford, W., Lewis, C., Solomon, Y., and Warin, J. (2001) *Family Understandings: Closeness, Authority and Independence in Mothers, Fathers and 11–16 Year Olds*, London: Policy Studies Centre, pp. 1–56.

Lloyd, N., O'Brien, M. & Lewis, C. (2003) *Fathers in Sure Start*, London: National Evaluation of Sure Start, London: Birkbeck College.

Lloyd, N. and Rafferty, A. (2006) *Black and Minority Ethnic Families and Sure Start Findings from Local Evaluation reports*, RR013, http://www.ness.bbk.ac.uk/documents/synthesisReports/1289 (accessed 25 May 2008).

Lupton, R. (2005) 'Social justice and school improvements: Improving the quality of schooling in the poorest neighbourhoods', *British Educational Research Journal*, 31 (5): 589–604.

Maddock, M. (2006) 'Children's personal learning agendas at home', *Cambridge Journal of Education*, 36 (2): 153–169.

NESS (2004) *Reaching Hard to Reach Families: An Evaluation for Sure Start Higham Hill Partners in Evaluation*, http://www.ness.bbk.ac.uk/documents/findings/834 (accessed 25 May 2008).

Ofsted (1999) *Handbook for Inspecting Primary and Nursery Schools*, London: HMSO.

Organization for Economic Cooperation and Development (2006) *Starting Strong II*, Paris: Organization for Economic Cooperation and Development.

Pomerantz, K.A., Hughes, M., and Thompson, D. (2007) *How to Reach 'Hard to Reach' Children: Improving Access, Participation and Outcomes*, Chichester: John Wiley and Sons.

Reay, D. and Mirza, H. (2002) *Doing Parental Involvement Differently: Black Women's Participation as Educators and Mothers in Black Supplementary Schooling*, Paper presented at ESRC Sponsored Seminar Series, 'Parents and Schools: Diversity, Participation and Democracy', University of Sunderland, 20 June.

SEBS (2008) *Social Emotional and Behavioural Skills Pilot Project in Secondary Schools* (http://www.bandapilot.org.uk/secondary/pages/sebs_pilot.html (accessed 10 October 2008).

Secretary of State for Children, Schools and Families (2007) *The Children's Plan. Building Brighter Futures*, Cm 7280, London: The Stationery Office.

Sheriff, N. (2007) *Supporting Young Fathers*, Brighton: Trust for the Study of Adolescence.

Shuayb, M. and O'Donnell S. (2008) *Aims and Values in Primary Education: England and other Countries. Interim Report*, Cambridge: University of Cambridge Faculty of Education.

Social Exclusion Taskforce (2007a) *Reaching Out: Progress on Social Exclusion*, http://www.cabinetoffice.gov.uk/social_exclusion_task_force/publications/reaching_out/progress_report.aspx (accessed 19 August 2008).

Social Exclusion Taskforce (2007b) *Reaching Out: Think Family*, http://www.cabinetoffice.gov.uk/~/media/assets/www.cabinetoffice.gov.uk/social_exclusion_task_force/think_families/think_families%20pdf.ashx (accessed 19 August 2008).

Solomon, Y., Warin, J., Lewis, C. and Langford, W. (2002) 'Helping with homework? Homework as a site of tension for parents and teenagers', *British Educational Research Journal*, 28 (4): 603–622.

UNICEF (2007) *Child Poverty in Perspective: An Overview of Child Well-being in Rich Countries*, Innocenti Report card 7, Florence: UNICEF Innocenti Research Centre.

Walker, B. and MacLure, M. (2001) *Home-school Partnerships in Practice*, paper presented at the ESRC Sponsored Seminar Series, 'Parents and Schools: Diversity, Participation and Democracy', University of East Anglia, 20 June.

Warin, J. (2000) *Early Excellence Centres. Evaluation Report 1999-2000*, Cumbria Early Excellence Network (available on request from the author).

Warin, J. (2007) 'Joined-up services for young children and their families: Papering over the cracks or re-constructing the foundations?', *Children and Society*, 21 (2): 87–97.

Warin, J., Solomon, Y., Lewis, C., and Langford, W. (1999) *Fathers, Work, and Family Life*, London: Family Policy Studies Centre, pp. 1–48.

Whalley, M. (1997) *Working with Parents*, London: Hodder and Stoughton.

Whalley, M. (2001) *Involving Parents in their Children's Learning*, London: Paul Chapman Publishing.

Wilson, P. and Refson, B. (2007) 'The hard to reach and the Place2Be' in G. Baruch, P. Fonagy and D. Robins (eds.), *Reaching the Hard to Reach: Evidence-based Funding Priorities for Intervention and Research*, Chichester: John Wiley and Sons.

# 9

# 'Health' and Safeguarding Children: An 'Expansionary Project' or 'Good Practice'?

Sue Peckover

## Introduction

The safeguarding children agenda has thrown up a myriad of challenges for health services. These include various organizational and performance requirements, such as joint working, statutory involvement in Local Safeguarding Children Boards (LSCBs), the establishment of child death review processes, staff vetting requirements and an array of measures to strengthen competence and provide supervision to front line workers (HM Government, 2006a; 2007). Such policy goods provide a framework for action for safeguarding children against which the National Health Service (NHS) will be judged (Department of Health [DoH], 2004a; HM Government, 2007). Alongside this lies considerable concern about the health of children and young people, and the need to improve standards of service delivery to ensure optimal outcomes for current and future generations (Association of Public Health Observatories, 2007; Blair *et al.*, 2003; DoH, 2004b). Constructing these as public health priorities enables initiatives aimed at improving the health and well-being of children and young people to be undertaken both separately and as part of wider developments concerned with safeguarding children.

There are policy, practice and conceptual overlaps here as safeguarding children and children's public health co-exist alongside one another. Disentangling these two priorities illustrates some of the complexities and challenges of safeguarding children within a health framework. It also serves to illustrate some ways in which the boundaries of 'health', whether that is understood in embodied conceptual terms or as professional and institutional practices, are expanding. These ideas will be explored in this chapter commencing with a

*Critical Perspectives on Safeguarding Children*   Edited by Karen Broadhurst, Chris Grover and Janet Jamieson
© 2009 John Wiley & Sons, Ltd

discussion of the organizational and performance requirements for safeguarding children for the NHS.

## The NHS and safeguarding children

While recent developments have ensured health services have clear responsibilities for safeguarding children (HM Government, 2007), this built upon an existing agenda for child protection with which the NHS was already engaged with variable success (Lupton *et al.*, 2001). Successive governments, often as a response to child abuse inquiries, implemented a series of policy and procedural guidance which had incrementally drawn health services and professionals into the child protection arena (DoH, 1991, 1999a). This effectively expanded the scope of health professional involvement with children and families, identifying new areas for inquiry, information sharing and intervention. Domestic violence, which became constructed as a child welfare issue, serves as an illustrative example (DoH, 2005). At the same time, awareness of, and responsibility for, protecting children became more widely dispersed across the health service. Once the preserve of a few professional groups, notably health visitors, paediatricians, general practitioners and child psychologists, the remit for protecting children became more widely spread and embraced primary, secondary, maternity and emergency care, and mental health and sexual health services. There was also an expansion of specialist posts for doctors and nurses with largely supervisory and training functions which aimed to address perceived 'shortcomings' in relation to information sharing/multi-agency work (DoH, 1991, 1999a; Polnay and Curnock, 2003).

Health professionals, particularly medical scientists and paediatricians, have also made an important contribution to expanding the knowledge base about child abuse, often in ways which shaped policy and practice beyond the gates of the health service. Here, the understanding and 'discovery' of child physical abuse (the 'battered baby') and child sexual abuse are key examples of the ways that child protection issues were constructed within medical discourses (Parton, 1985).

While an overview of health services involvement with protecting children suggests a lengthy engagement, the extent to which previous policy aspirations had been achieved in practice was often patchy and uncoordinated. Lupton *et al.* (2001), for example, have pointed towards the inherent tensions that arise because of centralized policy-making and local implementation, suggesting considerable gaps within overall NHS responses to the child protection agenda. The extent to which this has altered remains to some extent an empirical question, although there can be no doubt the raft of measures introduced post-Laming clearly intends to ensure the NHS is fully aware of its roles and responsibilities for safeguarding children (Chief Secretary to the Treasury, 2003).

Central to these is the requirement laid down in the Children Act 2004 (section 11) for the NHS and other public bodies 'to make arrangements to ensure that their functions are discharged with regard to the need to safeguard and promote the welfare of children' (HM Government, 2007). Key themes include the establishment of clear roles and responsibilities, and a clear line of accountability within each organization with regards to work on safeguarding and promoting the welfare of children, service development, staff training and development, safer recruitment and vetting procedures, and effective inter-agency working (HM Government, 2007). The reforms have also introduced new arrangements for the commissioning and delivery of services including initiatives such as Children and Young People's Strategic Partnerships and Children's Trusts. The establishment of LSCBs places strategic executive level responsibilities upon local NHS organizations and other partners for the coordination and monitoring of safeguarding children. Among the wider responsibilities of LSCBs is the requirement to establish child death overview arrangements, an area of work in which the NHS has been particularly involved (see Pearson, 2008). The emphasis within the reforms upon integrated working has drawn many health service providers into new organizational and working arrangements with children's services. At practice level there are many examples of professionals working closer together, such as co-locating health visitors into children's social care teams (Whiting *et al.*, 2008). Initiatives such as Children Centres, Extended Schools, disability services and drug intervention teams provide opportunities for closer professional working, although tensions inherent to co-location have been identified (Frost and Robinson, 2007; Schneiderman, 2005).

A central feature of the post-Laming reforms has been the emphasis upon the new accountabilities for safeguarding children. For the health services this has been a significant development and one that has ensured that safeguarding children is now more clearly prioritized. Consequently, considerable attention has been paid to organizational processes that have been implemented to fulfil legal and statutory responsibilities for safeguarding children. Integral to the introduction of these reforms is the performance management framework which in common with many other areas of public sector provision, shapes or dominates much activity within the NHS (DoH, 2004a). There is a Core Standard (C2) for safeguarding children which all NHS organizations are required to meet. Reflecting the requirements of *Working Together* (HM Government, 2006a) it states:

> Health care organisations protect children by following national child protection guidance within their own activities and in their dealings with other organisations. (DoH, 2004a, p. 28)

Such requirements include having in place 'effective processes . . . for identifying, reporting and taking action on child protection issues' and for working 'with partners to protect children' (DoH, 2004a; HM Government, 2006a). NHS organizations are also required to demonstrate that Criminal Records Bureau checks are conducted for all staff and students with access to children. Safeguarding children is also addressed within the National Service Framework for Children, Young People and Maternity Services (DoH, 2004b; HM Government, 2007), specifically standard 5, which states:

> All agencies work to prevent children suffering harm and to promote their welfare, provide them with the services they require to address their identified needs and safeguard children who are being or who are likely to be harmed. (DoH, 2004b, p. 145)

There are difficulties in judging the impact of new arrangements for safeguarding children, and compliance of the standards provides limited information, particularly as this is largely self-assessed rather than independently judged. Given these limitations, however, a recent inspection report (Ofsted, 2008, p. 21) suggests there have been positive developments in health services with regard to safeguarding children:

> In the NHS, the attention given to safeguarding children is increasing. NHS trusts have worked hard to raise the priority of children's issues. Most trusts (in 2006–07, 377 out of 394 – 95%) comply with the core standard for safeguarding children and young people monitored by the Healthcare Commission.

While evidence of increased senior NHS representation on Local Safeguarding Children Boards compared to Area Child Protection Committees (Ofsted, 2008, p. 13) suggests there has been an executive engagement with new working arrangements heralded by the reforms, less is known about the impact these are having at practice level. In particular, little is known about the cultural shift that is required to embed safeguarding children into everyday health service work.

Any commentary upon the intersection between the safeguarding children agenda and health service involvement must, of course, remain cognisant of the size and scope of health services in this country. The NHS is a large centralized organization, with responsibilities for provision and commissioning of local services clearly lodged with local NHS Trusts and Strategic Health Authorities. The nature of health care delivery is extensive and varied and includes primary, secondary and tertiary service provision. As such, children and their families may have wide-ranging contacts with health services, including, for example, general practitioners, midwives, health visitors, school nurses, child and adolescent mental health services (CAMHS), emergency services, specialist secondary services, sexual health and substance misuse services. The scope of health service provision creates difficulties for understanding and theorizing about the 'health' contribution to safeguarding. This is discussed in the following sections which critically examine notions of 'health' and the 'expansion of the clinical gaze' in the context of the safeguarding children agenda.

# Health concerns

The emphasis within the reforms for accountability, together with the regimes of inspection and grading, suggests it is highly improbable that NHS chief executives remain unaware of their organizational responsibilities in relation to safeguarding children. The discussion above, which has largely focused on procedural and systems issues and the standards-based performance management framework through which this is judged, suggests that the safeguarding children agenda has impacted upon the health services. What has not been addressed is the focus upon children's health and well-being, which is an integral part of the safeguarding children agenda, but which, of course, also represents core work for the NHS.

New Labour has introduced a raft of measures addressing service delivery issues for children, young people and their families. The National Service Framework for Children, Young People and Maternity Services, for instance, provides a standards-based approach and is aimed at all agencies involved with health care provision for children and young people (DoH, 2004b). Safeguarding children is specifically addressed by Standard 5 (see DoH, 2004b). Others address various aspects of care provision, such as medicines, mental health and psychological well-being, children with complex needs and children in hospital (DoH, 2003, 2004c, 2004d, 2004e). There are also various evidence-based guides and protocols, such as the child health promotion programme (DoH, 2008a) which provides a clinical framework for a range of activities concerned with prevention, early identification and health promotion activities. These developments encompass specialist and universal health care provision, are inter-disciplinary, and reflect a government attempt to ensure both quality standards based upon evidence and reducing opportunities for inequity in health service provision for children and young people. These have become the building blocks for health service provision for children and young people, and are central elements of the wider safeguarding children agenda. But beyond this and of key relevance to this discussion is the focus upon improving the overall health of children and young people which has developed within a public health context (Blair et al., 2003).

Concerns about the health of children and young people are certainly not new but reflect a societal concern with the health of the wider population. Just as late nineteenth-century campaigners and governments raised concerns about the poor health of recruits for the Boer War and the high rates of infant mortality associated with poor hygiene and feeding practices (Armstrong, 1986; Lewis, 1980), the recent interest stems from concerns about the health of the population due to a sharp rise in 'lifestyle diseases', such as diabetes and heart disease and rising health care costs due to increased demands. There is arguably a moral panic about the 'lifestyle diseases' facing children and young people, such as childhood obesity, diabetes, sexual health and teenage pregnancy, and mental health (Brooks and Shemmings, 2008), as well as concerns about implications for future adult health (Fawcett *et al.*, 2004; Parton, 2006b; Williams, 2004). There is also pervasive evidence of widening patterns of inequalities in the health of children and young people, which has raised policy alarm bells in the context of concerns about the inter-generational transmission of poor health patterns (Spencer and Law, 2007).

Discourses on child health are themselves socially constructed and influenced by paradigm shifts in thinking about health, children and childhood. The earlier prominence of psychologically and medically informed work, based upon notions of child development and which saw children as incomplete adults (Mayall, 1998), has been disrupted by a considerable body of theoretical work on childhood that views children as social actors (James *et al.*, 1998; Mayall, 2002). While this has informed some studies examining children's views about health and well-being (see for example, Hood, 2007; Mayall *et al.*, 1996; Morrow, 2000), difficulties remain in identifying, measuring and assessing all the elements that children consider important for their health and well-being. Moreover, as Green (2006) has noted, until recently discourses on child health have been located within a sickness, gender neutral medical model that has influenced both policy and everyday practice. Wills *et al.* (2008) provide a critical analysis of the adult-led nature of public health and health promotion agendas which they consider pays little attention to young people's conceptualizations and experiences of health and related behaviours. Drawing upon their own research conducted with young people they suggest that this lack of engagement with children's own perspectives on health has important implications for effectively tackling health priorities, such as obesity (Wills *et al.*, 2008).

A major theme running throughout public health discourses which focus upon children and young people is that of health inequalities. These can be demonstrated across a wide range of 'health-related' issues, including, for example, asthma, accidents, low birth weight infants, infant mortality, obesity and teenage pregnancy (Association of Public Health Observatories, 2007; Blair *et al.*, 2003; Bradshaw, 2002; Bradshaw and Mayhew, 2005; Spencer and Law, 2007). Despite government attempts to tackle them, many health inequalities persist and are in some cases widening (DoH, 2007a). Recognizing the determinants of health, such as income, housing, nutrition and activity, and socially patterned risk and protective factors that impact upon the health of children and young people, provides an important framework for understanding health inequalities (Blair *et al.*, 2003; Graham and Power, 2004; Spencer and Law, 2007). There are also important overlaps between the risks that children and young people may face in relation to their health, such as drug use, sexual activity and traffic accidents, and 'harms' they may need to be protected from within a safeguarding children framework. Moreover, the socially patterned nature of such 'risks' and 'harms' is an important point of synthesis and one which underpins much of government policy which aims to improve outcomes for children and young people (Department for Children, Schools and Families [DCSF], 2008).

## Expanding the clinical gaze?

While the contemporary policy frameworks promoting both children's public health and the safeguarding children agenda are widely considered as 'policy goods' they are also indicative of an expansion of health work. Debates about medical knowledge have been critical about the limited focus of Western medicine, but as health professionals engage with more socially oriented discourses and adopt more holistic understandings of health, this creates further tensions. This suggests a further expansion of the 'clinical gaze', an issue already well rehearsed by Armstrong (1995) who used the term 'surveillance medicine' to illustrate the expansion of medicine into previously private areas of social and family life. This can be illustrated by the ways in which issues such as parenting, and diet and exercise, while existing within a broader public health model, have nonetheless recently involved a high degree of medical engagement. Fitzpatrick (2001, pp. 171–2) has been particularly critical of the expansion of his own profession into areas previously beyond the gaze of medicine:

> The erosion of the boundaries between the public and the private spheres is one of the most ominous trends in modern society, and one in which doctors, with their unique access to the intimate aspects of personal life, play an important role. ... With their recommendations for changes in lifestyle and their invitations to screening, and their guidelines on tackling domestic violence, sexual abuse, defective parenting and numerous other social evils, doctors are at the cutting edge of the drive to extend professional regulation over personal life.

These concerns lie not only with an expanding medicalization of life (Ballard and Elston, 2005; Zola, 1972) but also with the ways that health professionals such as doctors, dentists, nurses and health visitors are involved in the surveillance and regulation of their clients (Bloor and McIntosh, 1990; May, 1992; Nettleton, 1991; Peckover, 2002; Silverman, 1987). Writing critically about public health, Lupton (1995) argues this also operates as a form of social regulation. In this context, we can point to the ways in which for those whose work brings them into contact with children and families the emphasis has been upon monitoring and assessing the quality of parenting, primarily that of mothers.

The safeguarding children agenda has created additional opportunities for health care professionals to enquire, assess and intervene in areas of family and social life that impact upon the health and welfare of children and young people. This can be illustrated by the following requirement that:

> All staff need to ensure, as part of their work with children and families and with adults who are parents or carers who are experiencing personal problems, that the needs of the children are considered and that where necessary they are assessed and appropriate referrals are made. (HM Government, 2007, p. 46)

What is significant here is the ways that the responsibilities for safeguarding children, now constructed as a broader and more elastic concept, implicate a wider and more diverse range of health care professionals who are required to enquire, assess and intervene in order to promote the welfare of children and young people. This expansion of the responsibilities placed upon health care staff coincides with an expansion in the discursive construction of children's risks, needs and vulnerabilities. In the context of health services, this both expands the remit of professional practice, and expands the scope of being concerned about children into areas of provision that previously had no involvement or interest in child welfare. How this is played out in practice is variable but has potentially far reaching consequences. It includes, for example, asking pregnant women about domestic violence (DoH, 2005) and checking the welfare of children when providing care to adults requiring mental health services (Cleaver *et al.*, 2007). Such initiatives take health care professionals into new arenas in which they often require support, training and persuasion to succeed. Indeed, professional reluctance to undertake these new responsibilities has been found in relation to midwives inquiring about domestic violence and NHS Direct nurses asking parents about their coping when they ring because their baby is crying (Mezey *et al.*, 2003; Smith, 2008).

At the same time we have seen an expansion of the specialist knowledge base for safeguarding children with additional requirements for named professionals, usually doctors, nurses or midwives, across all NHS and ambulance trusts, walk-in centres and NHS Direct (DoH, 2004a; HM Government, 2006a, 2007). While such roles are largely concerned with the provision of training and support to health care staff usually within a wider clinical governance remit, they do require specialist expertise in safeguarding children. Unsurprisingly, the expansion of these new roles has been associated with a process of professionalization that can be seen in the development of new job descriptions, skills and competencies aimed at ensuring standardization and conformity to regulation (Polnay and Curnock, 2003; Royal College of Paediatrics and Child Health, 2006). For nursing, in particular, the drive to establish the nurse consultant role provided additional opportunities to develop specialist professional roles in safeguarding children (Coster *et al.*, 2006; DoH, 1999b).

Interestingly, we are also witnessing a change in the way child maltreatment is being discussed within the health care field, with developments drawing upon medically oriented discourses concerned with promoting evidence-based practice. A number of publications have aimed to improve health care practitioners' identification of child maltreatment, especially in cases where there are physical signs or injuries (National Collaborating Centre for Women's and Children's Health, 2008; Royal College of Paediatrics and Child Health, 2006; Welsh Child Protection Systematic Review Group, undated). This includes a series of systematic reviews of the evidence base that informs the diagnosis of bruising, fractures, oral injuries, thermal injuries, human bites and central neurological system injuries (Welsh Child Protection Systematic Review Group, undated), and guidance to improve the ability of health care professionals to recognize child maltreatment (National Collaborating Centre for Women's and Children's Health, 2008). The latter aims to:

> provide a summary of clinical features associated with child maltreatment that may be observed when a child presents to the NHS. When used in routine practice, the guidance should prompt healthcare professionals who are not specialists in child protection to think about the possibility of maltreatment. (National Collaborating Centre for Women's and Children's Health, 2008, p. 14)

Writing about the prevention and early recognition of physical child abuse in babies, specifically non-accidental head injuries, Kemp and Coles (2003) argue that health professionals need to adopt a more proactive approach. This includes, for example, improved diagnostic skills, a lowering of the threshold for consideration of non-accidental head injury, intervention programmes which address the parenting skills of men, particularly those where violence and abuse has been a feature, and primary prevention activities that are multi-factorial and build upon successes of accident prevention programmes.

A contemporary theme within the child maltreatment literature emphasizes the importance of prevention and tackling the underlying causes, 'in other words a public-health approach' (Reading *et al.*, 2008, p. 52). Here, the emphasis is upon establishing the epidemiology of a condition and implementing policies and practice frameworks to ensure assessment, diagnosis, intervention and treatment (Gilbert *et al.*, 2008; Reading *et al.*, 2008; World Health Organization, 2006). While such public health discourses concerned with prevention and early identification are central to modern medicine, they are also reflected in the contemporary safeguarding agenda (Parton, 2006a). For example, the new responsibilities placed upon LSCBs to undertake child death reviews incorporates a public health approach in relation to the requirement to use the aggregated findings from all child deaths, collected according to a nationally agreed data set, to inform local strategic planning on how best to safeguard and promote the welfare of children in their area (DfES, 2006; HM Government, 2006a; Pearson, 2008). Indeed, one of the important overlaps between the two different approaches of safeguarding children and public health is the emphasis upon prevention and early intervention. While these have underpinned much public health work over the decades, they mark a somewhat new departure in the context of child welfare and represent a new direction for state intervention (Parton, 2006a).

It is also worth considering here the increasingly specialized demands placed upon health care professionals within the child protection field, particularly those cases involving court processes or high degrees of complexity. The emphasis upon scientific medical discourses, especially in cases of physical injury or death, requires a highly specific forensic knowledge. Recent high profile cases involving errors in medical opinion have served to shift public distrust of professionals to also include doctors and other health care workers. The legacy of this is currently being displayed with reported shortages of doctors willing to act as experts in child abuse cases, particularly if legal processes are involved (Hall, 2006; Turton and Haines, 2007). This uneasy alliance between medicine and child protection is also apparent in certain complex cases where, for instance, fabricated or induced illness is suspected (DoH, 2002).

Expanding the professional gaze of health care staff who have contact with children and families also requires developments in relation to their knowledge and skills. For health services the issue of training has become increasingly important, not only to fulfil this role effectively, but also in order to meet the requirements of the safeguarding children agenda (DoH, 2004a; HM Government, 2007). For health services, due to their size and complexity, the provision of appropriate child protection training is itself a complex task, and, as Long *et al.* (2006) have argued, requires the development of education and training standards. Baverstock *et al.* (2008), for example, describe the challenges of ensuring staff working in paediatric settings in a district general hospital had received appropriate training on child protection. Following an initial audit, measures introduced included additional investment in specialist posts and the provision of a tiered approach to training that was dependent upon the role and the level of experience of staff. The authors acknowledge the complexities of the issue for a large district general hospital due to the number and diversity of staff involved, and stress the importance of undertaking regular training audits.

The safeguarding children agenda has served to expand the knowledge and practices of health care staff. A related issue here is the difficulty in defining 'health' and, therefore, in establishing the limits of 'health' and 'health work'. The concept of health that can be defined in many ways – from an absence of disease to a more holistic approach encompassing emotional, social, physical, psychological well-being and fulfilment (see Blaxter, 2004; Taylor, 2003) – opens up possibilities for considering many aspects of life within health discourses. Simultaneously, the broader concept of safeguarding which is based upon discourses of 'harm', 'risk' and 'safety' focuses attention upon a wider range of harms facing children than that previously considered within child protection discourses. Therefore, it may not be surprising that a synthesis has developed between notions of 'health' and 'safeguarding', providing new opportunities for constructing hazards and risks facing children and young people in ways that cross the boundaries of both discourses.

## Safeguarding children in health care practice

The above section has focused upon the points of synthesis and tension between the safeguarding children and child public health agendas, suggesting they represent both opportunities for improved health care practice and an expansionary shift in the ways that health services and 'health' itself are constructed in public policy. The chapter now turns away from policy to examine some key elements

of the safeguarding children agenda in health care practice. It focuses upon two different areas of service provision: health visiting and mental health services.

## Health visiting and 'progressive universalism'

Health visitors play a key role in the contemporary safeguarding children agenda. Among the reasons for this is their longstanding involvement in child protection work, their provision of a near universal service to families with very young children, their professional orientation towards public health, and their preventative and early intervention models of working. They may also be particularly well placed because of professional and public uncertainty about the nature of their role as 'mother's friend' (Davies, 1988). This has enabled them to maintain state support and, perhaps to a lesser degree, public support to undertake a supportive, but regulatory, function with families with young children (seeMachen, 1996; Peckover, 2002; Taylor and Tilley, 1989).

One of the key developments within recent policy reforms is the requirement for universal services, such as health visiting, school nursing and midwifery, to provide tailored services that meet the needs of all service users while at the same time ensuring that children and young people with additional needs or risk factors receive extra or specialist services. The process of identifying which children and young people require additional services and what those services should be is a complex task. In policy it has been described as 'progressive universalism' which:

> means that those with high risk and low protective factors receive more intensive support and those with lower levels of need receive a lighter touch appropriate to their needs. (DoH, 2007b, p. 18)

Progressive universalism underpins the Child Health Promotion Programme (DoH, 2008a) which is framed in terms of focusing upon vulnerable children as a means of tackling inequalities that not only relate to children's health, but also to their well-being and achievement (DoH, 2008a, pp. 11–12). While poverty is identified as a key risk factor leading to poorer health outcomes, other risk factors suggest a multi-dimensional approach towards health and safeguarding:

> Children who come from families with multiple risk factors (e.g. mental illness, substance misuse, debt, poor housing and domestic violence) are more likely to experience a range of poor health and social outcomes. These might include developmental and behavioural problems, mental illness, substance misuse, teenage parenthood, low educational attainment and offending behaviour. (DoH, 2008, pp. 11–12)

There can be little doubt that the focus upon such 'risks' makes this a broad agenda, one that encompasses a multi-dimensional approach towards children's health and welfare. It does, however, raise a number of issues, not only in relation to the processes and tools associated with assessment and recognition, but also in terms of how it implicates universal health service providers into activities concerned with surveillance and risk categorization.

Health visitors are crucial to the activities of surveillance and categorization, for it is they who, particularly in the context of the child health promotion programme (DoH, 2008a), will be required to identify risk and protective factors, and to make judgements about the provision of additional services. This puts health visitors in an invidious position, for while they are expected to be 'mother's friend' they also have a central role in identification, surveillance and early intervention. This role involves not only a focus upon health concerns, but also a focus upon a wider set of vulnerabilities that children and young people face. While there is professional resistance to the idea that health visitors are engaged in the surveillance of families (Machen, 1996), it is undoubtedly the case that they are involved in such activities (cf. Abbott and Sapsford, 1990; Dingwall, 1977; Dingwall and Eekelaar, 1988; Dingwall and Robinson, 1993; Peckover, 2002). In such activities the role of the health visitor is important in the delivery of progressive universalism, for it is they who are making judgements about which families should have access to scarce welfare resources in the form of additional support.

Interestingly, there has been little critique or examination of the ways in which the idea of progressive universalism is likely to impact upon universal services, such as the NHS (see Greenway *et al.*, 2008). The process of identifying children and families with additional needs appears to lie in the exercise of good professional judgement supported by limited assessment tools. Appleton and Cowley (2004, 2008; also Appleton, 1994) have written extensively about the professional judgements of health visitors working with vulnerable children, suggesting that a reliance upon assessment tools is problematic. Of course, in the context of the safeguarding children agenda the Common Assessment Framework (CAF) is promoted as the standard tool to be used in order to assess needs and share information with other professionals in order to plan appropriate packages of care to enable children and young people to achieve the desired outcomes (DfES, 2006). Universal health service providers are heavily involved in using the CAF, although its variable implementation and shortcomings as an assessment tool have been identified (Peckover *et al.*, 2008; Pithouse, 2006; White *et al.*, 2008). They suggest that, rather than introducing a standardized approach to assessing needs, the deployment and use of CAF are dependent upon the local institutional and professional contexts in which practitioners operate (White *et al.*, 2008). In addition, the form itself, which is highly structured and domain specific, offers challenges to professionals who are involved in completing and reading it (Pithouse, 2006; White *et al.*, 2008). Nevertheless, the policy of progressive universalism and its tools require health visitors to engage in a complex filtering of cases in order to identify and assess clients with additional needs. In this sense, while progressive universalism is a new way of talking about service delivery, it is, in fact, one of a long line of concepts that have been used to avoid delivering, and undermining the efficacy of, universal welfare benefits and services.

The government commitment and interest in early intervention and prevention which runs throughout recent child welfare reforms has particular salience for groups of professionals, such as health visitors, who work with families with children under the age of five. Here, policy developments focusing upon improving health and social outcomes, including reducing the risk of social exclusion and future offending (HM Government, 2006b), have drawn health visitors into new roles with families.

A further important development is the newly established Family Nurse Partnership pilots (HM Government, 2006b) which provide intensive prenatal and infancy home visiting to 'high risk' families. Studies undertaken in the United States suggest these programmes can lead to improvements in maternal and child health and development, and reductions in child abuse and neglect (Olds *et al.*, 2002). As part of the health visiting narrative this is a particularly interesting development and one which has received little critical attention in the policy or professional world. It may simply reflect another stage in the unfolding history of health visiting in which ambiguity and uncertainty once again serve as a strength (Dingwall, 1977).

## Mental health services

Despite the obvious centrality of 'mental health' to the Every Child Matters reforms, there are shortcomings in both the accessibility and provision of services for children and young people, and in recognizing and addressing the needs of children whose parents are receiving mental health services. A number of government initiatives have attempted to tackle inequalities in the provision of CAMHS, including investment, the introduction of standards, and a strategic framework for planning, commissioning and delivering services based upon a four-tiered approach (DoH, 2004d; DoH, 2008b; Ford, 2008). Not surprisingly, and in line with other areas of policy development emphasis has been upon early intervention, overall health improvement and timely access to services, including those for children and young people with established or complex problems (DoH, 2004d, 2008b).

Despite these initiatives CAMHS service provision remains patchy (DoH, 2008b). While Ford (2008) suggests its development should be based upon epidemiological evidence, there are difficulties in establishing the extent of the problem due to definitional and reporting issues. Estimates suggest that at least 10 per cent of children and young people experience some form of mental distress (Green *et al.*, 2005; Meltzer, 2007). This covers a range of issues including, for example, emotional, conduct or hyperkinetic disorder, autism, eating disorders and dependency upon drugs and alcohol. While there are many reasons why children develop mental health issues some of the key associations include experiencing stressful life events, such as bereavement, family break up or serious disruption to their lives, such as experiencing domestic violence. Children whose mothers have poor mental health are also most commonly associated with emotional disorders. Children and young people particularly at risk of developing mental health problems include those who are more vulnerable such as children living in care, children in the criminal justice system, teenage parents, and those with an identified learning disability (DoH, 2008b, pp. 20–1). Once again, there is an overlap between the risk and protective factors associated with children's mental health, and those associated with safeguarding and social exclusion. Moreover, experiencing a mental disorder may impact upon a child or young person's capacity to engage with everyday life. In turn, this may affect their friendships and social relationships, their learning ability and their ability to cope with stresses and challenges, all of which may contribute to increased vulnerability and exclusion (DoH, 2008b).

Parental mental health, of course, also impacts upon the overall well-being of children and young people. However, difficulties remain in both the accessibility and uptake of services for this client group, and in the ability of adult mental health service providers to recognize and address the health, welfare and safeguarding needs of children and young people (Cleaver *et al.*, 2007; Greene *et al.*, 2008). For example, research undertaken by Kroll (2004) suggests that children living with parents who are substance misusers become invisible to service providers who are focused upon supporting parents. In contrast, Grant *et al.* (2008), in a study of the support needs of young people with care-giving responsibilities for parents with mental health problems, warn of the dangers of viewing them as passive recipients of interventions rather than as active social agents. Additional difficulties in addressing the mental health needs of children and young people arise due to the inherent complexity of service provison. This has traditionally been separated between adult, and child and adolescent services, between primary/community and secondary providers, and between mainstream and specialist services. Recent policy developments have further enhanced the multi-disciplinary nature of mental health service provision, which cuts across and embraces different professional groups, service providers and specialisms (DoH, 2008b). Disputes about how mental health is constructed and understood have contributed to movements concerned with resistance and advocacy for service users, as well as tensions arising from psychiatric, psychological and holistic discourses about mental health and well-being (Coppock and Hopton, 2001). All of this means that children and young people with mental health issues and their parents/carers, may not only receive services from different agencies and professional groups, but also across and between the tiered thresholds (DoH, 2008b). And, yet, despite these complexities mental health and psychological well-being is an essential element of 'health' and important to the current policy reforms, cutting across safeguarding children, social exclusion and children's public health agendas (DCSF, 2007, 2008).

# Summary

Promoting the health, welfare and safety of children and young people lies at the heart of the government's agendas for safeguarding and public health. These have been discussed in this chapter as overlapping, but distinct, areas of policy, practice and research, reflecting their different historical and genealogical roots. While remaining cognizant of the differences there are some important overlaps between the vulnerabilities, risks and protective factors that impact upon the health of children and young people and their need for safeguarding.

The contemporary safeguarding children agenda offers many opportunities and challenges for health services. Conceptualizing this as an expansionary project provides a means for examining more closely some of the tensions raised by this agenda, and the overlaps this has with wider public health concerns. In particular, it focuses attention upon the knowledge and power of health professionals who are charged with operationalizing this agenda in everyday practice. The agenda for safeguarding children also reveals new accountabilities for health services. This moves beyond more established concerns with child protection and legitimizes the health gaze upon broader dimensions of children's lives and well-being. That much of this falls outside the traditional medical model which underpins the work of the NHS becomes an irrelevance due to the inherent elasticity of concepts such as 'health' and 'safeguarding'. Also, policy imperatives emphasize identification and early intervention which draws more universally provided services into the filtering and categorization of families who, only if they coded as deserving enough, will get access to more specialist interventions.

An important theme running throughout the safeguarding children agenda is partnership working and the shifting roles and responsibilities placed upon agencies. This has placed huge demands upon a service such as the NHS, taking it into many new areas of work. Developments such as the CAF and LP, for example, require staff to engage with child welfare issues that may have previously been considered beyond their remit while opportunities to access services from specialist agencies such as social care remain open only to children requiring protection or who are clearly categorized as 'in need' (White et al., 2008).

While there is nothing new about boundary disputes between health and social care (Lewis, 2001), there are important differences arising from the Every Child Matters reforms. Previous major policy reforms, notably the introduction of community care legislation in the 1990s, were marked by a clear shift in responsibility between health and social care. Services providing for older people and those people with disabilities were separated, and often fragmented, and, most importantly, what counted as 'health' work reflected more medically oriented discourses, shifting away from anything that could be constructed as a social rather than a health care issue (Lewis, 2001; Twigg, 1997).

In contrast, the contemporary safeguarding children agenda has expanded the responsibility and accountability of health services towards children and young people. That this has occurred alongside a number of policy reforms that address children's public health and social exclusion is not a coincidence. It provides a framework for practice underpinned by a more elastic and holistic concept of what counts as health and therefore health work. While such developments reflect the emergence of the preventative surveillance state (Parton, 2006a), increased public distrust in child welfare professionals and the deepening economic crisis represent additional challenges for health services in responding to current and future requirements for safeguarding children and young people. At the same time, recent developments in health policy, such as the separation of commissioning and provider services, the Darzi review, and repeated reorganizations have created an increasingly complex environment. The impact of these developments for operationalizing the safeguarding children agenda remains to be seen (DoH, 2008c). Moreover, recent high profile child abuse cases, such as Baby P, has directed organizational and policy attention once again towards matters of child protection, and, although this is currently expressed within contemporary safeguarding children discourses, the future policy and practice implications arising from this remain to be seen.

# References

Abbott, P. and Sapsford, R. (1990) 'Health visiting: Policing the family?', in P. Abbott and C. Wallace, (eds.), *The Sociology of the Caring Professions*, Basingstoke: The Falmer Press.

Appleton, J. (1994) 'The concept of vulnerability in relation to child protection: Health visitors' perceptions', *Journal of Advanced Nursing*, 20 (6): 1132–1140.

Appleton, J. and Cowley, S. (2004) 'The guideline contradiction: Health visitors' use of formal guidelines for identifying and assessing families in need', *International Journal of Nursing Studies*, 4 (7): 785–797.

Appleton, J. and Cowley, S. (2008) 'Health visiting assessment: Unpacking critical attributes in health visitor needs assessment', *International Journal of Nursing Studies*, 45 (2): 232–245.

Armstrong, D. (1986) 'The invention of infant mortality', *Sociology of Health and Illness*, 8 (3): 211–232.

Armstrong, D. (1995) 'The rise of surveillance medicine', *Sociology of Health and Illness*, 17 (3): 393–404.

Association of Public Health Observatories (2007) *Child Health*, York: Yorkshire and Humber Public Health Observatory and the Eastern Region Public Health Observatory.

Ballard, K. and Elston, M. (2005) 'Medicalisation: A multi-dimensional concept', *Social Theory and Health*, 3 (3): 228–241.

Baverstock, A., Bartle, D., Boyd, B. and Finlay, F. (2008) 'Review of child protection training uptake and knowledge of child protection guidelines', *Child Abuse Review*, 17 (1): 64–72. Available at DOI: 10.1002/car.

Blair, M., Stewart-Brown, S., Waterston, T. and Crowther, R. (2003) *Child Public Health*, Oxford: Oxford University Press.

Blaxter, M. (2004) *Health*, Cambridge: Polity Press.

Bloor, M., and McIntosh, J. (1990) 'Surveillance and concealment: A comparison of techniques of client resistance in therapeutic communities and health visiting', in

S. Cunningham-Burley and N. McKegany (eds.), *Readings in Medical Sociology*, London: Tavistock.
Bradshaw, J. (ed.) (2002) *The Well-being of Children in the UK*, London: Save the Children Fund.
Bradshaw, J. and Mayhew, E. (eds.) (2005) *The Well-being of Children in the UK*, London: Save the Children Fund.
Brooks, F. and Shemmings, D. (2008) 'Guest editorial: Health and social care needs of children and young people', *Health and Social Care in the Community*, 16 (3): 219–221. Available at DOI: 10.1111/j.1365-2524.2008.00785.x.
Chief Secretary to the Treasury (2003) *Every Child Matters*, Cm 5860, London: The Stationery Office.
Cleaver, H., Nicholson, D., Tarr, S. and Cleaver, D. (2007) *Child Protection, Domestic Violence and Parental Substance Misuse: Family Experiences and Effective Practice*, London: Jessica Kingsley.
Coppock, V. and Hopton, J. (2001) *Critical Perspectives on Mental Health*, London: Routledge.
Coster, S., Redfern, S., Wilson-Barnett, J., Evans A., Peccei, R., and Guest, D. (2006) 'Impact of the role of nurse, midwife and health visitor consultant', *Journal of Advanced Nursing*, 55 (3): 352–363.
Davies, C. (1988) 'The health visitor as mother's friend: A woman's place in public health 1900–1914', *Social History of Medicine*, 1 (1): 39–60.
DCSF (2007) *The Children's Plan: Building Brighter Futures*, London: DCSF.
DCSF (2008) *Staying Safe: Action Plan*, http://publications.everychildmatters.gov.uk/default.aspx?PageFunction = productdetailsandPageMode = publicationsandProductId=DCSF-00151-2008and (accessed 13 January 2008).
DfES (2006) *Common Assessment Framework for Children and Young People: Practitioners' Guide*, London: DfES.
Dingwall, R. (1977) 'Collectivism, regionalism, and feminism: Health visiting and British social policy 1850–1975', *Journal of Social Policy*, 6 (3): 291–315.
Dingwall, R. and Eekelaar, J. (1988) 'Families and the state: An historical perspective on the public regulation of private conduct', *Law and Policy*, 10 (4): 341–361.
Dingwall, R. and Robinson, K. (1993) 'Policing the family? Health visiting and the public surveillance of private behaviour', in A. Beattie, M. Gott, L. Jones and M. Sidell (eds.), *Health and Well-being: A Reader*, Basingstoke: Macmillan.
DoH (1991) *The Care of Children: Principles and Practice Guidance and Regulations*, London: HMSO.
DoH (1999a) *Working Together to Safeguard Children: A Guide to Inter-agency Working to Safeguard and Promote the Welfare of Children*, London: DoH, Home Office, Department for Education and Employment.
DoH (1999b) *Making a Difference: Strengthening the Nursing, Midwifery and Health Visiting Contribution to Health and Healthcare*, London: DoH.
DoH (2002) *Safeguarding Children in Whom Illness Is Fabricated or Induced*, London: The Stationery Office.
DoH (2003) *Getting the Right Start: National Service Framework for Children, Young People and Maternity Services: Standard for Hospital Services*, London, DoH. Available at: http://www.dh.gov.uk/en/Healthcare/NationalServiceFrameworks/Children/DH_4089111 (accessed 6 January 2009).
DoH (2004a) *National Standards Local Action – Health and Social Care Standards and Planning Framework 2005/06–2007/08*, London: DoH.
DoH (2004b) *National Service Framework for Children, Young People and Maternity Services: Core Standards*, London, DoH. Available at: http://www.dh.gov.uk/en/Healthcare/NationalServiceFrameworks/Children/DH_4089111 (accessed 6 January 2009).

DoH (2004c) *National Service Framework for Children, Young People and Maternity Services: Disabled Children and Young People and those with Complex Health Needs*, London: DoH and DfES. Available at: http://www.dh.gov.uk/en/Healthcare/NationalServiceFrameworks/Children/DH_4089111 (accessed 6 January 2009).

DoH (2004d) *National Service Framework for Children, Young People and Maternity Services: The Mental Health and Psychological Well-being of Children and Young People*, London: DoH and DfES. Available at: http://www.dh.gov.uk/en/Healthcare/NationalServiceFrameworks/Children/DH_4089111 (accessed 6 January 2009).

DoH (2004e) *National Service Framework for Children, Young People and Maternity Services: Medicines for Children and Young People*, London: DoH and DfES. Available at: http://www.dh.gov.uk/en/Healthcare/NationalServiceFrameworks/Children/DH_4089111 (accessed 6 January 2009).

DoH (2005) *Responding to Domestic Abuse: A Handbook for Health Professionals*, London: The Stationery Office.

DoH (2007a) *Implementation Plan for Reducing Health Inequalities in Infant Mortality: A Good Practice Guide*, London: Health Inequalities Unit. Available at: http://www.dh.gov.uk/en/Publicationsandstatistics/Publications/PublicationsPolicyAndGuidance/DH_081337 (accessed 13 January 2009).

DoH (2007b) *The Government Response to Facing the Future: A Review of the Role of Health Visitors*, London: DoH. Available at: http://www.dh.gov.uk/en/Publicationsandstatistics/Publications/PublicationsPolicyAndGuidance/DH_080007 (accessed 27 November 2008).

DoH (2008a) *The Child Health Promotion Programme: Pregnancy and the First Five Years of Life*, London: DoH and DCSF. Available at: http://www.dh.gov.uk/en/Publicationsandstatistics/Publications/DH_083645 (accessed 27 November 2008).

DoH (2008b) *Children and Young People in Mind: The Final Report of the National CAMHS Review*, London: CAMHS Review, supported by the DoH and the DCSF.

DoH (2008c) *High Quality for All*, London: DoH.

Fawcett, B., Featherstone, B. and Goddard, J. (2004) *Contemporary Child Care Policy and Practice*, Basingstoke: Palgrave.

Fitzpatrick, M. (2001) *The Tyranny of Health: Doctors and the Regulation of Lifestyle*, London: Routledge.

Ford, T. (2008) 'How can epidemiology help us plan and deliver effective child and adolescent mental health services?', *Journal of Child Psychology and Psychiatry*, 49 (9): 900–914.

Frost, N. and Robinson, M. (2007) 'Joining up children's services: Safeguarding children in multi-disciplinary teams', *Child Abuse Review*, 16: 184–199.

Gilbert, G., Widom, C., Browne, K., Fergusson, D., Webb, E. and Janson, S. (2008) 'Burden and consequences of child maltreatment in high-income countries', *The Lancet*. Available at DOI: 10.1016/S0140-6736(08)61706-7.

Graham, H. and Power, C. (2004) 'Childhood disadvantage and health inequalities: A framework for policy based on lifecourse research', *Child: Care, Health and Development*, 30 (6): 671–678.

Grant, G., Repper, J. and Nolan, M. (2008) 'Young people supporting parents with mental health problems: Experiences of assessment and support', *Health and Social Care in the Community*, 16 (3): 271–281.

Green, H., McGinnity, A., Meltzer, H., Ford, T., and Goodman, R. (2005) *Mental Health of Children and Young People in Great Britain, 2004*, Basingstoke: Palgrave Macmillan.

Green, L. (2006) 'An unhealthy neglect? Examining the relationship between child health and gender in research and policy', *Critical Social Policy*, 26 (2): 450–466.

Greene, R., Pugh, R. and Roberts, D. (2008) *Black and Minority Ethnic Parents with Mental Health Problems and their Children*, Research Briefing 29, London: Social Care Institute for Excellence. Available at: http://www.scie.org.uk/publications/briefings/briefing29/index.asp (accessed 15 January 2009).

Greenway, J., Dieppe, P., Entwistle, V. and Meulen, R. (2008), '"Facing the future": The government's real agenda for health visitors', *Community Practitioner*, 81 (11): 29–32.

Hall, D. (2006) 'The future of child protection', *Journal of the Royal Society of Medicine*, 99 (1): 6–9.

HM Government (2006a) *Working Together to Safeguard Children: A Guide to Inter-agency Working to Safeguard and Promote the Welfare of Children*, London: The Stationery Office.

HM Government (2006b) *Reaching Out: An Action Plan on Social Exclusion*, London: The Cabinet Office.

HM Government (2007) *Statutory Guidance on Making Arrangements to Safeguard and Promote the Welfare of Children under Section 11 of the Children Act 2004*, London: The Stationery Office.

Hood, S. (2007) 'Reporting on children's well-being: The state of London's children reports', *Social Indicators Research*, 80 (1): 249–264.

James, A., Jenks, C. and Prout, A. (1998) *Theorising Childhood*, Oxford: Polity Press.

Kemp, A. and Coles, L. (2003), 'The role of health professionals in preventing non-accidental head injury', *Child Abuse Review*, 12 (6): 374–383.

Kroll, B. (2004) 'Living with an elephant: Growing up with parental substance misuse', *Child and Family Social Work*, 9 (2): 129–140.

Lewis, J. (1980) 'The social history of social policy: Infant welfare in Edwardian England', *Journal of Social Policy*, 9 (4): 463–486.

Lewis, J. (2001) 'Older people and the health–social care boundary in the UK: Half a century of hidden policy conflict', *Social Policy and Administration*, 35 (4): 343–359.

Long, T., Davis, C., Johnson, M., Murphy, M., Race, D. and Shardlow, S. (2006) 'Standards for education and training for interagency working in child protection in the UK: Implications for nurses, midwives and health visitors', *Nurse Education Today*, 26 (1): 11–22.

Lupton, D. (1995) *The Imperative of Health. Public Health and the Regulated Body*, London: Sage.

Lupton, C., North, N. and Khan, P. (2001) *Working Together or Pulling Apart? The National Health Service and Child Protection Networks*, Bristol: Policy Press.

Machen, I. (1996) 'The relevance of health visiting to contemporary mothers', *Journal of Advanced Nursing*, 24 (2): 350–356.

May, C. (1992) 'Nursing work, nursing knowledge, and the subjectification of the patient', *Sociology of Health and Illness*, 14 (4): 472–487.

Mayall, B. (1998) 'Towards a sociology of child health', *Sociology of Health and Illness*, 20 (3): 269–288.

Mayall, B. (2002) *Towards a Sociology of Childhood: Thinking from Children's Lives*, Buckingham: Open University Press.

Mayall, B., Bendelow, G., Barker, S., Storey, P. and Veltman, M. (1996) *Children's Health in Primary Schools*, London: Falmer Press.

Meltzer, H. (2007) 'Childhood mental disorders in Great Britain: An epidemiological perspective', *Child Care in Practice*, 13 (4): 13–326.

Mezey, G., Bacchus, L., Haworth, A. and Bewley, S. (2003) 'Midwives' perceptions and experiences of routine enquiry for domestic violence', *BJOG: An International Journal of Obstetrics and Gynaecology*, 110: 744–752.

Morrow, V. (2000) '"Dirty looks" and "trampy places" in young people's accounts of community and neighbourhood: implications for health inequalities', *Critical Public Health*, 10 (2): 141–152.

National Collaborating Centre for Women's and Children's Health (2008) *When to Suspect Child Maltreatment: First Draft for Consultation*, London: National Collaborating Centre for Women's and Children's Health. Available at: http://www.nice.org.uk/guidance/index.jsp?action=downloadando=42749 (accessed 29 January 2008).

Nettleton, S. (1991) 'Wisdom, diligence and teeth: discursive practices and the creation of mothers', *Sociology of Health and Illness*, 13 (11): 98–111.

Ofsted (2008) *Safeguarding Children: The Third Joint Chief Inspectors' Report on Arrangements to Safeguard Children*, London: Ofsted. Available at: www.safeguardingchildren.org.uk (accessed 19 January 2008).

Olds, D., Henderson, C. and Eckenrode, J. (2002) 'Preventing child abuse and neglect with prenatal and infancy home visiting by nurses', in K. Browne, H. Hanks, P. Stratton, and C. Hamilton. (eds.), *Early Prediction and Prevention of Child Abuse*, Chichester: Wiley, pp. 165–183.

Parton, N. (1985) *The Politics of Child Abuse*, Basingstoke: Macmillan.

Parton, N. (2006a) '"Every Child Matters": The shift to prevention whilst strengthening protection in children's services in England', *Children and Youth Services Review*, 28 (8): 976–992.

Parton, N. (2006b) *Safeguarding Childhood: Early Intervention and Surveillance in a Late Modern Society*, Basingstoke: Palgrave Macmillan.

Pearson, G. (ed.) (2008) *Why Children Die: A Pilot Study 2006*, London: Confidential Enquiry into Maternal and Child Health. Available at http://www.cemach.org.uk/getdoc/cc3d51cc-5043-4132-99b7-af5219276dce/Child-Death-Review.aspx (accessed 5 January 2009).

Peckover, S. (2002) 'Supporting and policing mothers: An analysis of the disciplinary practices of health visiting', *Journal of Advanced Nursing*, 38 (4): 369–377.

Peckover, S., Hall, C. and White, S. (2008) 'From policy to practice: Implementation and negotiation of technologies in everyday child welfare', *Children and Society*, 23 (2): 136–148.

Pithouse, A. (2006) 'A common assessment for children in need? Mixed messages from a pilot study in Wales', *Child Care in Practice*, 12 (3): 199–217.

Polnay, J. and Curnock, D. (2003) 'What's in a name? Named doctors in child protection – interpretation and implementation of the role', *Child Abuse Review*, 12 (5): 335–346.

Reading, R., Bissell, S., Goldhagen, J., Harwin, J., Masson, J., Moynihan, S., Parton, N., Santos Pais, M., Thoburn, J. and Webb, E. (2008) 'Promotion of children's rights and prevention of child maltreatment', *The Lancet*. Available at DOI:10.1016/S0140-6736(08)61709-2.

Royal College of Paediatrics and Child Health (2006) *Safeguarding Children and Young People: Roles and Competences for Health Care Staff*, Intercollegiate Document, London: Royal College of Paediatrics and Child Health. Available at: http://www.rcpch.ac.uk/Policy/Child-Protection/Child-Protection-Publications (accessed 2 January 2009).

Royal College of Paediatrics and Child Health (2008) *The Physical Signs of Child Sexual Abuse: An Evidence-based Review and Guidance for Best Practice*, London: Royal College of Paediatrics and Child Health.

Schneiderman, J. (2005) 'The Child Welfare System: Through the Eyes of Public Health Nurses', *Public Health Nursing*, 22 (4): 354–359.

Silverman, D. (1987) *Communication and Medical Practice*, London: Sage.

Smith, S. (2008) 'Is there something wrong? NHS Direct nurse practice in helping parents cope with crying babies', Unpublished PhD thesis, Huddersfield: University of Huddersfield.

Spencer, N. and Law, C. (2007) 'Inequalities in pregnancy and early years and the impact across the life course: progress and future challenges', in E. Dowler and N. Spencer (eds.), *Challenging Health Inequalities: From Acheson to 'Choosing Health'*, Bristol: Policy Press.

Taylor, S. (2003) 'Approaches to health, illness and health care', in S. Taylor and D. Field (eds.), *Sociology of Health and Health Care*, Oxford: Blackwell.

Taylor, S. and Tilley, N. (1989) 'Health visitors and child protection: Conflict, contradictions and ethical dilemmas', *Health Visitor*, 62 (9): 273–275.

Turton, J. and Haines, L. (2007) *An Investigation into the Nature and Impact of Complaints Made against Paediatricians Involved in Child Protection Procedures*, London: Royal College of Paediatrics and Child Health. Available at: www.rcpch.ac.uk (accessed 6 January 2009).

Twigg, J. (1997) 'Deconstructing the "social bath": Help with bathing at home for older and disabled people', *Journal of Social Policy*, 26 (2): 211–232.

Welsh Child Protection Systematic Review Group (undated) *A series of systematic reviews defining the evidence base behind the diagnosis of physical child abuse*, Wales: University of Cardiff. Available at: http://www.core-info.cf.ac.uk/index.html (accessed 2 January 2009).

White, S., Hall, C. and Peckover, S. (2008) 'The descriptive tyranny of the common assessment framework: Technologies of categorization and professional practice in child welfare', *British Journal of Social Work*. Advance access at DOI:10.1093/bjsw/bcn053.

Whiting, M., Scammell, A. and Bifulco, A. (2008) 'The Health Specialist Initiative: Professionals' views of a partnership initiative between health and social care for child safeguarding', *Qualitative Social Work*, 7 (1): 99–117.

Williams, F. (2004) 'What matters is who works: Why every child matters to New Labour. Commentary on the DfES Green Paper *Every Child Matters*', *Critical Social Policy*, 24 (3): 406–427.

Wills, W., Appleton, J., Magnusson, J. and Brooks, F. (2008) 'Exploring the limitations of an adult-led agenda for understanding the health behaviours of young people', *Health and Social Care in the Community*, 16 (3): 244–252.

World Health Organization (2006) *Preventing Child Maltreatment: A Guide to Taking Action and Generating Evidence*, Geneva: World Health Organization and International Society for Prevention of Child Abuse and Neglect.

Zola, I. (1972) 'Medicine as an institution of social control', *The Sociological Review*, 20 (4): 487–504.

# 10

# 'Be Healthy': Drugs, Alcohol and Safeguarding Children

Ian Paylor

## Introduction

There should be little doubt that the concerns about the consumption of illegal and legal drugs by children and young people are central to the safeguarding children agenda. So, all of the five Every Child Matters (ECM) outcomes – being healthy, staying safe, enjoying and achieving, making a positive contribution and economic well-being (Chief Secretary to the Treasury, 2003) – are impacted upon through the consumption of drugs, whether they are prescribed as being illegal (for instance, those covered by the Misuse of Drugs Act 1971) or legal (for example, alcohol), particularly if that drug use is deemed to be problematic. The evidence may not be clear cut. However, the arguments are compelling that problematic use of drugs and alcohol by children and young people not only presents short-term dangers to their health and well-being, but that these dangers may well have long-term implications that may prevent children and young people successfully achieving their full potential, not least from the government's perspective with regard to fulfilling their role of 'citizen-worker of the future' (Lister, 2003, p. 427).

This chapter explores the ways in which the consumption of legal and illegal drugs impacts upon issues of safeguarding by examining three issues. First, the chapter focuses upon the prevalence of the consumption of legal and illegal drugs among children and young people, and the risks that the consumption of such drugs exposes them to. Second, the chapter focuses upon recent policy initiatives that are aimed at addressing the consumption of legal and illegal drugs that range from more universally based interventions, such as drugs education, to more specialist services for those deemed to have drug use that is problematic enough to meet the threshold of treatment. Third, the chapter focuses upon the more problematic aspects of policies aimed at addressing the use of legal and illegal drugs among children and young people. Here the focus is upon the ways

*Critical Perspectives on Safeguarding Children*   Edited by Karen Broadhurst, Chris Grover and Janet Jamieson
© 2009 John Wiley & Sons, Ltd

in which the location of young people's consumption within crime and 'law and order' discourses creates tensions for safeguarding which is more concerned with the well-being of children and young people. In addition, the focus is on the ways in which policies related to problematic drug use tend to decontextualize it from its economic and social antecedents.

## The prevalence and harms of drug and alcohol use

A recent UNICEF (2007) report records that out of 21 countries, the UK is at the bottom of the league table for child well-being and that children in the UK have the highest incidence of risk-taking behaviour. In particular, the report suggests that British teenagers are among the heaviest drinkers in Europe and that they are the third highest users of cannabis. The findings from UNICEF are concerning, given that survey evidence from 8,200 school pupils in 288 schools throughout England in 2006 reveals a decline in the proportion of 11- to 15-year-olds reporting the use of drugs or alcohol in recent years (Fuller, 2007; see also Department for Children, Schools and Families [DCSF] *et al.*, 2008; Hoare and Flatley, 2008). With specific regard to drug use the survey found that 35 per cent of respondents reported ever having been offered drugs with 24 per cent of all pupils ever having taken drugs (Hills and Li, 2007, pp. 123–5). Most pupils do not take drugs frequently, with 17 per cent reporting using drugs during the last year; 10 per cent in the last month and 5 per cent reporting that they usually take drugs at least once a month, although the survey evidence also suggests that the prevalence of use increases with age. The young people were more likely to have taken cannabis in the last year than any other drug (10 per cent) followed by sniffing glue, gas, aerosols or solvents (5 per cent) and sniffing poppers (4 per cent). However, the use of other types of drugs by this age group was rare, with 4 per cent of pupils reporting having taken a Class A drug in the past year (*ibid.*). These findings resonate with those of the British, Scottish and Northern Ireland Crime Surveys which not only reveal that cannabis is by far the most commonly used drug, but also that more 16- to 24-year-olds report drug use in the last month and year than people in all other age groups (Hoare and Flatley, 2008; McMullan and Ruddy, 2006; McVie *et al.*, 2004).

Notwithstanding the ECM agenda's predominant focus upon reducing illicit drug use among young people, it would appear that the more pressing concern with regard to young people is that of alcohol consumption. Alcohol appears to be the 'drug' of choice for young people in the UK with the initiation of alcohol consumption typically occurring during adolescence (Bates *et al.*, 2007). By the age of 15 years many school children are drinking in excess of the recommended weekly and daily limits. According to a recent survey of 7,831 11- to 15-year-old school pupils in 273 schools throughout England, one in five pupils (20 per cent) reported having been drunk in the last 4 weeks (Bates *et al.*, 2007).

Indeed, drinking to intoxication appears to be a key feature of the drinking habits of young people in the UK with around a third (35 per cent) of the pupils who had drunk any alcohol in the last four weeks reporting that they had deliberately tried to get drunk. Young people's penchant for intoxication within the UK has been confirmed in consecutive European School Survey Project on Alcohol and Other Drugs (ESPAD) reports (Hibell *et al.*, 1997, 2000, 2004). For example, in comparing alcohol and drug use among 15- to 16-year-old students in 35 European countries, the ESPAD demonstrates that the UK has higher rates of regular drinking and drunkenness among 15-year-olds compared to most European countries (Hibell *et al.*, 2004).

It is important to note that for most young people the consumption of drugs and/or alcohol is simply not a problem (see Drugscope and Alcohol Concern, 2006). In many instances consumption of drugs and/or alcohol does not interfere with other aspects of the young person's life, rather their use is quite simply 'a rational lifestyle choice' (Muncie, 2004, p. 38). However, young people's drug and alcohol use is more often than not closely associated with diminished outcomes in terms of their health and well-being (DCSF *et al.*, 2008; Department for Education and Skills [DfES], 2005a; Matthews *et al.*, 2006; McIntosh *et al.*, 2006). With regard to the use of illicit drugs the government's 'Drug Harm Index' (DHI) reveals concerns related to drug-related deaths, overdoses, and mental health and behavioural problems, with additional health risks highlighted with regard to intravenous drug use in the form of HIV, Hepatitis B and Hepatitis (MacDonald *et al.*, 2005). Use of substances is also associated with youth crime, truancy and exclusion from school (DfES, 2004a). Likewise, in a synthesis of evidence with regard to young people's drinking Alcohol Concern (2004) reports that the effects of young people's drinking range from the unpleasant to the more serious. The unpleasant effects include hangovers and headaches and the more serious include absence from, and problems in, school, school exclusion and suspension, the engagement in various risk behaviours, including unsafe sex, crime and 'anti-social' behaviour, and, for a minority, the need for emergency medical attention to address severe intoxication and the accidents and injuries which occur as a consequence (Alcohol Concern, 2004). Moreover, increasing privatization of public space (Garland, 2001) and the regulation and criminalization of young people's 'anti-social' behaviour (Burney, 2005; Squires, 2008; Squires and Stephen, 2005) has served to push young drinkers into more isolated, dangerous spaces (Measham, 2008) which, in turn, increases the potential for personal harm should something go wrong (McIntosh *et al.*, 2008).

According to the ECM literature, the young people perceived at greatest risk of using drugs include children of problem drug users, persistent truants and school excludees, looked after children, young people in contact with the criminal justice system, homeless young people, young people abused through prostitution, teenage mothers and young people not in education, employment and training (DfES, 2005a, pp. 7–8). The risk factors associated with problem drinking among young people include poor parental supervision and discipline, truancy, living in a disadvantaged neighbourhood and early involvement in problem behaviour (Beinart *et al.*, 2002). The fact that the children and young people most 'at risk' of taking illicit drugs and engaging in problem drinking are those belonging to the most vulnerable, socially excluded groups in our society poses immense challenges with regard to promoting and safeguarding their well-being. This situation is exacerbated by estimates that between 200,000 and 300,000 children in England and Wales have one or more parents who misuse substances (Huxley and Foulger, 2008). While the relationship between parental substance misuse and neglectful parenting is complex, it is clear that parental intoxication (from either drugs or alcohol) not only presents acute risks in terms of incapacity to supervise and guard from hazardous situations, but also increases the risk of neglect, physical and emotional abuse and, to a lesser extent, sexual abuse (*ibid.*).

Official recognition that drug and alcohol use is prevalent among children and young people and that it is linked to poor outcomes in terms of their successful transition to adulthood has become a matter of growing concern across the health and social care spectrum, including criminal justice. Attention will now turn to how successive New Labour governments have sought to address this issue.

## Tackling drug and alcohol use among young people

Shortly after their election in 1997 New Labour issued *Tackling Drugs to Build a Better Britain* (Home Office, 1998), a 10-year strategy for tackling 'drug misuse' which focused on helping young people to resist drug misuse; protecting communities from the adverse consequences of drug-related behaviour; enabling those with drug problems to overcome them, and stifling the availability of illegal drugs, especially for 5- to 16-year-olds. This strategy was updated in 2002 to focus on reducing the harm caused by illegal drug use and, in particular, to reduce the use of Class A drugs and the frequent use of illicit drugs by all young people under 25 years, especially the most vulnerable groups of children and young people. It is of interest to note that the strategy focuses solely on illicit drugs – indeed, it was not until 2004 that an 'Alcohol Harm Reduction Strategy for England' was published (Cabinet Office Strategy Unit, 2004). Notwithstanding the government's aspirations towards addressing social exclusion and community-orientated drugs prevention and to improving drug-related education and treatment via its drugs strategy, it is clear that New Labour, like its Conservative predecessors, had chosen to retain law enforcement and crime reduction as central features within its approach to tackling drug use (South, 2007). Essentially, political will favours a punitive stance on drug issues (Parker *et al.*, 2001), and New Labour from the outset of its administration has primarily considered drug use as a matter of crime control (Crow, 2007). Thus, it is within a context in which drug (and alcohol) use is closely allied to a crime control discourse that the ECM change for children programme must be considered.

At first glance there appears a lot of positive safeguarding potential within the ECM programme with respect to children's and young people's use of substances, particularly since it aims to 'enhance the prevention of substance misuse ... as part of a holistic multi-agency outcomes-focused approach' (DfES, 2005a, p. 1). Indeed, in reading across the ECM policy series and related documents, it is possible to identify the following key strands to New Labour's approach in relation to drug use:

(1) Robust education and public awareness campaigns, delivered through schools and various media, namely *Blue Print* (Stead *et al.*, 2007) and *FRANK* (www.talktofrank.com)
(2) Earlier identification of children and young people using substances or who are deemed vulnerable to substance use, through the Common Assessment Framework (CAF) and the screening of individual children and young people involved in the criminal justice system.
(3) Increased investment in constructive activities and the creation of safe leisure spaces, as outlined in *Youth Matters* (DfES, 2005b).
(4) Greater integration of substance use issues within mainstream services and better coordination of relevant services to meet local and individual need, with Children's Trusts playing a key role.
(5) A personalized or tailored approach to meet the needs of those requiring more intensive or specialist help.
(6) Greater enforcement powers to tackle links between substance use, 'antisocial' behaviour and crime.

Since the launch of the ECM agenda in 2003, there has been a radical 'joining-up' of children's services, now underpinned by the legislative framework of the Children Act 2004 and founded on a vision of an *integrated* approach to service delivery (see chapter 2). Thus the Directors of Children's Services will be taking the local lead on action to reduce children's and young people's use of substances (DfES, 2005a; HM Government, 2008), with the Children's Trusts taking the lead role in delivering services for young substance users (National Treatment Agency, 2008). The priority placed on joined-up or partnership working is based on an increasing consensus that the problems faced by children and young people, who come to the attention of professional agencies, are multi-faceted (McArdle and Gilvarry, 2006; Vimpani, 2005). For example, with specific regard to young people's use of substances Vimpani (2005, p. 111) observes 'the pathways ... involve a complex interplay (against a background of developmental maturation) between individual biological and psychological vulnerability, familial factors and broader societal influences'. Thus, at a rhetorical level an integrated approach can be seen as a positive development for children with problems of substance use, given that the weight of research evidence indicates that it generally co-exists with other difficulties that are social, economic, health, educational or welfare related (McArdle and Gilvarry, 2006; Newburn and Shiner, 2001; Vimpani, 2005).

Moreover, the provision of preventative services for children and young people is also a generally welcome feature of the ECM programme for change agenda with regard to substance use, not least because of the universal nature of much of this provision. For example, a national FRANK website and helpline has been made available to provide accessible advice and information on drugs and services to children and families. All schools (primary, secondary, special schools and pupil referral units) should now have a drug education programme – addressing alcohol, tobacco, illicit drugs, medicines and volatile substances – which is appropriate to the age, maturity and ability of its pupils (DfES, 2004b; Home Office, 2005). Schools have also been tasked to ensure that pupils vulnerable to using drugs are identified and receive appropriate support either from within the school or through referral to other services (DfES, 2004b). Moreover, the Blueprint programme combining school-based education with parental involvement, media campaigns, local health initiatives and community partnerships has been delivered in 23 areas for the purpose of examining the effectiveness of a multi-component approach to drug education (Stead *et al.*, 2007). This 'mainstreaming' of substance use services is also evident in the new (2008–18) drug strategy, *Drugs: Protecting Families and Communities* (HM Government, 2008) which recognizes that earlier drug strategies had focused too much attention on the individual drug user rather than on the family and other environmental factors, such as income, housing, community, education and health. Thus, families are now the key focus and all relevant agencies are supposed to actively work with families to prevent drug use, reduce risk and promote treatment.

These universal preventative measures are to be accompanied by a range of more targeted approaches. For example, targeted youth services will be employed to divert children and young people from substance use through the use of constructive pro-social and diversionary activities (DfES, 2005a; HM Government, 2008). While vulnerable children and young people considered to be at particular risk of using substances, including children of 'problem drug users', 'persistent truants'; school excludees, looked after children and children in contact with the criminal justice, will be subject to early assessment in relation to substance use and targeted preventative strategies (DfES, 2005a; HM Government, 2008; Home Office, 2005). Treatment will also be closely targeted and, in particular, priority will be given to offenders, that is, those children and young people who are causing 'most harm to communities and families' (HM Government, 2008, p. 5). The overall aim is to increase the participation of young problem drug users in treatment programmes (DfES, 2005a).

A more punitive edge to addressing substance use is apparent from the Home Secretary's assertion in the foreword to the 2008 Drug Strategy that 'illegal drugs ruin lives and damage communities' (HM Government, 2008, p. 3). The punitive position of the government is reflected in the law, as demonstrated in the provisions of the Drugs Act 2005 which allows for compulsory drug testing of offenders when arrested; provides for intervention orders to be attached to Anti-Social Behaviour Orders; requires drug counselling, and allows presumption of intent to supply in cases of possession of a certain quantity of controlled drugs (South, 2007). Such actions raise difficult ethical issues and are also of dubious effectiveness (Gerada, 2005). With specific regard to children and young people, the Drug Interventions Programme (previously the Criminal Justice Interventions Programme) was launched in 2003 to pilot: arrest referral schemes for children and young people (10- to 17-year-olds) and on-charge drug testing of 14- to 17-year-olds in ten areas and – limited to only five areas – the piloting of the attachment of Drug Treatment and Testing Requirements to Action Plan Orders and Supervision Orders. On the basis of an evaluation of this pilot a wider rolling out of arrest referral has been recommended (Matrix Research and Consultancy and Institute for Criminal Policy Research, 2007). Additionally, all young people involved in the youth justice system who we have seen are considered a high risk group for substance use problems, will be screened through the assessment tool ASSET.

Children's and young people's use of alcohol has also come under increasing policy focus as a discrete category of substance misuse, requiring specific intervention and forms the subject of the recent Youth Alcohol Action Plan (YAAP) (DCSF *et al.*, 2008). The YAAP pays particular attention to unsupervised drinking by young people in public places and promises tough action to stop those who participate in what is deemed to be socially irresponsible behaviour and those who supply their alcohol. The YAAP offers a 'tiered' approach to the issue of underage public drinking offering increased powers with regard to under-18s who are drinking and behaving 'anti-socially', and the extension of 'Directions to Leave' powers to 10- to 15-year-olds (these currently apply to those aged 16 and over). Repeat instances of public drinking linked to 'anti-social' behaviour will elicit the use of Acceptable Behaviour Contracts, the wider use of Parenting Contracts and the extension of Arrest Referral Pilots. In the most serious cases the YAAP proposes maximizing the use of confiscation powers, resort to Anti-social Behaviour Orders and the creation of a specific offence for under-18s of persistently possessing alcohol in public places.

The YAAP also prioritizes partnership between parents, industry, criminal justice and law enforcement agencies. In particular, it contains a range of proposals focused on influencing parental attitudes and behaviour. These proposals range from those of establishing a new partnership with parents related to teenage drinking, including consultation and the offer of practical advice for parents on young people and alcohol, to utilizing formal interventions in the form of parenting contracts and orders in those instances where parents are judged not to be taking their responsibilities seriously (see chapter 7 for a discussion of the limitations of such approaches to 'good parenting'). Perhaps most significantly with regard to the safeguarding children agenda, the YAAP reveals government priorities with regard to early and intensive intervention in those families where parents and/or children have problematic drug use via Parenting Early Intervention Projects and the extension of Family Intervention Projects. In effect, not only do criminal justice responses pertain to the children whose alcohol use is deemed problematic but also to those parents and families who are adjudged to have failed these children and to have proved uncooperative with state authorities.

## Drugs, alcohol and safeguarding: a critique

In the previous section I examined the policy frameworks that structure the licit and illicit drug use of children and young people. It is clear that collaborative working, particularly through Children's Trust, is deemed to be *the* means through which services for young drug users is to be delivered. However, it has recently been argued that:

> there is little evidence that children's trusts, as required by the government, have improved outcomes for children and young people or delivered better value for money, over and above locally agreed cooperation. (Audit Commission, 2008, p. 4)

While the financial focus of the Audit Commission is useful,[1] it is nonetheless narrow and may not have captured the full picture of the Children's Trust. However, it is clear from more general research on collaborative working that it is often structured through a number of problems, including communication and hierarchy issues problems, poor understanding of roles and responsibilities and mistrust among professionals in sharing information (Horwath and Morrison, 2007). In this context, it difficult to see how the interests of children will be negotiated through partnerships that while engaging statutory and non-statutory bodies are more likely to be influenced by some of the former, most notably, primary care trusts, schools and the police, rather than the latter (Audit Commission, 2008).

It is also apparent from the preceding discussions that New Labour's idea of progressive universalism (see chapter 9 in this volume) helps to structure provision concerned with the 'Be Healthy' aim of *Every Child Matters*. Hence, there is provision of some services for all children and young people (for instance, FRANK and Blueprint) and the provision of more focused and specialist services (such as treatment services) for those children and young people deemed to be in the greatest need of intervention because of their alcohol and/or illegal drug consumption. While such a structure for intervention is portrayed as being benevolent, its premise upon early intervention that inevitably includes the identification of those deemed to be in, or at risk of being in need, of more

---

[1]   The Audit Commission (2008), for instance, demonstrates how there is little evidence of the pooling of financial resources through Children's Trust beyond collaborative working that pre-dated their introduction.

specialized interventions means that it is actually quite problematic, most notably because the study of risk factors is unable with any great accuracy to identify the offenders, or in our case, the drug users of the future (Goldson, 2005, see also chapter 11 in this volume).

While these two criticisms around collaborative working and progressive universalism are important, it appears that there may be more fundamental problems with New Labour's attempts to tackle the alcohol and drug use of children and young people. I shall focus upon two of these: the location of alcohol and drug use in crime discourses and the neglect of structural factors in explaining the alcohol and drug use of children and young people. In the case of the latter, the focus is upon drug use.

## Criminal justice discourse and interventions

There is a tension at the heart of policies designed to address drug and alcohol use among children and young people. While the safeguarding agenda is concerned with the well-being of such people, the discourse that constructs the use of drugs and alcohol among them is predominantly criminal justice focused. In the case of illegal drugs, for instance, the title of the most recent drugs strategy, *Drugs: Protecting Families and Communities* (HM Government, 2008) neatly demonstrates that it is illegal drugs, and by implication, illegal drug users, that are considered to be the threat, something that is made even more explicit in the detail of the report. Furthermore, while it is possible to argue that there is more ambiguity with regard to the construction of alcohol use by children and young people[2] than there is in their illicit drug use, it is the case that for children and young people, alcohol only appears as a social issue when it is defined as a 'law and order' problem. Hence, while the YAAP notes concerns with the health-related effects of 'unacceptable' alcohol use among young people, its main concern is with the risks that drunk children and young people pose in terms of crime and 'anti-social' behaviour. This means its ideas for tackling it are predominantly criminal justice related, for example, the extension of Directions to Leave powers to 10- to 15-year-olds 'so that police officers can effectively deal with *any* young person who is drinking in public places' (DCSF, 2008, para. 45) and the use of Acceptable Behaviour Contracts and Parenting Contracts.

Approaches that focus upon illegal drug and alcohol use among young people as a criminal justice issue have several implications for the safeguarding agenda. First, as we have noted, rather than seeing drug and alcohol use as a social welfare issue that has economic and social antecedents and, therefore, requires the

---

[2]   This is reflected in the Youth Alcohol Action Plan (DCSF, 2008, para. 4, emphasis added) that notes: '*While not all drinking by young people should be of concern*, some drinking by young people could put their health at risk and some is clearly unacceptable – particularly when they drink to get drunk and especially when this happens in public places. We will act to stop unacceptable drinking by young people under the age of 18...'.

support of social welfare organizations, they become activities that are defined because of their potential to challenge social order. The problem here is that the discursive framing of alcohol and drug use as criminal justice issues may act to further marginalize those children and young people involved and encourage them into more riskier spaces and activities. Measham (2008, p. 216), for example, argues that:

> Young people face limited access to private accommodation with growing numbers financially dependent on their parents into adulthood, resulting in limited private social space, whilst facing exclusion from licensed premises, greater surveillance on the streets and a host of restrictions in public space from playing ball games to wearing 'hoodies' and also drinking alcohol [resulting] in the displacement of underage drinking to less visible, more isolated and therefore potentially more dangerous outdoor locations.

The danger here, Measham (2008, p. 217) argues, is that pushing young people into more isolated and dangerous spaces may result in 'turning today's persistent young drinkers into tomorrow's furtive heavy drinkers'. Rather than safeguarding children the potential is that criminal justice interventions will encourage them into more problematic behaviours and scenarios that have long-term implications for their well-being.

In the case of illicit drugs, while the relationship between them and crime and disorder is complex and multi-faceted (see, for example, Bennett and Holloway, 2008; McSweeney *et al.*, 2007; Seddon, 2000, 2006), the main discourse remains that problematic illicit drug use is predominantly a crime control issue. This discourse is problematic because of the stigma that comes not only from problem drug use, but also from its association with crime and disorder. Research suggests that such stigma can lead to an erosion of problem drug users' support networks, such as family, friends and colleagues as the latter seek to disassociate themselves from the user and their deviant behaviour (Paylor *et al.*, forthcoming). Furthermore, problem drug users may come to recognize themselves as deviant and accept their ascribed role. This may lead to users' withdrawal from society as they exclude themselves from the places that 'normal people' go, and the things that 'normal people' do. This often leads to them becoming part of deviant subcultures (Schur, 1965). As Buchanan and Young (1998, p. 222) note, drug users 'are forced into an underworld of criminal networks and secrecy, which then exposes them to other drugs and other criminal activity'. The crime-drug discourse (to which alcohol may also be added) also has important implications for addressing illicit drug use through mainstream services that, we have seen, recent policy documents (for example, the most recent drugs strategy, *Drugs: Protecting Families and Communities*) places an emphasis upon. Shapiro (2008, p. 1), for example, argues:

> A public emphasis on the drugs-crime agenda simply reinforces in the public mind that drugs users are to be feared and marginalised. This can only impact adversely on the families and carers of drug users, the very groups that the government

say they are trying to help. Furthermore, professionals in the public sector and employers are also members of the general public and will be receiving this message loud and clear. Yet successful delivery of a mainstreaming agenda will require the engagement of doctors, nurses, social workers, housing officials and so on.

While not specifically about children, Shapiro's comments nonetheless have important implications for the safeguarding agenda as they demonstrate the potential of the association of drug use (and the argument can be extended to alcohol use) with crime to have a damaging effect upon the delivery of interventions through mainstream services. The implication is that if children and young people are to 'be healthy' through not engaging in problem alcohol and drug use, the delivery of mainstream services cannot be tainted by concerns about the service users who are routinely cast out as part of the 'criminal other'. If this does happen then young problem alcohol and drug users will not only be stigmatized because of their alcohol and/or drug use and its association with crime, but they will be marginalized to services that will be crucial to addressing their behaviour.

## Drug use as a structural issue

We have seen that there are various modes of intervention that are thought to be useful in addressing the consumption of licit and illicit drugs by children and young people. These range from universal forms of drugs 'education' that are taught within schools to more specialized forms of interventions aimed at treating the problem use of both alcohol and drugs. What unites these approaches is a focus informing and/or changing individual attitudes and behaviour. In this sense, attempts to ensure that children 'be healthy' by not engaging in the consumption of licit and illicit drugs is narrow in focus, with little consideration given to the broader environment in which problem drug use in particular occurs. Rivers *et al.* (2006, p. 24), for instance, note that:

> despite such understanding ... substance programmes continue to use strategies designed to bring about individual behaviour change with little regard for the structural factors that constrain people's choices and inhibit safer practices.

Such approaches are deeply problematic because it is clear that problem drug use is closely associated to the social and economic status of the users. While, of course, the extent of 'recreational' drug use undermines the argument that drug use *per se* is linked to poor economic and social circumstances, it is clear that problem drug use, particularly the consumption of heroin, is closely associated with poor material circumstances and prospects. Heroin, for instance, has been described as the 'poverty drug' (Seddon, 2006, p. 694). While this connection between heroin and poverty is problematized as being insensitive to the historical and cultural situatedness of its use, it is difficult to deny that there is a relationship between poor material circumstances and its use. Describing the '1980s heroin epidemic' Seddon (2006, p. 683), for instance, notes that:

> The socio-demographic profile of the new heroin users was significantly different too. They were primarily young unemployed people living in the poorest neigh-bourhoods and on the most impoverished housing estates. For the first time in Britain, heroin use was very strongly connected with social disadvantage.

In this context, accounts of drug use from young people themselves demon-strate how it is structured through not only poor material circumstances, but also a lack of hope for the future. It would, of course, be wrong to locate problem drug use just within social structure. Thankfully, the majority of young living in deprived circumstances are not, and will not become, problem drug use. Many are not even irregular users of what are often described as 'recreational drugs' (see, for example, MacDonald and Marsh, 2002).

This suggests that it is the intersection of the agency of individuals with their material condition and the opportunities that their structural position allows them, that explains problem drug use (MacDonald and Marsh, 2002; Seddon, 2006). Seddon (2006, p. 691), for example, notes that:

> there is a structurally influenced patterning and distribution of drug-related crime such that it is closely associated with socio-economic disadvantage. This is ev-idenced in the 'clustering' of problems of drugs and crime in neighbourhoods already suffering from multiple social difficulties. At a neighbourhood level, the central structural mechanism revealed by this research is the irregular economy. It is here that drugs and crime often come together as part of responses to a lack of opportunities in the legitimate labour market (Auld *et al.* 1984; 1986; Pearson 1987a). Involvement in drugs and crime is described in these studies very much in terms of active engagements with the irregular economy, hence the idea of in-volvement in heroin representing in part an 'active solution to the problem of unemployment'. (Auld *et al.* 1984, p. 3)

In this rather lengthy quote from Seddon he clearly makes the argument that in order for relationships between drug use and poor material circumstances to be appreciated an understanding of the structural position of the individual is crucial. As demonstrated in recent attempts in the current Drugs Strategy for the benefits system to support and incentivize those undertaking treatment pro-grammes (HM Government, 2008), interventions in Britain focus too much upon the individual and too little upon structural issues. Until the latter is brought into policies that aim to tackle problem drug use a very small, but nevertheless important, minority of children and young people will remain outside notions of safeguarding because of their drug use.

In this context, New Labour's concern with tackling worklessness and child poverty could be pointed to as being particularly helpful, because of their po-tential to address the poverty and exclusion of children and young people.

However, as Chris Grover points out in chapter 4, New Labour's attempts to address poverty are inadequate and have little chance of success. In addition, those schemes, such as the New Deal for Young People (NDYP) that are supposed to get young people on to the first rung of metaphorical employment ladder are derided by many young people living in those areas where problem drug use is of most concern. For many young people who were within the remit of the NDYP it has merely replaced what one of Craine's (1997, p. 140) respondents described as the 'Black Magic Roundabout'; 'runnin' round in circles an' gettin' nowhere ... like YOPs an' all that other shit'. While the focus in areas that are framed by multiple and high levels of deprivation is on reducing the employment expectations of young people through such schemes (Jeffs and Spence, 2000), they will do little to raise the hopes of them that society cares much about them and is willing to invest in them. This will do little to change the structural environment in which they are trying to negotiate decisions about the use, or not, of drugs.

## Conclusion

Problematic use of drugs and alcohol not only has a contemporaneous impact upon children and young people, but may also have a future impact as the cumulative effects of such substance use (licit and illicit) comes to fruition. While the attempt within the ECM and related policy programmes to integrate preventative and holistic 'joined up' approaches to the drug and alcohol use of children and young people is to be applauded, the momentum apparent towards criminal justice responses is very concerning. Criminalizing children's and young people's (unacceptable) behaviours not only serves to cut it off from its social roots, but historically has proven particularly unhelpful. Moreover, for those children and young people who feel 'trapped in a routinised, irrational and vicious cycle of surveillance, classification and regulation' (Smith, 2007, p. 175), the escalation towards criminal justice solutions to problematic drug and alcohol use may prove highly counterproductive to the prospects of safeguarding their well-being and future prospects.

## References

Alcohol Concern (2004) *Young People's Drinking: Factsheet 1 Summary*, London: Alcohol Concern. Available at: www.alcoholconcern.org.uk/files/20040706_145136_young%20people%20factsheet%20-%20updated%20March% (accessed 23 February 2009).
Audit Commission (2008) *Are We There Yet? Improving Governance and Resource Management in Children's Trusts*, London: Audit Commission.
Auld, J., Dorn, N. and South, N. (1984) 'Heroin now: Bringing it all back home', *Youth and Policy*, 9: 1–7.

Auld, J., Dorn, N. and South, N. (1986) 'Irregular work, irregular pleasures: Heroin in the 1980s', in R. Matthews and J. Young (eds.), *Confronting Crime*, London: Sage.

Bates, B., Clemens, S., Deverill, C. and Mackenzie, H. (2007) 'Drinking alcohol' in E. Fuller (ed.), *Smoking, Drinking and Drug Use among Young People in England in 2006*, London: The Information Centre for Health and Social Care. Available at: www.ic.nhs.uk/pubs/sdd07fullreport (accessed 23 February 2009).

Beinart, S., Anderson, B., Lee, S. and Utting, D. (2002) *Youth at Risk? A National Survey of Risk Factors, Protective Factors and Problem Behaviour among Young People in England, Scotland and Wales*, London: Communities that Care.

Bennett, T. and Holloway, K. (2008) 'Chain reaction', *Druglink*, 23 (2): 6–7.

Buchanan, J. and Young, L. (1998) 'Failing to grasp the nettle: UK drug policy', *Probation Journal*, 45 (2): 220–222.

Burney, E. (2005) *Making People Behave: Anti-social Behaviour, Politics and Policy*, Cullompton: Willan.

Cabinet Office Strategy Unit (2004) *Alcohol Harm Reduction Strategy for England*, London: Cabinet Office.

Chief Secretary to the Treasury (2003) *Every Child Matters*, Cm 5860, London: The Stationery Office.

Craine, S. (1997) 'The "Black Magic Roundabout": Cyclical transitions, social exclusion and alternative careers', in *Youth, the 'Underclass' and Social Exclusion*, London: Routledge.

Crow, I. (2007) 'Developments in work with drug using offenders', in G. McIvor and P. Raynor (eds), *Developments in Social Work with Offenders*, London: Jessica Kingsley.

DCSF, Home Office and Department of Health (2008) *Youth Alcohol Action Plan*, London: The Stationary Office. www.dcsf.gov.uk/publications/youthalcohol/ (accessed 23 February 2009).

DfES (2004a) *Every Child Matters: Change for Children*, London: DfES.

DfES (2004b) *Drugs: Guidance for Schools*, London: DfES. Available at: http://drugs.homeoffice.gov.uk/publication-search/young-people/guidance-for-schools (accessed 23 February 2009).

DfES (2005a) *Every Child Matters: Change for Children, Young People and Drugs*, London: DfES.

DfES (2005b) *Youth Matters*, London: DfES.

Drugscope and Alcohol Concern (2006) *Drugs: Guidance for the Youth Service*, London: Drugscope and Alcohol Concern. Available at: http://www.drugscope.org.uk/Resources/Drugscope/Documents/PDF/Education%20and%20Prevention/Drugs-guideservice.pdf (accessed 24 February 2009).

*FRANK website*: http://www.talktofrank.com/ (accessed 23 February 2009).

Fuller, E. (ed.) (2007) *Smoking, Drinking and Drug Use among Young People in England in 2006*, London: The Information Centre for Health and Social Care. Available at: www.ic.nhs.uk/pubs/sdd07fullreport (accessed 23 February 2009).

Garland, D. (2001) *The Culture of Control: Crime and Social Order in Contemporary Society*, Oxford: Oxford University Press.

Gerada, C. (2005) 'Random drug testing in schools', *British Journal of General Practice*, 55 (516): 499–501.

Goldson, B. (2005) 'Taking liberties: Policy and the punitive turn', in H. Hendrick (ed.), *Child Welfare and Social Policy*, Bristol: Policy Press.

Hibell, B., Andersson, B., Bjarnason, T., Kokkevi, A., Morgan, M. and Narusk, A. (1997) *The 1995 ESPAD Report: Alcohol and Other Drug Use among Students in 26 European Countries*, Stockholm: The Swedish Council for Information on Alcohol and Other Drugs and The Pompidou Group at the Council of Europe.

Hibell, B., Andersson, B., Ahlström, S., Balakireva, O., Bjarnason, T., Kokkevi, A. and Morgan, M. (2000) *The 1999 ESPAD Report. Alcohol and Other Drug Use among Students in 30 European Countries*, Stockholm: The Swedish Council for Information on Alcohol and Other Drugs and The Pompidou Group at the Council of Europe.

Hibell, B., Andersson, B., Bjarnasson, T., Ahlstrom, S., Balakireva, O., Kokkevi, A. and Morgan, M. (2004) *The ESPAD Report 2003: Alcohol and other Drug Use among Students in 30 European Countries*, Stockholm: The Swedish Council for Information on Alcohol and Other Drugs (CAN), The Pompidou Group at the Council of Europe.

Hills, A. and Li, N. (2007) 'Drug use' in E. Fuller (ed.), *Smoking, Drinking and Drug Use among Young People in England in 2006*, London: The Information Centre for Health and Social Care. Available at: www.ic.nhs.uk/pubs/sdd07fullreport (accessed 23 February 2009).

Hoare, J. and Flatley, J. (2008) *Drug Misuse Declared: Findings from the 2007/08 British Crime Survey England and Wales*, London: Home Office. Available at: www.homeoffice.gov.uk/rds/pdfs08/hosb1308.pdf (accessed 23 February 2009).

Home Office (1998) *Tackling Drugs to Build a Better Britain: The Government's Ten Year Strategy for Tackling Drug Misuse*, London: The Stationary Office. Available at: http://www.archive.official-documents.co.uk/document/cm39/3945/statemnt.htm (accessed 23 February 2009).

Home Office (2002) *Updated National Drugs Strategy*, London: Home Office. Available at: http://www.crimereduction.homeoffice.gov.uk/drugsalcohol/drugsalcohol60.htm (accessed 23 February 2009).

Home Office (2005) *Young People Substance Misuse Partnership Grant: Notification of Local Allocations*, London: Home Office. Available at: http://drugs.homeoffice.gov.uk/publication-search/young-people/YPSMPG-0506?view=Binary (accessed 19 February 2009).

Horwath, J. and Morrison, T. (2007) 'Collaboration, integration and change in children's services: Critical issues and key ingredients', *Child Abuse and Neglect*, 31: 55–69.

HM Government (2008) *Drugs: Protecting Families and Communities: The 2008 Drug Strategy*, London: Central Office for Information. Available at: http://drugs.homeoffice.gov.uk /publication-search/drug-strategy/drug-strategy-2008?view=Binary (accessed 23 February 2009).

Huxley, A. and Foulger, S. (2008) 'Parents who misuse substances: implications for parenting practices and treatment seeking behaviour', *Drugs and Alcohol Policy*, 8 (3): 9–16.

Jeffs, T. and Spence, J. (2000) 'New Deal for Young People: Good deal or poor deal?', *Youth and Policy*, 66: 34–61.

Lister, R. (2003) 'Investing in the citizen-workers of the future: Transformations in citizenship and the state under New Labour', *Social Policy and Administration*, 37 (5): 527–538.

MacDonald, R. and Marsh, J. (2002) 'Crossing the Rubicon: Youth transitions, poverty, drugs and social exclusion', *International Journal of Drug Policy*, 13: 27–38.

MacDonald, Z., Tinsley, L., Collingwood, J., Jamieson, P. and Pudney, S. (2005) *Measuring the Harm from Illegal Drugs using the Drug Harm Index*, Home Office Online Report 24/05, London: Research Development and Statistics Directorate, the Home Office. Available at: http://www.homeoffice.gov.uk/rds/pdfs05/rdsolr2405.pdf (accessed 23 February 2009).

Matrix Research and Consultancy and Institute for Criminal Policy Research, Kings College (2007) *Evaluation of Drug Interventions Programme Pilots for Children and young People: Arrest Referral, Drug Testing and Drug Treatment and Testing Requirements Home Office Online Report 07/07*, London: Home Office. Available at: http://www.homeoffice.gov.uk/rds/pdfs07/ rdsolr0707.pdf (accessed 20 February 2009).

Matthews, S., Brasnett, L. and Smith, J. (2006) *Underage Drinking: Findings from the 2004 Offending, Crime and Justice Survey*, London: Home Office Research Development and Statistics Directorate. Available at: http://www.homeoffice.gov.uk/rds/pdfs06/r277.pdf (accessed 23 February 2009).

McArdle, P. and Gilvarry, E. (2006) 'Drug and alcohol use in the young', *Psychiatry*, 6 (1): 30–35.

McIntosh, J., MacDonald, F. and McKeganey, N. (2008) 'Pre-teenage children's experiences with alcohol', *Children and Society*, 22: 3–15.

McKeganey, N., McIntosh, J., MacDonald, F., Gannon, M., Gilvarry, E., McArdle, P. and McCarthy, S. (2004) 'Preteen children and illegal drugs', *Drugs: Education, Prevention and Policy*, 11 (4): 315–327.

McMullan, S. and Ruddy, D. (2006) *Experience of Drug Misuse: Findings from the 2005 Northern Ireland Crime Survey*, Research and Statistical Bulletin 8/2006, Belfast: Northern Ireland Research and Statistics Agency. Available at: www.nio.gov.uk/bulletin_8_2006_experience_of_drug_misuse_findings_from_the_2005_ northern_ireland_crime_survey.pdf (accessed 23 February 2006).

McSweeney, T., Hough, M. and Turnbull, P. (2007) 'Drugs and crime: Exploring the links', in M. Simpson, T. Shildrick and R. McDonald (eds.), *Drugs in Britain*, Basingstoke: Palgrave.

McVie, S., Campbell, S. and Lebov, K. (2004) *Scottish Crime Survey 2003*, Edinburgh: Scottish Executive Social Research. Available at: www.scotland.gov.uk/Publications/2004/12/20379 (accessed 23 February 2009).

Measham, F. (2008) 'The turning tides of intoxication: Young people's drinking in the 2000s', *Health Education*, 108 (3): 207–222.

Muncie, J. (2004) *Youth and Crime*, 2nd edn, London: Sage.

National Treatment Agency (2008) *Interim Guidance on Commissioning Young People's Specialist Substance Misuse Treatment Services*, London: National Treatment Agency. Available at: http://www.nta.nhs.uk/areas/young_people/Docs/Commissioning_guid-ance_YP_Final_2008.pdf (accessed 23 February 2009).

Newburn, T. and Shiner, M. (2001) *Teenage Kicks? Young People and Alcohol: A Review of the Literature*, London: Public Policy Research Unit.

Parker, H., Aldridge, J. and Egginton, R. (eds.) (2001) *UK Drugs Unlimited: New Research and Policy Lessons on Illicit Drug Use*, Basingstoke: Palgrave.

Paylor, I., Measham, F. and Wilson, A. (forthcoming) *Social Work and Drug Use*, Buckingham: Open University Press.

Pearson (1987a) 'Social deprivation, unemployment and patterns of heroin use', in N. Dorn and N. South. (eds.), *A Land Fit for Heroin?*, London: Macmillan.

Rivers, K., Aggleton, P. and Ball, A. (2006) 'Young people, poverty and risk' in P. Aggleton, A. Ball and P. Mane. (eds.), *Sex, Drugs and Young People*, London: Routledge.

Schur, E. (1965) *Crimes without Victims: Deviant Behaviour and Public Policy-Abortion, Homosexuality, Drug Addiction*, New Jersey: Prentice-Hall.

Seddon, T. (2000) 'Explaining the drug-crime link: Theoretical, policy and research issues', *Journal of Social Policy*, 29 (1): 95–107.

Seddon, T. (2006) 'Drugs, crime and social exclusion: Social context and social theory in British drugs-crime research', *British Journal of Criminology*, 46: 680–703.

Shapiro, H. (2008) 'Editorial', *Druglink*, 23 (2): 1.

Smith, R. (2007) *Youth Justice: Ideas, Policy and Practice*, 2nd edn, Cullompton: Willan.

South, N. (2007) 'Drugs, alcohol and crime' in M. Maguire, R. Morgan and R. Reiner. (eds.), *The Oxford Handbook of Criminology*, 4th edn, Oxford: Oxford University Press.

Squires, P. (2008) *ASBO Nation: Anti Social Behaviour – Critical Questions and Key Debates*, Bristol: Policy Press.

Squires, P. and Stephen, D.E. (2005) *Rougher Justice: Anti-social Behaviour and Young people*, Cullompton: Willan.

Stead, M., Standling, B., MacKintosh, A., McNeil, M., Minty, S., Eadie, D. and the Blueprint Evaluation Team (2007) *Delivery of the Blueprint Programme*, Stirling: Institute for Social Marketing, University of Stirling.

Vimpani, G. (2005) Getting the mix right: Family, community and social policy interventions to improve outcomes for young people at risk of substance misuse, *Drug and Alcohol Review*, 24 (2): 111–125.

# 11

# In Search of Youth Justice

Janet Jamieson

## Introduction

> Young offenders are today more likely to be criminalised and subject to a greater
> level of intervention than before the 1998 reforms. If dealt with pre-court their
> warning is more likely to be accompanied by an intervention. They are more likely
> to be prosecuted. If convicted they are less likely to receive a discharge or fine. If
> subject to a community sentence it is more likely to be onerous. And last but not
> least, ... the number of children and young people sentenced to custody is 35%
> higher than a few years before the 1998 Act.
>
> (Morgan and Newburn, 2007, pp. 1046–7)

Successive New Labour governments have ardently pursued a diverse and expanding array of youth justice reforms and strategies in order to 'achieve the
governance of young people' (Muncie, 2006, p. 787). Since 2004 this reform
of youth justice has been informed by the Every Child Matters (ECM) agenda
(Department for Education and Skills [DfES], 2003, 2004a) which promises a
more universal approach to safeguarding and promoting the well-being of children (Goldson and Muncie, 2006; Payne, 2008). Notwithstanding the welfarist
overtures inherent to the ECM reform agenda, New Labour's approach to youth
justice has been characterized as consistently tough (Goldson and Muncie, 2006,
p. 210). Indeed, as the opening quotation attests, this toughness has been pursued since its initial foray into the reform of the youth justice system through
the 1998 Crime and Disorder Act, and has served to expand and intensify the
government's role with regard to the regulation, control and punishment of
young people in conflict with the law. In critically assessing the impacts of the
ECM reform agenda for the youth justice system and for the children and young
people involved, this chapter will reflect upon the 'ever more hybrid' nature of
youth justice (Muncie, 2006, p. 787). The chapter will explore the prospects
for enlightened policies and practices, and the exclusionary potential of coercive and punitive responses to young offenders and those considered 'at risk' of
offending. It will argue that the authoritarian imperatives that dominate youth

*Critical Perspectives on Safeguarding Children*   Edited by Karen Broadhurst, Chris Grover and Janet Jamieson
© 2009 John Wiley & Sons, Ltd

justice rhetoric, priorities and policies are unlikely to safeguard or promote the well-being of the children and young people targeted.

## The ECM reform agenda

Williams (2004, p. 407) asserts that the ECM reform agenda, and its laudable intent to place 'the child as one of the central subjects in New Labour's social policy', represents the 'biggest shake up' of statutory children's services since the 1960s. Echoes of New Labour's radical reform of the youth justice system in 1998 are evidenced in the concerns for clear leadership and accountability which permeate the 2004 Children Act. At a national level this concern has witnessed the creation of a Minister for Children, Young People and Families charged with responsibility for the cross-government agenda relating to children's well-being, safety, protection and care. It has also led to the appointment of an independent Children's Commissioner (for England) whose remit is to monitor legislation, policy and practice to gauge its effectiveness in safeguarding and promoting the rights and welfare of children (House of Commons, 2003). At a local level the 2004 Children Act led to the appointment of a Lead Member for Children's Services in each relevant local authority, who alongside a newly established Local Safeguarding Children Board and a Director of Children's Services (with responsibilities in relation to social services and education) was to facilitate intra- and inter-agency working across diverse partnerships (Payne, 2008). Overall, the ECM reform agenda includes a 10-year strategy for childcare, the development of Sure Start Children's Centres in deprived areas, a range of measures to help working parents, the development of integrated service frameworks and information services for all children and radical plans for work force reform. This wide portfolio of policies is focused on supporting and promoting the quality of children's and families' lives (DfES, 2003, 2004a; Payne, 2008; Smith, 2007; Williams, 2004). Performance will be measured against five key ECM outcomes – specifically, that children have the opportunity to: be healthy; stay safe; enjoy and achieve; make a positive contribution and achieve social and economic well-being (DfES 2003, 2004a) – which are incorporated within section 10 of the Children Act 2004 (Office of Public Sector Information [OPSI], 2004).

Williams (2004, p. 408) describes the ECM reform agenda as a 'hodge-podge mixture' of policies which simultaneously 'open up possibilities for the way society can transform the lives of children and young people' while also 'closing these off'. For youth justice the tensions integral to the 'dual logics' of the Children's Act 2004 regarding 'the protection of society from the child and protection of the child from society' are to the fore (Penna, 2005, p. 147). Ultimately, the provision of integrated children's services centred on the needs and well-being of children are underpinned by a set of expectations regarding children's and parental responsibilities. It appears that the government are willing to make 'help' available to facilitate social inclusion but only in return for individual compliance, for example, in the form of good behaviour, school attendance or appropriate parental discipline (see Young and Matthews, 2003). Those children and parents who are unable to, or fail to, live up to their responsibilities will inevitably experience the tougher side of the ECM reform agenda which seeks to enforce this 'responsibility' via early intervention strategies and an array of statutory orders. As Haworth (2008, p. 312) observes, this, in turn, raises questions about the need to safeguard children from and within the youth justice system itself.

## New Labour's youth justice

Events in the early 1990s were to prove particularly significant in the development of New Labour's youth justice agenda. In the context of a 'widespread and deep economic recession manifest in levels of unemployment unprecedented since the 1930s' (Hay, 1995, p. 202), a series of disturbances broke out in Cardiff, Oxford and North Shields in 1991, followed the next year by those in Bristol, Salford, Burnley and Carlisle. In the aftermath of this unrest Britain's societal folk devil was articulated through the discourse of a so-called 'underclass' masculinity living in Britain's 'thrown away places' (Campbell, 1993, p. 48), which coalesced with an ideological assault on single mothers (McRobbie, 1994) to create 'twin crises in the family and in childhood' (Scraton, 2007, p. 77). That the construction of these societal folk devils was to trigger a more punitive approach to issues of law and order in general, and for juvenile justice in particular, was ensured by the media and the police persistently highlighting the problems of joyriding; youth disorder; 'bail bandits' and 'persistent' young offenders (Gelsthorpe and Morris, 2002; Goldson, 2002; Muncie, 2004; Smith, 2007); doubts regarding the legitimacy of the criminal justice system (Hay, 1995), and the waning fortunes of the Conservative party (Goldson, 2002; Pitts, 2001). It was further exacerbated by a modernizing Labour Party, that under the increasing influence of Tony Blair, 'played the crime card' in a manner 'unprecedented in the history of the Labour party' (Brownlee, 1998, p. 33).

The arrest and charging of 10-year-old Jon Venables and Robert Thompson for the abduction and murder of 2-year-old James Bulger in February 1993 was to cement the 'authoritarian backlash' (Goldson, 2002, p. 131). This case focused attention on the 'vexed question' of the age of criminal responsibility (Worrall, 1997, p. 134). The consensus was that Venables and Thomson had committed an adult offence and as such needed to be treated as adults and be subjected to the full weight of adult sentencing. In the aftermath of the Bulger case childhood was deemed to be in 'crisis' (Scraton, 1997), a 'crisis' which was perceived to be so 'powerful' and 'pervasive' that it threatened 'the very fabric of social and moral order' (Scraton, 1997, p. xii). Within days of this 'extraordinary event' (Goldson, 2001, p. 133) John Major, the then Prime Minister, articulated the terms of the authoritarian backlash as necessitating society 'to condemn a little more and understand a little less' (cited in MacIntyre, 1993). This was to set in train a 'punitive renaissance' (Pitts, 2001, p. 13) in which law and order was to become 'a trophy', with the main political parties 'jockeying to show who is toughest on crime' (Kennedy, 1995, p. 4)

A punitive crusade against youth crime was initiated in March 1993, by the then Conservative Home Secretary, Kenneth Clarke who promised the creation of 200 places in secure training centres which could be utilized for the hard core of persistent and serious offenders, as young as 12, whose repeated offending made them 'a menace to the community' (Pitts, 2001, p. 14). It was to intensify with the appointment of Michael Howard to the position of Home Secretary in May 1993. Howard wasted no time in attempting to implement his party political soundbite that 'prison works' via a 'legislative onslaught' on issues of justice and punishment (Smith, 2007, p. 26). Furthermore, in the aftermath of yet another election defeat in 1992, the Labour Party came to view 'law and order' as 'a vehicle for the acquisition of and retention of power' (Pitts, 2001, p. 1), and breaking from its traditional welfarist concern which emphasized the link between crime and social and economic inequalities (Downes and Morgan, 1994) it sought to consolidate its tough on crime philosophy. Left 'Realist' criminology which emphasized the impact of crime on 'real' people and 'real' lives provided the critical paradigm which was to enable New Labour to champion the rights of the law-abiding majority and embrace ever more authoritarian approaches to questions of 'law and order' (Pitts, 2001).

In the wake of its landslide electoral success in May 1997, New Labour moved quickly to translate its law and order priorities into legislation in the form of the 1998 Crime and Disorder Act (OPSI, 1998). The 1998 Act heralded a 'root and branch reform' of the youth justice system (Home Office, 1997, p. 7), which under the overarching aim of preventing offending by children and young persons sought to improve the performance of the youth justice system and to rebuild safer communities (Johnston and Bottomley, 1998). It established the Youth Justice Board (YJB) to monitor the operation of the youth justice system and created Youth Offending Teams (YOTs) to coordinate the provision of youth justice services at the local level. The Act demonstrated New Labour's commitment to intervening early in the lives of young offenders, and those deemed to be at risk of becoming young offenders, through the replacement of the 'caution' with a reprimand and a final warning, and the introduction of Child Safety Orders, Local Child Curfews, Anti-social Behaviour Orders, and Parenting Orders. The Act also demonstrated the government's determination that young offenders should take responsibility for their offending via the abolition of the principle of *doli incapax* (incapable of evil) for 10- to 14-year-olds, and the introduction of a variety of evidence-based community punishments focused on criminogenic need which also incorporated opportunities for reparation. Finally, it illustrated the government's commitment to child imprisonment by widening court powers to incarcerate young offenders via the introduction of the Detention and Training Order (DTO) (see Morgan and Newburn, 2007; Smith, 2007).

The priorities established by the 1998 Act continue to resonate in 'the relentless stream of crackdowns, initiatives, targets, policy proposals, pilot schemes and legislative enactments' (Muncie, 2006, p. 771) that have been unleashed in its wake. Arguably, most significant are the ongoing prioritization of crime prevention and early intervention strategies; reparation and restorative justice; evidence-based interventions and the continued commitment to the juvenile secure estate. While New Labour's energetic reform of youth justice since 1998 has been characterized as consistently 'tough' (Goldson and Muncie, 2006, p. 210), a brief reprieve from the toughness agenda and a return to welfare values was briefly signalled by the premiership of Gordon Brown. Indeed, Brown's closest political ally, Ed Balls MP, has been frequently cited as recognizing that an effective approach to tackling youth crime needs to involve agencies other than those of criminal justice and must address the welfare needs of children (Balls, 2007; Travis, 2008a). However, Boris Johnson's successful London mayoral campaign – which exploited the electoral potential of the aggravation caused by 'hooliganism' and 'bad behaviour' on the capital's buses and tubes – and the Labour Party's humiliating performance in the local government elections in May 2008 have assured a return to a tough youth justice agenda. Indeed, in May 2008 Jacqui Smith, the then Home Secretary, reaffirmed the government's commitment to tackling the 'anti-social' behaviour of a 'hardcore' of troublemakers and persistent offenders via the 'harassment of daily visits, repeated warnings and relentless filming of offenders to create an environment where there is nowhere to hide' (*TimesOnline*, 8 May 2008).

The most recent articulation of the government's youth justice priorities is presented in the 'Youth Crime Action Plan' (YCAP), published in July 2008 (Secretary of State for the Home Department *et al.*, 2008). The YCAP sets out a 'triple track' approach to tackling youth crime premised on 'enforcement and punishment where behaviour is unacceptable, non-negotiable support and challenge when it is most needed and better and earlier prevention' (Secretary of State for the Home Department *et al.*, 2008, p. 1). Backed by £100 million of additional funding, it incorporates a diverse package of measures concerned with preventing and reducing young people's offending and unacceptable behaviour; increasing the reach of intensive family interventions; supporting young victims; improving the use of reparation; strengthening alternatives to custody and ensuring that custody is as effective as it can be in reducing reoffending and addressing underlying problems. Undoubtedly, the YCAP contains some laudable aims. Of particular note are the aims of reducing by a fifth the numbers of young people entering the criminal justice system by 2020 and ensuring that young people in the criminal justice system achieve the five ECM outcomes. However, in further extending the reach of existing youth justice provision, the implementation of the YCAP promises that 'interventions will be sooner, more pervasive and more intensive' (Broadhurst *et al.*, 2008). This continued commitment to 'toughness' within youth justice rhetoric and policy, with its potential for 'exclusionary' consequences, raises grave concerns about the capacity of the youth justice system to contribute the 'inclusive' imperatives of the ECM reform agenda.

## Youth justice and the safeguarding children agenda

Attention will now turn to the specificities of New Labour's youth justice policy and its potential to deliver with regard to safeguarding and promoting the well-being of children and young people who find themselves in conflict with the law. This discussion will be structured in accord with Muncie's (2006) identification of the complex and contradictory modes of youth governance which characterize contemporary youth justice policy (see also Goldson and Muncie, 2006; Muncie and Hughes, 2002). Therefore, it will address the relative opportunities and threats to the ECM agenda presented by the government's commitment to the neo-liberal imperatives of 'managerialism', 'risk management' and 'responsibilization', and the neo-conservative tendencies of 'remoralization' and 'authoritarianism' (Muncie, 2006).

### Managerialism

The report, *Misspent Youth* (Audit Commission, 1996), proved pivotal to New Labour's reform and reconfiguration of the youth justice system in England and Wales. The government 'enthusiastically embraced' (Muncie, 2006, p. 775) its 'excoriating criticisms of extant system' (Newburn, 2002, p. 456) and instigated a radical reconfiguration of the infrastructural provision and the mechanisms of accountability in the delivery of youth justice. In an effort to impose control from the centre, the 1998 Crime and Disorder Act created the YJB for England and Wales whose role was to involve the strategic monitoring of the youth justice system (Gelsthorpe and Morris, 2002; Newburn, 2002). It also established YOTs to coordinate the provision of youth justice services at the local level and to facilitate 'joined up', multi-agency and interagency working (Newburn, 2002). Goldson (2008, p. 28) asserts that the symbolic importance of the introduction of YOTS is to be found in the change of status from 'juvenile justice' to 'youth offending', which serves to cast the child primarily as an 'offender' and a 'threat', rather than as a 'child in need'. In practice, he maintains that this shift has served to 'systematically' and 'institutionally' distance youth justice from mainstream social care and child welfare services. Furthermore, the provision of youth justice services is to proceed within a context of time limits for the administration of justice, national standards, performance targets and the pursuit of 'what works' via evidence-based practice. Eadie and Canton (2002) argue that such managerial imperatives have served to constrain discretion on the part of the youth justice worker regarding the work they undertake and the issues they address with young people. Thus Jones (2001) suggests youth justice interventions have become geared to meeting targets rather than responding to the needs and circumstances of young offenders.

Ostensibly the ECM reform agenda and its radical reconfiguration of children's services raises the prospect of more enlightened and inclusive youth justice policies and practices in prioritizing child safety and holistic and multi-disciplinary services, which for youth justice has heralded further shifts in its infrastructural and practice arrangements. At a national level the YJB is no longer to be solely located within the criminal justice system, but rather jointly overseen by the Ministry of Justice and the Department of Children, Schools and Families (Haworth, 2008). At the local level, YOTS have been identified as a key partner agency – alongside the local authority, the police, probation, health, education and the Learning and Skills Council (until 2010 when it is to be replaced by local authorities taking on some of its work and a new National Apprenticeship Scheme – Secretaries of State for Children, Schools and Families and for Innovation, Universities and Skills, 2008) – with responsibilities to contribute to the planning and delivery of children's services. Indeed, the YCAP emphasizes the importance of an integrated approach, especially with regard to information sharing between key agencies, in order to effectively engage with 'young people at risk, young people already drawn into crime or 'anti-social' behaviour and parents in need of support and challenge' (Secretary of State for the Home Department *et al.*, 2008, para. 9).

However, while it is envisaged that the youth justice system will complement the ECM reform agenda as a whole, its primary focus will continue to be that of preventing offending and the tackling of factors underlying offending behaviour (DfES, 2004b). Hence, while there is an expectation that the youth justice system will contribute to the achievement of all five ECM outcomes, its key focus will be on the ECM outcomes of helping children to 'stay safe' and 'make a positive contribution', with particular regard to ensuring that children are safe from crime, exploitation, bullying, discrimination and violence, and to encourage them to engage in law-abiding and 'positive' behaviours (DfES, 2004b). Furthermore, the 2005 *Green Paper: Youth Matters* (DfES, 2005) reveals that all opportunities and support provided for those young people who get into trouble are contingent upon promoting young people's responsibilities. Likewise the 2008 YCAP's 'triple track' approach of enforcement, non-negotiable support and prevention is premised on sending a clear message to young people who offend, young people at risk of offending and their parents that 'youth crime will not be tolerated' (Secretary of State for the Home Department *et al.*, 2008, para. 40). Thus, notwithstanding the complex constellation of issues and adversities that young people in conflict with the law typically experienced, it would appear that the ECM reform agenda will continue to construct them as 'offenders' first and foremost, rather than as 'children in need'.

## Risk

New Labour's reconfiguration of youth justice has also witnessed the adoption of the actuarial penology of risk management and prevention as a means to overcome the 'nothing works' pessimism that had pervaded youth justice in the two decades before it first came to power (Muncie, 2006). The 'risk factor prevention paradigm' offers a pragmatic crime prevention model which involves identifying key domains in a young person's life – for instance, family, school, community and psycho-emotional aspects – that statistically increase (risk factor) or decrease (protective factor) the likelihood of crime (Case, 2007, p. 92). In contrast to traditional juvenile responses which seek to address youth offending via treatment, rehabilitation and opportunity reduction, the risk factor paradigm is premised on 'evidence-based' interventions that aim to reduce risk and prevent offending (Case, 2007, p. 92). Risk management strategies range from 'early preventative programmes (concentrating on parenting, "correcting" anti-social attitudes and behaviours and assisting families to lead more socially responsible lives) to intensive cognitive behavioural programmes (delivered either in the community or in custodial settings)' (Kemshall, 2008a, p. 310).

The government's robust commitment to developing systems to identify and intervene on the basis of risk assessment is reflected in the YCAP emphasis on the importance of a 'consistent approach assessment, early identification and targeted support' (Secretary of State for the Home Department *et al.*, 2008, para 9). In particular, the aim is to identify the minority of children who offend or who are deemed at risk of offending in order to 'address the root causes of their behaviour, which includes supporting and challenging their parents to meet their responsibilities' (Secretary of State for the Home Department *et al.*, 2008, para 6). Indeed, as a result of the implementation of the YCAP measures it is stated that 'all of the 110,000 families with children identifiably at risk of becoming prolific offenders will receive a targeted intervention' (Secretary of State for the Home Department *et al.*, 2008, para 18). The risk agenda is also at the forefront of the youth justice measures contained within the Criminal Justice and Immigration Act 2008, to be implemented in autumn 2009 (OPSI, 2008). In particular, the Youth Rehabilitation Order (YRO) will rationalize the array of community sentences available to address youth crime by providing a new simplified community sentence 'menu' that will allow magistrates to tailor a package of interventions to the individual criminogenic needs of the young person (DfES, 2003, 2004a). The YRO is to be complemented by the introduction of 'The Scaled Approach' which, it is claimed, will help youth justice practitioners to determine the appropriate level of YOT intervention necessary for each young person in order to reduce their likelihood of reoffending (YJB, 2008, p. 4).

Despite the undoubted political and electoral appeal of focused and targeted interventions, Haines and Case (2008, p. 7) assert that the evidence of their effectiveness is both 'limited and controversial'. Furthermore, serious reservations abound with regard to the likelihood of New Labour's particular interpretation of the risk factor prevention paradigm to safeguard or promote the well-being of the children targeted. Goldson (2005) argues that the provision of interventions on the basis of assessing young people as 'at risk', 'high risk', 'anti-social', or as posing a risk to themselves or others means that the entitlement to services is effectively being drawn along negative lines. Consequently, any conceptualizations of universal, transformative and rehabilitative provision have retreated into a 'context of classification, control and correction' (Goldson, 2005, p. 259). Children face assessment, judgement and exposure to formal state interventions 'not only on the basis of what they have done, but what they might do, who they are and who they are thought to be' (Goldson, 2008, p. 30). In this context, little regard to the legal principles of 'burden of proof', 'beyond reasonable doubt' and 'due legal process' are given (Goldson, 2008, p. 30), while children, young people and their families face 'diminished rights to refuse the regulation of the state' (Kemshall, 2008b, p. 28).

Furthermore, the quantitative emphasis of risk assessment and identification has also been robustly critiqued, not least for prioritizing 'immediate, proximate and individual' factors (Haines and Case, 2008, p. 11), while masking the structural, political and individual inequalities which often underlie recourse to criminal activities (Goldson and Muncie, 2006; Kemshall, 2008b; Squires and Stephen, 2005). Indeed, Kemshall (2008b, p. 22) argues that the government's focus on risk has served to blur the boundaries between social policy and criminal justice policy to the extent that 'crime control strategies are increasingly deployed to manage intractable social ills'. Hence children, families and neighbourhoods who are already socially, economically and politically excluded are being subjected to risk focused interventions which may not only exacerbate their disadvantage, but also subject them to stigma and criminalization (Goldson, 2000a; Haines and Case, 2008). In effect the preoccupation with risk facilitates increasing levels of surveillance and the provision of services and interventions which are ultimately neither inclusionary nor 'child centred' (Smith, 2007, p. 13).

## Responsibilization

Underpinning New Labour's preoccupation with 'risk' focused interventions, and indeed its broad social policy agenda, is the principle of 'responsibilization'. Developing alongside a critique of state dependency its responsibilization of citizens has served to legitimate its withdrawal from 'universal measures of state protection and welfare support' (Muncie, 2008a, p. 299) and the 'contraction of conventional child welfare services and partial withdrawal of social care agencies' (Goldson, 2008, p. 29). Comprising of an attempt to govern at a distance (Rose, 2000; Rose and Miller, 1992), New Labour's prioritization of responsibilization strategies is deeply engrained in its determination, since 1997, to forge a new political ideology of the 'Third Way' (Giddens, 1998; see also Chapter 1 in this volume), which favours the concept of an 'enabling state' with an emphasis firmly placed on the duties and responsibilities of citizens (James and

James, 2001). Responsibilization not only involves encouraging (and enforcing) individuals to take full responsibility for their actions, but also serves to shift the primary responsibility for crime prevention and public safety away from the state and towards employers, property owners, schools, communities, families and individuals (Muncie, 2006, 2008a).

Responsibilization strategies are evident in New Labour's modernization of a range of policy areas, including health; social care; education, training and employment; regeneration and neighbourhood renewal, and within the ECM reform agenda they are apparent in the emphasis upon interagency cooperation, partnership working and joined up government. For youth justice purposes the 'responsibilisation ethos finds its practical expression in the principles of restorative justice' (Muncie and Hughes, 2002, p. 4), which were consolidated within the youth justice system in England and Wales though the introduction of the Referral Order as part of the Youth Justice and Criminal Evidence Act 1999 (OPSI, 1999). The Referral Order comprises the primary sentencing disposal for all 10- to17-year-olds pleading guilty and convicted for the first time at court. Incorporating the principles of responsibility, reparation and restoration, it involves referring the young offender to a Youth Offending Panel (YOP) – usually comprising of two lay members of the community and a YOT representative. The YOP is intended to provide a constructive forum away from the formality of the court where the young offender, his or her family and, where appropriate, the victim, and his or her supporters, can discuss the young person's crime and its consequences. The aim is to agree a 'youth offender contract'.

From the outset referral orders attracted critical attention. Concerns have been raised with regard to their potential to distort the principles of restorative justice (Haines, 2000); to increase the jeopardy faced by minor and first offenders with regard to 'disproportionate sentencing' and more severe punishments should they be unable to fulfil their contract (Ball, 2000); and to undermine children's rights with regard to proportionality, the denial of legal representation, and fairness and justice. The latter indicates that the experience of young people in YOPs may be incompatible with international treaties, standards and rules for youth justice (Goldson, 2000b, 2008). Research evidence suggests that referral orders have proved relatively successful in responsibilizing young offenders and in enabling them to make reparation to their victims or the community as a whole (Crawford and Newburn, 2003; Gray, 2005). However, notwithstanding the multi-disciplinary expertise and resources at the disposal of YOTS, there is less evidence to show that referral orders have made any progress in addressing the social context of young people's offending in order to secure their reintegration into the 'law abiding' community (Gray, 2005). Overall, it would appear that the punitive focus on individual responsibility characteristic of the referral order is indicative of the government's ongoing commitment to exclusionary justice which undermines the government's rather contradictory aim of safeguarding and promoting the well-being of young offenders. Indeed, the government's propensity to view offending, and more generally social exclusion, as a consequence of individual deficits demonstrates its resistance to addressing the social problems and inequalities which underlie much youth crime, and the extent to which it has retreated from welfarist concerns (see Gelsthorpe and Morris, 2002; Gray, 2005).

## Remoralization

Accompanying the neo-liberal managerial, risk and responsibilizing concerns is the government's neo-conservative tendency towards remoralization (Muncie, 2006; Muncie and Hughes, 2002). 'Remoralization' imperatives arise from the perception that crime is 'greater than offending *per se*' representing the 'break-up of the moral fabric and cohesion of society' (Muncie and Hughes, 2002, p. 9). Its theoretical heritage draws variously on Wilson and Kelling's (1982) 'Broken Windows' thesis which advocates zero-tolerance approaches to minor incivilities; Putnam's (2000) ideas with regard to 'social capital' and its legacy of reciprocal social relations and – arguably most significantly – Etzioni's (1995) conservative variant of communitarianism which calls for a renewal and revital-ization of community values and institutions, and the prioritization of the needs and rights of victims and 'law abiding' citizens. The government's commitment to its communitarian influenced mantra that 'rights come with responsibilities' (Hudson, 2003, p. 78) is reflected in its propensity to utilize the state's disci-plinary powers to define, legislate and sanction in relation to the duties and obligations it views as fundamental to the membership rights of a 'law-abiding' citizenship (McLaughlin, 2002).

'Community' has become the 'central collective abstraction' in New Labour's reinvention of its social and criminal justice imperatives (Levitas, 2000, p. 191). Engaging in a process of 'regressive modernisation' (Hall, 1988, p. 2), the gov-ernment has ruthlessly utilized the discourse of community to mobilize nostalgia in order to 'crystallise and realise a vision of contemporary social arrangements' (Sim, 2009: 79), premised on the desirability of the 'work ethic', the 'normal or-derly family' and 'respect' (Muncie, 2006, p. 782). When this moralizing logic is applied to questions of non-compliance, parental deficits, disorder, 'anti-social' behaviour and youth crime the rights and responsibilities flow in one direction, that is, towards the 'law-abiding' community (Hudson, 2003). Thus, the gov-ernment's social and criminal justice policies prioritize the 'mutuality of trust' and the 'reciprocity of respect' (Scraton, 2007, p. 77). Accordingly, the ECM reform agenda – including the provision of more affordable nursery education, parenting support and measures to assist single parents back to work – and crime prevention and early intervention programmes, such as On Track, Splash, Youth Inclusion Projects (YIPs) and Youth Inclusion and Support Panels (YISPs) are provided as a means to 'micro-manage' behaviour in order to 'remoralise' the recipients (Muncie, 2006, p. 782).

The government's prioritization of remoralization strategies has witnessed the 'expansion of surveillant, correctional and ultimately punitive interventions'

(Goldson, 2008, p. 29), which are difficult to reconcile with the desire to safeguard and promote the well-being of children. The more holistic and potentially inclusionary ECM, crime prevention and early intervention initiatives have been characterized as 'tough love, compassion with a hard-edge' (Muncie, 2006, p. 782). However, it is the exposure of children, and in some cases their parents, 'to criminalizing modes of state intervention' (Goldson, 2008, p. 30) – without the necessity of a conviction, or even the commission of an offence – which have elicited most concerns. The intensification of authoritarian control over the lives of troublesome children and their families has been criticized with regard to due process (Hudson, 2003), net-widening (Pitts, 2003; Squires and Stephen, 2005) and its stigmatizing and criminalizing potential (Brown, 2004; Burney, 2005; Crawford, 1998; Jamieson, 2005). Not only is such authoritarian control likely to encourage intolerance and hostility, but it also serves to mask the often complex and diverse needs underlying 'parenting deficits' and the resort to 'anti-social' and criminal behaviours by children and young people. Furthermore, the emphasis upon, and enforcement of, individualized responsibility obscures the fact that the government and the 'law-abiding' community also have responsibilities, not least the responsibility for ensuring that social justice extends to all members of society, particularly those children and adults whose lived experiences undermine their ability and willingness to demonstrate respect and responsibility (Hudson, 2003; Squires and Stephen, 2005).

## Authoritarianism

The final strand of New Labour's youth justice policy is the neo-conservative authoritarian practice of incarcerating children (Muncie, 2006; Muncie and Hughes, 2002), and it is in this respect that the government's supposed commitment to safeguarding and promoting the well-being of children rings most hollow. The punitive turn in youth justice policy, apparent from the early 1990s, initiated a general trend towards penal expansion in respect to child incarceration in England and Wales. It has been consolidated by three successive New Labour administrations (Goldson, 2006, p. 145). The recent YCAP attests to the government's ongoing commitment to the use of child incarceration. The YCAP describes custody as the 'right response for serious or dangerous offenders or other persistent offenders where community punishments have not worked' (Secretary of State for the Home Department *et al.*, 2008, para. 12) and documents the ongoing expansion of the juvenile secure estate, including plans for a new Young Offenders Institute (YOI) at Glen Parva in Leicestershire.

Despite YJB attempts to increase the effectiveness of non-custodial options and to secure a reduction in the numbers of children in prison, the number of children in custody in England and Wales has remained around 2,800 since March 2001 (Solomon and Garside, 2008, p. 48), with 2,837 children detained on 29 February 2008 (UK Children's Commissioners, 2008, p. 33). Furthermore, despite the fact that Article 37(b) of the United Nations

Convention on the Rights of the Child (UNCRC) advises that the detention of children in custody should be applied only as 'a measure of last resort and for the shortest appropriate time' (cited in Goldson and Muncie, 2008, p. 63), the youth justice system in England and Wales incarcerates more children than any other country in Western Europe (Council of Europe, 2004), and there are growing numbers of children serving longer sentences (Goldson, 2006; UK Children's Commissioners, 2008). The government's law and order agenda has not only provided for the detention of younger children, but it has impacted disproportionately on girls, and black and minority ethnic groups boys (Goldson, 2006, p. 145). Moreover, Goldson (2006, p. 146) argues this expansionist drift 'bears virtually no relation to either the incidence or the seriousness of youth crime'.

The problems associated with sending young people to secure and custodial institutions are multiple and manifest. Child prisoners are routinely drawn from the most vulnerable, disadvantaged and socially excluded families, neighbourhoods and communities (Goldson, 2002, 2006; Goldson and Coles, 2005; Goldson and Muncie, 2008). As Goldson (2006, p. 146) observes:

> Approximately half of the children held in penal custody at any time will be or will have been, 'open cases' to statutory child welfare agencies as a result of neglect and/or other child protection concerns, a significant proportion will have biographies scarred by adult abuse and violation.

Such vulnerabilities may be compounded by the fact that children's experiences of incarceration are likely to incorporate risks with regard to bullying; intimidation; theft, extortion and robbery; physical and/or sexual assault; emotional and psychological abuse, and drug use (Goldson, 2006; Goldson and Muncie, 2008; Goldson and Peters, 2000). Furthermore, high numbers, strained levels of supervision – especially within the Young Offenders Institutions – and routine resort to the problematic practices of physical restraint, solitary confinement and strip searches have deleterious repercussions with regard to the conditions and treatment of child prisoners. Indeed, such is the concern regarding the use of restraint that in July 2008 the Court of Appeal prohibited the use of physical restraint methods on children in Secure Training Centres for the purpose of maintaining discipline (Equality and Human Rights Commission, 2008). Notwithstanding the recognition that physical restraint exposes children to the risk of inhuman and degrading treatment, in December 2008 the Ministry of Justice confirmed its continued commitment to the use of physical restraint 'in exceptional circumstances', albeit with a £4.9 million investment over 2 years to implement, allegedly, safer restraint techniques (Travis, 2008b). In short, child incarceration undermines the physical and mental well-being of child prisoners, which for some may lead to self-harm and/or suicide. Indeed, since 1990, 30 children have died in custody – all but two of these deaths were apparently self-inflicted (Goldson, 2006; Solomon and Garside, 2008).

In addition to such humanitarian concerns, child imprisonment has proved extraordinarily expensive, with a single place at a YOI and a Secure Training Centre respectively costing £977.00 per week (£50,800 per year), and £3,168 per week (£164,750 per year) (Goldson, 2006, p. 150). Moreover, with attempts to address offending behaviour and facilitate rehabilitation routinely undermined by institutional subcultures (Goldson and Peters, 2000), it is of no surprise that the reconviction rate of child prisoners stands at 80 per cent (Goldson, 2006, p. 150). As Goldson (2002, p. 160) eloquently asserts: 'to lock up a vulnerable child is a sign of failure. To lock up the number of children we do in England and Wales is failure in the extreme'. This failure is all the more galling given that government ministers and major state agencies 'comprehensively recognise' the personal and fiscal costs of imprisoning children (Goldson, 2006, p. 149).

## Looking to other UK jurisdictions

The developments in youth justice described within this chapter are not wholly unique to England and Wales, rather they may be viewed as part of a convergence of authoritarian and punitive approaches to criminal justice emanating from the USA and apparent in a range of Western European jurisdictions (Muncie, 2008b). However, youth justice policy is not uniformly envisaged, structured and implemented in all jurisdictions, rather it is 'mediated by distinctive national, regional and local cultures and practices' (Muncie, 2008b, p. 118). While, as we have seen, there is a pernicious encroachment of increasingly punitive responses to young people who offend across all UK jurisdictions, there are also contrary imperatives which provide some grounds for optimism and examples of progressive practice with regard to safeguarding and promoting the well-being of children in conflict with the law.

The Welsh Assembly has purposively decided to locate youth justice services within the portfolio of Health and Social Services rather than that of Crime Prevention and Community Safety. Its intention is to promote a 'child-centred ethos' (Cross *et al.*, 2003, p. 156). That this decision may signify the pursuit of a distinctive youth justice agenda for Wales is reflected in Edwina Hart's ministerial press statement with regard to the launch of the 'All Wales Youth Offending Strategy' (see Welsh Assembly Government and the YJB, 2004) in which she states, 'if children and young people have offended we must treat them as children first and offenders second' (YJB, 2004). Muncie (2008b, p. 118) argues that this emphasis on a UNCRC-inspired 'children first' mentality constitutes a stark contrast to the 'offender first' mentality evident in England. However, ethnographic work undertaken in two Welsh YOTs suggests that the philosophical tensions between the YJB's and the Welsh Assembly's approaches to children in conflict in the law are reflected in practice in the differing perspectives of experienced practitioners and social work students (Cross *et al.*, 2003). Cross *et al.* (2003, p. 158) argue that the practitioners have actively sought to preserve the 'children first' approach, while social work students have a clear tendency 'to construct young people as "young offenders" with the emphasis squarely placed on offending'.

In the North of Ireland the pursuit of the Youth Justice Service's primary aim to prevent offending has prioritized a concern for the child's welfare and encouraged the use of restorative justice approaches (UK Children's Commissioners, 2008). Furthermore, in the recent consultation on the substance of a Bill of Rights for Northern Ireland (Bill of Rights Forum, 2008), the working group on children and young people proposed that the pursuit of maximum protections with regard to youth justice would involve the use of detention only as a last resort; the development of effective alternatives to custody; the separation of detained children from adults; the removal of children from prison service custody and raising the age of criminal responsibility to 16 years (Convery *et al.*, 2008, p. 260). In spite of the movement towards restorative justice, the numbers of children detained in secure care and custody has remained above 400 since 2003, with particular concerns being identified with regard to the lack of gender-specific provision for girls, the practice of detaining children with adults and the over-representation of 'looked after' children within juvenile justice and young offenders centres (Convery *et al.*, 2008). The demonization and exclusion of children and young people within popular and political discourse has effectively stymied the realization of the maximum protection of children's rights (Convery *et al.*, 2008, p. 260). Indeed, the UK Children's Commissioners (2008, p. 34) have expressed serious concerns that recent attempts to bring legislation in line with the rest of the UK will result in the lowering of standards with regard to the application of children's rights within the North of Ireland.

Arguably it is within Scotland that the most child-centred pursuit of youth justice is to be found. Embracing the ethos of the 1964 Kilbrandon Committee of prioritizing the needs of the child, the Social Work (Scotland) Act 1968 introduced the Children's Hearings System to provide a unified response to children who offend and those deemed in need of care and protection. Premised on the 'best interests' of the child, the Hearings System seeks to offer holistic support and supervision 'in ways which do not stigmatise recipients' (McAra, 2006, p. 142). McAra (2006) observes that Scotland's longstanding commitment to welfarism is in stark contrast to the developments witnessed in youth justice in England and Wales and many other Western jurisdictions. However, McAra (2006, p. 131) also notes a range of developments which threaten the child-centred ethos of the Scottish approach to juvenile justice. In particular, she highlights the punitive edge contained within the powers of the 1995 Children (Scotland) Act which enables children's hearings to place the principle of public protection above that of the best interests of the child in those instances where the child concerned poses a risk to others. She also emphasizes the propensity of the fledgling Scottish Parliament to use crime control and penal practice as a means of building political capital. This is reflected in the punitive intolerance of the 2004 Anti-Social Behaviour Act which extends the use of ASBOs to children aged 12–15 years, gives the police additional powers in designated areas and introduces electronic tagging for children, and in the piloting of youth courts for 16- and 17-year-old persistent offenders which utilizes 'adult modes of justice' to respond to youth crime (Piacentini and Walters, 2006, p. 55). McAra (2006, p. 142) suggests that as a result of this process of 'detartanisation' the Scottish system of youth justice faces an uncertain future.

## Conclusion

The principle that youth justice should have regard to the welfare of the child was established by the 1933 Children and Young Person's Act, and 'remains untouched to the present' (Muncie and Hughes, 2002, p. 7). However, the overview of youth justice provided in this chapter demonstrates the ways in which 'welfare' has been envisaged with regard to questions of youth crime and justice and has been subject to considerable dispute over time and between the different jurisdictions of the UK. At first sight the ECM agenda appears to offer an enlightened, progressive and structural approach to the reform of children's services. Indeed, the concern to safeguard and promote the well-being of children across the full range of health, social care, education, training and employment, and youth justice services, alongside regeneration and neighbourhood renewal, is a welcome addition to debates regarding social and criminal justice policy (Goldson and Muncie, 2006). However, Penna (2005, p. 151) suggests that the ECM reform agenda merely serves as another means to assert the government's ideological, disciplinary and punitive priorities within an ongoing project to accomplish the governance of the public sphere. Herein the profound impacts of social, economic and political polarization and inequality are masked and diffused in the discourse of social exclusion, which in turn, perpetuates the view that crime and other social problems are firmly located in individual, family and community failings.

Notwithstanding the considerable financial investment and a multitude of new initiatives which have resulted from the ECM reform agenda, it is clear that rather than genuinely seeking to address the needs and promote the interests of all children, the provision of the more inclusive and progressive elements are to be selectively and conditionally applied (Goldson and Muncie, 2006). Indeed, the emphasis within the ECM agenda, and the subsequent YCAP, on individual deficits and provision being conditional on compliance, suggests that 'some children appear to "matter" more than others' (Goldson and Muncie, 2006, p. 213). Furthermore, in endorsing punitive youth justice discourse and practice and embracing further means by which to police and punish children, the ECM reform agenda has contributed to the cynical toughness of contemporary youth justice and its construction of 'responsibilised' and 'adulterised' young offenders rather than their construction as 'children in need' (Goldson and Muncie, 2006, p. 214). In the context of recent high profile reports that have condemned Britain as a bleak place to be a child (UNICEF, 2007; UK Children's Commissioner,

2008, see also Chapter 1 in this volume), the failure of the ECM agenda to challenge the authoritarian imperatives which have come to dominate youth justice rhetoric, priorities and policies means that Britain is an even bleaker place to be a young person in conflict with the law.

# References

Audit Commission (1996) *Misspent Youth: Young People and Crime*, Abingdon: Audit Commission.

Ball, C. (2000) 'R v B (Young Offender: Sentencing Powers): Paying due regard to the welfare of the child in criminal proceedings', *Child and Family Law Quarterly*, 10 (4): 417–24.

Balls, E. (2007) 'Foreword to the Children's Plan' in DfES, *The Children's Plan: Building Brighter Futures*, London: DfES.

Bennett, R. (2008) 'Law creates underclass of child criminals', *The Times*, 9 June.

Bill of Rights Forum (2008) *Recommendations to the Northern Ireland Human Rights Commission on a Bill of Rights for Northern Ireland*, Belfast: Bill of Rights Forum. Available at: http://www.billofrightsforum.org/ (accessed 11 February 2009).

Broadhurst, K., Grover, C. and Jamieson, J. (2008) *A Commentary on the Youth Crime Action Plan*, copy available from author.

Brown, A. (2004) 'Anti-social behaviour, crime control and social control', *The Howard Journal of Criminal Justice*, 43 (2): 203–211.

Brownlee, I. (1998) 'New Labour – new penology? Punitive rhetoric and the limits of managerialism in criminal justice policy', *Journal of Law and Society*, 25 (3): 313–335.

Burney, E. (2005) *Making People Behave: Anti-social Behaviour, Politics and Policy*, Cullompton: Willan.

Campbell, B. (1993) *Goliath: Britain's Dangerous Places*, London: Methuen.

Case, S. (2007) 'Questioning the 'evidence' of risk that underpins evidence-led youth justice interventions', *Youth Justice*, 7 (2): 91–106.

Convery, U., Haydon, D., Moore, L. and Scraton, P. (2008) 'Children, rights and justice in Northern Ireland: Community and custody', *Youth Justice*, 8 (3): 245–263.

Council of Europe (2004) *Space 1, Council of Europe Annual Penal Statistics, Survey 2004*, Strasbourg: Council of Europe.

Crawford, A. (1998) 'Community safety and the quest for security: Holding back the dynamics of social exclusion', *Policy Studies*, 19 (3/4): 237–253.

Crawford, A. and Newburn, T. (2003) *Youth Offending and Restorative Justice: Implementing Reform in Youth Justice*, Cullompton: Willan.

Cross, N., Evans, J. and Minkes, J. (2003), 'Still children first? Developments in youth justice in Wales', *Youth Justice*, 2 (3): 151–162.

DfES (2003) *Every Child Matters*, London: DfES.

DfES (2004a) *Every Child Matters: Next Steps*, London: DfES.

DfES (2004b) *Every Child Matters: Change for Children in the Criminal Justice System*, London: DfES.

DfES (2005) *Youth Matters Green Paper*, London: DfES.

Downes, D. and Morgan. R. (1994) 'Hostages to fortune? The politics of law and order in post-war Britain', in M. Maguire, R. Morgan and R. Reiner (eds.), *The Oxford Handbook of Criminology*, 1st edn, Oxford: Oxford University Press, pp. 183–232.

Eadie, T. and Canton, R. (2002) 'Practising in a context of ambivalence: The challenge for youth justice workers', *Youth Justice*, 2 (1): 14–26.

Equality and Human Rights Commission (2008) *Commission calls for an end to degrading child restraint rules after win in Court of Appeal Case against the government*, 28 July 2008. Available at: http://www.equalityhumanrights.com/en/newsandcomment/Pages/Commissioncallsforendtodegradingchildrestraintrule.aspx (accessed 11 February 2009).

Etzioni, A. (1995) *The Spirit of Community: Rights, Responsibilities and the Communitarian Agenda*, London: Fontana Press.

Gelsthorpe, L. and Morris, A. (2002) 'Restorative youth justice: The last vestiges of welfare?' in J. Muncie, G. Hughes and E. McLaughlin (eds.), *Youth Justice: Critical Readings*, London: Sage, pp. 238–254.

Giddens, A. (1998) *The Third Way: The Renewal of Social Democracy*, Cambridge: Polity Press.

Goldson, B. (2000a), 'Whither diversion? Interventionism and the new youth justice', in B. Goldson (ed.), *The New Youth Justice*, Lyme Regis: Russell House, pp. 35–57.

Goldson, B. (ed.) (2000b) *The New Youth Justice*, Lyme Regis: Russell House.

Goldson, B. (2001) 'The demonization of children: From the symbolic to the institutional', in P. Foley, J. Roche and S. Tucker, (eds.), *Children in Society: Contemporary Theory, Policy and Practice*, Basingstoke: Palgrave.

Goldson, B. (2002) 'New punitiveness: The politics of child incarceration', in J. Muncie, G. Hughes, and E. McLaughlin (eds.), *Youth Justice: Critical Readings*, London: Sage, pp. 386–400.

Goldson, B. (2005) 'Taking liberties: Policy and the punitive turn', in H. Hendrick (ed.), *Child Welfare and Social Policy*, Bristol: Policy Press, pp. 255–268.

Goldson, B. (2006) 'Penal custody: Intolerance, irrationality and indifference', in B. Goldson and J. Muncie (eds.), *Youth Crime and Youth Justice: Critical Issues*, London: Sage, pp. 139–156.

Goldson, B. (2008) 'New Labour's youth justice: A critical assessment of the first two terms', in G. McIvor and P. Raynor (eds.), *Developments in Social Work with Offenders*, London: Jessica Kingsley, pp. 23–39.

Goldson, B. and Coles, D. (2005) *In the Care of the State? Child Deaths in Penal Custody in England and Wales*. London: INQUEST.

Goldson, B. and Muncie, J. (2006) *Youth Crime and Youth Justice: Critical Issues*. London: Sage.

Goldson, B. and Muncie, J. (2008) 'Children in custody', in B. Goldson (ed.), *Dictionary of Youth Justice*, Cullompton: Willan, pp. 62–64.

Goldson, B. and Peters, E. (2000) *Tough Justice: Responding to Children in Trouble*, London: The Children's Society.

Gray, P. (2005) 'The politics of risk and young offenders experiences of social exclusion and restorative justice', *The British Journal of Criminology*, 45 (6): 938–957.

Haines, K. (2000) 'Referral Order and Youth Offender Panels: Restorative approaches and the new youth justice', in B. Goldson (ed.), *The New Youth Justice*, Lyme Regis: Russell House.

Haines, K. and Case, S. (2008) 'The rhetoric and reality of the "risk factor prevention paradigm" approach to preventing and reducing youth offending', *Youth Justice*, 8 (1): 5–20.

Hall, S. (1988) *The Hard Road to Renewal: Thatcherism and the Crisis of the Left*, London: Verso.

Haworth, S. (2008) 'Safeguarding', in B. Goldson (ed.), *Dictionary of Youth Justice*, Cullompton: Willan, p. 312.

Hay, C. (1995) 'Mobilization through interpellation: James Bulger, juvenile crime and the construction of a moral panic', *Social Legal Studies*, 4 (2): 197–223.

Home Office (1997), *No More Excuses*, Cm 3809, London: Home Office. Available at: http://www.homeoffice.gov.uk/documents/jou-no-more-excuses?view=Html (accessed 10 February 2009).

House of Commons (2003) Children's Commissioner for England, London: The Stationary Office. Available at: http://www.publications.parliament.uk/pa/cm200203/cmbills /121/2003121.pdf (accessed 10 February 2009).

Hudson, B. (2003) *Justice in the Risk Society: Challenging and Re-affirming Justice in Late Modernity*, London: Sage.

James, A. and James, A. (2001) 'Tightening the net: Children, community and control', *British Journal of Sociology*, 52 (2): 211–228.

Jamieson, J. (2005) 'New Labour, youth justice and the question of respect', *Youth Justice*, 5 (3): 180–193.

Johnstone, G. and Bottomley, K. (1998), 'Labour's crime policy in context', *Policy Studies*, 19 (3/4): 173–184.

Jones, D. (2001) 'Misjudged youth: A critique of the Audit Commission's reports on youth justice', *British Journal of Social Work*, 31 (1): 57–79.

Kemshall, H. (2008a) 'Risk factors' in B. Goldson (ed.), *Dictionary of Youth Justice*, Cullompton: Willan, pp. 309–310.

Kemshall, H. (2008b) 'Risks, rights and justice: Understanding and responding to youth risk', *Youth Justice*, 8 (1): 21–38.

Kennedy, H. (1995) *Banged Up, Beaten Up, Cutting Up: Report of the Howard League Commission into Violence in Penal Institutions for Young People*, London: Howard League for Penal Reform.

Levitas, R. (2000) 'Community, Utopia and New Labour', *Local Economy*, 15 (3): 188–197.

MacIntyre, D. (1993) 'Major on crime: "Condemn more, understand less"', *Independent on Sunday*, 21 February. Available at: http://www.independent.co.uk/news/major-on-crime-condemn-more-understand-less-1474470.html (accessed 2 March 2009).

McAra, L. (2006) 'Welfare in crisis? Key developments in Scottish Youth Justice' in J. Muncie and B. Goldson (eds.), *Comparative Youth Justice*, London: Sage, pp. 127–145.

McLaughlin, E. (2002) '"Same bed, different dreams": Postmodern reflections on crime prevention and community safety', in G. Hughes, and A. Edwards (eds.), *Crime Control and Community: The New Politics of Public Safety*, Cullompton: Willan, pp. 46–62.

McRobbie, A. (1994) 'Folk devils fight back', *New Left Review*, 202: 107–116.

Morgan, R. and Newburn, T. (2007) 'Youth justice', in M. Maguire, R. Morgan and R. Reiner (eds.), *The Oxford Handbook of Criminology*, 4th edn, Oxford: Oxford University Press, pp. 1024–1060.

Muncie, J. (2004) *Youth and Crime: A Critical Introduction*, 2nd edn, London: Sage Publications.

Muncie, J. (2006) 'Governing young people: Coherence and contradiction in contemporary youth justice', *Critical Social Policy*, 26 (4): 770–793.

Muncie, J. (2008a) 'Responsibilisation', in B. Goldson (ed.), *Dictionary of Youth Justice*, Cullompton: Willan, pp. 299–300.

Muncie, J. (2008b) 'The "punitive turn" in juvenile justice: Cultures of control and rights compliance in Western Europe and the USA', *Youth Justice* 8 (2): 107–121.

Muncie, J. and Hughes, G. (2002) 'Modes of youth governance: Political rationalities, criminalization and resistance', in J. Muncie, G. Hughes and E. McLaughlin, (eds.), *Youth Justice: Critical Readings*, London: Sage, pp. 1–18.

Newburn, T. (2002) 'The contemporary politics of youth crime prevention', in J. Muncie, G. Hughes and E. McLaughlin (eds.), *Youth Justice: Critical Readings*, London: Sage, pp. 452–463.

208   *Critical Perspectives on Safeguarding Children*

OPSI (1998) *The Crime and Disorder Act 1998, Chapter 37*, London: The Stationery Office. Available at: http://www.opsi.gov.uk /acts/acts1998/ukpga_19980037_en_1 (accessed 17 December 2008).
OPSI (1999) *Youth Justice and Criminal Evidence Act 1999*, London: The Stationary Office. Available at: http://www.opsi.gov.uk/acts/acts1999/pdf/ukpga_19990023_en.pdf (accessed 17 December 2008).
OPSI (2004) *The Children's Act 2004*, London: The Stationary Office. Available at: http://www.opsi.gov.uk/acts/acts2004/ukpga_20040031_en_1 (accessed 17 December 2008).
OPSI (2008) *Criminal Justice and Immigration Act, 2008*, London: The Stationary Office. Available at: http://www.opsi.gov.uk/acts/acts2008/pdf/ukpga_20080004_en.pdf (accessed 17 December 2008)
Payne, L. (2008) 'Every Child Matters (ECM)', in B. Goldson (ed.), *Dictionary of Youth Justice*, Cullompton: Willan, pp. 162–63.
Penna, S. (2005) 'The Children Act 2004: Child protection and social surveillance', *Journal of Social Welfare and Family Law*, 27 (2): 143–157.
Piacentini, L. and Walters, R. (2006) 'The politicization of youth crime in Scotland and the rise of the "Burberry Court"', *Youth Justice* 6 (1): 43–60.
Pitts, J. (2001) 'Korrectional karaoke: New Labour and the zombification of youth justice', *Youth Justice*, 1 (2): 3–16.
Pitts, J. (2003) 'Youth justice in England and Wales', in J. Young and R. Matthews, (eds.), *The New Politics of Crime and Punishment*, Cullompton: Willan, pp. 71–99.
Putnam, R. (2000) *Bowling Alone: The Collapse and Revival of American Community*, New York: Touchstone.
Rose, N. (2000) 'Government and control', *British Journal of Criminology*, 40 (2): 321–339.
Rose, N. and Miller, P. (1992) 'Political power beyond the state: Problematics of government', *British Journal of Sociology*, 43 (2): 173–205.
Scraton, P. (ed.) (1997) *'Childhood' in 'Crisis'?*, London: UCL Press.
Scraton, P. (2007) 'The neglect of power and rights: A response to "problem solving"', in Z. Davies and W. McMahon (eds.), *Debating Youth Justice: From Punishment to Problem Solving?*, London: Centre for Crime and Justice Studies. Available at: http://www.jbutts.com/pdfs/whoseproblem.pdf (accessed 11 February 2009).
Secretary of State for Children, Schools and Families and Secretary of State for Innovation, Universities and Skills (2008) *Raising Expectations: Enabling the System to Deliver*, Cm 7348, Norwich: The Stationery Office.
Secretary of State for the Home Department, Secretary of State for Children, Schools and Families and Lord Chancellor and Secretary of State for Justice (2008) *Youth Crime Action Plan*, London: The Stationery Office.
Sim, J. (2009) *The Carceral State*, London: Sage.
Smith, R. (2007) *Youth Justice: Ideas, Policy and Practice*, Cullompton: Willan.
Solomon, E. and Garside, R (2008) *Ten Years of Labour's Youth Justice Reforms: An Independent Audit*, London: Centre for Crime and Justice Studies. Available at: http://www.crimeandjustice.org.uk/opus647/youthjusticeaudit.pdf (accessed 11 February 2009).
Squires, P. and Stephen, D. (2005) *Rougher Justice: Anti-social Behaviour and Young People*, Cullompton: Willan.
Travis, A. (2008a) 'Planned changes to youth justice system aimed at keeping more children out of jail', *Guardian*, 17 July. Available at: http://www.guardian.co.uk/society/2008/jun/17/youthjustice.justice1 (accessed 28 July 2008).
Travis, A. (2008b) 'Jails get go-ahead to continue using pain to control children', *Guardian*, 16 December. Available at: http://www.guardian.co.uk/society/2008/dec/16/youth-justice-restraint-independent-review (accessed 11 February 2008).

UK Children's Commissioners (2008) *UK Children's Commissioners' Report to the UN Committee on the Rights of the Child*, London/Belfast/Edinburgh/Colwyn Bay: 11 Million/NICCY/SCCYP/Children's Commissioner for Wales.

UNICEF (2007) 'Child poverty in perspective: An overview of child well-being in rich countries', *Innocenti Report Card 7*. Florence: UNICEF Innocenti Research Centre.

Welsh Assembly Government and the YJB (2004) *All Wales Youth Offending Strategy*, London: YJB and Welsh Assembly Government.

Williams, F. (2004) 'What matters is who works: Why every child matters to New Labour. Commentary on the DfES Green Paper *Every Child Matters*', *Critical Social Policy* 24 (3): 406–427.

Wilson, J. and Kelling, G. (1982) 'Broken Windows', *Atlantic Monthly*, March: 29–38.

Worrall, A. (1997) *Punishment in the Community: The Future of Criminal Justice*, London: Longman.

YJB (2004) *All Wales Youth Offending Strategy*, 16 August. Available at: www.yjb.gov.uk/engb/News/llWalesYouthOffendingStrategy.htm (accessed 17 December 2008).

YJB (2008) *Youth Justice: The Scaled Approach, A Framework for Assessment and Interventions*, London: YJB. Available at: http://www.yjb.gov.uk/publications/Resources/Downloads/Youth%20Justice%20-%20The%20Scaled%20Approach.pdf (accessed 17 December 2008).

Young, J. and Matthews, R. (2003) 'New Labour, crime control and social exclusion', in J. Young and R. Matthews (eds.), *The New Politics of Crime and Punishment*, Cullompton: Willan, pp. 1–32.

# 12

# Looked After Children and the Criminal Justice System

Claire Fitzpatrick

## Introduction

Vulnerable by virtue of their 'looked after' status, as well as because of the reasons that brought them into 'care' in the first place, children in the care of the state represent one of the most disadvantaged and marginalized groups in society. As a result, they have been a prime target for the New Labour policy machine over the past decade and are an obvious focus for attention within the wider 'safeguarding children' agenda. A plethora of initiatives ranging from the Quality Protects programme in 1998, to the Care Matters plan in 2008, have emphasized the crucial need to improve outcomes for looked after children as a group and reduce the gaps of achievement between them and their peers. Meanwhile, a number of key policy changes have occurred in statute, aimed at promoting placement stability and educational attainment, and enabling children to remain in care beyond the age of 16. The Children and Young Person's Act 2008 has been passed through Parliament, with the aim of further strengthening the legislation underpinning the care system.

In spite of all of this policy activity, the needs of some looked after children, such as those who come into contact with the criminal justice system, remain comparatively neglected. Indeed, the government has had curiously little to say about these particular young people. While the majority of looked after children are *not* involved in offending behaviour, this chapter argues that the welfare and needs of those who are accused of criminal offences should be a key focus for attention. This is particularly important in light of recent evidence that they are at risk of being criminalized for minor offences in some residential settings (Home Office, 2004; Nacro, 2005) and potentially denied access to key leaving care services and support if placed in custody (Nacro, 2008). These issues are considered in further detail below, following a general discussion of the impact of recent policy.

*Critical Perspectives on Safeguarding Children*   Edited by Karen Broadhurst, Chris Grover and Janet Jamieson
© 2009 John Wiley & Sons, Ltd

## Disadvantage and social exclusion

The unprecedented focus on looked after children in recent years has undoubtedly been a positive development in the sense that they are now, at least, *on* the policy agenda. Yet while good legislative intentions are commendable, they are meaningless if they do not lead to actual change on the ground. So how much has actually changed in practice? In launching *Care Matters: Time to Deliver for Children in Care* in March 2008 (a guide for local authorities on improving the lives of children in care) (Department for Children, Schools and Families [DCSF], 2008a), the then Children and Young People's Minister, Beverley Hughes, commented that 'for too long children have languished in a care system that allowed them too fail' (see DCSF, 2008b). It is telling that such comments are still being made after over a decade of government policies, programmes and initiatives aimed at improving this very system. Furthermore, the guide's subtitle of *Time to Deliver* raises the question that if it is time to deliver in 2008, what exactly has been going on since 1997?

There have been a number of developments in recent years. Key pieces of legislation include the Children (Leaving Care) Act 2000, which finally enabled looked after children to remain in care, if they wished to, beyond the age of 16. In addition, the Act placed a range of new duties on local authorities, such as the duty to assess and relieve the needs of 16- and 17-year-olds who are in care or care-leavers and the duty to maintain contact with 18- to 21-year-olds, and provide them with support and financial assistance. The Leaving Care Act was hailed as a historic development by the government, which would, at last, ensure positive changes for care-leavers that were long overdue (Standing Committee A, 2000, col. 3). Yet, a number of provisions under the legislation were problematic. For example, with respect to the new financial arrangements for care-leavers, Grover *et al.* (2004) raise several concerns about the issue of sanctions for care-leavers who are judged to be uncooperative and disengaged from their pathway plans. Commenting on the withdrawal of entitlement of 16- and 17-year-old care-leavers to claim income support and housing benefit, they argue that, in the most extreme cases, when the relationship between a young person and the social services department breaks down, care-leavers may become even more excluded than they were previously (Grover *et al.*, 2004; see also Grover and Stewart, 2004).

Findings from a large-scale empirical study by Broad (2005) on the implementation of the Leaving Care Act reveal that while the increased number of care-leavers entering post-16 education, employment and training is a significant development, overall progress in implementing the provisions of the Act has been far slower than might be expected. According to Broad (2005), the provision and scope of leaving care services remains akin to a lottery, with vastly differential access to services around the country. He further warns that 'longer-term investment especially in terms of planning and service delivery from 2004 will become problematic, and a return to the inadequate pre-investment days appears a real threat' (Broad, 2005, p. 382). Clearly, the Children (Leaving Care) Act 2000 has not had the impact on the ground that had been hoped for.

In terms of other policy developments, the *Every Child Matters* Green Paper, which led to the Children Act 2004, highlighted the government's vision for a major reform of children's services. Among other things, the Children Act 2004 placed a new duty on local authorities to promote the educational achievement of looked after children, with the aim of ensuring that this links in with decisions about placements and stability in care.

In short, policies aimed at allowing children to remain in care until they themselves are ready to leave, and that emphasize their educational potential, are certainly positive in theory. However, in practice, progress in improving outcomes has been incredibly slow. While the proportion of looked after children doing well has increased on certain measures, there has been little progress on reducing the gap between looked after children's achievement and that of their peers, and many of the government's own targets have been missed (Department for Education and Skills [DfES], 2006a).

Some of the headline figures are as follows:

- In 2007, only 13 per cent of looked after children obtained at least five GCSEs (or equivalent) at grades A\*–C compared with 62 per cent of all children (DCSF, 2008c).
- In 2006, 20 per cent of looked after children were unemployed the September after leaving school compared to 5 per cent of all school-leavers (DfES, 2007).
- A study by the Youth Justice Board (YJB) showed that 41 per cent of children in custody had some history of being 'looked after' (Hazel *et al.*, 2002).

Furthermore, reports on the social exclusion faced by many care-leavers highlights that they continue to be over-represented among the unemployed, the homeless, the mentally ill and the prison population and are more likely to experience drug and alcohol dependency than their peers (for example, Sergeant, 2006). The list goes on, and the findings sound depressingly familiar, as they are reflected in a large body of previous research (for instance, Biehal *et al.*, 1995; Social Services Inspectorate, 1997; Stein and Carey, 1986). For too many individuals, it seems that the care system simply serves to reinforce early disadvantage, rather than enabling looked after children to overcome it. Referring to government activity aimed at improving state care in the foreword to the *Care Matters* Green Paper, the then Secretary of State for Education and Skills, Alan Johnson MP, explained the situation in the following way:

> Quite simply, it is now clear that this help has not been sufficient. The life chances of all children have improved but those of children in care have not improved at the same rate. The result is that children in care are now at greater risk of being left behind than was the case a few years ago – the gap has actually grown.
>
> (Johnson, 2006, p. 3)

The failure to close the gap between looked after children and their peers, and reduce the former's experiences of future social exclusion, indicates that looked after children as a whole are still not being safeguarded. In some respects it is difficult to understand why the intense activity and relentless government initiatives over recent years have not made more of an impact. There are a number of possible explanations.

First, the government began from an extremely low base with respect to improving the outcomes for looked after children and care-leavers (cf. Colton, 2002), and consequently there is a great deal of ground to be made up. Second, while government attention has continually emphasized the need for organizational and bureaucratic change within children's services, at a wider level there has not been enough emphasis on the structural changes required to reduce the early experiences of poverty and social deprivation that many young people bring with them into care, and which are in themselves factors associated with future disadvantage and exclusion (cf. Berridge, 2007). Third, there has been a lack of attention paid to the needs of specific groups within the looked after population because policy-makers continue to direct their lens at the care population as a whole. Yet, it is a fallacy to treat children in care as a homogenous group, and policies that lump these children together as one fail to recognize the great variety of children and the diversity of their individual care careers (Sinclair *et al.*, 2007; Taylor, 2006). For example, in a recent study of more than 7000 looked after children, Sinclair *et al.* (2007) identified a number of distinct groups within the care system. These included: abused adolescents, adolescent graduates (first admitted under the age of 11 but now older than this and still looked after), children seeking asylum, disabled children and young entrants (under the age of 11).

As Malcolm Hill and Peter Hopkins illustrate in chapter 13 in this volume, treating looked after children as a homogenous group has resulted in a failure to address the specific needs of, and support required by, certain subgroups. In the remainder of the current chapter, I focus on the subgroup of looked after children who come into contact with the criminal justice system, arguing that they are often the least likely to have their well-being safeguarded. Curiously, New Labour governments have had little to say about this particular group of children. This is arguably because its policies on children in need and children in trouble are a very long way from being joined up and do not sit comfortably together (cf. Goldson, 2002).

## Offending rates of looked after children

Before commenting on the offending rates of looked after children, it is important to reiterate that only a minority of looked after children offend and come to the attention of the police. Many do very well (often *in spite of*, rather than *because of* their care experience) and are incredibly resilient despite earlier adversity and disadvantage in their pre-care lives (cf. Taylor, 2006). However, according to official figures, looked after children of the age of criminal responsibility are more than twice as likely to be cautioned or convicted of an offence compared to their peers (DCSF, 2008c). Interestingly, the gap between looked after children and all children has narrowed, partly because of a decrease in the figures for looked after children, but also because of an increase in the number of final warnings and convictions for all children (DCSF, 2008c). Yet there has still been a failure to achieve the following target set in the 2002 spending review: 'To reduce the proportion of children in care who were cautioned or convicted in the year to 30 September by a third from 10.8% to 7.2% by 2004, and maintained until 2006' (DfES, 2006b, p. 12).

In fact, according to the latest government figures (DCSF, 2008c), 9.5 per cent of children looked after for a year or more, who were aged 10 or over, had been convicted or subject to a final warning or reprimand in the year to September 2007. This compares with a figure of 4.1 per cent for all children. Having said this, the national figure regarding offending by looked after children masks a wide variation across the country. For example, between 2002–3 and 2004–5, offending rates among such young people rose from 13 per cent to 25 per cent on the Isle of Wight, but fell from 10 per cent to zero in Ealing, West London (McCormack, 2006). It is unclear what accounts for such a difference between the best and worst performing authorities.

In interpreting some of the local figures, it is important to sound a note of caution and emphasize that some areas have very low numbers of looked after children. Therefore, a small change in the number of crimes can cause large changes in percentage rates. Furthermore, the comparability of the figures for *all* children with looked after children is also problematic, because the figures for all children are for police force areas, which do not necessarily follow the same boundaries as individual local authorities (which the looked after children data are based on) (DfES, 2006b).

While the limitations above are important to be aware of, collecting data on offending rates still provides us with some useful baseline information and is a starting point for examining the issues further. Of course, what the statistics can never do is provide reasons and explanations for particular types of outcome, and we can interpret the national data on offending rates in a number of ways. For example, do they indicate that looked after children are more likely to be criminal, more likely to come under official surveillance or more likely to have their behaviour reported to the police? Clearly there is a need to move beyond the statistics and recognize that they do not tell the full story in understanding exactly what is going on. For example, in explaining the offending rates of young people in residential care, the situation is complex and there are a whole host of factors at play that may include bullying, peer pressure, lack of staff continuity and support, low aspirations for young residents, as well as their own behaviour (Taylor, 2006). One particular issue of concern is considered below.

## The prosecution of minor offences in children's homes

The routine prosecution of minor offences in children's homes has emerged as a particular problem in recent years, and there is increasing evidence to suggest that residential care staff may rely on police involvement as a means of controlling behaviour (Home Office, 2004; Nacro, 2005). One inevitable consequence of this is that looked after children can be unnecessarily criminalized for behaviour that is highly unlikely to result in an official intervention for those living at home with their parents. As Nacro recently found:

> Because the threshold for calling the police to deal with looked after children can be low, some enter the criminal justice system earlier and for less serious offences than their peers. This situation widens the gap between the number of reported offences by looked after children, and that by children generally. (Nacro, 2005, p. 34)

Of particular concern is the policy that many local authorities have had of routinely reporting to the police incidents of criminal damage and assault in care homes. While such policies may well exist to protect staff and the general home environment, they need to be used with caution, and there must be clear agreement about what actually constitutes 'criminal damage' and 'assault' (Taylor, 2003). As Stanley (2006, cited in McCormack, 2006, p. 19) notes, 'magistrates were seeing children in court for having thrown a cup across the room. They were saying "we do not know what to do with these children". Court was not the solution for them'. Comments from care leavers echo such concerns:

> I was messing about in the kitchen ... and I wouldn't get down off the side, I was looking for something ... And I just got down and I was like in a hyper mood and I pushed the door to get out the way and it just hit her on the shoulder ... she took me to court. (Care-leaver, aged 16, cited in Taylor, 2006, p. 89)

The low threshold described above is incredibly worrying for looked after children, not only because it means that this vulnerable group may be discriminated against, but also because of the wider policy climate. We are living in an age where many young people are appearing before the courts and custodial rates for children are unacceptably high (Bateman, 2005). There is great concern about net-widening generally (cf. Jamieson, 2005) and the fact that young people entering the criminal justice system today are at increased risk of receiving a custodial sentence (cf. Smith, 2003). As a recent report by the Children's Rights Alliance for England (2008, p. 3) has highlighted, 'our treatment of children in conflict with the law is deeply punitive and abusive'.

Rod Morgan (in Ahmed, 2006, p. 14), former Chair of the Youth Justice Board, has noted that, 'too many cases are being brought to courts that could be dealt with more speedily and cheaply in other settings'. He expressed particular concern about children being criminalized for minor offences in children's homes, and argued that staff should be trained to deal with their behaviour rather than resort to prosecution.

Given that children are receiving custodial sentences for more and more minor offences, it is clear that the actions of carers who routinely prosecute children in their care may contribute, however unintentionally, to increasing the population of these children in prison. Added to this, of course, is the fact that routinely prosecuting minor offences does not resemble anything remotely approaching normality as it is highly unlikely that birth parents would respond to the behaviour of their children in the same way. Unfortunately, this is not the only difficulty for those trying to reduce the offending rates and safeguard the welfare of looked after children.

## Different agencies with different priorities

The experience of looked after children is structured by a lack of joined-up thinking in policy terms. While it may be argued that this is the case for most children, the experiences of disjunctures between policy areas and interventions are likely to be felt more acutely by children in care, especially those engaged in the criminal justice system as well as the looked after system. We can see this, for instance, in relation to 'intensive fostering', which, in addition to being available for those children deemed 'at risk' of harm, are also referred to in recent policy documents as potential criminal justice tools. The *Every Child Matters* Green Paper (DfES, 2003), for example, refers to the use of 'intensive fostering' for young offenders, including for 10- and 11-year-old persistent offenders. 'Intensive fostering' placements are regarded as an alternative to custody for very young offenders, yet this blurring of the boundaries between parenting and punishment highlights something of the disjointed nature of policies relating to children in the care and criminal justice systems.[1]

There is, then, a serious need for relevant agencies to understand each other's priorities, policies and practices. So, for example, the National Crime Recording Standard (NCRS) was introduced as a more victim-oriented approach to crime recording in 2002, and requires that all reports of incidents to the police, whether from victims, witnesses or third parties, be recorded. Clearly the introduction of the NCRS may limit police discretion in response to reported offending in children's homes. This obligation to record reported incidents is something that residential care staff must be made aware of, particularly those who may rely on police involvement as a means of control (cf. Home Office, 2004). This is particularly important because: 'Many care staff felt the contraction of the residential care sector and emphasis on adoption and foster placements meant that the *resident population now tends to represent the more challenging end of the looked-after spectrum*' (Home Office, 2004, p. 4, original emphasis).

---

[1]   The use of 'intensive fostering' in this manner also raises questions about how such a scheme could successfully operate given the national shortage of carers. In addition, there are concerns that, in the current climate, intensive fostering may be used in addition to custody, instead of as an alternative to it (Kenny, 2005)

Not only is there a need for links to be made between the priorities of the police and residential care workers, but also between the police and youth justice workers. Morgan (in Ahmed, 2006) argues that the police should be given incentives for diverting young people away from the criminal justice system. As he notes, the police do not have targets for restorative justice work, but for how many cases they bring to justice. As he rightly observes, 'if we want to see police work dovetailing with youth justice, they must be rewarded for spending time on other measures' (Morgan, in Ahmed, 2006, p. 14). Indeed, it is often only when the police and other practitioners deviate from their 'official' priorities that genuinely positive joined-up working can actually occur. This tends to happen when committed individuals are prepared to devote time and energy to work that is supplementary to requirements, and that they will not necessarily be rewarded for.

A nationally recognized initiative from the Lancashire police constabulary aimed at reducing 'young runaway' cases has demonstrated how the police, in partnership with care providers and local authorities, can help to reduce the incidence of children repeatedly going missing from care (see Middleham, 2005). One of the benefits of this approach is to mitigate the exposure of young people running from care to the dangers of drug and alcohol abuse, as well as sexual exploitation and crime. Clearly, looked after children who run away from care may be at particular risk of coming into conflict with the law, and this is another route that may lead to their involvement in the justice system. Once on the run, offences may be committed as a means of survival in an effort to obtain money for food and lodgings. Sleeping rough is also likely to expose children to older homeless populations who may themselves be involved in varying degrees of illegal activity.

The Lancashire initiative highlighted that children running away from residential care homes dominate the repeat runaway problem (those running three times or more) and put themselves at increased risk of involvement in crime, as both victims and offenders. Yet establishing protocols for joint working in this area has led to a 25 per cent cut in the number of repeat missing cases (Mickel, 2008). However, the police have no targets to deal with the problem of runaways, and when resources are low, other areas where there are targets to be met inevitably take priority. Clearly there is a need to ensure that relevant agencies have the capacity to make progress in working together, rather than having conflicting priorities that dominate their attention. This is particularly pertinent with respect to safeguarding looked after children in custody.

## Supporting looked after children in custody

Looked after children and care-leavers are over-represented in our prisons, despite the fact that prison is not an appropriate place for any children, let alone some of the most vulnerable children in our society. As Goldson (2001, p. 79) points out, 'we are literally awash with evidence which confirms time and time again that youth custody is corrosive, damaging, expensive and spectacularly counter-productive'. Despite this, the number of 15- to 17-year-olds in prison over the last 10 years has more than doubled, and there is a great concern generally about the creeping inflation of sentences for non-violent and petty offences (Prison Reform Trust, 2006).

Given current concerns about the routine prosecution of minor offences in children's homes, it is arguable that the punitive emphasis in the current political climate bodes particularly badly for looked after children. Thus, looked after children may find themselves at disproportionate risk of a prison sentence and all that this entails (including the consequences of trying to build a stable life on release). Many, of course, are still entitled to a certain amount of support from their local authority, for example, under the Children Act 1989 and Children (Leaving Care) Act 2000, although the quality of this support is incredibly variable (see, for instance, Broad, 2005 on financial support). In one recent case, Mr Justice Munby (2005, para. 39) ruled that a local authority's plans for a looked after child in prison were 'little more than worthless'. Worryingly, evidence suggests that some looked after children will never receive any support at all because of the inherent problems in identifying looked after children in custody (Hart, 2006).

A recent study by the National Children's Bureau (Hart, 2006), commissioned by the DfES, has highlighted a number of barriers to joined up working between the relevant agencies. Of particular concern is the fact that there are two distinct planning systems in operation with no formal links between them: the looking after children system and the sentence planning system. As Hart (2006, p. 4) argues, a 'fundamental difficulty in planning for looked after children in custody is the fact that we do not know how many there are or what their exact care status is. The reason for this lack of data lies in the way each agency defines, collects and shares information'.

She goes on to identify some specific difficulties in this area:

- ASSET (the assessment system used by Young Offender Institutions) does not effectively capture children's care status, in particular their entitlement to services under the Children (Leaving Care) Act 2000. While the introduction of the Common Assessment Framework may assist in this respect, it also throws up a number of potential problems for practitioners with regard to the duplication of data and the potential for misunderstanding of key terms (such as 'risk' and 'harm') used in different ways by those working in Children's Services and the Youth Justice system (see YJB, 2006).
- There are confusing and poorly understood legal definitions of the 'care' status of looked after children who enter custody. For example, children accommodated by agreement under section 20 of the Children Act 1989 are not regarded as 'looked after children' when they are in prison.

While Hart (2006) reports that moves are afoot to improve information sharing between key agencies, this does not address the issue of why children accommodated under section 20 are regarded as 'looked after' right up until the point that they enter prison. Further anomalies in the law with respect to looked after children in custody have been highlighted by Nacro (2008), who note that not only do those children looked after under section 20 lose their 'looked after' status when they enter custody, but this status is not automatically reinstated upon release. This obviously has implications for whether individuals are entitled to leaving care support. To add further complexity, there is little uniformity from area to area in the treatment of those on remand:

> Those on remand face a complex range of legal provisions which can seem to be, and sometimes are, unjust. Looked after status can be gained, denied or lost according to age, gender, assessed vulnerability, placement type and availability and the approach of individual local authorities (regarding applications for secure accommodation orders). (Nacro, 2008, p. 3)

So while those accommodated under 'section 20' lose their looked after status on entry to custody (possibly forever), the entitlement of those on remand to looked after services is a complete lottery. Furthermore, Nacro (2008) highlight that particular neglect of duties can arise when a child is subject to long-term detention or an indeterminate sentence and reaches the age of 18 while in custody. Such anomalies in the law seem nonsensical in many respects, and when combined with the lack of information-sharing between relevant agencies, serve only to increase the likelihood that looked after children who enter custody may become lost in the system and denied access to key support services that they are entitled to. Many may already face particular difficulties as a result of being brought up in the care of the state, such as inadequate preparation for independent living. This can result in young people finding comfort in an institutional setting such as prison (cf. Carlen, 1987; Taylor, 2006), as highlighted in the following comment from a care-leaver serving his fifth custodial sentence.

> I worry more about getting out than I do about coming in ... Because when you get out you're getting out and you haven't even got nowhere to live, you know what I mean? Cos I can't go and stay with me mum or dad, so then I've got to go to a hostel and wait in there on a council waiting list. And then I've got to wait for a flat, and it takes whatever, however long. And once you've got your flat you've gotta find the money to like decorate it, buy furniture and like all the things you need and all that. You get grants but like it's not enough. (Care-leaver, aged 18, cited in Taylor, 2006, p. 167)

With respect to looked after children and care-leavers in prison, it is absolutely crucial that Children's Services continue to be involved, particularly as the primary aim of the youth justice system is to prevent offending, and not to safeguard children's welfare. It is noteworthy that the White Paper, *Care Matters:*

*Time for Change* (DCSF, 2007, p. 64) proposes introducing a notification requirement so that 'Youth Offending Teams must inform the responsible local authorities where their children in care, whether or not they share formal parental responsibility for them, enter custody'. This could potentially go some way to ensuring that children are actually visited and not simply forgotten about.

## Protocols and restorative justice

So how can we avoid some of the difficulties described above and divert young people in care from the criminal justice system? Detailed examination of the tensions between the safeguarding agenda and criminal justice priorities is arguably an important first step. In addition, improved sharing of information could overcome some of the difficulties of identifying, and planning for, looked after children in custody. However, there is also a pressing need to address the issues that involve looked after children being unnecessarily involved in the justice system in the first place. This returns us to the issue of the prosecution of minor offences in children's homes. Concern over this issue prompted the Crown Prosecution Service (2008) to recently issue legal guidance that states:

> A criminal justice disposal, whether a prosecution, reprimand or warning, should not be regarded as an automatic response to offending behaviour by a looked after child, irrespective of their criminal history. This applies equally to Persistent Young Offenders and adolescents of good character. A criminal justice disposal will only be appropriate where it is clearly required by the public interest.

The Crown Prosecution Service guidance (2008) goes on to note that informal disposals such as restorative justice conferencing, reparation and acceptable behaviour contracts may well be sufficient to satisfy the interests of the public, as well as reduce the risk of future offending behaviour. Indeed, one way in which the routine prosecution of minor offences is being reduced in some areas is through the development of protocols between residential care staff and the police (cf. Nacro 2005), which outline guidelines for staff on how best to respond to disruptive behaviour. The protocols encourage staff to question when it is actually appropriate to respond to an incident by calling the police, and allow for incidents to be divided into levels of seriousness.

A short, three-month study by the Home Office (2004) in three local authorities examined some of these issues further, and assessed three protocols between social services and the police for the reporting and management of incidents in children's homes. It concluded that such protocols could be beneficial because considerable reductions in reported incidents and offences were recorded. For example, in one local authority, the proportion of offences by looked after children had more than halved in two years. One of the benefits of having a formal protocol written down is that all parties involved, including young people, care home staff and the police can be made aware of exactly what type of incident or behaviour will warrant police intervention. An additional finding from the Home Office study was that protocols could lead to 'a more reflective, consistent, considered and preventative approach – making staff think what could be done differently' (Home Office, 2004, p. 12). In other words, they could encourage staff to question whether having a young person arrested was always the right response. An alternative approach developed by some local authorities has been the promotion of restorative justice.

Nacro (2005) found that one local authority in their study had provided residential staff with training in restorative skills and interventions. The course included focusing on active listening, dealing with challenging situations, mediating others' conflicts and facilitating conferencing and problem-solving circles. 'Feedback from the staff showed that their confidence grew, the team developed a strong bond, and new skills were developed. Anecdotal feedback from managers, six months later, stated that the police were called in less to deal with disruption and problems' (Nacro, 2005, p. 37).

Similarly, one local authority in the Home Office study had adopted a restorative justice approach because home staff, police and magistrates were dissatisfied with their present system. It was felt that 'police are too often used as an agent of control, called out too frequently for what they perceive to be "care issues", and forced to arrest young people for want of any alternative' (Home Office, 2004, pp. 8–9). Rather than training home staff, this local authority aimed to provide trained staff from outside the home to be on call to respond to incidents in the homes. The idea was that these staff would offer mediation between perpetrators and home staff, and consider how young people could 'pay' for their behaviour without being arrested.

The *Care Matters* Green Paper (DfES, 2006c) refers to the use of restorative justice as an alternative form of behaviour management. Further research is required to explore exactly how effective the interventions described above are in reducing offending rates in a range of care settings. Yet, they do at the very least highlight that residential care staff have a range of options available to them when responding to 'disruptive' behaviour. Calling the police should never be the default response, as this can have consequences that last a lifetime for the looked after child.

## Discipline from someone who cares

None of the above discussion is intended to suggest that looked after children should never be punished when they are involved in more serious offences, or that police involvement is always inappropriate. Of course, there will be times when young people need to be disciplined. However, as I have argued elsewhere (Taylor, 2006) this discipline is most likely to be most effective in reducing offending when it comes from someone who cares, and who the young person, in turn, cares about. This is most likely to occur when carers and young people have the opportunity to develop bonds of trust and respect for one another, and when clear and consistent boundaries about acceptable behaviour are provided. In this situation, where strong attachment relationships may develop, punishment and reintegrative shaming are possible while maintaining bonds of respect (cf. Braithewaite, 1989).

Unfortunately, the development of secure attachments is notoriously difficult to achieve in residential care, in particular where a lack of staff continuity, peer group pressure and a generally more challenging care population can seriously hinder the development of stability, security and safety. While this chapter has focused on the residential care experience in particular, it is important to acknowledge that different types of care experience may lead to very different outcomes. In this respect, the potential of foster care is noteworthy – in encouraging the development of secure attachments, as well as in diverting young people from criminal behaviour. Interviews with care-leavers highlight that certain sorts of foster care experience, such as those associated with stability, security and a quality relationship with foster carers, can help to protect against involvement in crime (Taylor, 2006).

Notwithstanding the earlier comments made about intensive fostering, the potential of specialist foster care schemes to divert young people on remand from criminal behaviour must not be overlooked. A recent evaluation of one of the National Children's Home's specialist remand fostering services considered the success of the service as an alternative to custodial or residential accommodation for young people on remand. Results from the evaluation revealed that over 70 per cent of the young people did not commit any offences during their placement, despite persistently offending before (Lipscombe, 2006). Similarly, an evaluation of a specialist fostering scheme in Scotland (Walker *et al.*, 2002), offering placements to young people who would otherwise be in secure residential accommodation, highlighted that young people could benefit from such schemes. Benefits were highest for those who established long-term relationships with carers and who would be able to rely on their support into adult life.

As commentators continually observe, the 'most likely means of translating stability in care into felt security, and into ongoing social support, is through the continuity of relationships, acceptance and the normality of these young people's daily lives' (Cashmore and Paxman, 2006, p. 239). Indeed, discipline is likely to be particularly effective when it is carried out by someone who cares, and it goes without saying that routinely reporting looked after children to the police is not anything remotely approaching normality or acceptance by carers.

## Conclusion

This chapter has focused on policy and practice relating to looked after children who represent some of the most vulnerable and disadvantaged individuals in society. New Labour governments have expressed a clear commitment to improving outcomes for children in care and after as part of its wider 'safeguarding children' agenda, and this commitment is certainly to be welcomed. However, in practice, progress has been incredibly slow and children in care are now at greater risk of being left behind than was the case a few years ago (Johnson, 2006). Furthermore, the government has failed to seriously address the complex needs of those who may find themselves straddling the care and criminal justice systems simultaneously. Ironically, it is these individuals who may be at particular risk of marginalization and social exclusion in the future. While specialist fostering schemes may offer a way of diverting young people from the criminal justice system, it is unfortunate that appropriate resources, such as specialist carers, remain in short supply.

It has been argued here that a range of factors may contribute to the criminalization of looked after children (other than their own behaviour), and there has been a particular focus on the routine prosecution of minor offences in children's homes. Evidence suggests that the police are often called inappropriately as a means of control, and looked after children may find themselves prosecuted for behaviour that would not necessarily result in an official intervention for those living at home with their parents. However, there are other factors too. The lack of joined-up working between relevant agencies has been highlighted as a particular problem. This issue is often exacerbated by the fact that agencies tend to have different priorities, different targets to meet and different performance measurements to monitor. Indeed, there is a clear conflict between top-down nationally set targets and the need to join-up services bilaterally via effective close working relationships in order to safeguard children and young people (cf. Newman, 2001). Currently, relevant agencies are rarely working towards the same goal. Nowhere is this more apparent than when looked after children end up in prison custody.

In November 2007 a joint governmental youth justice unit was launched with the aim of bringing together the agendas of the Ministry of Justice and the DCSF. It is not yet clear whether this new unit will be able to deal with any of the issues discussed above, but it is sincerely hoped that it will recognize the diversity of individual care careers and focus on meeting the needs of all looked after children. At present, the disjointed policy assumptions relating to children in need and children in trouble means that the situation looks particularly bleak for those who come into contact with the justice system. This is unlikely to change unless the government leads the way in ensuring that every child really does matter. Until then we will continue to see an over-representation of care-leavers in the criminal justice system and in prisons up and down the country.

While this chapter has highlighted a degree of concern with respect to policy and practice relating to looked after children, it is nevertheless important to end on a note of optimism, as it is the firm belief of the author that things do not have to be this way. There is nothing inevitable about looked after children faring poorly in the care system and beyond. Research with young people themselves highlights that some do very well, are incredibly resilient in spite of previous adversity and can have very positive experiences of care. There is no reason why this could not be the case for a far greater proportion of children in the care of the state. Emphasizing the need to safeguard the welfare of *all* looked after children, including those who come into contact with the criminal justice system, would arguably go some way to ensuring that positive experiences of care become the norm rather than the exception.

# References

Ahmed, M. (2006) 'Too many cases that go to court could be dealt with elsewhere', *Community Care*, 4–10 May: 14.

Bateman, T. (2005) 'Reducing child imprisonment: A systemic challenge', *Youth Justice*, 5 (2): 91–105.

Berridge, D. (2007) 'Theory and explanation in child welfare: Education and looked after children', *Child and Family Social Work*, 12 (1): 1–10.

Biehal, N., Clayden, J., Stein, M. and Wade, J. (1995) *Moving On: Young People and Leaving Care Schemes*, London: HMSO.

Braithewaite, J. (1989) *Crime, Shame and Reintegration*, Cambridge: Cambridge University Press.

Broad, B. (2005) 'Young people leaving care: Implementing the Children (Leaving Care) Act 2000?' *Children and Society*, 19: 371–384.

Carlen, P. (1987) '*Out of care, into custody*' in P. Carlen and A. Worrall (eds.), *Gender, Crime and Justice*, Milton Keynes: Oxford University Press.

Cashmore, J. and Paxman, M. (2006) 'Predicting after-care outcomes: The importance of felt security', *Child and Family Social Work*, 11 (3): 232–241.

Children's Rights Alliance for England (2008) *United Nations Committee on the Rights of the Child: Third Examination of the UK, 2008, Summary June 2008*, London: Children's Rights Alliance.

Colton, M. (2002) 'Factors associated with abuse in residential child care institutions', *Children and Society*, 16 (1): 33–44.

Crown Prosecution Service (2008) 'Offending behaviour in Children's Homes' in *Legal Guidance on 'Youth Offenders'*. Available at: http://www.cps.gov.uk/legal/v_to_z/youth_offenders/#a22 (accessed 11 November 2008).

DCSF (2007) *Care Matters: Time for Change*, London: DCSF.

DCSF (2008a) *Care Matters: Time to Deliver for Children in Care*, London: DCSF and the Association of Directors of Children's Services and the Local Government Association.

DCSF (2008b) 'Children in care to get school pics and passports', *Press Notice 2008/0057*. Available at: http://www.dcsf.gov.uk/pns/DisplayPN.cgi?pn_id = 2008_0057 (accessed 11 November 2008).

DCSF (2008c) *Outcome Indicators for Children Looked After: Twelve Months to 30 September 2007, England*, London: DCSF.

DfES (2003) *Every Child Matters*, Cm 5860, Norwich: The Stationery Office.

DfES (2006a) *The Children Act 1989 Report: 2004 and 2005*, London: DfES.

DfES (2006b) *Outcome Indicators for Looked After Children, Twelve Months to 30 September 2005 – England*, London: DfES.

DfES (2006c) *Care Matters: Transforming the Lives of Children and Young People in Care*, Cm 6932, London: DfES.

DfES (2007) *Outcome Indicators for Looked After Children, Twelve Months to 30 September 2006 – England*, London: DfES.
Goldson, B. (2001) 'A rational youth justice? Some critical reflections on the research, policy and practice relation', *Probation Journal*, 48 (2): 76–85.
Goldson, B. (2002) *Vulnerable Inside: Children in Secure and Penal Settings*, London: The Children's Society.
Grover, C. and Stewart, J. (2004) 'Care leavers: Financial support and the 2000 Children (Leaving Care) Act', *Benefits: A Journal of Social Security Research, Policy and Practice*, 12 (2): 107–111.
Grover, C., Stewart, J. and Broadhurst, K. (2004) 'Transitions to adulthood: Some critical observations of the Children (Leaving Care) Act 2000', *Social Work and Social Sciences Review*, 11 (1): 5–18.
Hart, D. (2006) *Tell Them Not to Forget about Us: A Guide to Practice with Looked After Children in Custody*, London: National Children's Bureau.
Hazel, N., Hagell, A., Liddle, M., Archer, D., Grimshaw, R. and King, J. (2002) *Detention and Training: Assessment of the Detention and Training Order and Its Impact on the Secure Estate across England and Wales*, London: YJB.
Home Office (2004) *Preventative Approaches Targeting Young People in Local Authority Residential Care*, Home Office Development and Practice Report 14, London: Home Office.
Jamieson, J. (2005) 'New Labour, youth justice and the question of "respect"', *Youth Justice*, 5 (3): 180–193.
Johnson, A. (2006) 'Foreword' in *Care Matters: Transforming the Lives of Children and Young People in Care*, Cm 6932, London: The Stationery Office.
Kenny, C. (2005) 'Special report on intensive fostering', *Community Care*, 5 May 2005. Available at: http://www.communitycare.co.uk/Articles/2005/05/05/49220/special-report-on-intensive-fostering.html (accessed 12 November 2008).
Lipscombe, J. (2006) *Care or Control: Foster Care for Young People on Remand*, London: British Association for Adoption and Fostering.
McCormack, H. (2006) 'High thresholds for referral to criminal justice system are key to cutting offending', *Community Care*, 25–31 May: 18–19.
Mickel, A. (2008) 'Advantageous liaisons', *Community Care*, 27 March: 20–21.
Middleham, N. (2005) 'Nowhere to run to', *Police Professional*, 20 October.
Munby, The Honourable Mr Justice (2005) in R (J) v Caerphilly County Borough Council, 12 April 2005, *2005 WestLaw 836348*, para. 39.
Nacro (2005) *A Handbook on Reducing Offending by Looked After Children*, London: Nacro.
Nacro (2008) 'Children in custody: Local authority duties, responsibilities and powers', *Youth Crime Briefing March 2008*, London: Nacro and Howard League for Penal Reform.
Newman, J. (2001) *Modernising Governance: New Labour, Policy and Society*, London: Sage.
Prison Reform Trust (2006) *Bromley Briefings: Prison Factfile April 2006*, London: Prison Reform Trust.
Sergeant, H. (2006) *Handle with Care: An Investigation into the Care System*, London: Centre for Young Policy Studies.
Sinclair, I., Baker, C., Lee, J. and Gibbs, I. (2007) *The Pursuit of Permanence: A Study of the English Care System*, London: Jessica Kingsley.
Smith, D. (2003) 'New Labour and youth justice', *Children and Society*, 17 (3): 226–235.
Social Services Inspectorate (1997) *When Leaving Home Is also Leaving Care: An Inspection of Services for Young People Leaving Care*, Wetherby: Department of Health.

Standing Committee A (2000) *Children (Leaving Care) Bill [Lords]*, First sitting, London: The Stationery Office.

Stein, M. and Carey, K. (1986) *Leaving Care*, Oxford: Basil Blackwell.

Taylor, C. (2003) 'Justice for looked after children?', *Probation Journal*, 50 (3): 239–251.

Taylor, C. (2006) *Young People in Care and Criminal Behaviour*, London: Jessica Kingsley.

Walker, M., Hill, M. and Triseliotis, J. (2002) *Testing the Limits of Foster Care: Fostering as an Alternative to Secure Accommodation*, London: British Association for Adoption and Fostering.

YJB (2006) *The Common Assessment Framework, Asset and Onset: Guidance for Youth Justice Practitioners*, London: YJB.

# 13

# Safeguarding Children Who Are Refugees or Asylum Seekers: Managing Multiple Scales of Legislation and Policy

Malcolm Hill and Peter Hopkins

## Introduction

This chapter is concerned with children who have sought, or are seeking, refuge in the UK on account of major threats to their welfare and possibly lives in their countries of origin. Initially, when such children arrive in the UK, they are classified as asylum-seekers. The majority of these come with a parent or other responsible adult, but some are 'unaccompanied', giving rise to needs concerning immediate care in addition to that of asylum. An asylum seeker is someone who has left her/his country of origin because of persecution and who applies to be recognized formally as a refugee in the UK. If and when asylum seekers are granted leave to stay in the UK, then they become 'refugees', although that is not necessarily a label that they or others would wish to emphasize. All young refugees have therefore been young asylum-seekers at some point, and were successful in their application to be given refugee status. It is very important that the terms 'refugee' and 'asylum seeker' should be distinguished from the term 'economic migrant', as the first two terms are associated with protection issues, while economic migrants are associated with moving in order to work.

Children who are seeking asylum or who are refugees apart from their families may be separated for different reasons. Some are sent abroad by their parents in order to save their lives; others are left behind when parents return home or re-settle elsewhere (Kidane, 2001; Whande, 1993). A particularly vulnerable sub-group of refugee children are those who have entered the country as a result of 'trafficking'. In other words, those who are in the UK against their wishes and possibly those of their parents (Bokhari, 2008).

*Critical Perspectives on Safeguarding Children*   Edited by Karen Broadhurst, Chris Grover and Janet Jamieson
© 2009 John Wiley & Sons, Ltd

This chapter explores how safeguarding the well-being and rights of refugee and asylum-seeker children is the product of a complex interaction between, on the one hand, immigration and asylum policies and, on the other hand, children's policies. While the latter are centrally concerned with promoting children's welfare and protecting them from harm, the former represent an uneasy compromise between humanitarian impulses and a desire to control or restrict the number and types of individuals entering the country or becoming citizens. This complex interaction is further complicated by the ways in which legislation and policy at various scales – international, European, British and devolved levels (for example, Scotland and Wales)   influences the ways in which practitioners work to maximize the well-being of the children they work with.

## Multiple scales of immigration, asylum and citizenship policy: International, European, British and devolved strategies

In order to explore the complex scaling of legislation and policies for asylum seeking and refugee children in the context of safeguarding, we now explore relevant policies at the international and European, UK and devolved levels.

### International and European policies

Focusing upon international policy, the 1951 Convention on the status of refugees states that the term 'refugee' shall apply to any person who:

> owing to well-founded fear of being persecuted for reason of race, religion, nationality, membership of a particular social group or political opinion, is outside the country of his nationality and is unable or, owing to such fear, is unwilling to avail himself of the protection of that country; or who, not having a nationality and being outside the country of his former habitual residence as a result of such events, is unable or, owing to such fear, is unwilling to return to it. (UNHCR, 1951)

As such, a refugee is a person 'whose asylum application has been successful and who is allowed to stay in another country having proved they would face persecution back home' (Refugee Council, 2004, p. 1). An asylum seeker is a person who has fled persecution in their country of origin, has identified themselves to the relevant authorities and is exercising their right to apply for refugee status.

European policy has been having an increasing impact on various aspects of legislation in recent years, thereby adding an additional layer of policy to worldwide agreements. The European Union has a long-standing interest in the movement of people, though the focus has been on adult workers, with children accompanying them as dependents (Hantrais, 1995; Hill, 1990). A central policy principle has been to promote the free movement of labour as part of an internal market aimed at improving prosperity. At the same time, an emphasis has been placed on controlling inward migration. Thus, internal borders within the EU have weakened, while external borders have been strengthened, at least in theory. Certain policies have been developed affecting children as by-products of fostering labour movement and equalizing costs for workers. For instance, a Directive from 1977 sought to ensure that children of migrant workers are educated in the same way as others (Ruxton, 1996). Also, some steps have been taken to combat racism (Pringle, 1998).

At a summit in 1999, European Union member states agreed to establish a Common European Asylum System (CEAS) (Refugee Council, 2004). Part of the process of harmonization of member state policies towards this goal has been the establishment of a Council Directive (2003/9/EC) on 27 January 2003 'laying down the minimum standards for the reception of asylum seekers'. This covers the reception of families (Article 8), the schooling and education of minors (Article 10), housing (Article 14), as well as the reception of unaccompanied minors (Article 19). In 2003, the Council of the European Union also established a Directive (2003/86/EC) 'on the right to family reunification'. This states that Member States 'shall authorise the entry and residence for the purposes of family reunification of his/her first-degree relatives', as well as suggesting that Member States may also do this for the legal guardian or other family members of an unaccompanied asylum-seeking child. Also, the European Council Directive 2004/83/EC, of 29 April 2004, set out minimum standards for qualification, status and the nature of the protection that should be granted, including, for instance, rights to travel, employment and education. This directive was transposed into UK law on 9 October 2006 by the introduction of 'The Refugee or Person in Need of International Protection (Qualification) Regulations 2006' and new paragraphs of the Immigration Rules.

The European Convention on Human Rights and the five Protocols associated with this also outline a range of articles that should guide efforts to maximize the well-being and welfare of asylum-seeking and refugee children. Article 3, for example, states that 'no one shall be subjected to torture or to inhuman or degrading treatment or punishment'. Article 6 outlines an individual's right to a free trial and Article 8 is about the right to respect for private and family life. Protocol 1, Article 2 also clarifies that 'no person shall be denied the right to education'. A number of these articles can be drawn upon by lawyers in their attempts to secure refugee status for the asylum-seeking children they work with.

The Council of Europe is a more informal association with less power than the EU, so that its influence is exerted mainly by guidance and persuasion. For example, it has taken a lead role in devising standards for safeguarding the interests of asylum-seeking and refugee children. In particular, it has advocated that all countries should assign guardians to unaccompanied asylum-seeking children to supervise their care arrangements and advocate on their behalf. The

Council of Europe has a Convention designed to protect adults and children from trafficking and its consequences. The UK has signed but not ratified this Convention (Bokhari, 2008).

Just as international agreements about asylum sometimes refer to children, so documents concerned with children as a whole may include specific reference to asylum seekers and refugees, as well as define universal obligations towards children that should include those who have sought refuge. The leading document in this respect is the UN Convention on the Rights of the Child (UNCRC, 1989). This has been ratified by nearly all nation states, which are thereby expected to adhere to its provisions. The individual articles and terms are sometimes quite general, however, and so open to varying interpretations (Archard, 2003; Asquith and Hill, 1994). Moreover, states are able to register exemptions, as the UK has done with respect to certain immigration issues. Furthermore, certain countries have incorporated the Convention directly into their domestic legislation, but many, including the UK, have not done this, though they have imported selected principles into statutes.

The UNCRC sets out a wide range of children's rights, which governments are expected to respect and respond to. They are often grouped into three or four categories. Prominent among these is the right to protection. Others relate to participation, provision of services and promotion of development (Verhellen, 1997). These are meant to apply to all children and are governed by an overarching principle of non-discrimination set out in Article 2. This specifies that all the rights covered by the Convention are to be applied without discrimination, that is, irrespective of a child's characteristics or background. The list of features that should not be used as a basis of discrimination includes race and national origin, which are very pertinent for refugees. The UNCRC also covers refugee children explicitly. Section 22 stipulates that governments should ensure that a child seeking refugee status or considered a refugee receives appropriate assistance and protection. Such children are deemed to have the same rights as any other (for example, to protection, services, education and participation). The relevant government has a duty to seek to reunite separated refugee children with their families. Where this is not possible, then such children should be afforded the same protection as any other separated child.

As noted above, EU policy has for the most part ignored children because it has been mainly concerned with economic and political matters, from which children are excluded. However, an exception is the Directive (2003/86/EC) 'on the right to family reunification'. This requires Member States to 'authorise the entry and residence (of a child) for the purposes of family reunification of his/her first-degree relatives'. It also suggests that Member States may for the same reason accept the legal guardian or other family members of an unaccompanied asylum-seeking child.

The Council of Europe devised its own Convention on the Exercise of Children's Rights to supplement the UNCRC (Marshall, 1997). It applies only to judicial family proceedings. A major thrust of the Convention is that children should enjoy clear procedural rights (for example, to information about any legal matter) and that they should be active participants whose views ought to be taken seriously.

## UK policy

At the heart of the UK's immigration policy is a desire to control both the number and 'types' of people adding to the population through inward migration. At times of labour shortage, immigration has often been encouraged, but demographic and racist fears have often fuelled more restrictive policies (Smith, 1989). Cemlyn and Briskman (2003, p. 164), for instance, state that 'asylum policy in Britain has been built on the racist foundations of previous immigration policy'. The last 50 years have seen fluctuating trends in the UK with both large inward movements and restrictive legislation. Since 2000 the position has been mixed with a large expansion in immigration from Eastern Europe as a result of EU expansion and of asylum-seekers due to the large number of conflict zones and the easier (though not necessarily easy) means of travel to Europe. Serious efforts have been made to restrict the numbers of asylum-seekers while adhering to international obligations. Efforts to stem an increase in the admission of refugees has also occurred in Ireland, even though it has had a very different history, with net immigration only recently replacing a century of substantial emigration (Christie, 2003).

Asylum-seeker and refugee children's entitlements to enter the UK or to stay are largely determined by asylum policy, which originates in international law rather than immigration legislation (CARIS, 2007). Domestic law has been passed to incorporate the relevant international conventions and set out national procedures and enforcement mechanisms. The two basic principles are:

(1) refugees should not be returned to persecution
(2) the government must provide an asylum applicant with a procedure to make a claim to stay.

Immigration law is mainly concerned with planned applications for entry and citizenship rather than the emergency and persecution basis of asylum seeking. However, the contents and debates surrounding immigration policies have helped express and shape the cultural and attitudinal context that impinges on the everyday lives of young people who have sought refuge in the UK. Negative images of incomers to the country have been central to policies aiming to control immigration and the location of immigrants, including policies to disperse asylum seekers away from London, and to restrict access to financial and health services (Cohen *et al.*, 2002).

The Immigration Act 1971 is the main statutory source of modern immigration law, setting out provisions, for example, related to the leave to enter and the right of abode (CARIS, 2007). It also contains enforcement procedures, and details of immigration-related offences, including helping an asylum seeker to enter the UK unlawfully. The Immigration and Asylum (Treatment of Claimants) Act 2004 set out altered arrangements for dealing with asylum claims, prompted in part by public and media concerns about the growth in applications from asylum seekers and long delays in reaching decisions about them (see, for instance, Article 19, 2002). A policy paper of 2005 spoke of intentions to 'enforce strict controls to root out abuse', reflecting concerns about deception, as well as fears of newcomers (Dennis, 2007, p. 22).

In the last few years, a new strand has been added to policy debates and actions concerning immigration and asylum, namely the question of whether or not it is desirable to require prospective and new citizens to demonstrate knowledge of Britishness. This in turn has been linked to statements that 'multi-culturalism' has failed, because it has encouraged some immigrants (and their descendants) to avoid becoming 'British'. As a result, the government through the Nationality, Immigration and Asylum Act 2002 introduced courses and tests that need to be attended and passed to obtain UK citizenship, as well as ceremonies to mark the award of that status. This follows the example of other countries like the USA, Canada and Australia (Bloemraad, 2006). Critics have argued that the attack on multi-culturalism has been misguided since it is aimed at integration based on respect for difference, not segregation (Modood, 2007). Furthermore, the emphasis on Britishness has evoked concern that this relies on fixed traditional notions that are unhelpful at a time when many people experience multiple or ambiguous identities, some of which are related to overseas descent (Hopkins, 2007; Modood *et al.*, 1994), though others are not, most notably in Northern Ireland, Scotland and Wales.

With regard to UK policy and law about children, while these are largely devolved (although a few matters, like child benefit, are reserved to the UK level), there is considerable commonality in the children's legislation for England, Wales, Scotland and Northern Ireland. The UK as a whole did opt out of a few parts of the UNCRC when this was ratified in 1991. This meant that the UK retained the right to pass laws concerning asylum and immigration without having to take account of the rights of any children affected. This in itself highlights Government priorities. The opt out has been interpreted to mean that any measure of immigration control is unaffected by the UNCRC (CARIS, 2007). It has also added to concerns of practitioners that this seems to restrict the rights of the children affected (Dennis, 2007). On the other hand, Home Office policy says that no unaccompanied minor will be removed from the UK unless it is satisfied that adequate reception and care arrangements are in place in the country to which he/she is to be removed. If it is not possible for satisfactory reception arrangements to be made for a child under 18, the presumption is that discretionary leave will be granted for three years or until the child reaches 18, whichever comes first. Critics have cast doubt on the adequacy of arrangements for some children who have been removed, suggesting that they should have been allowed to stay to safeguard their welfare and safety (Watters, 2008). Moreover, children who are permitted to stay temporarily can experience acute anxiety about their uncertain status and fears for their future (Chase *et al.*, 2008; Hopkins and Hill, 2008).

More generally, in recent years it has been possible to identify a crystallization of 'children's policy', separate from 'family' policy and wider than 'child welfare policy' (Wasoff and Hill, 2002; see also chapter 2 in this volume). Both legislation and government departmental organization have given greater priority to children in their own right and aimed to integrate legislation and provision that previously dealt separately with, for instance, child protection and looked after children, education, early years services, divorce/separation and family support. This trend has been prompted and accompanied by an acceptance by many professionals and politicians that many problems and needs in relation to children and families are interconnected, and that there should be close links between universal and more specialist or targeted services. As Taylor in this volume notes, a related theme has been a widening, and indeed revision, of the concept of child protection towards the notion of safeguarding (see also Walker and Thurston, 2006).

Reflecting and helping to constitute this broadening process the revised ECM framework (Department for Children, Schools and Families [DCSF], 2008, p. 1) emphasizes that the five outcome statements apply to 'every child and young person, whatever their background or circumstances'. Indeed, unaccompanied asylum-seeking children were identified in ECM as being among those in greatest need. It committed the government to enhanced support from the Immigration Service, social services and the police. ECM recognized the important role of the Refugee Council's Children Panel, as well as its capacity to support only a minority of children. The Panel has focused support largely in the South East of England, lacking resources to cover, for instance, Scotland (Hopkins and Hill, 2006). However, with rare exceptions, asylum-seeking and refugee children have been marginal within policies and practice concerned with both child protection and children in need (see, for example, Munro, 2002).

## Devolved contexts

With reference to devolution in the UK, legislation about immigration and nationality is a reserved matter and so powers to create such policies lay with Westminster rather than with the devolved governments, and such policies are applied to the whole of the UK. There are, therefore, no specifically English, Scottish or Welsh legislation that applies to the asylum seeking or refugee children with regards to their immigration status. However, most of the legislation about children *is* devolved to England, Scotland and Wales, and this also includes policies about education. This means that tensions can arise not only between different government departments, but also between different levels of government, especially as the responsibility for implementing legislation mainly rests with a large number of local authorities.

The leading piece of children's legislation, the Children Act 1989, only applies to England and Wales apart from a few sections (Hill and Aldgate, 1996). However, the Children (Northern Ireland) Order of 1995 is almost identical. The Children (Scotland) Act 1995 shares many principles and some terminology with the 1989 Act, for example, with regard to the duties of local authorities and others to promote and safeguard the welfare of children, and take their views into account provided they have sufficient age and understandings (Hothersall, 2006). Also, the concept of children in need has been adopted from the 1989 Act. However, Scotland also has important differences, notably that matters of child protection and crime by young people are dealt with in the hearings system rather than by youth or family courts as in England and Wales (Hill *et al.*, 2005). Similarly, Scotland and North of Ireland have separate Education Acts and there are significant differences, for example, with regard to examinations and core curriculum.

The Scottish Executive produced a vision statement for all Scotland's children that noted they need to be: achieving, active, healthy, included, nurtured, respected, responsible and safe. These are very similar to the outcomes of ECM. The Scottish strategy document, equivalent to ECM in England, is *Getting it Right for Every Child* (Scottish Executive, 2003). It aims to build better childhoods for children in Scotland, encourage inter-agency cooperation and services with a 'whole child' approach, and link the needs and rights of vulnerable children with those of all children. On the whole, the programme has concentrated on broad principles and changes in organizations and cultures, rather than specific groups of children, but refugee children are entitled to the same 'child-centred', integrated assessment and services as any other child.

## Safeguarding children in the context of multiple scales of legislation

Having explored the multiple scales and interweaving levels of policy and legislation for asylum-seeking and refugee children in the UK, we now consider the ways in which these policies are played out with reference to four issues of salience to the safeguarding of asylum-seeking and refugee children: housing and accommodation; education; family contact and needs arising from past trauma.

### Housing and accommodation

With reference to safeguarding asylum seeking and refugee children, an issue of paramount importance is housing and accommodation, and this has also been identified as a key dimension of the integration process:

> The housing conditions and experiences of refugees clearly play an important role in shaping their sense of security and belonging, and have a bearing on their access to healthcare, education and employment. The ability to access safe, secure and affordable housing is also likely to have an impact on community relations, the level of secondary migration by refugees, and the development of a migrant household's capacity for secure and independent living. (Phillips, 2006, p. 539)

For a number of years asylum-seeking families who arrive in the UK have been dispersed to a variety of locations across the country. The 1999 Asylum and Immigration Act has a number of objectives which contributed to the formation of the National Asylum Support Service (NASS). This organization is responsible for assessing whether or not asylum seekers are entitled to welfare benefits and services, for allocating such entitlements and for dispersing asylum seekers to local authorities who have a NASS agreement. NASS then pays the housing and accommodation costs to the local authority in which asylum seekers have been dispersed (Robinson, 2003). Children who arrive in the UK as part of an asylum-seeking family are, therefore, dispersed with their family. Concern has been raised about the suitability of dispersal areas for the reception of refugees and asylum seekers (Robinson, 2003). Furthermore, in terms of safeguarding the welfare of refugee and asylum-seeking children, an important concern here is the extent to which access to services such as education and healthcare are available in the areas that children are dispersed to. As the dispersal areas typically make available housing that is not required by local residents, another consideration also relates to the suitability of this accommodation for asylum seeking and refugee children. Also, it has been suggested that asylum seeking and refugee children may experience hostility, racism and social exclusion from unwelcoming local children and families in such neighbourhoods (Robinson, 2003).

Immigration and asylum legislation in 1999 and 2002 exempted certain children from entitlements to support as 'children in need' under the Children Act 1989 (and its counterparts in Scotland and Northern Ireland). Unaccompanied minors seeking asylum should get the full range of support, but local authorities are prohibited from helping families with children under 18, who are provided for by NASS. If NASS withdraws support (for instance, because the family has been causing nuisance or the application for asylum has failed) then a local authority may assist. A court judgement in 2004 clarified that a local authority has a power to assist a person unlawfully present in the UK with a dependent child who was a UK citizen (*M* v *Islington London Borough Council* (Court of Appeal, 2 April 2004).

Although children who arrive with their family are allocated housing through NASS, unaccompanied children are not, and so their housing and accommodation situation is often less secure. This is concerning, particularly since these children do not have some of the structures of support available to children who arrive as part of a refugee or asylum-seeking family. The EU Directive (2003, Article 19(2)) lays down the minimum standard for the reception of asylum seekers and states that:

> Unaccompanied minors who make an application for asylum shall, from the moment they are admitted to the territory to the moment they are obliged to leave the host Member State in which the application for asylum was made or is being examined, be placed:
>
> (a) with adult relatives;
> (b) with a foster-family;
> (c) in accommodation centres with special provision for minors;
> (d) in other accommodation suitable for minors
>
> Member States may place unaccompanied minors aged 16 or over in accommodation centres for adult asylum seekers.
>
> As far as possible, siblings shall be kept together, taking into account the best interests of the minor concerned and, in particular, his or her age and degree of maturity. Changes of residence of unaccompanied minors shall be limited to a minimum.

The duties and powers of local authorities to accommodate children and young people when circumstances and their best interests require it are also unaffected. The local authorities where unaccompanied minors arrive are responsible for their welfare, and so they should be allocated a social worker and provided with appropriate accommodation according to their age. Research has shown, however, that this is often a complex process that depends on issues such as the availability of appropriate accommodation and the age of the children involved (Hopkins and Hill, 2006; Wade *et al.*, 2005). Unaccompanied children under 16 are normally accommodated in a children's unit or less often in a foster home. In 2003, about 2,400 young people were looked after in this way in England. Two-thirds were in London and many of the rest in south-east England (Kohli, 2007). Those aged 16 or 17 are usually housed in youth hostels or other residential units. Some have been accommodated for periods in hostels for homeless people and/or bed and breakfasts. Wade *et al.* (2005) showed that outcomes tended to be better for children (mainly aged under 16) who were accommodated by local authorities as being fully looked after (Children Act 1989, section 20), compared with those (mainly aged 17 or 18) who were given more limited community support (section 17). Clearly the accommodation provided to unaccompanied minors has important implications for their safety, security and well-being, as well as their ability to create a new life for themselves in a new place. In particular, the use of hostels and bed and breakfast establishments has been long criticized for exposing vulnerable young people to further risks of isolation, exploitation or abuse (Dixon and Stein, 2005).

Similarly, local authorities have duties to provide assistance after the age of 18 under the Children Leaving Care Act 2000, though the accompanying Guidance embodied ambiguity by stating that local authorities should take account of the young person's immigration status (Dennis, 2007). This does not apply in Scotland, but analogous responsibilities do apply.

Referrals and action in relation to child abuse and neglect may be taken with respect to asylum seeker and refugee children in the same way as it is with any other child. Such measures may be necessary to protect children from a person associated with their entry to the country (for instance, by trafficking) or who has provided care subsequently. Assessment, supervision and alternative care in such circumstances are intended to safeguard a child's welfare, but have been criticized for, at times, being unnecessarily intrusive and forming an extension of state surveillance (Parton *et al.*, 1997). Moreover, the arrangements made may result in additional harm, whether through direct abuse by substitute carers, discontinuities of care or lack of personalized support (Sen *et al.*, 2008; Thomas, 2000; Tunstill, 1999).

Thus there are dangers that children and young people who have experienced oppression in one country may feel oppressed anew within the British child welfare system. On the other hand, developments in both practice and theory have sought to accord agency to young people and respect their views, rather than simply treat them as objects of concern and welfare (D'Cruz and Stagnitti, 2008; Parton and Wattam, 1999). This approach fits with a resilience perspective concerning refugee children that portrays them as individuals with capacities to meet challenges, as well as needs and vulnerabilities (Kohli and Mather, 2003; Wade *et al.*, 2005). Indeed, some have criticized traditional perspectives on adult refugees as focusing too much on loss and trauma, and insufficiently on strengths and durability (Watters, 2008). In reality, refugee children and young people normally have a mix of emotional needs and robustness, with a wide variation in the combination of the two (Chase *et al.*, 2008; Hopkins and Hill, 2006; Wade *et al.*, 2005). There are opposite risks of imposing notions of psychological damage inappropriately and of ignoring the ongoing impact of past physical or emotional hurt.

Clearly then, in terms of safeguarding asylum-seeking and refugee children, housing and accommodation issues represent a somewhat unequal landscape in which a variety of issues such as availability, existence or not of other family members, and the age of the young person can have significant implications on how asylum seeking and refugee children experience their everyday lives in the UK.

## Family contact

The EU Directive (2003, Article 19(2)) laying down the minimum standard for the reception of asylum seekers states that unaccompanied minors who arrive with siblings should, as far as possible, be kept together. The same applies to children arriving as part of an asylum-seeking or refugee family. In the past when children have been separated from parents, policy and practice has at times focused on rescuing children and offering a complete break from adverse circumstances, but nowadays the emphasis is generally on seeking to sustain contact between parents and children, provided this is consistent with the child's welfare (Cleaver, 2000). As Trinder (2003) notes, there is a 'presumption in favour of enduring parent-child relationships'. This is reinforced by legal duties to promote contact with parents, provided this is consistent with the child's interests. Recent attention to kinship care highlights the importance of other relatives when parents are unavailable or unable to care (Aldgate and McIntosh, 2006; Broad, 2001). Sometimes the child feels closest to unrelated adults who have acted like kin. The person who helped a child enter the country may have an uncertain relationship to the child and the legal status may be unclear (Hopkins and Hill, 2008), but the wishes and needs of the child should be critical in making decisions about what level of contact and care is appropriate. This approach, for instance, informed specialist work with unaccompanied children undertaken by social work staff in Kent. Following careful assessments they were able to place about three-quarters of children with parents or, more commonly, other kin (Kearney, 2007).

The issue of family contact is clearly very relevant for unaccompanied minors, though professionals and experts have rarely considered them when discussing this topic. A recent text on contact between children and parents includes reference to children separated from one or both parents in a wide range of circumstances, but not unaccompanied refugee children (Bainham *et al.*, 2003). One chapter addresses contact across international boundaries, but in relation to divorce and abduction rather than asylum (Smith, 2003).

Some unaccompanied children have lost their families in very traumatic circumstances, including witnessing family members being killed in front of them (Hopkins and Hill, 2008). Many others do not know where their family members are, if they have moved from their original home or if they are seeking asylum in the same or another country. The Red Cross International Tracing and Messaging Service may, therefore, be a useful way for unaccompanied children to attempt to make contact with family members. Care is required, however, since some children will have reservations about the reactions of family members, while in other cases information may be hard to gain or be upsetting. Even so, many young people do support efforts to trace relatives on their behalf, though quick results are not common (Wade *et al.*, 2005).

## Education

In recent years particular attention has been drawn to the interaction of asylum arrangements, including temporary accommodation and financial support, and the responsibilities towards children of other services, notably those provided by the NHS and local authorities. In many respects, children in asylum-seeking families and unaccompanied asylum-seeking children have been deemed to have the same rights of access to education and health services, although those in detention centres have had to receive these services apart from other children.

In consequence, in the UK, local authorities have mostly attempted to integrate asylum-seeking and refugee children into mainstream provision, except where children have been detained with their parents prior to adjudication of status or deportation. In some other countries in Europe, children have been educated in separate centres, which doubtless provides a sense of commonality and gives access to specialist help, but militates against social integration (Watters, 2008).

Several studies have found that many young asylum seekers and refugees are highly motivated to do well educationally and have an ability to learn fast. Understandably, given their often limited English language skills and unfamiliarity with British curricula, teaching practices and wider culture, their performance is generally well below average, although certain individuals and groups appear to do well (Rutter, 2002 and 2006, cited in Watters, 2008). Some have initial difficulties gaining access to appropriate schooling, but others have been given excellent support (Hopkins and Hill, 2006; Wade *et al.*, 2005). In some European countries, specialist teachers have been provided for young people to assist them in making the transition to unfamiliar settings, curricular, languages and so on. While such dedicated services can make it easier for the young person to adapt, Lorenz (1994) comments that this should not be used as a means to put all the responsibility for adjustment on to the young person. Schools and colleges, too, need to be responsive, as indeed some have been (Hopkins and Hill, 2006).

Some commentators and campaign groups have suggested that the educational needs of refugee children are more related to ethnicity than mode of entry to the country. In other words, the teaching needs to be cognisant of racism and cultural diversity, as well as specific linguistic needs that may arise (Watters, 2008).

## Needs arising from past trauma

In terms of safeguarding asylum-seeking and refugee children an important issue relates to considering their needs arising from previous experiences of individual persecution, persecution of family members, and/or war or other such traumas that are often associated with the pre-flight experiences of asylum-seeking and refugee children (Hopkins and Hill, 2006). Refugee children may also be exposed to abuse or exploitation after entry to the host country, especially if they were unaccompanied. Commonly, the purpose of trafficking is to make children available as cheap or slave labour, or for sexual gratification of adults (Bokhari, 2008). Clearly, the needs arising from these experiences will vary according to the specific experiences and maturity of the children concerned, and the extent to which any children are accompanied by family members who protect them and help them to cope.

A commonsense approach to safeguarding asylum-seeking and refugee children with needs arising from past trauma would suggest that they should be offered counselling services as soon after arriving in the UK as possible. However, Kohli (Research in Practice, 2005) advocates deferring such support. He argues in favour of a chronology for different types of help as follows: 'the normal pattern of resettlement is present first, the future next and the past last' (Research in Practice, 2005). In other words, asylum-seeking and refugee children may be best safeguarded by dealing with immediate issues and thinking about their plans for the future months and years, before looking back to deal with the past.

Like anyone who has undergone maltreatment, there can be a reluctance to confide resulting from feelings such as shame or a wish to avoid reliving past pain. Some children who have been recently trafficked or exploited may be fearful of retaliation if they speak honestly (Bokhari, 2008). In Sweden, a condition known as 'severe withdrawal behaviour' has been recognized among children in asylum-seeking families. This can include refusal to eat or talk, as well as a tendency towards social isolation (Watters, 2008).

Most commentators suggest that intensive individual counselling is only appropriate for a minority who have experienced extreme trauma (Watters, 2008). As with all counselling, but especially in view of the inhibitions mentioned above, there is a need to start from the child's position and proceed at a pace that is comfortable for the child. When a therapist or other professional co-works with an interpreter such work needs to be particularly carefully planned with careful debriefings (Raval, 2007). For children who have experienced less severe stress or have coped better, it may be that help is better provided through group work and approaches that are strength-enhancing (Watters, 2008). Kohli (2007) suggests that a range of methods can be appropriate depending on the child's history, needs and wishes, but the critical ingredient is the development of trust between the child and worker.

## Conclusion

The principal theme of policy with regard to asylum-seeking children and young people has been a tension between refugee and immigration policy on the one hand and children's legislation on the other. The former has had a defensive emphasis on restricting numbers and, hence, discouraging or even punishing those with claims perceived to be marginal, while the latter includes the positive duty to promote the welfare of any child in the UK. This dualism in policy is related to different conceptions of children. Watters (2008) refers to an 'immigration control trajectory' affected by perceptions that refugee children are *untrustworthy*. It may be suspected by state agencies that their or their parents' claims about persecution are false, or that the children have been given a story to tell about the pre-flight experiences in order to assist their claims for refuge (Anderson,

2001). Even if genuineness is conceded, concern may still arise from general fears about the acceptability of 'alien' people and the perceived need to limit their number. Watters (2008) suggests there is a parallel and conflicting 'welfare trajectory'. This is based on a view of refugee children as psychologically and emotionally *damaged* and, therefore, requiring specialized intervention. Some writers have recognized a third construction, the *resilient* child, whose personal and network strengths have made possible a hazardous journey to safety and can be built on in the admitting country (Kohli and Mather, 2003). Elements of all three conceptions may be present at the same time or in a single service.

In addition to these competing priorities and images of children, service providers have had to negotiate and respond to policy measures at multiple levels of government that have frequently been in tension. As a whole, the UK has international obligations towards child asylum seekers and refugees. These are reinforced by European level commitments. In recent decades children's legislation and ministerial rhetoric about children has also emphasized placing their welfare first and positively promoting their well-being. Two significant exceptions apply. The first concerns youth crime and 'anti-social' behaviour (see, for example, Tisdall, 2006). The second has been the subject of this chapter – immigration – where government and public anxieties have at times over-ridden the principle of children's best interests. This is demonstrated most starkly in one of the few reservations made in the UK's ratification of the UNCRC, which exempts immigration policy from the application of the Convention's principles. Although this exemption was included by a Conservative government, subsequent Labour governments have shown no inclination to revoke it.

Differences and conflicts have also been evident between the UK, the devolved and the local levels. It is only fair to point out that the UK government has put resources into additional services for asylum-seeking and refugee families and children, though professionals and commentators have suggested this has not been adequate. Both central and local government have, at times, been resistant to the provision of accommodation, though legal action has clarified responsibilities. Especially sharp instances of differences were illustrated when asylum-seekers were dispersed to Scotland. The Scottish Executive was uncomfortable but largely passive over action taken by the Home Office to detain children at Dungavel in what were seen as prison like-surroundings and to deport certain families. However, along with teachers and children, the Scottish Commissioner for Children and Young People criticized such measures and claimed they were incompatible with children's and human rights, as embodied in international treaties.

These difficulties cannot simply be attributed to politicians, since they reflect wider ambiguities and ambivalence in the public at large. There are significant deficiencies which, at worst, may have resulted in some children through deportation being re-exposed to risks they came here to escape. On the other hand, the great majority of those who have arrived recently appear to find helpful the services and professionals they encounter, as well as peer support (Chase *et al.*,

2008; Hopkins and Hill, 2006). In the future we shall need to know more about how these individuals' lives unfold in adulthood. However, the signs are that many will go on to lead satisfying lives and to make positive contributions to our society and economy, as policy-makers wish in their aims and visions for children.

# References

Aldgate, J. and McIntosh, M. (2006) *Looking after the Family: A Study of Children Looked After in Kinship Care in Scotland*, Edinburgh: Social Work Inspection Agency.

Anderson, P., (2001) '"You don't belong here in Germany ...": On the social situation of refugee children in Germany', *Journal of Refugee Studies*, 14 (2): 187–199.

Archard, D. (2003) *Children: Rights and Childhood*, London: Routledge.

Article 19 (2002) *What's the Story? Samgatte: A Case Study of Media Coverage of Asylum and Refugee Issues*, London: Article 19.

Asquith, S. and Hill, M. (eds.) (1994) *Justice for Children*, Dordrecht: Martinus Nijhoff.

Bainham, A., Lindley, B., Richards, M. and Trinder, L. (eds.) (2003) *Children and their Families: Contact, Rights and Welfare*, Oxford: Hart.

Bloemraad, I. (2006) 'Becoming a citizen in the United States and Canada: Structured mobilization and immigrant political incorporation', *Social Forces*, 85 (2): 667–695.

Bokhari, F. (2008) 'Falling through the gaps: Safeguarding children trafficked into the UK', *Children and Society*, 22 (3): 201–211.

Broad, B. (2001) *Kinship Care*, Lyme Regis, Russell House.

CARIS (2007) *Child Asylum and Refugee Issues in Scotland*. Available at: www.savethechildren.org.uk/caris/ (accessed 1 August 2008).

Cemlyn, S. and Briskman, L. (2003) 'Asylum, children's rights and social', *Child and Family Social Work*, 8 (3): 163–178.

Chase, E., Knight, A. and Statham, J. (2008) *Promoting the Emotional Wellbeing and Mental Health of Unaccompanied Young People Seeking Asylum in the UK*, London: Thomas Coram Research Unit.

Christie, A. (2003) 'Responses to asylum seeking children in Ireland', *Child and Family Social Work*, 8 (3): 223–232.

Cleaver, H. (2000) *Fostering Family Contact*, London: The Stationery Office.

Cohen, S., Humphries, B. and Mynott, E. (2002) *From Immigration Controls to Welfare Controls*, London: Routledge.

D'Cruz, H. and Stagnitti, K. (2008) 'Reconstructing child welfare through participatory and child-centred professional practice: a conceptual approach', *Child and Family Social Work*, 13 (2): 156–165.

DCSF (2008) *Revised ECM Outcomes Framework*, London: DCSF. Available at http://www.everychildmatters.gov.uk (accessed 1 August 2008).

Dennis, J. (2007) 'The legal and policy frameworks that govern social work with unaccompanied asylum seeking children in England', in R. Kohli and F. Mitchell (eds.), *Working with Unaccompanied Asylum Seeking Children*, Basingstoke: Palgrave Macmillan.

Dixon, J. and Stein, M. (2005) *Leaving Care, Through care and After care in Scotland*, London: British Association for Adoption and Fostering.

Hantrais, L. (1995) *Social Policy in the European Union*, Basingstoke: Macmillan.

Hill, M. (ed.) (1990) *Social Work and the European Community*, London: Jessica Kingsley.

Hill, M. and Aldgate, J. (1996) *Child Welfare Services*, London: Jessica Kingsley.

Hill, M., Walker, M., Moodie, K., Wallace, B., Bannister, J., Khan, F., McIvor, G. and Kendrick, A. (2005) *Fast track Children's Hearing Pilot: Final Report of the Evaluation of the Pilot (Abridged Version)*, Edinburgh: Scottish Executive.

Hopkins, P. (2007) '"Blue squares," "proper" Muslims and transnational networks: Narratives of national and religious identities amongst young Muslim men living in Scotland', *Ethnicities*, 7 (1): 61–81.

Hopkins, P. and Hill, M. (2006) *This Is a Good Place to Live and Think about the Future*, Glasgow: Scottish Refugee Council.

Hopkins, P. and Hill, M. (2008) 'The pre-flight experiences and migration stories of unaccompanied asylum-seeking children and young people', *Children's Geographies*, 6 (3): 257–268.

Hothersall, R. (2006) *Social Work with Children, Young People and their families in Scotland*, Exeter: Learning Matters.

Kearney, M. (2007) 'Friends and family care of unaccompanied children', in R. Kohli and F. Mitchell (eds.), *Working with Unaccompanied Asylum Seeking Children*, Basingstoke: Palgrave Macmillan.

Kidane, S. (2001) *I Did Not Choose to Come Here*, London: British Association for Adoption and Fostering.

Kohli, R. (2007) *Social Work with Unaccompanied Asylum Seeking Children*. Basingstoke: Palgrave Macmillan

Kohli, R. and Mather, R. (2003) 'Promoting psychosocial well-being in unaccompanied asylum seeking young people in the UK', *Child & Family Social Work*, 8 (3): 201–212.

Lorenz, W. (1994) *Social Work in a Changing Europe*, London: Routledge.

Marshall, K. (1997) *Children's Rights in the Balance*, Edinburgh: The Stationery Office.

Modood, T. (2007) *Multiculturalism*, Cambridge: Polity Press.

Modood, T., Beishon, S. and Virdee, S. (1994) *Changing Ethnic identities*, London: Policy Studies Institute.

Munro, E. (2002) *Effective Child Protection*, London: Sage.

Parton, N., Thorpe, D. and Wattam, C. (1997) *Child Protection*, Basingstoke: Macmillan.

Parton, N. and Wattam, C. (eds.) (1999) *Child Sexual Abuse*, Chichester: John Wiley.

Phillips, D. (2006) 'Moving towards integration: The housing of asylum seekers and refugees in Britain', *Housing Studies* 21 (4): 539–553.

Pringle, K. (1998) *Children and Social Welfare in Europe*, Buckingham: Open University Press.

Raval, H. (2007) 'Therapeutic encounters between young people, bilingual co-workers and practitioners', in R. Kohli and F. Mitchell (eds.), *Working with Unaccompanied Asylum Seeking Children*, Basingstoke: Palgrave Macmillan.

Refugee Council (2004) *Briefing of the Common European Asylum System*, London: Refugee Council.

Research in Practice (2005) *On New Ground: Supporting Unaccompanied Asylum-seeking Children and Young People*, Audio Series 9 (transcript).

Robinson, V. (2003) 'Dispersal policies in the UK', in V. Robinson, R. Andersson and S. Musterd, *Spreading the 'Burden'? A Review of Policies to Disperse Asylum Seekers and Refugees*, Bristol: Policy Press.

Ruxton, S. (1996) *Children in Europe*, London: National Children's Home.

Scottish Executive (2003) *Getting it Right for Every Child*, Edinburgh, Scottish Executive. Available at http://www.scotland.gov.uk/children's services/girfec (accessed 1 August 2008).

Sen, R., Kendrick, A., Milligan, I. and Hawthorn, M. (2008) 'Historical abuse in residential care in Scotland 1950–1995: A literature review', in T. Shaw, *Historic Abuse Systemic Review*, Edinburgh: Scottish Government.

Smith, D. (2003) 'Making contact work in international cases', in A. Bainham, B. Lindley, M. Richards and L. Trinder, *Children and their Families: Contact, Rights and Welfare*, Hart: Oxford.

Smith, S. (1989) *The Politics of 'Race' and Residence*, Cambridge: Polity Press.

Thoburn, J., Chand, A. and Procter, J. (2005) *Child Welfare Services for Minority Ethnic Families*, London: Jessica Kingsley.

Thomas, N. (2000) *Children, Family and the State*, Basingstoke: Macmillan.

Tisdall, K. (2006) 'Antisocial behaviour legislation meets children's services', *Critical Social Policy*, 26 (1): 101–120.

Trinder, L. (2003) 'Introduction', in A. Bainham, B. Lindley, M. Richards and L. Trinder, *Children and their Families: Contact, Rights and Welfare*, Hart: Oxford.

Tunstill, J. (1999) *Children and the State*, London: Cassell.

UNCRC (1989) *Convention on the Rights of the Child*, New York: UN General Assembly.

UNHCR (1951) *Convention Relating to the Rights of Refugees*, Geneva: UNHCR.

Verhellen, E. (1997) *Convention on the Rights of the Child*, Leuven: Garant.

Wade, J., Mitchell, F. and Baylis, G. (2005) *Unaccompanied Asylum Seeking Children*, London: British Association for Adoption and Fostering.

Walker, S. and Thurston C. (2006) *Safeguarding Children and Young People*, Lyme Regis: Russell House.

Wasoff, F. and Hill, M. (2002) 'Family policy in Scotland', *Social Policy and Society*, 1 (3): 171–182.

Watters, C. (2008) *Refugee Children*, Abingdon: Routledge.

Whande, N. (1993) 'General issues relating to refugee children', in S. Asquith and M. Hill (eds.), *Justice for Children*, Dordrecht: Martinus Nijhoff.

# 14

# Conclusion: Safeguarding Children?

Karen Broadhurst, Chris Grover and Janet Jamieson

As we draw together observations and analyses from our contributors, a series of high-profile deaths of children at the hands of their parents or carers has once again drawn 'safeguarding' firmly under the spotlight. In particular, the case of Baby P has prompted a flurry of intense activity at every level of the workforce implicated in safeguarding. Moreover, searching questions are being asked about the effectiveness of the ambitious Laming reforms enacted through the Every Child Matters (ECM) agenda, given the very obvious similarities between the death of Baby P and Victoria Climbié – the latter case having set in motion the very significant transformation of children's services that we are now witnessing.

So far, central government responses to what appears to be a mounting crisis in confidence about new integrated services are disappointing, as the following extract from a letter from Lord Laming (task with reviewing the effectiveness of the current arrangements for safeguarding children) to Ed Balls (Secretary of State for Children Schools and Families) illustrates:

> You may wish to know that I have taken the opportunity to review some of the legal and parliamentary reports preparatory to the 1989 Children Act and the subsequent legislation and practice guidance. I have been struck by the robustness of the foundation on which current children's services are based. There is now a coherent system that incorporates the policy, law and guidance. From that I conclude that the main challenge is to ensure that the system is fully implemented so as to ensure that good practice becomes standard practice everywhere and in every service. (Laming, 2008)

Of course, reviewing safeguarding through the lens of the latest tragic death of a child, will inevitably throw the spotlight on compliance with procedures and protocols – both the inspectorial regime and serious case review processes encourage this kind of focus. However, Lord Laming's conclusion that: 'there

*Critical Perspectives on Safeguarding Children*   Edited by Karen Broadhurst, Chris Grover and Janet Jamieson
© 2009 John Wiley & Sons, Ltd

is now a coherent system ... and the main challenge is to ensure that the system is fully implemented' is glaringly narrow and tautological. The chapters in this volume offer alternative explanations of the limitations of the safeguarding project that have less to do with local implementation problems (that Laming's analysis points to) and far more to do with the political and conceptual foundations of the safeguarding project. In this concluding chapter by discussing analytic themes that we consider cut across the chapters, we focus on (a) the 'welfare' foundations of the New Labour safeguarding project, (b) responsibility and conditionality within safeguarding and (c) successes and failures of 'joined up' government with respect to safeguarding children.

## The 'welfare' foundations of the safeguarding project

Let us start with an alternative formulation of the life of Baby P.

The recent tragic case of Baby P was used in a speech by Martin Narey, the chief executive of the children's charity Barnardo's, to highlight the material deprivation that many children in the UK endure:

> It saddens me that the probability is that had Baby P survived, given his own deprivation, he might have been unruly by the time he had reached the age of 13 or 14.

> At which point he'd have become feral, a parasite, a yob, helping to infest our streets. The response for his criminal behaviour would have been to lock him up – but we [Barnardo's] believe these children deserve better. (Narey, 2008)

Narey's comments are as controversial as they are overly deterministic because the perjorative language that he uses to describe an imagined future for Baby P had he lived ('feral, a parasite, a yob') is not the language usually associated with the leaders of charitable organizations for children. However, his words do raise what we consider to be overarching and foundational issues for any government aiming to safeguard children and that is the relationship between children's vulnerability and socio-economic deprivation. Reading across the chapters of this volume, a central and cross-cutting theme is that the lives of many children and young people who are likely to come to the attention of safeguarding services (in the broadest sense) are framed by acute and multiple levels of deprivation and poverty, yet the 'welfare' commitments of New Labour do not place this deprivation central to the safeguarding project.

While there can be little doubt that New Labour inherited from the Conservative governments of the 1980s and 1990s stubbornly high and stagnant levels of poverty, it has had over a decade to make at least some inroads into them. For analysts and commentators change can always come more quickly. However, the efforts of New Labour to tackle what it holds out as the most problematic aspect of poverty – child poverty – have been inadequate, failing to have any significant impact on those most in need, as Chris Grover has discussed in chapter 4 of this volume. Moreover, at a time when all the constituent nations of the UK have entered what by all accounts (except that of the government) will be a long and deep recession, it is difficult to see how, in the medium term at least, any government will be able or willing to tackle structural disadvantages that continue to frame the lives of many children. As a number of chapters have discussed, New Labour's idea of a Social Investment State may have drawn a vocabulary of child poverty back into mainstream politics. However, because it also retains of the neo-liberal commitments of previous Conservative administrations – for example, the acceptance of the sovereignty of the free market (albeit with some modest flanking measures) – it does not appear to hold out much promise for tackling socio-structural inequalities.

In considering the future of safeguarding, the indications are that we cannot expect any change in either Labour or Conservative party commitment to capitalism and its inherent inequalities. Indeed, both parties attribute current economic difficulties to external financial shocks, most notably the default of poor mortgagees in the USA and the rapid pace of expansion in some countries that in 2008 imported price inflation into the UK. In this context, in which the operation of capitalism goes unquestioned, it is particularly worrying that on entering recession the government argued that it was time for stepping up the pace of welfare 'reform', rather than stepping back from it (and here again, we see a consensus between political parties on the left and the right). In what would be a laughable logic if it were not so serious, when it is estimated that 20,000 people per week will lose their jobs over 2009 and well into 2010, the government continue to argue that paid work is the best way of tackling child poverty and the best form of welfare more generally (Secretary of State for Work and Pensions, 2008). This approach, through the extension of conditionality, marks a high degree of continuity with the principle of 'less eligibility' that has framed social welfare policy for the past two centuries. This principle suggests that working-class people will only work and provide for their dependants on the threat of poverty. Such an approach is antithetical to safeguarding children, because it condemns many children – about a third – to living in households where the income is less than the amount that the government uses as its own measure of poverty. If safeguarding is to be successful then there needs to be a focusing of effort upon the risks that children and young people face because of structural inequalities and inequities that exist in contemporary society. Reading across the chapters in this volume, whether our contributions derive from philosophy, geography, social policy, social work, criminology, health or education, all draw attention to flaws in New Labour's policies with regard to social inequalities.

The death of Baby P was newsworthy, among other things, because he was killed in the same area of London (Haringey) and subject to the care of the same social services department, as was Victoria Climbié. However, both government and public concerns with Haringey Social Services, now and in the case of the Climbié Inquiry, are focused narrowly on context with respect to manager, worker, procedure, file and so forth. Note the following extract from the Climbié report:

> it is not enough to consider the omissions and failings of individual practitioners in Haringey without considering the context in which they were working at the time. It is also necessary to understand the extent to which the organisation in which they served, and the working practices of the organisations, can, and must, shoulder the blame for serious lapses in individual professional practice. (Laming, 2003, Part 2, para 6.2, Cm 5730)

There is of course a far broader organizational context, which should be of interest to the public and policy-makers and which clearly impacts on the ability of local authorities to meet local need.

Haringey Borough Council operates in one of the most deprived and socially divided boroughs in London. It ranks 18 out of 354 local authorities in terms of area deprivation (where 1 is the most deprived). Within the Haringey border are a number of the most deprived wards in the UK, with 39 falling in the top 10 per cent of the most deprived (Government Office for London, 2008). More than a third of Haringey's population are eligible for free school meals and the impoverished east side of the borough contains some of the worst housing problems in the UK (Government Office for London, 2008). Haringey is a borough marked by social divisions and inequality (Hudson *et al.*, 2007). The Association of Public Health Observatories (2008) found that in Haringey, the fourth most deprived borough in London, percentage rates for child poverty, statutory homelessness, educational under-achievement, violent crime, mental illness and infant deaths, were all significantly higher than national averages for England. As chapters in this volume clearly reveal, indicators of socio-economic deprivation such as these are clearly associated with poor outcomes for children. But somehow, this context is missed in government and public analyses of safeguarding systems. Extreme cases of child homicide/manslaughter, throw the spotlight on issues of individual culpability, be that of parents/carers or professionals, but it is important to retain a focus on the broader socio-economic circumstances that frame the lives of a larger, but far less visible, population of vulnerable children and young people.

## Safeguarding: rights, responsibility and conditionality

In examining how 'citizenship' and 'social rights' are conceptualized within New Labour's particular imagining of the neo-liberal welfare state, we shall highlight a range of concerns which we see as significant to the government's approach to rights, responsibilities and the conditionality of support within its safeguarding children agenda.

Given New Labour's clear interests in child well-being, a concern to pay due respect to the issue of children's rights would appear to be a crucial element of its safeguarding agenda. Indeed, following a report published by the Gulbenkian Foundation: *Effective Government Structures for Children* (Hodgkin and Newell, 1996), that outlined how central government might become more responsive to the needs and rights of children, a number of changes were made in England to the structures of government with specific respect to children. A Parliamentary Select Committee for children was established, a statutory and independent office of the Children's Rights Commissioner was set up, and a cabinet minister was given specific responsibility for children. However, as commentators have cautioned, we need to be careful not to overstate the significance or likely impact of such new structures (Payne, 2007; Warin, 2007).

As several contributors to this volume have highlighted children's rights do not appear to fit easily with the New Labour's political priorities. In chapter 3, David Archard asserts that children's views are afforded 'limited' or 'insignificant' value within the development of the safeguarding children policy agenda, despite New Labour's language of a 'stakeholder' society. Rather, expert voices and views have dominated and – as has historically been the case in social welfare – policy has been structured through the purview of professionals. Moreover, in characterizing the five ECM outcomes – to be healthy, to stay safe, to enjoy and achieve, to make a positive contribution, and to achieve economic well-being – as desired outcomes rather than as entitlements, Archard asserts New Labour have fallen significantly short of adopting a children's rights-based agenda. The tensions and inconsistencies integral to achieving the United Nations Convention on the Rights of the Child, to which the UK has been a signatory since 1990, are also highlighted across a range of other chapters in the clear breaches of children's rights within specific areas of practice, most significantly in criminal justice and the treatment of refugee and asylum-seeking children. In particular, in chapter 13 Malcolm Hill and Peter Hopkins reveal how a concern to promote children's rights is compromised by the government's desire to restrict the numbers and types of individuals entering the UK and becoming citizens.

For New Labour 'rights' are premised on 'responsibilities' whereby individuals secure their own well-being through the taking of the opportunities of education, employment and community engagement offered by the state. Thus, and shifting away from a significant redistributionist role, great store is placed on the state's role in the inculcation of an ethic of self-responsibility in its citizens. As Hartley Dean (2006, p. 5) describes, in part, this reflects long-standing British liberal concerns with the moral conduct of its citizens, but under New Labour there is also a distinctly 'illiberal desire to enforce the civic responsibilities of workers and/or citizens'. Enforcement of civic responsibilities is achieved through a creeping conditionality – the provision of state social benefits and/or services that are conditional upon recipients' compliance with workfare, educational or rehabilitative 'opportunities'. So how does enforcement and creeping conditionality impact on safeguarding?

The chapters in this volume demonstrate that New Labour's intention to inculcate an ethic of self-responsibility is manifest in the increasing regulation of both childhood and parenting. However, we can also see from our contributors' analyses of parenting or problematic drug and alcohol use in children and young people or the prevention of 'offending' and/or the 'management' of young asylum seekers, the *sharper* edge of New Labour's 'enabling state'. Most notably, where criminal justice meets safeguarding, we see the flip side of New Labour's activation policies and 'opportunity structures' (Dean, 2006, p 5). It is here that the coercive and iatrogenic effects of New Labour's early intervention agenda that seeks to steer children and young people down the path of active citizenship, are undoubtedly evident and inconsistencies in the safeguarding agenda very clear.

The shift away from a social protectionist ethic for the welfare state, towards an ethic of self-responsibility (Dean, 2004, 2006) appears to have particular ramifications for children, who given even a weak association with criminality, for example, via drinking alcohol in public spaces, can forfeit their rights to being safeguarded. Indeed, New Labour's tendency towards implementing tough responses to the problematic behaviours of children and young people have been highlighted by a number of contributors to this volume. In chapter 10 Ian Paylor highlights the escalation towards criminal justice responses in relation to drug and alcohol use among children and young people, while in chapter 12 Claire Fitzpatrick draws attention to the intolerant responses evident with regard to 'looked after' children. Both contributors' emphasize the stigmatizing and criminalizing potential of such reactions to children and young people who are disproportionately drawn from the most marginalized, excluded and vulnerable sections of the population. In a similar vein, in chapter 11 Janet Jamieson emphasizes the damaging repercussions integral to the punitive imperatives of New Labour's youth justice policy. It is perhaps within the detention and incarceration of children and young people that the inconsistencies in the safeguarding agenda are drawn most sharply into focus. However, the government have proved remarkably resistant to changing practices in this regard despite both national and international campaigns that point to the failure of UK governments to safeguard the well-being of detained and incarcerated children and young people.

New Labour's preoccupation with what Frank Furedi (2006) has described as 'behaviour politics' is not limited to the problematic behaviours of children and young people, but rather extends to their families, in particular, to perceived deficits in parenting. As Goldson and Jamieson (2002, p. 85) argue, parenting deficits have historically been derived from a 'pathological construction' of working-class families wherein the need to address individual deficiencies has proved the justification for the increasing incursion of state intervention into family life.

The recent high profile child maltreatment case of Shannon Matthews is illustrative of the populist construction of the pathological parent. In this case, the focus of attention has been on her mother, Karen Matthews, rather than the child herself. However, and of particular note, media coverage, internet blogs and the like, have focused less on Karen's offences – child neglect and seeking to pervert the course of justice – but rather on Karen's lifestyle and behaviour. Re-invigorating notions of 'broken Britain', this case has sparked a number of headlining media reports, that on the face of it might appear unconnected with the issue of child neglect. For example, the *News of the World* forcefully suggests the need to 'force low-life to work for a living' (7 December 2008), while the *Independent on Sunday* discusses the paternity of Karen's children in some detail under the the headline 'Five fathers, one mother and a muddled family saga' (13 April 2008). Of course, there is also frequent references across the popular press to her 'fiddling' benefits, TV watching and spending her money on 'booze and fags'. The moral outrage sparked by this case, and the frequent reference to feral or dysfunctional families indicates that perjorative notions of the 'underclass' have far from disappeared under New Labour – the public is quick to condemn an imagined population of benefit claimants who lead squalid and irresponsible lives. Karen's case is not considered an isolated extreme, but rather symptomatic of 'broken Britain' and a larger imagined population who exist 'in the murkiest, darkest corners of this country' (*News of the World*, 7 December 2008) as the following extract indicates:

> A whole legion of people who contribute nothing to society yet believe it owes them a living – good-for-nothing scroungers who have no morals, no compassion, no sense of responsibility and who are incapable of feeling love or guilt.
> (*News of the World*, 7 December 2008)

The burgeoning interventions apparent in the area of parenting, and the conditionality attached to the support offered, attests to New Labour's commitment to pathological constructions of family life. However, as discussed by Karen Broadhurst in relation to parenting support in chapter 7 and by Jo Warin with regard to education in chapter 8, New Labour's tendency to pathologize and punish what it perceives to be 'inadequate' parenting is unlikely to secure parental support and cooperation in safeguarding the welfare of their children. Moreover, both contributors note that the policies New Labour have implemented to get parents to conform to its particular version of the responsible parent fails to account for the often immensely difficult social and material circumstances these parents face in bringing up their children.

On the basis of detailed analysis of child protection in Anglophone countries, Lonne *et al.* (2009, p. 171) suggest, that the presence of controlling and punitive imperatives within policies directed at safeguarding the welfare of children are likely to result in systems which 'hurt more people than they help'. In our disappointment with New Labour's safeguarding agenda, we share Lonne *et al.*'s conviction that state support and help must be premised on much more ethical and humanitarian principles than are currently evident in responding to the difficulties faced, and the problems posed, by the children and families who comprise the prime constituency for New Labour's responsibilization project.

## Joined up government?

So, finally we turn to the issue of 'joined-up government'. As we stated in the introduction to this volume, early in office New Labour made clear that it aimed to 'modernize' in response to the perceived failings of traditional forms of bureaucracy and political structures (Cabinet Office, 1999). The new government was to shift further towards dispersed government, emphasizing the importance of regional actors and offices that would coordinate the delivery of central government initiatives, albeit adapted to local needs. In addition, local government actors and offices would play a key role in ensuring the local co-ordination of mixed markets of public, private and voluntary sector services. In this context, new issues of 'governance' have come to the fore, that arise from attempts to manage political goals at a distance and across diverse sectors of the market, with each having their own organizational operating codes and priorities. Thus, issues of coordination, to do with joint planning, agreeing protocols, information sharing and so forth, have become central political and policy concerns.

There is now a growing appreciation that New Labour's attempts to 'modernize' have been and continue to be fraught with problems and tensions (Catney, 2009; Jessop, 1999). In addition, the problems of New Labour's dispersed government, while different from those exhibited under old Labour's statism or the New Right's turn to the market, do not appear to hold out the promise of more effective government. Of course, nowhere are the failings of new forms of governance more visible that in relation to safeguarding, where the very public nature of particular forms of child death (intra-familial) make failings in new structures particularly newsworthy.

Problems arising from new forms of governance are not particular to New Labour. Given the rise of neo-liberalism as a global phenomenon, and attempts in many advanced economic societies to cut across the public–state divide through stakeholder or what Bob Jessop (1999) describes as 'heterarchic' approaches to government, problems of new forms of governance are widespread. However, New Labour does exhibit the following particularities with respect to its failures of governance.

First, New Labour has been keen to be seen as a party of action, an impulse that has arguably led to what Carolyn Taylor described in chapter 2 as 'initiativitis'. As Stoker (2005, p. 159) states, early in office New Labour '"looked for quick wins", and launched initiative after initiative from the centre'. In relation to safeguarding children such initiativitis resulted in Sure Starts, followed by a range of local projects set up under the Children's Fund and local projects set up through funding streams made available to tackle particular aspects of social exclusion (for example, teenage pregnancy). A multiplicity of policy initiatives were also launched in order to impact on child poverty, youth crime, educational attainment, parenting and so forth. However, the pace of change that has come to characterize New Labour's approach to policy-making has created acute difficulties in both establishing connections between initiatives and the coherence of local strategies.

Second, New Labour has met failures of local implementation and coordination with more governance. This is symptomatic of late modern attempts to govern at a distance (Jessop, 1999), but New Labour has been particularly reactive and, indeed, hyperactive in this respect. In addition, New Labour has relied heavily on the proxies of New Public Management to attempt to engineer compliance among its local stakeholders. This latter tendency has resulted in the proliferation of public service indicators and performance targets, together with unremitting revisions to inspection regimes, that, while attempting to draw local actors into working with the grain of central government agendas, appear distracting, confusing and demoralizing (Barton, 2008; Catney, 2009).

In chapter 9, Sue Peckover reminds us of the size and scope of the health service, identifying a complexity that New Labour appears to have missed in its ambitious attempts to integrate services for children and families under ECM. Similarly, in chapter 5, Andy Pithouse and Karen Broadhurst highlight the limits of the Common Assessment Framework (CAF) to facilitate and manage heterarchic relationships around children with 'additional needs'. They usefully point out that assumptions within ECM may be over-deterministic in relation to the presumed impact of new forms and protocols. In chapter 6, Sue White makes a number of important and related points, identifying the centrality of individual professionals and their sense-making practices in effective collaboration. The cross-boundary partnerships that Labour encourages in its heterarchic approach to governance, have been described as complex, costly and often dysfunctional (Dowling *et al.*, 2004; McMurray, 2007). Nowhere is this more evident than in New Labour's attempt to create an e-infrastructure for safeguarding. The development of the integrated children's system (ICS) has required local authorities to enter into costly and contentious relationships with IT providers that many report are posing very significant problems both of implementation and practicability. Plans for *ContactPoint* have been repeatedly stalled and appear fraught with complications that relate not just to financial costs or practicalities, but also raise, as contributors to this volume discuss, ethical considerations related to do privacy and security of personal information. Of course, critical commentators will draw parallels between the ambitious e-plans for safeguarding, and earlier, but failed attempts to thus engineer other public services (at significant cost to the tax payer). The Child Support Agency (CSA) provides a case in point – following a long and difficult relationship with the IT provider EDS, that saw serious delays in the processing of child support applications, this over-ambitious project was phased out with a more simple and streamlined solution.

While not disputing the utility of IT solutions for safeguarding, it is problematic that the problems that appeared in the piloting of ICS appear to have gone unheeded by a government intent on rolling it out (Bell *et al.*, 2007; Broadhurst *et al.*, 2009;). Despite research and evidence about the shortfalls of New Labour's approach to policy making (Catney, 2009; Jessop, 2003), New Labour appears to continue to steam ahead with ambitious reforms that demonstrate a continued lack of appreciation of their likely local impact or how new policies will embed in local policy agendas (for example, the raft of initiatives outlined under *Care Matters: Time for Change* [DCSF, 2006]). New Labour demonstrates limited capacity for reflexivity, although arguably this is the very attribute that it seeks to promote in its dispersed local government actors through performance management feedback loops.

New Labour demonstrates an incorrigible resistance to insight. While quick to berate local governments for implementation failures (see Haringey in relation to Baby P), it is slow to identify its own self-serving but over-ambitious claims. A focus on local implementation failures or poor IT providers draws attention away from problems of New Labour's own making to do with the combination of increasing market proxies into the public sector, the extension of methodologies of New Public Management and the pace and process of policy-making. Failings in the government's ability to critically reflect on its own performance are very important because limited public funds mean that money mis-spent on governance is at the expense of perhaps more straightforward (but arguably 'statist') notions of direct support to families through the provision of social housing, childcare and income maintenance. Unfortunately, New Labour's mis-spending is likely to leave a lasting legacy, given that in the midst of recession, there will be little money available to remedy policy muddles.

## Future research priorities

We end with a few questions that might shape future research agendas or that might in some small way inform thinking about government. These are largely to do with balance, and acknowledging the legacy of New Labour and The Third Way. First, given that it is likely that future governments will continue to chart a path between the market and the state, how can an effective balance be achieved between competition and cooperation? This is a tension that will inevitably face governments of any political persuasion. Second, how can government concede less to populism and what kind of constitutional reforms might be necessary such that governments desist from short-term gains? Third, how might a dispersed or more honest stakeholder government work? This would require a reconsideration of the balance between local and central government; between state direction and professional autonomy, as well as a consideration of how effective participation of service users can be achieved. Fourth, how might we more effectively measure the impacts of our investment in children, such that both the iatrogenic, as well as positive impacts of services, are rendered visible?

# References

Association of Public Health Observatories (2008) *Health Profile Haringey, 2008*. Available at: http://www.apho.org.uk/resource/item.aspx?RID=52440 (accessed 10 December 2008).

Barton, A. (2008) 'New Labour and untrustworthy professions', *Public Policy and Administration*, 23 (3): 263–277.

Bell, M., Shaw, I., Sinclair, I., Sloper, P. and Rafferty, J. (2007) *An Evaluation of the Practice, Process and Consequences of the ICS in Councils with Social Services Responsibilities*, Report to the Department for Education and Skills and Welsh Assembly Government. Available from author, York University.

Broadhurst, K., Wastell, D., White, S., Hall, C., Peckover, S., Thompson, K., Pithouse, A. and Davey, D. (2009) 'Performing "initial assessment": Identifying the latent conditions for error at the front-door of local authority children's services', *British Journal of Social Work*. Advance access published on 18 January 2009. DOI:10.1093/bjsw/bcn162

Cabinet Office, The (1999) *Modernising Government*, London: The Stationery Office.

Catney, P. (2009) 'New Labour and joined up urban governance', *Public Policy and Administration*, 24 (1): 47–66.

DCSF (2006) *Care Matters: Time for Change*, London: The Stationery Office.

Furedi, F. (2006) *Save Us from the Politics of Behaviour: How Long before British Adults Will Need a Licence to Parent their Children?* Available at: http://www.spiked-online.com/index.php?/site/article/1638/ (accessed 16 January 2009).

Dean, H. (2004) 'Popular discourse and the ethical deficiency of "Third Way" conceptions of citizenship', *Citizenship Studies*, 8 (1): 65–82.

Dean, H. (2006) 'Activation policies and the changing ethical foundations of welfare', paper presented at ASPEN/ETUI conference: Activation Policies in the EU, 20–21 October 2006, Brussels. Available at: LSE Eprints: http://eprints.lse.ac.uk/3784/ (accessed, 5 December 2008).

Dowling, B., Powell, M. and Glendinning, C. (2004) 'Conceptualising successful partnerships', *Health and Social Care in the Community*, 12 (4): 309–317.

Goldson, B. and Jamieson, J. (2002) 'Youth crime, the "parenting deficit" and state intervention: A contextual critique', *Youth Justice*, 2 (2): 82–99.

Government Office for London (2008) *Borough Information*. Available at: http://www.go.london.Gov.uk/boroughinfo/borough.aspx?bid = 14 (accessed 10 December 2008).

Hodgkin, R. and Newell, P. (1996) *Effective Government Structures for Children*, London: Calouste Gulbenkian Foundation.

Hudson, M., Phillips, J., Ray, K., and Barnes, H. (2007) *Social Cohesion in Diverse Communities*, Joseph Rowntree Foundation. Available at: http://www.jrf.org.uk/ (accessed 10 December 2008).

*Independent on Sunday* (2008) 'Five fathers, one mother and a muddled family saga', 13 April.

Jessop, B. (1999) 'The dynamics of partnership and governance failure', in G. Stoker (ed.), *The New Politics of Local Governance in Britain*, Oxford: Oxford University Press, pp. 11–32.

Jessop, B. (2003) 'From Thatcherism to New Labour: Neo-liberalism, workfarism, and labour market regulation', in H. Overbeek (ed.), *The Political Economy of European Unemployment: European Integration and the Transnationalization of the Employment Question*, London: Routledge.

Laming, Lord (2003), *The Victoria Climbié Inquiry: Report of an Inquiry by Lord Laming*, Command 5730, London: The Stationery Office.

Laming, Lord (2008) Letter to Ed Balls, 1 December. Available at: http://www.dcsf.gov.uk/localauthorities/_documents/content/0112080005_Lord%20Laming%20letter%20to%20Ed%20Balls.pdf (accessed 10 December 2008).

Lonne, B., Parton, N., Thomson, J. and Harries, M. (2009) *Reforming Child Protection*, London: Routledge.

McMurray, R. (2007) 'Our reforms, our partnerships, same problems: The chronic case of the English NHS', *Public Policy and Management*, 27 (1): 77–82.

Narey, M. (2008) 'Damage to Baby P could have turned him into a yob, says Barnardo's boss', *Guardian*, 26 November. Available at: http://www.guardian.co.uk/society/2008/nov/26/baby-p-barnardo-s (accessed 10 December 2008).

News of the World (2008) 'Force low-life to work', 7 December.

Payne, L. (2007) 'A "children's government" in England and child impact assessment', *Children and Society*, 21 (6): 470–475.

Secretary of State for Work and Pensions (2008) *No One Written Off: Reforming Welfare to Reward Responsibility*, Cm 7363, Norwich: The Stationery Office.

Stoker, G. (2005) 'Joined-up government for local and regional institutions', in V. Bogdanor (ed.), *Joined-up Government*, Oxford: The British Academy in Association with Oxford University Press, pp. 156–157.

Warin, J. (2007) 'Joined-up services for young children and their families: Papering over the cracks or re-constructing the foundations?', *Children and Society*, 21 (2): 87–97.

# Index